Sharp Knife

Recent Titles in
Native America: Yesterday and Today
Bruce E. Johansen, Series Editor

Daughters of Mother Earth: The Wisdom of Native American Women
Barbara Alice Mann, editor

Iroquois on Fire: A Voice from the Mohawk Nation
Douglas M. George-Kanentiio

Native America, Discovered and Conquered: Thomas Jefferson, Lewis & Clark, and Manifest Destiny
Robert J. Miller

The Praeger Handbook on Contemporary Issues in Native America
Volume 1: Linguistic, Ethnic, and Economic Revival
Volume 2: Legal, Cultural, and Environmental Revival
Bruce E. Johansen

The Tainted Gift: The Disease Method of Frontier Expansion
Barbara Alice Mann

Frontier Newspapers and the Coverage of the Plains Indian Wars
Hugh J. Reilly

Lethal Encounters: Englishmen and Indians in Colonial Virginia
Alfred A. Cave

Reservation "Capitalism": Economic Development in Indian Country
Robert J. Miller

Land and Spirit in Native America
Joy Porter

Resource Exploitation in Native North America: A Plague upon the Peoples
Bruce E. Johansen

American Indian Identity: Citizenship, Membership, and Blood
Se-ah-dom Edmo, Jessie Young, and Alan Parker

Urban American Indians: Reclaiming Native Space
Donna Martinez, Grace Sage, and Azusa Ono

Sharp Knife

Andrew Jackson and the American Indians

Alfred A. Cave

NATIVE AMERICA: YESTERDAY AND TODAY
Bruce E. Johansen, Series Editor

BLOOMSBURY ACADEMIC
NEW YORK • LONDON • OXFORD • NEW DELHI • SYDNEY

BLOOMSBURY ACADEMIC
Bloomsbury Publishing Inc
1385 Broadway, New York, NY 10018, USA
50 Bedford Square, London, WC1B 3DP, UK
29 Earlsfort Terrace, Dublin 2, Ireland

BLOOMSBURY, BLOOMSBURY ACADEMIC and the Diana logo
are trademarks of Bloomsbury Publishing Plc

First published in the United States of America by ABC-CLIO 2017
Paperback edition published by Bloomsbury Academic 2024

Copyright © Bloomsbury Publishing Inc, 2024

Jacket design by Silverander Communications
Cover photo: Andrew Jackson, head-andshoulders portrait, facing slightly right. Between 1850 and 1900. Photograph. (Retrieved from the Library of Congress, https://www.loc.gov/item/93500745/)

All rights reserved. No part of this publication may be reproduced or
transmitted in any form or by any means, electronic or mechanical,
including photocopying, recording, or any information storage or retrieval
system, without prior permission in writing from the publishers.

Bloomsbury Publishing Inc does not have any control over, or responsibility for,
any third-party websites referred to or in this book. All internet addresses given
in this book were correct at the time of going to press. The author and publisher
regret any inconvenience caused if addresses have changed or sites have
ceased to exist, but can accept no responsibility for any such changes.

Library of Congress Cataloging-in-Publication Data
Names: Cave, Alfred A., author.
Title: Sharp Knife: Andrew Jackson and the American Indians / Alfred A. Cave.
Other titles: Andrew Jackson and the American Indians
Description: Santa Barbara, California: Praeger, an imprint of ABC-CLIO, LLC, [2017] |
Series: Native America: yesterday and today | Includes bibliographical references and index.
Identifiers: LCCN 2017023416 (print) | LCCN 2017023953 (ebook) |
ISBN 9781440860409 (ebook) | ISBN 9781440860393 (alk. paper)
Subjects: LCSH: Jackson, Andrew, 1767–1845—Relations with Indians. | Indians of North America—Wars—1815–1875. | Indian Removal, 1813–1903. | Indians of North America—Government relations—1789–1869. | United States—Politics and government—1829–1837. | Jackson, Andrew, 1767–1845—Public opinion. | Public opinion—United States. | United States—Race relations.
Classification: LCC E382 (ebook) | LCC E382 .C29 2017 (print) | DDC 973.5/6092—dc23
LC record available at https://lccn.loc.gov/2017023416

ISBN: HB: 978-1-4408-6039-3
PB: 979-8-7651-1984-6
ePDF: 978-1-4408-6040-9
eBook: 979-8-2161-4477-9

Series: Native America: Yesterday and Today

To find out more about our authors and books visit www.bloomsbury.com
and sign up for our newsletters.

Contents

Series Foreword	vii
Preface	xi
1. A Man on the Make	1
2. Militia General and Indian Fighter	21
3. Empire Builder	51
4. A Backwoods Napoleon?	81
5. Candidate	113
6. President	133
Epilogue: Andrew Jackson, Ethnic Cleansing and Genocide	189
Notes	193
Index	235
About the Author	243

Series Foreword

One of President Donald J. Trump's first interior decorating decisions in the Oval Office was the installation of a large portrait of Andrew Jackson, who served between 1829 and 1837 as the United States' seventh president. The portrait has become a familiar fixture as President Trump shows off his executive orders for the cameras. A no-nonsense former Army general, Jackson led an insurgency by frontier farmers, miners, and traders (the "forgotten men" of the 1820s) against the East Coast elite, led by former president John Quincy Adams.

Beyond a surface affinity, I wonder how much about Jackson's life and times Trump knows, most notably regarding the treatment of Native Americans. He could learn something from Professor Alfred Cave's new book, *Sharp Knife: Andrew Jackson and the American Indians*.

Jackson was a self-made millionaire (worth billions of dollars in today's money), gained by trading in the two most valuable commodities of his preindustrial time: real estate and human beings. Jackson had a temper and was generally intolerant of contrary opinion. He was accustomed to issuing orders, not seeking consensus. Jackson provided the Democratic Party with its iconic donkey, co-opting it after an opponent called him a "jackass."

Jackson's main campaign pledge involved his own deportation policy, called "Removal," which required forced marches of southeastern Native American peoples (and others) westward to "Indian Territory," now Oklahoma. The best known of many forced marches involved the Cherokees, about 16,000 of them, a quarter of whom died on the trail, and an equal number dying of starvation and disease within two years of arrival in what was, to them, a foreign land. Men, women, and children, deprived of sufficient food, clothing, and shelter, died by the thousands.

Jackson had an inflated self-image, imagining himself as a friend of the Native peoples he was forcing into exile. He argued that removal was an act of paternal kindness and certainly preferable to extermination. In today's language, Jackson employed "alternative facts," and his "base," whose members stood to receive the lands that had belonged to the Native peoples, supported him fervently. "The safety and comfort of our citizens have been greatly promoted by their removal," he said. "The remnant of that ill-fated race has been at length beyond the reach of injury or oppression. . . . The paternal care of the Government will thereafter watch over them and protect them" (Jackson, 1837).

Jackson's racism is raw to our ears—no "political correctness" here. He proclaimed that Native peoples were incapable of civilization, as he proclaimed: "What good man would prefer a country covered with forests and ranged by a few thousand savages to our extensive Republic studded with cities, towns, and prosperous farms . . . filled with all the blessings of liberty, civilization, and religion? The policy [of Removal] is not only liberal, but generous" (Jackson, 1830).

The Cherokees did not leave their homeland without opposition. They sued the state of Georgia, and the U.S. Supreme Court under its founding chief justice John Marshall, largely upheld their position. President Jackson then ignored Marshall's majority opinion. A constitutional scholar might argue that Jackson had engaged in contempt of the Supreme Court, an impeachable high crime or misdemeanor. There is no contemporary evidence that Jackson said "The chief justice has rendered his decision, now let him enforce it." The outcome was the same, however. Jackson was no stickler for constitutional fine points.

Despite considerable opposition to his stiffing of the Supreme Court, Jackson was not impeached by the House of Representatives. As today, the United States was deeply divided during the 1830s. One of the most divisive issues, especially among Jackson's southern base, was states' rights. When Jackson ignored the U.S. Supreme Court in the Cherokee case, he was taking the side of the state of Georgia, which sought to seize their land and give it away to non-Indians in a lottery. Had Jackson sided with the Court (and Marshall's ruling in favor of the Cherokees), the Civil War might have started during the 1830s, rather than the early 1860s.

This is the face into which President Trump has chosen to look when he walks into the Oval Office. In *Sharp Knife*, readers will meet Jackson full-front, as he sought to (using current Trumpian political rhetoric) "make America great." While many Anglo-Americans celebrate "Old Hickory" as the original Democrat, who broadened participation in the political system, many Native Americans regard him as the author of a barbaric policy that victimized their ancestors.

Was it "genocide"? Cave finds that largely a semantic argument. The term was not invented until many generations after Jackson and the many trails of tears. The law of genocide requires stated intent (such as Hitler's vow to wipe out the Jews and others), which is absent in Jackson's case. Hitler in his way was less delusional than Jackson, who believed he was *saving* Native people from extermination. Regardless, the toll in human death and suffering was monumental.

Nonetheless, Native American people survived Jackson and Removal, just as the Jews (and many others) outlived Hitler and his own deadly delusions.

Read *Sharp Knife* and enter the mind of the man who was as preoccupied with Removal as President Donald Trump has been with his own attempts to screen out Muslims and build a "great, great wall" along the United States' Mexican border. The past will inform the present.

I am honored to again welcome Alfred Cave to our series, "Native America: Yesterday and Today." He published *Lethal Encounters: Englishmen and Indians in Colonial Virginia* in 2011. My sense of honor is enriched by the fact that Professor Cave has been informing me about American history for the better part of four decades, since I was a doctoral student.

Bruce E. Johansen
Frederick W. Kayser University Research Professor
Communication and Native American Studies
University of Nebraska at Omaha

FURTHER READING

Jackson, Andrew. "Second Annual Message to Congress, 1830." The American Presidency Project. http//www.presidency.ucsb/?pid=67087.

Jackson, Andrew. "Farewell Address." 1837. The American Presidency Project. http//www.presidency.ucsb/?pid=67087.

Preface

On President's Day 2012, the *Indian Country Media Network* named Andrew Jackson the nation's "worst president," claiming that, among other atrocities committed in the course of his career, Jackson during the Creek War had "recommended that troops systematically kill women and children after massacres to complete the extermination." One reader, commenting on that story, confided that "I can't touch a $20 bill without getting the creeps." Another agreed that "blatant bigotry and ruthless blood thirst rightfully earn him a top spot of the worst U.S. Presidents. It's a travesty that his face is on the $20 bill."[1]

Andrew Jackson's unpopularity among Native Americans is hardly new and certainly not surprising. Early in his career as an Indian fighter, they gave him a name—Sharp Knife—that evoked their sense of his ruthlessness and cruelty. But in white America's historic memory, Jackson was Old Hickory, an iconic hero, tough, fearless, and intrepid, the fierce defender of the Republic and of the common (white) man from the treachery of savages, foreigners, and homegrown aristocrats. Belief that he was the chosen agent of divine providence is given its most striking expression in Herman Melville's *Moby Dick*. The narrator invokes "the great democratic God who didst pick up Andrew Jackson from the pebbles, who didst hurl him upon a war horse, who didst thunder him higher than a throne."[2] In a similar if less mystical vein, Frederick Jackson Turner early in the 20th century described Old Hickory as "that fierce Tennessee spirit, who broke the traditions of conservative rule, swept away the privacies and privileges of officialdom, and, like a Gothic leader, opened the temple of the nation to the populace."[3] That belief in his heroic role in American history was not shared by all his contemporaries. Far from it. Jackson was never without critics who deplored various aspects of conduct as a general and as president. But prior to the late 20th century,

Jackson's Indian wars were usually portrayed as necessary and justifiable, and his Indian removal policy, although always controversial, was seldom considered a major issue in the evaluation of his presidency.

Of the handful of presidents usually ranked by historians as "great" or "near great," none in recent years have fared as poorly as Andrew Jackson.[4] In the early spring of 2016 when Secretary of the Treasury Jacob Lew announced, after many months of controversy, that Jackson's portrait would be removed from the face of the $20 bill, to be replaced by Harriet Tubman, an escaped slave, abolitionist activist, and feminist, the American press responded, for the most part, with choruses of approval for Tubman and declarations of reprobation against Jackson. A commentator in *The New York Times* proclaimed simply that Jackson had been "a bad President."[5] Kari Winter, writing in the *Washington Post* concluded that "Jackson represented the worst side of American history."[6] In the same paper the following day, Eugene Robinson reminded readers that not only was Jackson a racist and a slaveholder but was personally responsible for "forcing the mass migration of thousands of Native Americans from the southwest to the west, an exodus called the Trail of Tears that can be described only as genocidal."[7] In the same vein, the *Los Angeles Times* declared that through Jackson's actions "Indians died by the thousands from hunger, cold, and disease."[8] The Fort Worth *Star Telegram* quoted historian Edward Baptist: "Harriet Tubman is what is good about America. Andrew Jackson is what is problematic in our history."[9] The *Dallas Daily News* editorial found in the removal of Jackson and the celebration of Tubman "proof that America is finally recalibrating the image it sees when it looks in the mirror. It is a correction slow in coming and long overdue." Jackson, though a "war hero and a milestone president" is "also inextricably linked to the shame of America's inhumanly harsh treatment of Native Americans during his time on stage."[10] A cartoon in the *Los Angeles Times* portrayed a $20 bill with a scowling Andrew Jackson complaining that "it's that damned musical that got Hamilton spared and got me banished." A skeleton wearing an Indian robe and feather hairdress replies, "Strange. You'd think genocide would've been enough."[11] The *Salt Lake Tribune* bluntly declared Jackson "the war criminal on our $20 bill."[12]

Until recently, American historians generally avoided use of the term "genocide." It has not been a traditional part of our collective sense of the American past. The word was not to be found in the textbooks given to school children. It was rarely invoked in narratives or specialized monographs published by scholars. A few radicals (notably Ward Churchill and David Stannard) claimed that Indians at the hands of European invaders and pioneer settlers suffered a catastrophe comparable to the Nazi Holocaust. But they were ignored by a profession generally committed to the celebration of American Exceptionalism.

Times have changed. One fall afternoon, several years ago, my granddaughter informed me that the family gathering about to occur should not be called "Thanksgiving." "My friends," she explained, "call it Genocide Day." As Alex Alvarez noted in 2014, there is now "a great deal of resistance to the idea of perceiving the history of Native America [in its contacts with Europeans] as consisting of anything other than genocide." To do so, it is feared, might somehow discount and minimize Native American "suffering and victimization."[13] A recent news story in the *New York Times* on racial slurs referred, without further comment or explanation, to "the fact of sustained genocide" as a fundamental reality of Native American experience.[14] That is the assumption underlying the editorial celebrations that accompanied Andrew Jackson's recent "demotion" on our currency quoted above. American politicians now seldom claim him as a role model. President Trump's declaration of admiration for that "amazing figure in American history" made the headlines and did nothing to reassure Trump's many critics.[15]

Was Andrew Jackson, aka Sharp Knife, guilty of the crime of genocide? Before trying to answer that question we need to define the term. On that matter there has been surprisingly little agreement over the years. As one prominent genocide scholar has written, "few ideas are as important in public debate, but in few cases are the meaning and scope of a key idea less clearly agreed."[16] Let us begin with the origins of the word itself. Coined by Raphael Lemkin in 1943, it combines "the Greek *genos* (race, tribe) and the Latin *cide* (killing)." Lemkin defined its meaning "as the destruction of a nation or of an ethnic group."[17] But by "destruction" he meant not only mass killing but also a lethal assault on "the way of life and institutions of a people." A genocidal invader not only occupies territory and kills those who resist but also undertakes the degradation and displacement of its indigenous inhabitants. Their collective cultural identity is first crippled, then destroyed, to be replaced by culture of the invader. The survivors may be killed, exiled, or reduced to a servile state. His reading of documents relating to the Nazi plan for the incorporation of much of Eastern Europe into the Reich through "Germanization" of both its culture and population afforded Lemkin the key model for this process.[18] But the Nazis, in his view, were not original or unique. Genocide was of ancient origin. A trail of blood, Lemkin believed, flowed from ancient Rome to the present day.[19]

Lemkin's historical inquiries into recurrent patterns of conquest characterized by efforts to bring about "the destruction of the way of life of a people" predated the Nazi Holocaust. Born in 1900, Jewish by ethnicity, a Pole by citizenship, trained as a lawyer, Lemkin, a man of deep convictions and wide-reaching scholarly interests, since childhood had shown a particular interest and concern with the persecution of ethnic and religious groups. (At age 10, he read with fascination and horror the popular novel *Quo Vadis* with its vivid account of Nero's atrocities against the Christians). In the early 1930s he advocated, in a report to an international gathering of jurists in Madrid, the establishment of international laws prohibiting "barbarity" and "vandalism" (the terms he used before his coinage of "genocide"). In the early 1940s, after Hitler invaded Eastern Europe, Lemkin suffered the loss of all of his family, including parents and siblings, in the Holocaust.[20]

Finding refuge in the United States, he devoted the remainder of his life to lobbying for the creation of an international rule of law that would declare genocide in all of its manifestations criminal and make possible the individual punishment of its perpetrators. Attending the Nuremberg War Trials, Lemkin tried to persuade the tribunal to recognize genocide as an international crime. He failed. Genocide was not one of the formal charges in the indictments of the war criminals, although there were some allusions to that term in connection with "crimes against humanity" throughout the course of the trail. Returning to New York City, Lemkin then lobbied the newly formed United Nations. Finally with much difficulty, and after some compromises, he won support for a resolution defining and outlawing genocide. In 1948, in response to that resolution, the United Nations Convention on Genocide declared that "genocide means any of the following acts committed with intent to destroy, in whole or in part, a national, ethnical, racial, or religious group as such:

a. Killing members of the group
b. Causing severe bodily harm
c. Deliberately inflicting on members of the group conditions of life calculated to bring about its destruction in whole or in part
d. Imposing measures intended to prevent births within the group
e. Forcibly transferring children of the group to another group."

The declaration, it must be noted, was by no means as comprehensive as Lemkin's concept. In response to political pressures from the United States, the United Kingdom, and the Soviet Union, whole categories of victims were omitted and thus denied protection. The convention failed to declare state-sponsored mass killing to eliminate a political group, or an economic class, acts of genocide. Thus, in years to come, the work of right-wing death squads in Latin America, the slaughter of suspected leftists in Indonesia after the fall of Sukarno, Pol Pot's bloody campaign of class extermination in Cambodia, to name only a few examples, all technically fell outside the definition set in 1948. The UN Declaration also failed to do justice to Lemkin's thinking about "cultural genocide."[21]

Given the shortcomings of the UN Declaration, it is not surprising that there have been over 20 proposed new definitions, most of which broaden, others which narrow, the meaning of the word.[22] Historian Jeffrey Ostler notes that conservative definitions emphasize intentional actions and policies of governments that result in very large population losses, usually from direct killing. More liberal definitions call for less stringent criteria for intent, focusing more on outcomes. They do not necessarily require sanction by state authorities; rather they identify societal forces and actors. They also allow for several intersecting forces of destruction, including dispossession and disease.[23]

We will not try to resolve all the points of disagreement, as on some issues related to the genocide question matters of ideological conviction, as well as commitments to various philosophical assumptions and personal loyalties, render resolution not only unlikely but probably impossible. However, it is important to note that most, if not all definitions, discussions, and analyses of genocide assume its advocates and perpetrators are driven by a conviction that, because of certain perceived racial, moral, intellectual, cultural, or religious deficiencies or tendencies, there are groups of people residing in their midst who are unworthy of inclusion in the community and do not deserve its protection and support. Their deficiencies and propensities render them at best a threat to the community's well-being and at worst endanger its survival.

Reviewing the voluminous documentary records of Andrew Jackson's long career as an Indian fighter, treaty negotiator, and president, from his earliest years on the Tennessee frontier to his last days at the Hermitage, leaves us no reason to doubt that he was a ruthless opponent of Indians who, in his view, threatened the United States. As we shall see in the pages to come, private letters, military dispatches, and public speeches over the years are consistent in their view of such Indians as cruel, treacherous, irrational, and inhuman brutes who must never be trusted. During his military campaigns against the Creeks and the Seminoles, he insisted that there was no obligation, indeed, nor reason, to respect the laws of war when dealing with "savages." Sharp Knife frequently called for the "extermination" of entire Indian nations who took up arms. The frontier Indian wars were nasty and brutal. Indians and whites alike could—and often did—tell stories that illustrated the inhumanity of the enemy, stories that told of scalpings, torture of prisoners by fire, and of disembowelments, impalements, and castrations. Noncombatants were not always spared. The records of the period indicate that Andrew Jackson's talk of "extermination" was not just rhetorical. To cite one example, we will investigate in more depth in a subsequent chapter, Sharp Knife in his first Indian War ordered the killing of all the Creek prophets (religious leaders) and described in detail in letters to his wife the slaughter of the surviving warriors at Horseshoe. The records also tell us that Jackson's men sometimes boasted about killing Indian infants and the elderly. No one under Jackson's command was ever disciplined for atrocities committed against Indian noncombatants. Jackson personally kept as mementos several scalps lifted during the Creek War.[24]

But there is another side to this story. Hundreds of Indian warriors from several nations fought as Jackson's ally against other Indians, and he called a number of their chiefs his friends. He adopted an Indian boy orphaned during one of his campaigns. He frequently portrayed himself as the friend and benefactor of those Indians who remained at peace with the United States. Ronald Satz, the historian of Jacksonian era Indian policy argues that Andrew Jackson harbored no feelings of animosity toward the Indian. Jackson was not the merciless Indian hater most historians have portrayed. Although he was a ruthless opponent in battle, Old Hickory demonstrated great paternalism in his dealings with Indians as territorial governor of Florida. He also openly sanctioned Indian-white marriages, adopted an Indian orphan, whom he treated as his own son, and counted hundreds of full bloods as personal friends.[25]

All that is true. But as we ponder claims regarding Sharp Knife's paternalistic benevolence, we should bear in mind that Jackson throughout his career was opposed to Indian-white coexistence within the states. Even a cursory reading of Jackson's letters, speeches, and private memoranda reveals his lifelong belief that Indian communities must not be allowed to remain east of the Mississippi River. Jackson and his supporters argued that his removal program was humane, intended not to damage, kill or impoverish Indians but to save them by removing them from harm's way. A few scholars have agreed, and declared Old Hickory the friend and benefactor of the Indians who without his paternal concern would have perished in even greater numbers.[26] But they are now as minority. The record of his many interactions with Native American peoples simply does not support his self-image as a humanitarian.

You will recall that the 1948 UN Convention required that it be demonstrated that the perpetrators acted with the deliberate intent to do grievous harm to the victim group. Those who deem Jackson guilty of genocide find the strongest evidence in support of their case in the records regarding Jackson's efforts to expedite the Indian Removal program. His Indian removal treaties were obtained through intimidation, fraud, and bribery. More to the point, as a result of his work first as a negotiator and later as president, Native Americans driven from their homelands, sometimes at the point of a bayonet, were subjected to "conditions of life" so harsh that thousands perished before they reached the new territories they had been promised, and many others, their health shattered by the ordeal, died soon thereafter. Jackson was well aware of the deprivation and suffering those measures brought to thousands of the dispossessed. Indeed, and this is a crucial point, Jackson acted in collusion with state officials who condoned, or in some cases engaged, in their harassment. As president, he systematically removed from office federal Indian agents deemed too sympathetic to Indians and too protective of their rights.

Throughout his career, Andrew Jackson used, and often abused, his power and authority to force Native American abandonment of their homelands. To cite a crucial example of his abuse of power, Jackson as president, in defiance of all precedent, maintained that the federal government had no jurisdiction over Indians living within the boundaries of the states or any responsibility to them other than the payment of annuities for past land cessions. He, therefore, refused to carry out the duty, given to him under the Constitution, to uphold long-standing treaty guarantees regarding their physical safety, their territorial boundaries, and their rights to limited self-government. He made his position clear to both the states and to Native American communities, advising the latter that they would be secure from harm only if they left their traditional homelands.

Denial of the protection of the law to the proscribed group is a fundamental characteristic of a genocidal regime. To reiterate and expand a point made earlier, advocates and defenders of genocide, however they may disagree on other particulars, invariably argue that the targeted group is unworthy of inclusion in the community, that its continued presence is in some way a threat, either to the security or prosperity of the dominant group, and that means must therefore be found to effect its diminishment or removal. Andrew Jackson's lifetime agreement with those premises will be documented in depth in the pages to come.

Gary Clayton Anderson maintains that Jackson's Indian removal program was not genocide, in that its object was not the physical extermination of Native

Americans but rather ethnic cleansing on a very large scale.[27] I have argued elsewhere that ethnic cleansing is a form (or perhaps one should say, an early phase) of genocide, as it targets all members of the group indiscriminately, results in increased mortality, and is rooted in the belief that certain populations because of their inherent group characteristics must not be allowed to remain within the community. By defining genocide as "deliberately inflicting upon members of a group conditions intended to bring about its physical destruction in whole or in part" the 1948 UN Convention of Genocide in effect implicitly included "ethnic cleansing." Bear in mind that the term itself was not in use in 1948.[28] While we do need to recognize that the Indian removal programs in early 19th-century North America were in many ways unlike the genocides of the 20th century, it does not follow that they were not genocidal. Benjamin Lieberman has argued that we can distinguish ethnic cleansing from genocide, as the former does not involve advocacy of physical extermination. He adds, however, that "extreme forms of ethnic cleansing overlap with genocide" when the process results in a marked increase in mortality. In the same vein, historian Christopher D. Haveman noted that "at its most extreme, ethnic cleansing is genocide."[29] But ethnic cleansing almost always leads to increased mortality (this writer cannot think of an exception), so this distinction is of limited value. What percentage of the dispossessed must die as a result of the brutal conditions inflicted upon the victims of forced removal before we call it "genocide?"

Some writers have claimed that the key to separating ethnic cleansing from genocide is intent, maintaining that only if there is clear evidence that the framers of removal policies intended to kill, as opposed to dispossessing, indigenous peoples can we claim that they have initiated a program of genocide. But we encounter several problems when we try to apply that standard to specific historical circumstances. The perpetrators often deny their guilt, either by covering up the evidence or declaring (as did Andrew Jackson) that the removal program was a humanitarian undertaking designed to protect and uplift the dispossessed group. They not infrequently claim that they acted righteously, as removal saved backward peoples from extinction. On the other hand, in some ethnic cleansing-genocide programs, we find no effort to deny that the policy in question is murderous. Instead the indigenous peoples are described as subhuman, treacherous, a danger to decent and civilized people. To kill them, it is argued, is to do the work of God. Public defense of group annihilation is not commonly found in the declarations of Anglo-American leaders but it is by no means totally absent from our history. There have been places and times in the American past when clergymen (for example, Puritan New England early 16th century), governors and semiofficial killing squads (early in the history of Texas and California), and newspaper columnists (the South and the West, 19th century) cried for the "extermination" of some or all of the Indian tribes in their region.

The debate over the distinction between genocide and ethnic cleansing has been of only limited value in explaining the circumstances that led to these horrendous events. A more promising line of inquiry, I suggest, has been proposed by the proponents of the "settler colonialism" school.[30] Their examinations of the economic and social evolution of the British colonies and the states and territories of the independent United States indicate that within a few generations their settlers had largely abandoned the original patterns of colonialism, and in doing so radically marginalized the indigenous peoples. As Walter L. Hixson has written, "what primarily distinguishes settler colonialism from colonialism proper is that the settlers came not to exploit the original population for economic gain but rather to remove them from the colonial space."[31] Tony Barta, a leading Australian scholar, has pointed out that colonial settlements that marginalize indigenous peoples because of their need to appropriate their land and resources soon find themselves in a relationship "that implicitly rather than explicitly, in ways that were inevitable rather than intentional," becomes "a relationship of genocide." The origins of genocide are most often to be found, not in the examination of original statements of intent, which may contain no hint of plans for extermination but in the ongoing economic conditions and social realities in colonies that derived little or no profit from the protection and exploitation of indigenous labor.[32] A. Dirk Moses, also an Australian and a pioneer in the study of settler colonialism, notes that "occupation policies that are not initially murderous can radicalize or escalate in an exterminatory direction when they are resisted."[33] "Settler colonial projects," remarks Lorenzo Veracini, "are specifically interested in turning indigenous peoples into refugees."[34] His comment is one we should keep in mind as we assess Andrew Jackson's dealings with Native Americans.

As the *Dallas Daily News* suggested in the column previously cited, the current popular revulsion at Jackson's conduct of Indian relations does offer some "proof that America is finally recalibrating the image it sees when it looks in the mirror. It is a correction slow in coming and long overdue." But while it is useful, indeed, essential, that we face with honesty and with humility the evidence of a very dark part of our past we've too long worked hard to ignore, simply condemning Jackson, stamping the dread word "genocide" on his image, is not enough. We must bear in mind that labeling does not necessarily lead to better understanding. Sometimes it is an obstacle. We need to ask why Andrew Jackson, and his many supporters, regarded the thorough ethnic cleansing of the eastern United States, through removal of most of its Indian population, as essential to the security and well-being of both whites and Indians. That requires that we look very closely at the voluminous evidence we have concerning Andrew Jackson's thoughts as well as his actions during his long career as an Indian fighter and Indian ally, Indian negotiator, territorial governor, and finally president. It goes without saying that we need to place him within his historical context. Few public policymakers are either original or solitary thinkers or actors and Andrew Jackson was no exception. We must attend, also, to the testimony of those who opposed Jackson's Indian policy, ponder the alternatives they offered, and seek to understand their objectives and the reasons they failed. By pursuit of those questions, we may indeed help recalibrate that image we see in the mirror. We may also be surprised by what we find there.

Chapter 1

A Man on the Make

Andrew Jackson's origins, as Melville suggests in his image of a man "picked up from the pebbles" by "the great democratic God," were humble. Jackson was born in 1767 to an impoverished family of Scotch-Irish immigrants, a family that offered none of the social advantages and economic resources usually available to aspiring young leaders in the early years of the Republic. Andrew first saw the light of day in a small farmhouse belonging to a relative and located in a backcountry district known as the Waxhaws some miles to the south of Salisbury. It is uncertain whether that birthplace was located in North or South Carolina, but Andrew Jackson believed that he was a South Carolinian by birth and the burden of scholarly opinion supports that view. His father, a hardscrabble farmer who worked but apparently never owned a piece of marginally fertile land near Twelve Mile Creek, died either shortly before or soon after the birth of his third son, Andrew. The infant's widowed mother abandoned the family's rude cabin and the red clay field her husband had struggled to cultivate and moved in with a sister, whom she now served as a housekeeper. Local lore maintains that she hoped Andrew would be called to the Presbyterian ministry, but those stories also tell us that the young man seemed unsuited for the cloth. Even as a child, he had a hair-trigger temper and a foul mouth, frequently flooding "a room with bloodcurdling oaths that frightened his listeners half to death." He was also remembered as a boisterous, fun-loving boy fond of games and pranks. He developed early on a love of horses and of wagering on horse races. The high-spirited young Andrew in some recollections was a bully, and in others, a defender of the vulnerable, particularly of those who sought his protection. He matured rapidly into a lean, tall, redheaded youth, not as strong as many of his fellows but as tough as any of them. One classmate later related that in wrestling matches he "could throw him three times out of four, but he would never *stay throwed*."[1]

Jackson had some schooling between the ages of 8 and 13 and briefly again in his mid-teens. He later recalled studying "the dead languages." Throughout his life, Jackson occasionally inserted a Latin phrase or a reference to Shakespeare into his correspondence. (Three come to mind: "Cathago est Delenda" [sic], "Something is rotten in the state of Denmark," and "Et tu, Brute.") But while he was never the semi-illiterate frontier barbarian described by his political enemies, Jackson was, in comparison to early presidents, poorly educated. He was not, however, unintelligent, and in later life his letters and his communiqués, and, as president, his own drafts of state papers, although deficient in spelling and sometimes awkward in both grammar and syntax, displayed a passionate commitment both to republican ideals and to the expansion of the Republic. Although not a learned man, Jackson came to respect learning and later in life stressed in advice to a nephew the importance of "having a good library." His own library at the Hermitage numbered some 800 volumes. He urged the study of history and regarded the stories of the Scottish chiefs "as particularly instructive."[2] One recent scholar conjectures that Jackson came to see himself as a Thane, a heroic self-made leader committed to fight evil and uphold honor.[3]

The coming of the American Revolution to the Waxhaws effectively ended Andrew Jackson's childhood. The Jacksons were staunch supporters of independence. When British armies occupied South Carolina, Jackson's older brothers fought for the resistance. In June 1779, Hugh died of heatstroke and battle fatigue shortly after the battle of Stono Ferry. Less than a year later, in the Waxhaws, Lieutenant Colonel Banastre Tarleton's army overcame the patriot forces commanded by Abraham Buford and, ignoring their white flag of surrender, massacred 113 and grievously wounded about 150 others. Survivors were cared for at the Waxhaws log meeting house. Andrew's mother Elizabeth was among those who nursed them. Andrew, although still a child of 13, joined the revolutionaries as a messenger. With his surviving brother Robert, he was taken prisoner when the British raided the Waxhaws again in April 1781 and burned the meeting house. Held for a time in a local house belonging to Thomas Crawford, a cousin, both boys were ordered to clean a British officer's boots, and both refused. As Jackson many years later recalled the scene, the officer then struck him in the head with a saber. He tried to deflect the blow with his hand. "The sword point," he wrote, "reached my head and has left a mark there as durable as the scull, as well as on the fingers." Robert was also struck by the saber, receiving a deep cut on his scalp.[4]

Jackson was embittered by the British treatment of prisoners of war. Confined with about 250 others in the Camden Jail, he recalled that "no attention whatever was paid to the wounds or the comfort of prisoners, and the small pox having broken out among them, for want of proper care, many of them fell victim to it. I frequently heard them groaning in the agonies of death and no regard was paid to them."[5] Both brothers became gravely ill. During a prisoner exchange, their mother came to take them home. Robert died. Andrew was bedridden for many months. When he was out of danger, his mother joined other women of the Waxhaws in journeying to Charleston to nurse American prisoners held in

British hulks in the harbor. The ships were riddled with cholera. Elizabeth caught the disease, sickened, died, and was buried in an unmarked grave. Her surviving son received a small bundle containing his dead mother's clothes. Throughout his lifetime, Jackson detested the British. In 1813, he remarked to a close friend that he had been "brought up under the tyranny of Britain."[6]

Young Jackson's loathing of the British was matched by his detestation of their Indian allies. During his childhood, Jackson had formed a view of Indians as barbaric, cruel, and treacherous, a view that mirrored the convictions and prejudices of his kinsfolk and neighbors. Susan Alexander, an elderly lady who had known Jackson's mother, claimed in 1845 that Elizabeth Jackson was "at dreadful enmity with the Indians." She related that "Mrs. Jackson and her son Andrew came to our house . . . they were inveterate haters of the Indians, on account of their barbarities—both he and his mother." Mrs. Alexander added, "Oh, we all suffered by those horrid Indians, and the remembrance of it is not gone out of me yet."[7] Like other children growing up in the Carolina backcountry, young Andrew heard and on occasion retold some truly sickening stories of Indian atrocities committed elsewhere, in earlier times and other places. Those stories spoke not only of killing and scalping of innocent white women and children, as well as adult male settlers, but also of rape, castration, disembowelment, and other horrors. A hint of their tenor is found in the report of two prominent Cherokee leaders who met with President Jackson in the White House in 1831. Remembering the Indian lore of his childhood, Old Hickory informed his guests that their old rivals the Catawba, though now "poor, miserable, reduced in numbers" through long association with whites, in their days of power regularly "threw captives in the fire and, when their intestines were barbequed, ate them."[8]

Such Indian atrocity stories had been common currency in the British colonies long before Andrew Jackson's birth. They led the British cleric (and cofounder of Methodism) John Wesley, who served as rector of a church in South Carolina in 1735–1736, to hold up American Indians as extreme examples of human depravity. "The natural religion of the Creeks, Cherokees, Chickasaws and all other Indians," Wesley wrote, "is to torture all of their prisoners from morning to night till at length they roast them to death . . . it is a common thing among them for the son, if he thinks his father lives too long, to knock out his brains."[9]

Those who accepted such stories of savagery easily came to believe that killing an Indian was a meritorious act. Consider the now forgotten case of the folk hero Tom Quick, who died in 1795, the year when 28-year-old Andrew Jackson was elected a delegate to Tennessee's constitutional convention. Historian Patrick Griffin relates that Quick had devoted his life to avenging his father's murder by a Delaware Indian. Over a three decade period, Quick

> killed Indians hunting, sleeping, eating, drinking. He shot, tomahawked, stabbed, and bludgeoned Indians. He pushed Indians off of cliffs. He slaughtered them when sober and when drunk. He butchered men, women, and children,

as well as whole families. As he put it after he had dashed out the brains of an infant, "Nits make lice." He preyed on some close to his home, including the Delaware who had scalped his father, and ambushed others far away.

Quick had hoped to kill at least 100, but by the time of his terminal illness in 1795, he "was one short of his grisly goal." He reportedly asked that an Indian be dragged to the foot of his sick bed, so he could shoot his final victim, but no Indian could be found in the vicinity. After his death, Quick was transformed into a folk hero. Throughout the 19th century, his bloody career was celebrated and often embellished in books, stories, and even stage dramas. Quick's cruelty was justified as a necessity in the ongoing battle against the savage, and his excesses as a killer were not only excused but glorified. A monument "In honor of Tom Quick, the Indian slayer, the Avenger of the Delaware" was erected in 1889 in his hometown in Pennsylvania, at a celebratory dedication covered by the *New York Times*. There it remained for over a century until in 1997 "unknown assailants" finally tore it down. By then, it had become a civic embarrassment. But in earlier times, writes Patrick Griffin, "Quick epitomized the triumph of civilization and democratic values over savagery."[10]

Andrew Jackson was the child of the culture that produced and celebrated Tom Quick. From the mid-18th century onward, political leaders in British North America had found in their common struggles against savages the key to transcending the many diverse and conflicting interests and identities that divided them. "Patriot" leaders during the American Revolution, in promoting the belief in of a "common cause" unifying the colonies against British tyranny charged that the Mother Country was actively promoting not only slave rebellions but Indian massacres. In revolutionary rhetoric praise of the Rights of Man was accompanied by strident invocations of racial prejudice and fear.[11]

Throughout his life, Andrew Jackson regarded the removal of the Indian as essential to the peace, security, and prosperity of the West. It is not surprising that his first written commentary on Indian affairs, penned a few years after he settled in Tennessee, denied that Indians can be trusted to honor treaty commitments or follow "the law of nations." To negotiate with savages, Jackson argued, was to give them "a more easy Road to [commit] Murder with impunity."[12] Jackson never really abandoned that view of Indian character. Although he would use Indian allies in his wars, in his treaty negotiations, and in his land deals, even cursory survey of his papers and correspondence leaves no doubt that he believed throughout his life that for the most part they were not to be trusted. They had no sense of honor. Jackson did make some exceptions, for a very few who did his bidding (the Creek chieftain and slaveholder McIntosh is an example), but they were infrequent.

Orphaned in his early teens, Jackson had few prospects. He lived for a time in the Waxhaws with relatives, assisting in a saddler's shop. He received a small inheritance from his grandfather, which he squandered trying to play the role of a high living young gentleman in Charleston. In 1782, he went back to school in the Waxhaws, studying with Robert McCulloch, then in 1783–1784 reputedly taught grammar school for a time himself. But he had little reason to remain there, lacking, it would appear, any close personal ties to his relatives in the region. In later life, he seldom mentioned and never visited his South Carolina kinfolk. In fact, he often claimed, falsely, he had no living kinfolk in America.[13] At age 17, Jackson moved on to Salisbury, North Carolina, where he read law with two locally prominent attorneys, Spruce McCay and John Stokes. In 1787, he received his law license, set up practice in Martinsville, but found the opportunities there limited. A year later he moved west, to serve as public prosecutor for the western district in the future state of Tennessee, an unenviable and daunting task in that very rough and semi-lawless region.

A decade after his death biographer James Parton, searching for eyewitnesses who could shed light on his early years, visited the town of Salisbury, North Carolina, where Jackson in his late teens had read law in preparation for admission to the bar. For the most part, the respectable people of Salisbury whose recollections Parton related did not have particularly fond memories of the young aspiring lawyer. Many remembered him as a wild and irresponsible hell-raiser and professed astonishment at his political success. He was, they reported, considered "the most roaring, rollicking, game-cocking, horse-racing, card-playing, mischievous fellow that ever lived in Salisbury" but was not regarded as a man of much promise. A prankster, Jackson, it was recalled, had spoiled a holiday celebration by inviting two prostitutes to a fancy Christmas ball. One lady, learning some years later that he was running for the presidency of the United States, had exclaimed, "Andrew Jackson? The Jackson that used to live in Salisbury? Why, when he was here he was such a rake that my husband would not bring him into the house! It was true that he *might* have taken him into the stable to weigh horses for a race, and might drink a glass of whiskey with him *there*. Well, if Andrew Jackson can be President, anybody can!"[14]

While researching the first volume of his Jackson biography, Parton also came upon a story that probably wasn't true, but that nonetheless is of value to our understanding of the role Indian fighting would play in the making of Andrew Jackson's political career. In the early fall of 1788, Andrew Jackson, a 21-year-old lawyer newly appointed to the post of public prosecutor for the western district of North Carolina (now in Tennessee), joined a 120 other pioneers traveling under armed guard from Jonesborough through Indian country to the tiny frontier settlement at Nashville. Some 70 years later, his biographer James Parton recorded a very remarkable story about young Jackson's rescue of the party from massacre. The account came "from the lips of Thomas Searcy, the clerk of the Superior Court, who rode by Jackson's side." After a particularly arduous 36-hour march through the most hazardous part of the newly opened road to Nashville, the company, believing it had traveled beyond immediate danger, stopped to make camp for the night. After posting sentinels, most of the travelers fell asleep. Jackson, although not on guard duty, remained awake, listening to the hooting of owls in the nearby woods. Suddenly, from a distance, he heard a loud owllike sound. That, he thought, was too loud. Suspicious, he woke up Searcy.

As Parton records the story, Jackson whispered, "Searcy, raise your head and make no noise."

"What's the matter?" asked Searcy.

"The owls—listen—there—there again. Isn't that a little too natural?"

"Do you think so?" asked Searcy.

"I know it," replied Jackson. "There are Indians all around us. I have heard them in every direction. They mean to attack us before daybreak."

Jackson and Searcy then "roused . . . the more experienced woodsmen" who "confirmed the young lawyer's surmise." On Jackson's advice, the camp was broken up and the party marched on through the night. But an hour after they left, several hunters made camp at the site they had abandoned. All but one were killed by the Indians before daybreak. The following spring, Judge John McNairy, having "no Jackson in his retinue," nearly lost his life in an Indian attack "near the same spot." Three members of his party, including "one friendly chief and his son," perished.[15]

James Parton believed that story. But it is not very plausible. We must ask why did it not become part of the Jackson lore until so long after Old Hickory's death? Of the hundreds of people who knew Jackson and were interviewed by Parton, how is it that only Searcy remembered this astounding episode in the life of his hero? If woods were indeed full of Indians that night, why was the party not attacked at the time it was most vulnerable, awakening from sleep, striking tents, gathering children and possessions? As Parton notes, Andrew Jackson was not an experienced wilderness guide. But that raises a question as to how it is that he understood the fraudulent nature of owl hoots that the more seasoned hands missed? James Parton's biography is a treasure trove of recollections of Andrew Jackson. But he was sometimes rather credulous.[16] This tale is not really believable.

But that is not really the point. Like all stories of the early deeds of heroes, this story, so readily believed by Parton's readers, tells us a great deal about the nature of the Jackson myth and the role of Indians in that myth. As a young man, Jackson, as he sought to build a life and career on the newly opened frontier of the upper south, entered a world in which the Indian was an object of fear, fear rooted in a recent and continuing history of conflict marked by sickening atrocities committed against Indians and by them. The massacre that Jackson allegedly averted could easily have happened. Jackson's preeminent modern biographer Robert Remini gives the Searcy tale some credibility. While conceding that "some of its details" might be "exaggerated," he finds it "appropriate to the Jackson legend."[17] While this story was, as far as we can tell, not part of that legend during Jackson's lifetime, its portrayal of Jackson as a man of great intuitive insight who knew who the people's enemies were, and took bold and decisive action to thwart them, was at the core of the Old Hickory legend. Parton's retelling of the Searcy story, with its emphasis on Jackson's clear understanding of the threat posed by Indians and on his preternatural ability to sense and deal with that threat, tells us much about the popular image of the man who would become first the nation's preeminent Indian fighter and later the president responsible for a program to rid the eastern United States of the Indians' presence.

When Andrew Jackson took up residence in Nashville in 1788, the town, which within a little more than a decade would emerge as "a center of fashionable life for the old west," had only a few hundred inhabitants.[18] There was a crude one room log courthouse, a distillery, a pair of taverns, two stores, and a very few houses. Most of the still beleaguered population made do in rude cabins, tents, and other "non-descript shelters."[19] The first church (Methodist) was not built until 1796. Prior to 1797, there was no mail service linking Nashville with the rest of the world; nor was there a newspaper. Both made their first appearance in that year. The town possessed only one brick house at that time. Most residents still lived in small log cabins, protected from the Indians by makeshift stockades.[20] The Indian raids continued well into the 1790s and claimed scores of lives in the region each year. To cite but one example, in 1792, two families, James Thompson's and Peter Caffrey's, were attacked within five miles of Nashville. All the adults, men and women alike, and most of the children perished. Two smaller children were spared, after being told by one of their English-speaking assailants that they'd be back to finish the job and kill them once they grew up.[21]

Jackson lore maintains that after such incidents the newcomer often took command of retaliatory raids. An historian of Tennessee, writing in 1859, claimed that Jackson from his first days in Nashville was filled with "great ambition for encounters with the savages" and engaged in Indian fighting to "his heart's content."[22] There may be some exaggeration here. We cannot find evidence in contemporary documents that he actually commanded war parties at this time, but it is highly likely that he participated in raids led by older, more experienced Indian fighters. It is clear that he shared their belief that "killing Indians and driving them south and west was the only way to safeguard the Tennessee frontier."[23] In a letter critical of federal treaty making written in 1794, Jackson complained that "they have been Constantly infesting our frontier."[24]

Although the victims of Indian raids, their kinfolk, and frontier politicians saw in such atrocities proof of innate Indian savagery, they are better understood as acts of resistance against those who sought to drive them from their homelands. On the southwestern frontier, fortunes were made through speculation in those lands, often even before Indians had entered into treaties or purchases extinguishing title. Although for practical reasons Indian lands were sometimes bought, usually for a pittance, it was widely assumed, particularly in the west, that Indians really had no land rights, either because of their savagery and backwardness, or because they had often supported the British during the Revolution and were therefore now a conquered people. An editorial writer in the *Knoxville Gazette* in 1792 declared bluntly "the original right of these aborigines to the soil . . . is a right of which I have never thought with much respect. It is like the claim of children . . . I first saw it. . . ."[25] During the Confederation years, states often laid claim to tracts of land still occupied by Indian tribes, using some of that land to settle their debts to Revolutionary War veterans, making the remainder available for public purchase. The original owners were simply driven out.

The infamous North Carolina land grab of 1783, engineered by Jackson's future political sponsor William Blount, had opened up to white purchase and occupation vast tracts in Tennessee, including regions still owned and occupied by Indian tribes. Many of the dispossessed fought back, aided by the Spanish governor of Louisiana who supplied them with guns. The Chickamauga band of Cherokee, led by Dragging Canoe, struck isolated frontier settlers, provoking bloody reprisals. To placate the Indians, North Carolina officials promised to hold a treaty conference and arrange payment for the lands they had seized. That promise was never kept. The federal treaty of Hopewell of 1785 restored title to some Tennessee land to the Cherokee, but most of the roughly 3 million acres at issue remained in the hands of white land speculators. Blount was the most voracious of those speculators. One distinguished historian writes of Jackson's patron: "The entire Southwest was his hunting grounds and he stuffed his pockets with the profits of his speculations in land. In the maw of his incredible ambition—or greed—there originated land grabs involving thousands of choice acres."[26] The North Carolina land grab was neither the first nor the last Blount land seizure, but it was among the most lucrative to those in a position to exploit its potential.

Most settlers were unable to share in the largess made possible by Indian dispossession. Land purchase warrants, as historian Thomas Abernethy noted, "could be secured only after a tract had been visited and located roughly by marking its boundaries," and warrants for that purpose had to be obtained from a land office within seven months of the passage of the act. Even if the settler had the necessary funds to buy the land, the difficulties of carrying out surveys in remote regions not accessible by road and then meeting the deadline for entering the claim meant that "the average citizen had little chance to profit from this legislation. . . ."[27] But land speculators who could hire surveyors earned fabulous profits. The father of the future Rachel Jackson, the late Colonel John Donelson, "and his numerous children . . . obtained much of the best land in the Cumberland Valley, often at the expense of original settlers who lacked the means to file for the land they were on." One of his sons, Shockley, took advantage of his position as a state surveyor to acquire, among other properties, some 20,000 acres near the site of the future city of Chattanooga.[28]

Jackson's connections with the Donelsons paved the way for his emergence as member of the fledgling state's elite. Although his own origins were humble and obscure, soon after his arrival in Tennessee in 1788, he quickly formed attachments and alliances with people of prominence. He boarded at the home of the widow of Colonel Donelson, a founder of Nashville, and became the protector and later the husband of Donelson's daughter Rachel, then married to the dour and abusive Lewis Robards. The irregularities of his subsequent marriage to Rachel, too well known to require recounting here, would later be a source of some embarrassment to Andrew Jackson, but affiliation with the one of Nashville's leading families brought many advantages. He formed close friendships with some of the territory's most prominent citizens. Jackson was among the young men who caught the eye and won the favor of the territory's powerful and wealthy governor, William Blount, a man Indians nicknamed "the Dirt King" for his success in acquiring their land. A shrewd operator with an eye for the main chance, the rising young attorney soon aligned himself with the powerful Blount faction.

Jackson earned a good living in Nashville, for while his position as district attorney for the Mero district carried no stipend, he soon developed a very successful private practice representing creditors who had previously been unable to collect on debts. During the first few years of his residence, Jackson "handled between one-fourth and one-half of all cases on the docket" in Davidson County, including virtually all of the suits against debtors.[29] His practice involved extensive travel over crude and dangerous backcountry roads and required both courage and toughness. In one celebrated incident in Sumner County, one defendant tried to bully Jackson by stepping on his foot. Jackson grabbed a piece of wood and knocked out his larger would-be assailant.[30]

Despite the primitive conditions, the work proved lucrative. As currency was scarce, he was often paid for his services in land. His new land holdings, acquired in a variety of ways, soon made him a man of prominence and influence. Despite later rumors of irregularity, Jackson's business dealings were generally legitimate. But on at least one occasion, he did accept a bribe from land speculators during his short term as a U.S. senator. A promoter for the notorious Yazoo land company added Jackson's name to a list of politicians who were to be given gifts of land from the company's fraudulent claim at Muscle Shoals on the Tennessee River. Jackson was down for a thousand acres, but the fraud was exposed, and he did not profit from this venture.[31] However, most, although not all, of Jackson's land transactions were very lucrative. To cite one well-documented example, in 1798 he acquired, for $100, a half interest in 500 acres at the Chickasaw Bluffs, on the Mississippi, land then occupied by the tribe of that name. He immediately sold half of that holding (some 250 acres) for $312, yielding a profit of $262, well over 500 percent. Jackson held on to the remainder until 1818. In that year, serving as chief federal negotiator with the Chickasaw, he obtained a treaty that, among other things, provided for Chickasaw removal and white settlement of the territory at Chickasaw Bluff. He then placed the remainder of his old Chickasaw purchase on the market and sold it for $5,000. His profit: some 5,000 percent.[32]

Jackson's closest friend in Nashville, John Overton, with whom he had shared lodgings at the Donelsons when he first arrived in the area, was among those who grew wealthy through Tennessee land acquisition. Jackson was one of Overton's business partners, at one point acquiring co-title to some 50,000 acres at the site of the future city of Memphis. But for Jackson the road to wealth was not always a smooth one. In 1795, he went to Philadelphia to sell that land along with another tract owned by John Rice. He planned to use the proceeds to buy slaves for Overton (who was a prospering slave trader) as well as goods for a commercial operation that Jackson himself planned to launch.[33] The trip did not go as planned. He could not find buyers willing to pay in cash and accepted instead the promissory notes of a Blount associate David Allison, who soon thereafter went bankrupt.[34]

Jackson had used the notes to purchase merchandise for his store. The suppliers, unable to collect from Allison, demanded that Jackson pay the debt.[35] Returning to Tennessee, Jackson exchanged his store and its goods for some 33,000 acres of undeveloped land, then sold that land to raise money for partial settlement of the Allison obligation. After that, he expanded his acquisitions, "picking up large parcels of land all over Tennessee, from Powell's Valley in the eastern district to the Obion River in the western district," as well as Lewis Robards's former holdings at Hunter's Hill, some "640 acres on the south side of the Cumberland River." Robards had never occupied Hunter's Hill, probably because of fear of Indian attack. All in all, in some two months in the spring of 1796, Andrew Jackson acquired some 29,228 acres of Tennessee land. But once again he had difficulty finding buyers in Philadelphia. He then repeated his mistake, turning to Allison and to Blount, who took the land off his hands and gave Jackson more promissory notes, rather than money or goods, in exchange. Neither ever made good on those notes, and this sorry affair almost ended with Andrew Jackson "sitting in debtor's prison." It took him some years to settle this matter and left him with a deep distrust of paper transactions.[36] It did not, however, lessen his interest in land speculation. The Allison-Blount fiasco was only one episode in an active and varied business career. Between 1793 and 1797 Jackson bought some 16 tracts of land, at a cost in modern purchasing power of over a million dollars, and acquired with that land 16 slaves. He was barely 30 years old. He would acquire much more wealth in the years to come.[37]

We must now return to the matter of Indian raids on white settlements. Although not a popular viewpoint on the frontier, leading members of the Washington administration believed that peace and security could not be gained by force of arms alone but required enforcing treaties that excluded land hungry settlers from areas reserved for Indians. Thus in 1791, when Andrew Jackson was appointed attorney general for the Mero District, the territorial governor William Blount, under pressure from the federal government, directed him "to prosecute vigorously white violations of the treaty with the Cherokee," some of whose lands previously seized by North Carolina had been restored to them under the federal treaty of Hopewell of 1785.[38] We do not know how vigorously Jackson complied with those instructions; the record is silent. We do know he had little faith in treaty making. In January 1793, Jackson had complained to Tennessee's commissioner to the Cherokee about the federal government's efforts to negotiate a peace on the frontier, declaring that Indians would only use such proceedings "to lull the peo[ple to] sleep" so that they could "commit Murder with impunity." On May 16, 1794, he responded to a report of a pending peace settlement with the disaffected Indians of the region by declaring "their Peace Talks are only Delusions . . . to put us of[f] our Guard: why Treat with them ? Does not Experience teach us that Treaties answer no other Purpose than opening an Easy door for the Indians to pass [through to] Butcher our Citizens. . . ." He went on to lambast the U.S. Congress for its misplaced belief that "humanity" required making peace with Indians. If Congress were really concerned with "humanity," Jackson argued, it should take steps to "Punish the Barbarians for murdering her innocent Citizens." But instead of protecting Americans on the frontier from the savages, the government, he complained, had "Prosecuted" those who had marched on Indians towns and killed Indians in retribution for their outrages. Jackson suggested that if Congress did not provide "a more amp[le] protection this Country will have at length [to break] or seek a protection from some other Source. . . ."[39]

Jackson's disdain for federal peacemaking reflected the views of other prominent Tennesseans. In 1794, Governor William Blount in effect looked the other way when militia general James Robertson defied federal orders not to attack the Chickamauga and, in the so-called Nickajack expedition, put a number of their villages to the torch. Robertson was rapped on the knuckles, went through the motions of resigning, but was not actually replaced by the governor. He remained in command. To gain more control over Indian policy, Blount and others championed the cause of statehood. But they also pondered the possibility of becoming an independent nation, should that status be denied.[40] Within four months after his arrival in Tennessee, Jackson had personally become involved in conversations with local leaders who openly discussed the possibility of some special relationship with the Spanish who still occupied some of the American Southeast and claimed ownership of much of it. Perhaps, they hoped, the Spanish officials who had encouraged Indian resistance to American settlement might be induced to place the American settlements under their protection and use their good offices to secure the frontier.[41]

Jackson was soon in a position to influence congressional policy directly. In 1796, with Tennessee now admitted to the union as a state, he was elected as its first representative to the U.S. House of Representatives. A year later, he was elevated to the Senate. The circumstances of his election to the upper house were unusual. His patron William Blount, one of Tennessee's original senators, had been impeached after a compromising letter came to light in 1797, which revealed that he was implicated in a conspiracy to enlist British and Indian support in attacking the Spanish in the Mississippi Valley and in Florida. The plot, aimed at preventing a rumored transfer of Louisiana and Florida to France by seizing the territories for England and the United States, was apparently designed, in part at least, to protect Blount's overextended land speculation schemes. When Tennessee's other senator William Cocke refused to vote against Blount's expulsion from the Senate, the pro-Blount Tennessee legislature retaliated by replacing him with Blount loyalist Andrew Jackson.[42]

Jackson's congressional career was undistinguished. Lacking some of the gentlemanly polish he would acquire later in life, he made a poor impression on some of his colleagues at Philadelphia. Albert Gallatin, then representing western Pennsylvania in the House, recalled him as "a tall, lank, uncouth-looking personage, with long locks of hair hanging over his face, and a queue down his back tied in an eel skin, his dress singular, his manner of deportment those of a rough backswoodsman."[43] As a congressman, Jackson's one notable achievement was the winning of reimbursement for Tennessee militiamen commanded by John Sevier who, in response to a Chickamauga assault on the frontier post at Buchanan's station, had conducted a raid, unauthorized by the federal government, against several Cherokee towns in 1793. The Chickamauga, a branch of the Cherokee, had made common cause with the Creek in seeking to drive whites from the Cumberland. The Washington administration nonetheless considered the Sevier raid unduly provocative, and accordingly had refused to pay for the expedition unless forced to do so by Congress. Taking issue with Secretary of War Timothy Pickering's characterization of Sevier's action as unwarranted, Jackson defended Tennessee's right to undertake what he described as a "defensive" campaign against a "savage" aggressor. The Indians, Jackson cried, were waging war against the state. Congress must understand that "the knife and the tomahawk were held over the heads of women and children . . . peaceable citizens were murdered." Tennessee consequently had no choice but to recognize that "it was time to make a resistance." Although an earlier investigation by the House's Committee on Claims had raised questions about whether Tennessee was really in such imminent danger as to justify disregard of the federal prohibition against attacking Indians, the committee subsequently declared the Sevier expedition necessary for the defense of the frontier. Congress thus accepted Jackson's argument, and the claim was paid.[44]

Jackson's senatorial record, as his leading biographer notes, "is nearly blank."[45] He delivered no recorded speeches. The presiding officer, Vice President Thomas Jefferson, who came to see him as "a dangerous man," many years later, in a conversation with Daniel Webster, described "his passions" as "terrible," adding that in the Senate "he could never speak on account of the rashness of his feelings. I have seen him attempt it repeatedly, and as often choke with rage."[46] Even allowing for some element of hyperbole and hindsight in Jefferson's account, there is no reason to doubt that Jackson in 1797 was an angry man, and that much of that anger came from his conviction that the Washington and Adams administrations by coddling Indians were placing the frontier in jeopardy. As a congressman, he was one of three representatives who had refused to vote to commend the Father of His Country on the occasion of his retirement from the presidency. Jackson believed that Washington was indifferent to the sufferings of Tennessee settlers threatened and killed by Indians. Holding the British and the Spanish responsible for inciting Indians, Jackson was angered by Jay's Treaty and outraged by the generally conciliatory policy toward those powers pursued by the administration.

The senator from Tennessee was even more offended by the federal government's presumed pro-Indian partiality in cases involving conflicts over treaty rights. On March 5, 1798, Jackson joined with the other members of the Tennessee congressional delegation, Joseph Anderson and William C. Claiborne, in protesting the arrest and detention by federal military authorities of Judge David Campbell, who had been accused of trespassing on Indian land. Although the judge was held only for one evening, Jackson and his colleagues described the action as an "Outrage against the Dignity of the State, and the rights of Civil liberty." Demanding "redress," the Tennesseans called on President Adams to protect their fellow citizens from "Such wanton violence . . . Such Military Tyranny."[47]

Although Adams soon thereafter negotiated a new Indian treaty that brought a greater measure of peace and security to the Tennessee frontier, Jackson remained "disgusted with the administration of the government."[48]

Jackson's frustration over Indian policy, however, does not explain his sudden resignation from the Senate after a single session. Andrew Jackson in 1798 was a troubled man, lonely for his wife Rachel, out of place among the more experienced and polished politicians in the nation's capital, and deeply in debt. He had become involved in speculative schemes that had gone bad. Hounded by creditors, in poor health from a severe knee injury that left him crippled for some seven months, Jackson returned to Tennessee to rebuild his fortunes.[49]

He may have been an outsider in Philadelphia, but that was far from the case in his home state, where his relationship with Blount and other notables in the past had led to a seat in the Tennessee constitutional convention, and then to election, as we have seen, first as a federal congressman, then to the U.S. Senate. But national politics no longer had much appeal to the young attorney. His future, he believed, lie in Tennessee. As an aspiring and ambitious Southern gentleman, Jackson had no intention of limiting himself to the practice of law or the pursuit of office. Years earlier, while waiting as the McNairy expedition to Nashville was being assembled in Jonesborough, he had bought a young female slave named Nancy, recognizing that "a gentleman needs a servant."[50] The key to financial success and social status, men of his generation and place believed, was in the acquisition of land and of slaves to cultivate that land. But the land needed to meet the needs and aspirations of the ambitious could be had only through Indian dispossession.

While the Washington administration deplored the aggressive tactics of the frontier, its officers had no illusions about the necessary final outcome. The Indian, they agreed, must be moved aside. Secretary of War Knox hoped this could occur without resorting to violence. "As the settlements of the whites shall approach near to the Indian boundaries established by treaties," Knox argued, "the game will be diminished, and the land being valuable to the Indians only as hunting grounds, they will be willing to sell further tracts for small considerations." Very soon, he concluded, "the Indians will, by the invariable operation of causes which have hitherto existed in their intercourse with the whites, be reduced to a very small number."[51] Through wise management of Indian affairs, the west could be occupied not only without much if any bloodshed but also at a very low cost.

That process was well underway by the time Andrew Jackson returned to Tennessee. The Robertson raid of 1794 had demoralized the Chickamauga. To the south, the more militant Creek warriors who hoped for aid from the Spanish in their resistance to American expansion were disappointed, and dissuaded from war, by the Treaty of San Lorenzo (1795), which settled the boundary dispute between the United States and Spain. An uneasy peace descended on the Cumberland, as white population soared from around 3,000 to some 20,000 by the decade's end. The demoralizing impact of that influx on the tribal warriors and chiefs is well documented. Throughout the new state, alcohol, disease, depredation, and despair took their toll on the indigenous population. Knox's prophecy was accurate. The Indians were quickly being diminished in both numbers and power.[52] They were now well on the road to dispossession if not extinction.

During his first decade in Tennessee, Jackson had made money and gained social status through involvement in law, politics, commerce, and land speculation. After leaving Philadelphia, he resumed those pursuits. He may have lacked some of the business acumen of his close friends John Overton and John Coffee, both of whom regularly advised him, but like them Andrew Jackson saw in land acquisition and sale the real key to power, prominence, and affluence in frontier Tennessee.[53] He would remain an avid land speculator throughout most of his adult life. But his immediate circumstances on returning to Tennessee were somewhat problematic. Much of his property had to be sold to settle the Allison debts, including the plantation he had begun at Hunter's Hill. The setback in his fortunes proved temporary. Jackson was soon earning a reasonable income from various ventures, although he remained burdened with debt for many years. While Jackson and his family lived for a number of years in a fairly small two story log house several hundred yards from the site of his future mansion at the Hermitage (which was not built until 1821), he was by no means a simple frontier farmer. His parlor, although very modest in size, was well furnished, and his possessions included fine silver vessels and expensive dining ware. While the records do not permit a full reconstruction of all his investments in land, we can say with much certainty that over the years he made substantial profits. It has been estimated that his cumulative gains from land speculation during the first two decades of the 19th century totaled around $100,000, equivalent to several millions of dollars in modern currency. By the time he emerged as a national political figure, Andrew Jackson was "a fairly rich man."[54] But, given the heavy demands for financial support from his adopted son and several wards, as well as a series of bad investments, he was often short of cash. At no point in his life did he feel completely secure financially.[55]

The economy of middle Tennessee had undergone a surprisingly rapid and dramatic transformation since Jackson's early years in Nashville. Once dependent on subsistence agriculture, hunting, and the fur trade, the region by 1800 was producing substantial crops of cotton and tobacco. The Cumberland land was rich and fertile and yielded handsome returns. But it was owned by a small minority. Seven out of eight white men owned no land at all but were tenants. Below them in status were slaves, who comprised some 20 percent of the region's population. The wealthy few now built fine brick homes reflecting their station in life and imported luxury goods from the East Coast and overseas. Nashville and environs in the early 19th century was not an egalitarian frontier. It had been shaped and dominated by a land holding elite from the beginning.[56] For most settlers living conditions remained crude. Francis Baily, a British visitor to Nashville in 1797, described single story houses so poorly constructed that the floors, laid directly on the ground, usually had huge gaps that allowed snakes free entry into the home. One of his hosts told Baily that the snakes sometimes crawled into bed with him. When a slave spotted an "enormous snake" under Baily's bed, he was assured that he need not worry; it was harmless. Baily was even more appalled by the practice of sleeping several to a bed in Nashville's best inn, and by the general shortage of good food available to travelers.[57]

After his return to Tennessee in 1798, Jackson's continuing affiliation with the powerful Blount faction secured him election by the legislature to a seat on Tennessee's Superior Court. The post paid well. Among public officers, only the governor made more. Jackson knew very little about legal precedents, let alone the finer points of the law, but his decisions, as an early biographer tells us, although "short, untechnical and unlearned, sometimes ungrammatical," were "generally right."[58] As a jurist, he won wide respect for his efficiency, clearing dockets with remarkable speed, for his fairness, and also for his personal courage. Presiding over a court in a remote settlement, he was defied by a ruffian named Russell Bean, who refused to come before the bar to answer charges of disorderly conduct. When the local sheriff reported they could not force Bean to come to court, Jackson demanded that he personally be summoned to bring the malefactor to justice. The sheriff did so reluctantly, fearing for the judge's safety. Outside, Bean, big, mean, and well armed, loudly promised to kill anyone who tried to bring him in. Jackson pointed two pistols at the culprit, and, according to Jackson lore, shouted "Now, you infernal villain, this very instant, surrender, or I'll blow you through!" Bean, to everyone's surprise, surrendered. It was reported that when he was asked later why he gave in, he said, "Why, when he came up, I looked him in the eye, and I saw shoot, and there wasn't shoot in nary other eye in the crowd; and so I says to myself, says I, hoss, it's about time to sing small, and so I did."[59]

If the confrontation with Russell Bean enhanced Jackson's reputation as a man of courage and honor, a duel fought several years later brought both into question in some circles. The quarrel began with a horse race.[60] Ever since his childhood, Andrew Jackson had been a great fancier of horse flesh. By 1806, Jackson, now a general in the Tennessee militia, was making substantial profits from racing his five-year-old stallion Truxton. A race between Truxton and Captain Joseph Erwin's horse Plowboy, scheduled for November 28, 1805, with a $2,000 prize at stake, had to be cancelled when Plowboy went lame, making Erwin liable for a forfeit penalty of some $800. A dispute between Erwin and Jackson over which notes would be accepted in payment was initially settled, after some difficulties, fairly amicably. But Erwin's son-in-law, Charles Dickinson, who had a stake in the wager, reportedly, while drinking in a tavern, made some comments about Jackson that included a slur against Rachel Jackson.[61] Infuriated, Jackson confronted Dickinson, and received an apology, the younger man claiming that he had been drunk, could not recall what he said, but intended no injury. Jackson accepted that apology, but subsequent reports that Jackson had claimed Erwin was not keeping his word about the notes to be given in satisfaction of the forfeit re-inflamed the controversy.[62]

Hearing the story about his alleged insinuations from Thomas Swann, Dickinson confronted Jackson, who denied that he had questioned Erwin's honor. Swann, resentful at being called a liar, then challenged Jackson to a duel.[63] But Jackson, refusing to recognize Swann as a social equal, threatened to cane him first and then carried out that threat when he encountered him in a Nashville tavern.[64] Soon thereafter, Swann again demanded the satisfaction of a duel and published in the local newspaper a piece labeling Jackson a liar and a coward.[65] Jackson replied by dismissing Swann as "the puppet and lying varlet for a worthless, drunken, blackguard scoundrel." In addition to that allusion to Dickinson, he also impugned the integrity of Dickinson's friends, one of whom, the brother of Jackson's longtime friend Judge McNairy, now published an insulting demand that "the braggadocio General" accept Swann's challenge. He included a slur on Jackson's close friend and business associate John Coffee, who promptly challenged McNairy to a duel, which ended with Coffee wounded in the leg and McNairy unhurt. The seconds of both men charged that the other had violated the rules by firing prematurely.[66] Soon thereafter, Charles Dickinson added to the already ample ill-feeling by sending the local newspaper a diatribe against Andrew Jackson.

Jackson's friends got advance word of Dickinson's piece and informed the general who demanded to see it before it was published on May 24. He found that Dickinson had described him as a "worthless scoundrel," and, quoting Swann's phrase, declared him "a poltroon and a coward."[67] Jackson, still unwilling to grant a gentleman's status to either Swann or McNairy, now challenged Dickinson, even though Dickinson also, in Jackson's words, did "not merit it," as he was presumably not a gentleman either.[68] In the duel that ensued, Jackson, although severely wounded in the first fire by Dickinson, killed his opponent. Jackson's first shot had misfired as the hammer had stopped at half-cock. Though bleeding profusely, he recocked his pistol, pressed the trigger, and fired a second time. Struck below the ribs, Dickinson bled to death, dying in agony several hours later. Jackson was severely wounded. Dickinson's bullet had shattered two of his ribs and was lodged near his heart.[69] For the rest of his life he "suffered from abscesses caused by the bullet in his chest." For years to come, Jackson "kept the pistol with which he had killed Dickinson, showing it off and recounting details of the duel" to visitors to the Hermitage. He boasted that he would "have hit him [even] if he shot me through the brain."[70]

But while his triumph in the Dickinson duel exemplified the legendary force of Jackson's will, for a time it seriously damaged his reputation. His second shot, many said, was not only unnecessary, as honor had already been satisfied, but improper by the code governing duels between gentlemen. Jackson, stung by those accusations, protested that he had had no choice. It was self-defense, he claimed, as Dickinson had boasted about his intention to kill his challenger and had placed a $300 bet with a local merchant, Thomas Wagaman, that he would succeed in doing so. In further evidence that his life was in danger, Jackson related that Dickinson had delayed "the meeting for eight days to make himself more perfect in the art of Shooting" and had "marked the genl. On a tree and boasted how often he had hit him" in practice.[71] But even though he may have been correct in his assessment of Dickinson's intentions, the public for the most part found

Jackson's protestations unpersuasive. James Parton, after interviewing Tennesseans who still recalled the controversy, concluded that "it is certain that at no time between the years 1806 and 1812, could General Jackson have been elected to any office in Tennessee that required a majority of the voters of the whole state." From the Dickinson duel Jackson gained a reputation for violence and vindictiveness he never quite shook off.[72]

Jackson had resigned his judicial position two years earlier (on July 24, 1804) and never resumed the practice of law. He aspired to greater wealth than the law could provide and sought his fortune instead as a merchant, a planter, and a land speculator. In 1802, he had entered into partnership with Thomas Watson and John Hutchings, both of them relatives of his wife Rachel. The partners owned three stores, a distillery, and a cotton gin. A dispute over accounting led to the termination of the relationship with Watson a year later and the formation of a new partnership with John Coffee. At a place called Clover's Bottom on a branch of the Cumberland River the new firm of Jackson, Coffee, and Hutchins built a store (located in the blockhouse where Coffee lived), a boatyard, a tavern, and a racetrack. Jackson's small log house on the estate he called the Hermitage was about four miles away, and "each morning Jackson rode over . . . and worked all day at the store."[73] Dry goods such as blankets, fabric, and kitchen and farm implements were brought in from Philadelphia and sold at a 300 percent markup. Jackson also sold salt, coffee, rum, and gunpowder. There was little money in circulation in Tennessee in the first decade of the 19th century; therefore, much of the firm's business was by barter, with the locals offering the products of farm and forest: cotton, corn, wheat, tobacco, pork, skins, and furs, which the partners sent down river for sale at New Orleans.

At first the company prospered and opened several branch stores. But a combination of bad debts, lack of access to reliable market data, high transportation costs, and general bad times soon led to large losses. Jackson sold his interest in the venture to John Coffee, receiving in return some long-term promissory notes which, some later said, he tore up when Coffee married Rachel's niece. Whatever the truth of that story, Jackson did not prosper as a merchant. His wealth would come from land speculation, horse raising, the cultivation of cotton, a federal military salary, and, on some occasions, slave trading.[74]

Jackson never expressed any moral reservations about slavery. In one of his earliest private cases as a lawyer in Nashville, he was engaged to recover, or obtain compensation for, some five slaves, described as "One Negro fellow Daniel about 28 years old, One Wench Kate, 32, One Boy Joe, 11, One Boy Bob, 9, One Boy Pompey between one & two years, with a net value estimated at 720 British pounds."[75] While the evidence is scant, his papers from this period indicate that Jackson as an attorney was a participant in other litigation involving property in slaves.[76] Later, as a merchant, Jackson sometimes, on request of customers or friends, engaged in the sale or purchase of slaves.[77]

Jackson as a slave owner from time to time expressed anxiety about the mistreatment of his slaves by overseers. While president, he wrote in a letter to Andrew

J. Hutchings, "I could not bear the idea of inhumanity to my poor negroes."[78] In another letter to Andrew Jackson Jr., he demanded that his overseer at the Hermitage be made to "treat them with great humanity, feed and clothe them well, and work them in moderation." If he did not, "he must be discharged."[79]

But Jackson himself could be very harsh in his treatment of disobedient or insolent slaves, placing runaways in irons until they could be sold. In an advertisement in the *Tennessee Gazette* dated September 26, 1804, Jackson offered a reward of $50 for the return of a runaway, with "ten dollars extra for every hundred lashes any person will give to the amount of three hundred." Such a lashing could well have been lethal.[80] He also on one occasion wrote to his ward Andrew Jackson Donelson of the need to arrange a public flogging of Rachel's maid who, in Jackson's words, "had been putting on some airs and had been guilty of a great deal of impertinence." He did confess that he found it "humiliating" to have to resort to the lash, but he did so nonetheless from time to time.[81] Advising on the need to discipline one of his slaves, he remarked that while she had the potential of being a good servant, "she must be ruled with the cowhide."[82] Jackson told his nephew Andrew Donaldson, who was in charge at the Hermitage during his absence, that if the steward did not administer the 50 lashes he prescribed for that slave's misconduct, he was to be discharged.[83] However, he was enraged when his overseer Ira Walton, in 1827, killed a manacled runaway who was resisting a whipping Jackson had ordered. He fired Walton and attempted, unsuccessfully, to have him indicted.[84]

Jackson saw himself as a benevolent father to his slaves, just as he would later cast himself in the role of Great Father to the American Indians. But, as one writer has noted, occasional statements concerns for slave welfare notwithstanding, Jackson's "most frequently expressed intention was to get the maximum amount of labor from each Negro . . . all other considerations were either related or secondary to that role."[85] Historian Mark Cheathem, reviewing Jackson's correspondence, finds that "benevolent expressions towards his slaves were rare, much more frequent was the episodic violence that he authorized or endorsed."[86] As Jackson prospered, he bought more slaves. According to available records, he owned 10 in 1794 and 15 in 1798. By 1820, the number had risen to 44. By the end of his life, Jackson owned over 150.[87] Their acquisition was a mark of his success and of his hard won status as a Southern gentleman. Their labor had made him one of the wealthiest men in America.

Jackson had no tolerance for those who challenged the prerogatives of slave holders in any way. When the Indian agent Silas Dinsmore insisted that whites transporting slaves through Choctaw Territory carry proof of ownership, Jackson labeled the agent a "petty Tyrant" who violated the "rights secured to us by the bravery and blood of our forefathers."[88] Journeying through Choctaw country in late 1811 in order to retrieve "a number of Negroes which had been sent to that country for sale" but which had remained unsold, Jackson defied Dinsmore by refusing to present papers to his subagent. To avoid a violent confrontation with Jackson and his well-armed band, the man let him pass.[89] Jackson was not placated but continued a vendetta that ended with the agent being dismissed from service and financially ruined. "Poor Dinsmore," Remini writes, "was reduced to wandering in poverty among the Indians he had once protected. Several years later, Dinsmore tried to effect a reconciliation with the general, but the stern, unbending Jackson simply glared his contempt and turned away."[90] In his later career, Jackson gave some support to the American Colonization Society's plan to resettle free blacks in Africa but remained a vehement foe of critics of the South's "Peculiar Institution." His order as president authorizing postmasters to destroy abolitionist literature is often noted. It is even more telling that during his presidency, the United States rejected invitations to join with other nations in assisting the British navy's campaign against the international slave trade, leaving this country alone in its refusal "to cooperate in ending the despicable trade in human cargo."[91]

In 1796, Jackson's quest for prominence and power in Tennessee had led him to seek election as major general of the state's militia. He was only 30 years old at the time, had no military training, and no experience as a commander in frontier Indian warfare. He did have the support of William Blount's powerful political faction. However, the retiring major general, Governor John Sevier, no fan of Blount or of his favorites, believed Jackson to be unsuited for the militia's highest command post and therefore maneuvered to block his selection by politicking among the ranking officers who elected their commander. Jackson, by a narrow margin, lost to Sevier's favored candidate, George Conway.

Jackson protested Sevier's meddling in the militia election. Sevier dismissed his complaint by describing Jackson as a "poor pitifull petty fogging Lawyer." The feud between the two was temporarily patched over but continued to fester.[92] When Sevier, after leaving the governor's office in 1802, ran for his old post as major general, he lost to Andrew Jackson by the deciding vote of the new governor who broke a tie. Jackson in the years since his loss to Conway had worked very hard to win the support of the ranking militia officers, and it paid off in a surprising upset. But that upset was not solely the product of Jackson's charm. In fact, he won the nod from Governor Archibald Roane by exposing Sevier's role in the notorious Glasgow land fraud, using information that he had had in his possession since 1797 but had earlier kept in confidence. While the exact timing of that revelation is not entirely clear, Jackson's efforts to undermine Sevier's reputation at this juncture are well documented.[93]

Sevier's friends in the legislature robbed Jackson of part of his victory by establishing a second major generalcy and thereby dividing the command. The feud culminated in a duel after both men unleashed a torrent of insults in the course of which, among other things, Sevier implied that Jackson had committed adultery with Rachel prior to their marriage and Jackson, in a much quoted retort, had bellowed "Great God! Do you mention her sacred name?" The duel itself was a bloodless farce, ending with Sevier cowering behind a tree.[94] Given Sevier's great popularity in the state, it was Jackson's good fortune that he did not wound or kill his opponent. But, though no one could foresee it at the time, his win over Sevier was the most significant militia election outcome in American history, for now he was General Andrew Jackson.

CHAPTER 2

Militia General and Indian Fighter

The new general was eager to take the field. An ardent expansionist and vehement foe of both the British and the Spanish, Jackson applauded Jefferson's Louisiana purchase. Rumors that "the Dons" would fight to prevent American occupation of the territory inspired Jackson to issue to the Tennessee militia under his command a general order declaring that, in light of the "hostile appearance and menacing attitude" of the Spanish forces, they "should be in complete order and at a moment's warning ready to march." In his communiqué to his troops, the general charged the Spaniards with various offenses "degrading to our national character," including tearing down the nation's flag, imprisoning five of its citizens, and expelling a party sent by the government to explore the Red River region.[1] But the Spanish, while denouncing the purchase as illegal, did not actually resist its implementation. A peaceful transfer of power placed the vast territory under American rule.

Under circumstances that soon proved to be embarrassing, Jackson reissued those orders verbatim three years later, repeating his 1803 charges against the Spanish.[2] His action had been prompted by a visit from former vice president Aaron Burr. Two years earlier, his killing of Alexander Hamilton in a duel had led authorities in New York and New Jersey to issue orders for his arrest as a murderer. Following the expiration of his term as vice president, Burr, no longer welcome or safe in his northeastern homeland, had traveled throughout the west seeking to raise money and men for a military venture, the exact nature of which remains controversial. Urbane, polished, and quietly eloquent but never overbearing, Burr possessed not only "the common touch" but also a rare charisma. As one Burr biographer notes, his "contemporaries uniformly acknowledged his personal appeal. Small, trim and handsome, he had the gift of transfixing both sexes."[3] During his visit at the Hermitage, Burr had charmed Andrew Jackson, who soon came to believe that he was on a secret government mission to enlist an expeditionary force to attack the Spanish in Florida and Mexico. Sharing the former vice president's impatience with Jefferson's cautious foreign policy, Jackson was eager to use his militia to assist Burr in a grand campaign to drive "the hated Dons" from the continent. On the day he issued his order alerting his troops, he wrote to Captain William P. Anderson directing him to meet personally with Burr and also help arrange meetings with other Tennessee militia officers, including Generals Overton and Robertson.[4]

Insight into Jackson's frame of mind at the time of his first involvement with Burr's scheme is found in a letter he wrote in the late summer of 1806 to General James Winchester, who was then serving as one of his brigadiers. Jackson declared that since the Jefferson administration's negotiations for the purchase of Florida had failed, immediate war with Spain was the only answer to America's security needs and territorial aspirations. It should be a war of conquest and occupation that would seize not only the Floridas but Texas and Mexico as well. Jackson added that he hoped to raise on "short notice . . . at least two thousand Volunteers" to join in the invasion of Spain's North American possessions and thereby "give freedom and commerce to those provinces and establish peace, and a permanent barrier against the inroads and attacks of foreign powers on our interior." Invoking the mystique of battlefield glory, Jackson proclaimed that a Spanish war "will be a handsome theatre for our enterprising young men, and a certain source of acquiring fame." He closed by expressing the hope that Winchester himself would "partake in the campaign."[5] After seeking the support of some other Tennessee militia officers, Jackson hosted a lavish reception for Burr at Nashville's finest hotel, arranged for the purchase of provisions and of boats to transport Burr's men and supplies, and compiled for Burr's use a secret list of his most reliable officers.[6]

Jackson was soon disillusioned, hearing from a number of authorities and informants that Burr not only had no official authorization for his activities but was said to be plotting the separation of the west from the United States and the creation of a new western empire under his personal rule. He was stunned by talk that Burr would soon seize New Orleans, a city now part of the United States, as the first step in his campaign. There was also talk of Burr's collusion with either Spain or Great Britain. Jackson, alarmed and no longer certain of Burr's loyalty to the United States, immediately wrote several letters warning of danger, including one to Senator Daniel Smith expressing his strong conviction that plans were "already afoot" to seize New Orleans and then, with Spanish assistance, break up the Union. The conspiracy, Jackson believed, involved "many high charectors from New York to Neworleans."[7] To President Thomas Jefferson, he dispatched a rather vague but bombastic message proclaiming his own loyalty and offering his services against any who would endanger the Republic.[8]

On November 12, Jackson wrote to William C. C. Claiborne, the territorial governor of Louisiana, to warn him that "your government, I fear is in danger, I fear there are plans on foot—inimical to the Union—whether they will be attempted to be carried into effect or not I cannot say but rest assured that they are in operation or I calculate badly—beware the month of December—I love my Country and my Government. I hate the Dons—I would delight to see Mexico reduced, but I will die in the last ditch before I would yield a part to the Dons, or see the Union disunited." But while Jackson, on hearing the rumors about Burr, initially suspected him of plotting to commit treason, he soon persuaded himself that the former vice president was not aware of the real nature of the conspiracy but was being misled, and used, by General James Wilkinson, a man of gigantic ego, limited competence and questionable character whom Jackson had long detested. "Be upon alert," he admonished Governor Claiborne, "keep a watchful eye on our General, [Wilkinson] and beware of an attack from your own country as from Spain. I fear there is something rotten in the state of Denmark."[9]

Jackson was not alone in his apprehensions. On December 19, 1806, Secretary of War Dearborn advised Jackson that he should keep his forces in readiness should there be "some unlawful enterprise . . . on the western waters."[10] A few weeks later, Dearborn heard rumors of an imminent attack. Accordingly, Jackson was ordered to mobilize the militia under his command. He quickly mustered his troops, paraded them through Nashville, and sent out a reconnaissance party to locate Burr's forces. The party found only a handful of men making their way down river toward New Orleans on 10 small boats. Burr never had the 100 boats and 1,000 men he was rumored to command. There was no hostile army, no real danger. Aaron Burr, declared a traitor by President Jefferson himself, was now a fugitive, not an empire builder.

By the time of Burr's trial for treason at Richmond the following year, Jackson was convinced that Burr was not disloyal, and that the real traitor was General James Wilkinson. Burr had personally assured him of his innocence, affirming, as Jackson related, "with the most sacred pledges" that "he had not nor ever had views inimical or hostile to the United States" and certainly never had "the intention of separating the union." It was Wilkinson's denunciation of Burr that had led to the former vice president's arrest on a charge of treason. Jackson was now certain Wilkinson was lying.[11] Burr, he believed, had been deceived and betrayed by Wilkinson and other conspirators. Jackson was alarmed to discover his own conduct was questioned in some circles and wrote to Secretary of War Dearborn to complain, in rather intemperate terms, that the secretary had libeled him by reporting rumors of his collusion with Burr in a scheme to divide the Union. In that letter, Jackson proceeded to charge Dearborn with duplicity in not admitting that he had in fact authorized Burr's "adventures." But the real traitor, he insisted, was Wilkinson. Jackson suspected (correctly turns out) that the general was in the pay of Spain.[12]

While his distrust of Wilkinson was well founded, his conclusions about Burr's innocence are less tenable. Contrary to the story he told Jackson, Burr had not consistently limited his activities to planning ways of supporting the United States in the event of a war with Spain. Some of the men Burr visited during his western journey related conversations with Burr that suggest that at various times he had offered his services to agents of both Great Britain and Spain and had spoken to both of the possible future disunion of the eastern and western states. Some informants related that Burr spoke of engineering the breakup of the American Union through encouraging the secession of the Mississippi valley. Others reported that he planned to invade Mexico and rule it as an "emperor." But to some who questioned his intentions, Burr claimed that his only interest was in the settlement of a tract of land in Louisiana the title of which had presumably been obtained legally from the Spanish. It is likely that Burr himself revised his plans as circumstances changed. The surviving letters that passed between Burr and Wilkinson suggest collusion in schemes both later wished to conceal. Wilkinson very carefully edited the copies of that correspondence made public after Burr was charged with treason to obscure his own role.[13]

After Burr's arrest, Jackson traveled to Richmond and testified on his behalf to the grand jury. But he embarrassed the defense attorneys and irritated the administration by his loud and intemperate protestations, outside the courtroom, that an innocent man was in the dock. He was not called as a witness in the trial but continued his public denunciations of Wilkinson. Jefferson and his supporters found his behavior highly offensive, particularly since some of his off-the-cuff comments personally impugned the president and other members of his administration. Jackson had been warned by Senator Daniel Smith some months earlier that Jefferson would not believe his accusations against Wilkinson.[14] As for the president, he may not have questioned Jackson's personal loyalty to the Union, but he now had grave misgivings about his judgment. Others shared Jefferson's reservations about Jackson. In December 1807, Jackson wrote to Senator Smith to complain that Wilkinson was spreading false rumors about his lack of patriotism, rumors which he feared some men of prominence found credible. The real traitor, Jackson insisted again, was Wilkinson himself.[15]

He would continue his campaign against Wilkinson for some years to come. Throughout the years Jackson "diligently and laboriously gathered documentary evidence wherever he could find it, and passed it along to influential friends." Astounded that his accusations were dismissed by the administration, Jackson came to believe that Jefferson and Dearborn both were fully aware of Wilkinson's disloyalty and his conspiracy against the Union but chose to cover it up. The affair deepened his long-standing reservations about the trustworthiness of the federal government.[16]

As tensions with the British and conflicts with the western Indians intensified during the years that followed Burr's downfall, Jackson remained eager to go to war. His services were not in demand. In late November 1811, when word of the clash at Tippecanoe between troops led by Indiana territorial governor William Henry Harrison and the followers of Tecumseh and the Prophet reached Tennessee, Jackson wrote the governor to offer his aid. "*The blood of our murdered Countrymen,*" Jackson declared, "*must be revenged.*" The Indian "*banditti* ought to be swept from the face of the earth," he told Harrison, and with them "the secret agents of great Britain," who had encouraged their nefarious schemes. He told the governor that if his services were needed, he would muster men immediately.

Harrison had only to tell him "at what point I can meet with supplies" and "I will have the number required at a short day at the appointed place." To his disappointment, Jackson's offer was not accepted.[17]

The belief, expressed in his letter to Harrison, that the British were still working behind the scenes to encourage Indian insurrections and provoke the massacres of frontier settlers was, for Andrew Jackson, an article of faith. Thus, prior to the declaration of war against Great Britain in 1812, Jackson was among the most ardent of the supporters of the War Hawks. In a response to a congressional call for volunteers several months before the actual war declaration, General Jackson issued a communiqué to his militia forces that proclaimed "the hour of national vengeance is now at hand." Americans would soon "fight for the reestablishment of our national character, misunderstood and vilified at home and abroad" and "seek some indemnity for past injuries, some security for future aggressions, by the conquest of all the British dominions upon the continent of North America." In this crisis, Jackson proclaimed, we see "a free people compelled to reclaim by the power of their arms the rights which god has bestowed upon them, and which an infatuated King has said they shall not enjoy." But Americans would not "crouch before the slaves of a foreign tyrant." Warming to his subject, he rhapsodized that Canada would soon be conquered, and the young Tennessee volunteers who marched to glory in that "distant country" would soon "view the stupendous works of nature, exemplified in the falls of the Niagara and the cataract of Montmorence" and "tread upon the consecrated spot on which Wolf and Montgomery fell."[18]

Jackson hoped to be at the head of their historic and heroic march. Some months before the war declaration in June, Jackson, through newly elected Tennessee governor Willie Blount, had offered to the secretary of war his services in leading 4,000 volunteers in the conquest of Quebec. But when war came, Jackson was not among the Tennessee officers called into national service. Instead, his brigadier James Winchester was ordered to take two regiments north to support Harrison's campaign against the British and against the Indians led by Tecumseh in the northwest. President Madison, after a perfunctory acknowledgement, did not act on Jackson's request to be called to duty. The reasons were probably both personal and political: lingering suspicion about his role in the Burr affair and resentment over his support of James Monroe against Madison in the contest for the Democratic Republican presidential nomination.[19] When the time came to raise troops for the defense of New Orleans, the federal authorities in communication with Governor Blount did not name Jackson among the officers they recommended be called into service. The governor, half-brother of Jackson's old mentor William Blount and a political ally, disregarded that hint and Jackson was mustered into the national force as a major general.[20] But he was placed under the command of his old enemy General James Wilkinson, who took pains to see to it that Jackson saw no action.

Jackson marched his men down the Mississippi valley in bitterly cold weather in January 1813. Encamped a few miles from Natchez, he received from Wilkinson stern orders to move no further. He had earlier advised the secretary of war that his troops "will rejoice at the opportunity of placing the American eagle on the ramparts of MOBILE, PENSACOLA AND FORT SAINT AUGUSTINE, effectively banishing from the southern coasts all British influence."[21] But when the immediate threat to New Orleans was deemed to have passed, Jackson, instead of being ordered to attack Spanish Florida as he hoped, was told by the Secretary of War John Armstrong to discharge his troops and give up his command at Natchez. All "articles of public property" were to be turned over to General Wilkinson. His men, should they not choose to enlist under Wilkinson, were to make their way home on their own, without government assistance. In his reply to the secretary on March 15, Jackson protested that they were being "dismissed eight hundred miles from home, deprived of arms, tents and supplies for the sick,—of our arms and supplies for the well . . . these brave men certainly deserve better fate and return from their government." Under the orders he received to demobilize at Natchez, his men were to be disarmed and left "to pass through the savage land where our women and children and defenseless citizens are daily murdered" without the means to protect themselves. Jackson told the secretary that he would not let that happen.[22]

He led his men, many of them very sick, on a long, hard march home. The Jackson legend, the legend of Old Hickory, was born on that march. With both toughness and compassion, he took care of his charges, walking on foot with his officers so the sick might ride horses, cheering the downcast, and sharing their privations. His soldiers, touched and inspired by his example, declared him tough as hickory wood. Thereafter, Andrew Jackson was known as "Old Hickory."[23]

Old Hickory would soon see the action he craved, but the foe would not be the hated Spanish or British but Creek Indians whom he also detested. Five years earlier, Jackson had responded to a false report of a Creek Indian massacre of white settlers near the mouth of the Duck River by issuing orders, on April 20, 1808, to his militia to stand ready to take the field. He told the troops that he had heard "that 25 of our innocent Citizens have fallen victims, to the ruthless hands of Savage barbarity, and from strong circumstances it appears that the Creeks who have perpetrated this horrid massacre has been excited to this hellish act, by the instigation of white men, agents under foreign influence, who have stimulated these barbarians to lift the scalping knife and Tomahawk against our defenseless women and Children." The report of this atrocity, Jackson continued, was brought to Nashville by Thomas Meadows, who claimed that 420 Creek warriors accompanied by "twelve white men" had wiped out "three whole families . . . three miles below the mouth of the Duck." The general declared his belief that the murderers had acted under the "orders of Great Britain" and exhorted his troops that the "blood of our innocent citizens must not be shed with impunity—prepare then for retaliation." He was confident that "the relation of this horrid scene will rouse our countrymen."[24]

On the same day, he wrote to President Thomas Jefferson to warn of "the alarming and hostile attitude of the Creek Indians" and of British incitement of Creek "hostilities against the United States." He enclosed Meadows's written report of the incident, adding that while he did not personally know Meadows and could not yet verify that report, he had been told he was a man of good character. In fact, Meadows was lying. Nothing is presently known of his identity or motives. But the discovery that the attack had not occurred did not change Jackson's views of the Anglo-Creek threat.[25]

Four years later, Creek Indians did massacre six American settlers near the place where the Duck River flows into the Tennessee. They also took captive Mary Crawley, the mother of two children they had killed. On receiving news of the raid after returning from a trip to Georgia, Jackson wrote to Governor Willie Blount: "My heart bleeds within me at the news of the horrid cruelty and murders committed by a party of Creeks, on our innocent, wifes and little babes since I left home." The Creeks, he insisted, "were urged on by british agents and tools . . ." Jackson called on the authorities to order an immediate military reprisal "and demand the perpetrators at the point of the Bayonet." Should the Creeks refuse to comply, then "make reprisals and lay their Towns in ashes."[26]

Hearing that some of the Creeks, with Mrs. Crawley in tow, had traveled through the Chickasaw Nation, Jackson also wrote to its pro-American chief George Colbert to threaten, in the name of the president of the United States, reprisals if he did not assist in apprehending the malefactors. "The whole Creek nation," Jackson predicted, "shall be covered with blood, fire shall consume their towns and villages, and their lands shall be divided among the whites" if they did not surrender immediately the warriors responsible for the Duck River massacre. The Chickasaw, he hinted, might suffer a comparable fate if they did not cooperate and report the names and whereabouts of the offending Creeks.[27]

But Jackson, in his vision of blood, fire, and land seizure, was not speaking for Thomas Jefferson. The national administration, preoccupied with the coming struggle with Great Britain, did not share the Tennesseans' hunger for an Indian war over Duck River. There was no immediate response from Washington, D.C., to the appeals from Governor Blount and General Jackson. Frustrated and angry, Jackson then published a letter in the *Democratic Clarion* on July 7, 1812, condemning the national government for its inaction and threatening independent action. He complained that Tennessee's governor, although eager to meet the threat, "is not permitted to march out and disperse the wretches who are laying waste his country and threatening to storm his capital!" Jackson, resurrecting an old controversy (the Nick-a-Jack affair), recalled that "in the settlement of Kentucky and Cumberland, in the wars between the whites and the Indians, every expedition by the former into the country of the latter, was made not only without the consent of the general government, but in defiance of its prohibition." He declared it time for Tennesseans to act independently once again, as they cannot "permit the assassins of women and children to escape with impunity and with triumph. . . . What then can we do but to imitate the conduct of those who marched to Nick-a-Jack and terminated with one blow the war which had so long depopulated the infant settlements of Tennessee." He ended with a question that was in effect a battle cry: "*Are you ready to follow your general to the heart of the Creek nation?*"[28] His call received a loud affirmation in Tennessee. *The Clarion* rejoiced that the Creeks "have supplied us with a pretext for a dismemberment of their country." The legislature called for the raising of an army large enough "to exterminate the Creek nation."[29]

Jackson's letter declaration displayed little understanding of the real situation in the so-called Creek Nation. There were no actual Creek war parties threatening to storm the state's capital after laying waste to its settlements. The Duck River killings were neither ordered by nor condoned by the leaders of the Creek National Council, most of whose members were strongly committed to maintaining peace with the United States. Indian agent Benjamin Hawkins reported to Washington, D.C., on May 12, 1812, that he had found the Creek chiefs determined to remain neutral in the event that tensions with Great Britain should lead to a new Anglo-British war. They promised to take steps to "prepare the minds of their young people to be neighborly and friendly" in all their relations with the Americans.[30] Hawkins had insisted, as a condition of peace, that they execute the Indians who had killed white settlers. The chiefs reluctantly complied. Hawkins on September 7, 1812, reported that they had put to death eight Creeks for the Duck River murders, as well as punishing the perpetrators of two earlier incidents in which two white travelers had died.[31]

That fall, Tandy Walker, a white blacksmith living among the Creeks, secured the help of a prominent Creek chief in locating and securing the release of Mrs. Crawley, who though "very feeble" and rather traumatized by her kidnapping and captivity, soon recovered in mind and body.[32] On October 12, 1812, Hawkins wrote to assure his superiors that the Creek leaders told him that "they are unanimously determined to preserve the friendship of the United States. Traveling [in Creek country] appears to be quite safe . . . since the execution of the murderers."[33] He reiterated that assurance in a letter to Secretary of State Monroe dated January 11, 1813, and to Secretary of War Armstrong on March 1. In the letter to Armstrong, Hawkins related that "the distinguished chiefs" of the Creek Executive Council, unanimous in their desire to remain at peace, had complained bitterly of false rumors circulated by their "white neighbors."[34] In the light of Hawkins assurances, federal authorities, now caught up in the waging of a war against Great Britain, understandably chose not to yield to the clamor in Tennessee for a punitive campaign against the Creek.

Events would soon reveal that Hawkins, like Jackson, had a deficient understanding of the true situation in Creek country. If Jackson overstated the danger, Hawkins underestimated it. To understand the origins of the Indian war that would soon break out and afford Andrew Jackson his first opportunity for military glory, as well as an occasion for the annexation of vast tracts of Indian land, we must digress and review the troubled history of the so-called Creek Nation. In the European sense, it had never been a nation. The national council, which in 1812 purported to speak for the Creek, was a relatively recent innovation, probably established in the late 18th century to assist Alexander McGillivray's bid for power. While Hawkins tried to use the council as a sort of superior court and legislature, it had not traditionally had the coercive power with which he wished to endow it. The term "Creek" itself had no native equivalent, but was first used by English traders to designate the people living near Ochese Creek in Georgia. The term was later extended to designate between 50 and 100 autonomous groups living in the interior regions of Georgia, Alabama, and Mississippi. There was no single Creek language, nor did they all have common points of origins. A majority spoke dialects of the Muskogean language group, but there were a number of Creek villages that did not. Their inhabitants had migrated from other areas where their communal lives had been disrupted by the collapse of the old Mississippian chiefdoms and by the continuing depredations of slave traders.

Creek villages located in Alabama in the vicinity of the Coosa and Tallapoosa Rivers the English came to designate as Upper Creeks; the Lower Creeks lived to the east in Georgia along the Chattahoochee and Flint Rivers. Although the Upper and Lower Creeks sometimes followed common policies in their relations with other tribal groups and with Europeans, neither at the time of contact had a unified political structure, nor did they develop one for many years thereafter. The Creeks, both Upper and Lower, were tied together to some degree by their sharing of rituals, such as the Green Corn ceremony, the use of Black Drink as a powerful purifying emetic, and of customs such as division of towns into red war towns and white peace towns. Some unity was provided by a clan system that cut across tribal and village boundaries, but Creek villages, although sometimes acting in unison through agreement of their chiefs, were essentially autonomous.[35]

Contact with Europeans—English, Spanish, and French—brought changes. In the 18th century, British colonial authorities sought to identify a principal Creek chief or "emperor" with whom they could deal, but the Creek resisted. In 1752, when a local headman named Tunape tried to assume the English granted title of King of the Creek, some of his erstwhile subjects poisoned him, leaving their "monarch" paralyzed for life. But several headmen did become adept at the European power game, playing the English, Spanish, and French off against one another. In the early 18th century, Chief Brims of Coweta was reputed to be "as great a politician as any governor in America." Late in the century, Alexander McGillivray, son of a Scotch trader and a Creek mother, made a powerful bid to lead the Creek in a series of elaborate diplomatic maneuvers that entailed at first an alliance with Spain and then, as the power situation in the Southeast shifted, with the United States. Successful relations with the intruding powers came to be essential not only for the protection of Creek Territory but for their economic well-being as well.[36]

British traders had entered Creek country in the late 17th century, exchanging a variety of goods for deer skins and, in the early years, for Indian slaves the Creeks obtained in raids against neighboring peoples.[37] Although the items the traders supplied were at first seen as nothing more than remarkable novelties, European trade within a very few decades had a profound effect on their way of life, bringing at first prosperity and power and later severe social disruption. As to the negative aspects of trade, most immediately destructive were the infectious diseases brought by the traders, diseases for which Native Americans had no natural immunity. Throughout North America, Indian villages were decimated by waves of disease (small pox was an especially virulent killer) that in some areas reduced the local population by 90 percent or more within the first century of contact. Also lethal were the effects of alcohol, supplied in quantity to peoples totally unfamiliar with its use. A French Jesuit missionary reported from New France that the Indians with whom he worked, normally "the gentlest and most tractable of men, become when intoxicated, madmen and wild beasts. They fall upon one another, stab with their knives, and tear one another. Many have lost ears and some portion of their noses in these tragic encounters."[38]

Comparable reports came from every part of North America, with traders sometimes relating that soon after they provided their Indian clients with rum, they would find along the trails dead Indians killed either by alcohol poisoning or by other Indians crazed with drink.[39] Among the Creek, it was widely believed that alcohol led to madness and that those who were under its influence were not to be held responsible for their actions. Alcohol was valued by warriors for the frenzy and the ferocity it could help evoke in battle.[40] In the early 19th century, George Stiggins, a Creek writer, deplored the demoralizing effects of alcohol addiction among his people, which he declared affected even tribal chiefs. "Common men and women," he wrote, "will wallow in filth and mire so long as they can raise the means to purchase spirits to drink." In lines reminiscent of the Jesuit fathers testimony half a century earlier, he reported that when drunk "they will fight each other indiscriminately frequently taking each others lives and when the fracas is over they attribute the whole scene to the spirits they had drank, very truly saying it was not them but the liquor what was in them that fought." Sober, the Creek, Stiggins reported, were of "peaceable disposition."[41] From the earliest years of contact, British authorities and Indian leaders recognized the malevolent effects of the alcohol trade. But efforts to ban or restrict that trade proved ineffective. On the Indian side, despite the misgivings of tribal leaders, demand was too great. On the British, the opposition of traders and land speculators accustomed to use of rum as most effective tool in the defrauding of Indians in trade transactions and in the securing of land concessions proved much too powerful.

Other aspects of the trade relationships with the newcomers seemed far more positive, at least initially. The replacement of stone, wooden and bone tools, utensils and weapons with trade items made of metal greatly improved the material quality of life. Metal tipped arrows and spears, and knives and swords of steel, were far more effective than those previously fashioned for hunters and warriors. The acquisition of European guns was particularly empowering. To survive and prevail in local power struggles, an Indian community now required a new kind of armament. The traditional weapons fashioned from wood and stone could no longer guarantee a village's safety. To live comfortably in that village, replacement of Indian stone vessels and woven baskets by their European copper and iron equivalents was now deemed a necessity. European woven textiles, blankets, and items of clothing came to be esteemed, as they were lighter and, in some eyes, more attractive than animal fur and leather. Then there were items for personal adornment: glass beads, medallions, medals, jewelry, mirrors, some of which in the early years were believed to possess magical powers and which later became important symbols of status. As time went on, imported items replaced local handicrafts, and the skills that once were used in the making of pottery, clothing, weapons, and other essential items were slowly lost. By the end of the 18th century, as Braund notes, the Creeks no longer provided their young "traditional training in the native crafts and manufactures."[42] Like many other Indian peoples within the European trading orbits, they had been reduced to a state of economic dependency.

The growing demand in Creek communities for European trade goods led to aggression against neighboring peoples. From the early years of contact onward, "the Creeks slowly enlarged their effective hunting territories via wars against the Florida tribes, the Cherokee and the Choctaw."[43] The nature of hunting shifted from subsistence harvesting of only those animals needed locally for food and pelts to a larger scale commercial hunt for peltry for sale to British traders. It has been estimated that by 1750, the deerskin trade resulted in the killing of 400,000 deer annually. The overkilling of game led to a radical decline in local populations of deer and other desirable fur-bearing animals, forcing hunters to range over larger areas and spend a greater part of each year away from their home villages. Moreover, not only were deerskins harder to come by, the price they brought on the market declined by some 50 percent between 1775 and 1792. While European trade at first brought prosperity and power, by the late 18th century many Creek villages were impoverished.[44]

The growth of the white population in the lower South in second half of the 18th century posed an even graver challenge to the Creek way of life. Following the defeat of Great Britain in the war for American independence, the newly independent states demanded that the Creek leadership cede and evacuate great tracts of tribal land. The North Carolina constitution explicitly declared the state the owner of all western lands included in its old colonial charter, thereby negating any and all Indian claims to land title. Other states were less explicit, but whatever their theoretical views concerning the legal status of land claims, none were willing in practice to recognize, respect, and protect Indian rights. Western settlers and some others sometimes argued that since Indians, like the British, had been defeated in the revolutionary war, they had lost their sovereignty in areas granted to the United States in the Treaty of Paris. It was also commonly believed that as savages Native Americans had failed to use the land in a truly productive manner and should therefore give way to the civilized. "By the law of nations," Tennessee's John Sevier declared, "it is agreed that no people shall be entitled to more land than they can cultivate."[45] The Indians were, to Sevier and other men of the West, no more than "tenants-at-will," with no right to the vast hunting lands contained within their tribal territories, entitled to use those lands only on the sufferance of whites. In practice, however, both the states and later the federal government in dealing with Indian tribes found it expedient to negotiate land cession treaties anyway and "pay small amounts bit by bit for the territory it already claimed, particularly since such payments conformed to Indian custom and helped insure peace." It was often argued that the governments were not acknowledging Indian ownership, as "payments for land were no more than presents to sweeten the Indian mood and prevent hostilities."[46]

Representatives of the Creeks first ceded land to the state of Georgia in the treaty of Augusta in 1783 and granted additional tracts to the state at the Treaty of Galphinton in 1785 and at the Treaty of Shoulderbone Creek in 1786. Under the new constitution of 1787, federal negotiators and Creek representatives led by Alexander McGillivray at New York in 1790 confirmed most of those cessions but restored to the Creeks some of the land taken from them by the Galphinton treaty. The Georgia negotiators had dealt with small, unrepresentative groups of chiefs in those earlier negotiations and resorted "strong arm tactics to intimidate and coerce."[47] Although the Washington administration sometimes deplored such tactics, they were not unlike those that would be employed by federal negotiators (most notably by Andrew Jackson) in numerous proceedings in the years to come. A Creek spokesman at Fort Colerain, Georgia, in 1796, confronted with new demands, protested that "if we part with any more of our lands . . . the white people will not suffer us to keep as much as will bury our dead."[48] But the federal government in the decades that followed continued to require more Creek land, and the Creeks were again and again forced to yield. Bitterness against the leaders who agreed to those demands was a prime cause of the Creek War. A Creek spokesman, confronted with a new land demand at treaty negotiations at Fort Wilkinson in 1802 exclaimed: "The thing that was asked us to part with, was like asking ourselves to cut ourselves in two."[49] But the process the chief compared to the dismemberment of the body continued, with further Creek land cessions demanded, often in payment of debts to white merchants, and granted, resentfully, in 1804, 1805, and 1811.

The treaties did not bring peace to the southeast frontier. Throughout the early 1790s, Creek Indians, unhappy with the land cessions or angered by white incursions on lands not ceded, joined disaffected Cherokees in striking isolated settlements. Whites retaliated in kind, with the territorial militia as noted earlier mounting a major unauthorized raid in 1792. Territorial governor William Blount and his land speculator associates were not satisfied with the pace of Indian dispossession and regularly pressed for a full-scale war. In 1794, Blount declared in a letter to the secretary of war that "if the citizens of the United States do not destroy the Creeks, they will kill the citizens of the United States: the alternative is to kill or be killed."[50]

Blount and other western war mongers systematically collected stories of Indian atrocities against white settlers and sent them to Congress and the executive, thereby providing a lurid picture of the Creek menace. While some of the atrocity stories were fabricated or exaggerated, others were not. But however much they might deplore Indian atrocities, western empire builders found them very useful in building a case for Indian dispossession. Andrew Jackson, as he reflected late in life on the violence of the early Tennessee frontier, declared that "every war we had with the Indians was brought on by frontier ruffians, who stole their horses, oppressed, or defrauded, or persecuted, the Indians."[51] But Jackson was only partly right. Those actions which he belatedly admitted provoked frontier wars were not solely the work of lawless elements. The records indicate Jackson's own patron Governor Blount personally inspired "the Indian violence he pretended to deplore, by encouraging, even ordering, expeditions against unoffending Indians."[52] His failure to enforce treaty provisions protecting Indians from the depredations on their land of white owned livestock, which often destroyed Indian crops, and of white land poachers, who sometimes simply seized the Indian lands they coveted, provided further provocation. After federal Indian agent Benjamin Hawkins urged the governor, who was also the territory's superintendent of Indian affairs, to curb such abuses, Blount quietly wrote to one of his agents, James Carey, to ask that the Creeks be encouraged to ask the president for Hawkins's removal, "for if he stays in the Creek nation he can and will do great injury to our plan." He ordered Carey to burn the letter after he had read it, which Carey neglected to do.[53] Hawkins believed Indians were entitled to the full protection promised them in treaties. That did not accord with Blount's land schemes, nor later with Andrew Jackson's.

Benjamin Hawkins, like Blount (whom he knew well and regarded as a friend) was a former federalist senator from North Carolina. Appointed to his post in Indian country by President George Washington, he was not opposed to the western expansion of white settlement. Far from it. He was in fact executing a carefully conceived long-term plan that, if consummated, would, in the administration's estimation, free up most of the territory occupied by the Southern Indian tribes for white possession and settlement, and do so in a humane and peaceful manner, without war, without bloodshed. The plan, generally associated with Washington's Secretary of War Henry Knox, envisioned a total economic, political, and social transformation of tribal life. It called for instructing Indians in Euro-American agricultural techniques, persuading them to replace reliance on hunting with animal husbandry and to abandon communal land ownership and usage in favor of individually owned farm plots. In a letter to William Augustus Bowles, a white adventurer and opponent who had declared himself emperor of the Creeks, he explained that "the plan of the Government entrusted to my agency is benevolent in the extreme: it is to introduce the wheel, the loom and the plough, to turn the attention of the Indians to raising Cattle, hogs and horses and to facilitate to them the means of procuring them; to promote Civilization among them and peace toward their neighbors."[54]

Under the new order, the vast hunting territories previously so essential to the traditional Indian economy would no longer be needed and would be available for occupation by white settlers. Hawkins envisioned a new Indian society motivated by the spirit of enterprise and individual profit, no longer committed to the old communal values he associated with backwardness and savagery. The Creek

Nation as a political entity, in his plan, was to be transformed as well, centralized, placed under the rule of a strengthened national council, with a national police force and a legal system that replaced the old clan law of individual retribution against family members with a Euro-American system of punishments limited to the guilty. Hawkins's innovations brought comfort and prosperity to a new Creek elite, who became under his tutelage ranchers, planters, merchants, and in some cases slave-holding cotton growers. But there were warning signs. As Hawkins reported, many Creeks resisted, saying that his scheme "did not comport with the ways of red people."[55] He did not understand that the problem was not merely that they were recalcitrant. The new economy was replacing traditional communalism with capitalist individualism, and thereby fostered a concentration of wealth, with an acculturated minority, often of mixed blood, numbering no more than a fifth of the population controlling 60–70 percent of "the accessible wealth in Creek country, goods such as cattle, cotton and spinning wheels. The bottom 50% in contrast, owned only between 8 and 15% of the wealth." Historian Claudio Saunt writes that "this astounding degree of inequality among a people who only thirty years earlier had disdained the accumulation of property and the centralization of power explains to a great extent why Red Sticks took up arms in 1813."[56]

Bitterness over the wealth of the new elite was exacerbated by their refusal to share resources in times of adversity (a betrayal of Creek tradition) and by agent Hawkins's lack of sympathy for the poor. In a report to the secretary of war in 1804, the agent acknowledged that many who had not adapted themselves to new economy were beginning to starve to death but declared he would not help those who would not help themselves by embracing "farming, spinning and stock raising."[57] Hawkins hoped that the pangs of hunger would force the Creeks to conform to his plan for their future. But he was mistaken. Within the Creek Nation, opposition to land cessions and to adoption of the customs of the whites grew in intensity as conditions worsened, and led, as we shall see, to violence against those who had abandoned the old ways and to the Creek War.

Although many Creeks honored their chiefs' commitment to remain neutral in the Anglo-American War of 1812, a substantial number did not. Among the Upper Creeks in particular, the militant nativist teachings of Tecumseh and his brother the Shawnee Prophet reinforced their deep disaffection with those who cooperated with white expansionists. In 1811, at a time when the nation was bitterly divided by the federal agent's demand that a new road for white commerce be cut through their homelands, Tecumseh had visited the Creeks and had won some converts to his cause.[58] When war broke out in the following year, some Creeks joined Tecumseh's forces in support of the British in Upper Canada. The party that attacked the Duck River settlement in 1812 was returning from Canada. Its leader, Little Warrior, had heard that the Creek Nation was already at war with the United States. Among those executed to placate Hawkins was a woman accused of spreading the rumor that Tennesseans had attacked the Creek Nation. Little Warrior, however, was not apprehended, nor were his followers intimidated.[59] In February 1813, another band of Tecumseh's supporters, led by two Creek chiefs, struck a small white settlement. James Robertson, Indian agent to the Chickasaw, reported "seven families have been murdered near the mouth of the Ohio, and most cruelly mangled, shewing all the savage barbarity that could be invented. One woman was cut open, a child taken out, and stuck on a stake."[60] As historian Frank Owsley Jr. notes, the result was "panic on the frontier."[61]

Hawkins wrote to all the Upper Creek chiefs to demand that they turn over to the United States those responsible, or face the hostility of the United States. "Of all the murderous acts committed by savages against the people of the United States, this is the most outrageous," Hawkins raged. "It is not done by thoughtless, wild young people, but deliberately, by a party under the command of two Chiefs. . . . You must get together one and all, turn out your warriors, apprehend the two Chiefs and their associates and deliver them to me, or to some other officer of the United States commanding on the frontiers, to be punished according to the Laws of the United States. . . . The affair will not admit delay. The guilty must suffer for their crimes, or your nation will be involved in their guilt."[62]

The Upper Creek chiefs chose to kill the accused themselves. Among those they executed were Little Warrior, who, as we have noted, was implicated in the Duck River killings the year before, and Tuskegee warrior, who allegedly boasted before he died that "he had killed and eaten white people."[63] Soon thereafter the Creek chiefs were also forced to deal with the killers of two whites on a road near a place called "the Wolf-warrior's path." The Creek leader Big Warrior reported to Hawkins on the Creek Council's actions: "We have killed eight for the murder on the Ohio, two for the murder on the Wolf Path; one for last year, for the murder on the Duck River, in all eleven," but he added that to avert future difficulties U.S. Indian agents should see to it that no Shawnees were permitted to enter Creek Territory and that steps must also be taken to prevent further violations of Creek lands by American settlers.[64]

Hawkins was well aware of problems created by some of his lawless fellow citizens, but he believed that he now had the situation under control. On May 10, he reported to General Armstrong, with much satisfaction, that a subcontractor who had recently traveled through the Creek agency related that following the executions, the roads were as safe "as in the white man's country." Hawkins commented that "as the chiefs have acted with spirit in putting these Indians to death, we think that it will have the effect of deterring others from the commission of similar crimes."[65] On June 7, he wrote again to Armstrong to deny Governor Blount's claim that Indians were massacring whites, a claim supposedly supported by the discovery in a Seminole village of "three hundred fresh scalps of men, women, and children." Hawkins, who deplored such rumor mongering, added, "If my fellow citizens on the frontiers will withdraw their intrusions on Indian rights, and be honest, they have but little to apprehend." The chiefs, he concluded, are "as well convinced as I am, that their existence as a nation depends upon their observance of their treaty stipulations with the United States."[66]

Hawkins did not foresee that the executions that he hoped, indeed believed, would secure the peace would instead help precipitate a civil war. Despite his long residence among the Creeks, he did not understand the implications of disregarding their customs in dealing with homicides. Such matters were traditionally handled by the clans, not by a national council. The killings "created immense political discontent" and antagonized "many Creeks not otherwise sympathetic to the Red Sticks."[67] Hawkins took comfort in a report from his interpreter Alexander Cornells who on June 22, 1813, advised him that the "prophets party" had influence only among "the Alabamas, who although of the Creek Confederacy, are not Creeks." As to the response of the Creeks themselves to the prophets' plan, most, Cornells assured the agent, "looked upon it as a sort of madness and amusement for idle people."[68]

Cornells was wrong. A few weeks later, Hawkins received a very different account from the Upper Creek chiefs. Their lives, he was now told, were in danger. The adherents of the prophets were killing those who had "aided and assisted" in the executions. Nine had already been slain, "one of them a woman." The prophets party had burnt the village of Hatchechubbee and several detached settlements, destroying cattle, hogs, horses, and corn. The chiefs now feared that "All who are friends of the United States are doomed to destruction." The Americans must send troops to help defend them. They were willing to give up to the whites "the lands on the Alabama" to defray the expense.[69]

The chiefs were not exaggerating the danger. In late July, Hawkins reported to the secretary of war that the prophets' warriors had laid waste to several Upper Creek towns, killing not only many of the inhabitants but "all the cattle, hogs, and fowl." Near one town, they had staged a demonstration of the "Dance of the Lakes," which they had learned from Tecumseh, invited a number of chiefs to watch the spectacle, and at its conclusion encircled and butchered several of the spectators. The Red Sticks' objective, Hawkins concluded, was "to destroy everything received from the Americans, all the chiefs and their adherents who are friendly to the customs and ways of white people, to put to death every man who will not join them, and by these means unite the nation in the aid of the British."[70]

The idea that the Creek prophetic movement was conceived "in aid of the British," and would not have come about without British encouragement, although widely held by American officials, was as fanciful as the claim that they were supported only by a few "idle people." The prophets were nativist shamans driven by a powerful vision of the restoration of the traditional Creek way of life free from the control and corruption of the whites and their toadies. They claimed to be in direct communication with the Creator, the Maker of Breath, who taught them new rituals of empowerment and endowed them with the capacity to protect their followers from the white man's bullets. To many, who had suffered deprivations and felt powerless in the new order represented by Hawkins and the compliant chiefs, the prophets' message was a compelling one. Their promise that the sacred power that had once sustained the people could be reclaimed through the violent purging of the alien and the corrupt brought them new hope.[71]

There was now a civil war in the Creek Nation, and the prophets were winning it. As one historian writes of the summer of 1813 in the nation, "everywhere dead livestock rotted. In the cattle range of Tuckabatchee the stench continued for fifteen miles. Towns were destroyed, people slaughtered."[72] Twenty-nine of the thirty-four Upper Creek towns were allied with the Red Sticks, as the prophets' people were now called, probably in reference to the painted war clubs they wielded. In numbers, they commanded around 3,000 warriors. The Lower Creek towns, debilitated by a recent epidemic, were less sympathetic to the Red Sticks, with many seeking to remain neutral. Some fought back, defending some territory and killing a few of the prophets and their followers, but they lacked the means to win the war. They also told Hawkins and other American officials that without the intervention of the United States, the Red Sticks would wipe them out.[73]

Hawkins at first was reluctant to summon troops to the Creek Nation, and particularly hoped to avoid involvement of the state militias, fearing that they might well abuse and alienate the Creeks. He tried for a time to appeal to the Red Sticks, warning that they would be destroyed if they did not cease their raids and make peace.[74] To no avail. Hawkins was soon forced to call for help from the federal army. But the first blow struck by whites against the Red Sticks was struck by militia under the command of Colonel James Caller. Having received word that a group of Red Sticks led by the prophet Peter McQueen was returning from Florida with some gun powder, lead, and other supplies given to them by the Spanish governor, Caller on July 22 attacked at Burnt Corn Creek. The outcome was an American rout, with Caller deserting the field and hiding in the woods for the next two weeks.[75]

Emboldened, a Red Stick war party then struck Fort Mims near Mobile and, in the worst Indian massacre of noncombatants in the nation's history, wiped out the poorly defended garrison and slaughtered more than 200 refugees—white, mixed blood, and Creek, who had taken refuge within its walls.[76] Accounts of the mutilation of the dead once again inflamed the southeastern frontier. Fort Mims proved a pyrrhic victory for the Red Sticks. For one thing, the magic that their prophets promised would protect against American bullets failed them. The attackers suffered high casualties. George Stiggins estimated half were killed or wounded. For another, the Fort Mims massacre precipitated a major American armed invasion of the Creek Nation. Indian agent Hawkins now warned that Red Stick belief in the power of their supreme deity "has permitted a conquering spirit to rise among them like a storm and it shall ravage like a storm." The United States, he now argued, must respond in force.[77] Debate over the handling of relations with the Creek Nation was now over. No one any longer imagined that the Creek leadership could handle the Red Stick problem.

The Fort Mims massacre strengthened the hand of those who clamored for Indian removal. Gregory A. Waselkov, the leading authority on this bloody episode, writes that "the prevailing attitude of white Americans towards Indians shifted significantly in the wake of the battle, away from the government's policy of cultural assimilation and toward a new style of American colonialism."[78] In the Southeast, the cultural assimilation policy had never been popular. Some of the region's leaders actually welcomed the Red Stick attack. An article, in the *Nashville*

Clarion, probably written by Andrew Jackson, declared it fortunate that "the crimes of this nation have supplied us with a pretext for the dismemberment of their country." The writer rejoiced that "imagination looks forward to the moment when all the Southern Indians shall be driven across the Mississippi; when the delightful countries now occupied by them shall be covered with a numerous and industrious population, and when a city, the emporium of a vast commerce, shall be seen to flourish on the spot where some huts, inhabited by lawless savages, now mark the junction of the Alabama and Tombigbee rivers. The present is a favorable moment of accomplishing part of this grand design."[79]

Four armies were ordered to strike and defeat the Red Sticks. From Tennessee, an East Tennessee force commanded by General John Cocke and a West Tennessee army commanded by General Andrew Jackson were to merge under Jackson's command and enter Creek country from the North. They were to be joined by the Third Regiment of the U.S. Army, initially commanded by General Thomas Flournoy, by the Mississippi militia under General Ferdinand L. Claiborne, and by the Georgia militia under General John Floyd. After several months of confusion, overall command of the operation was given to federal general Thomas Pinckney. The orders to all of the units were to burn the pro-Red Stick villages, destroy their food supplies, kill all their warriors, and build and garrison forts to secure the country. Given the overwhelming superiority in numbers and firepower of the American forces, the war, as one scholar notes, should have been over "in two or three months." Because of supply problems, poor coordination of effort, and "a constant turnover of militia," it took 10 months. But the outcome, as we will see, was a crushing defeat not only for the Red Sticks but also, thanks to Andrew Jackson, for those Creeks who had supported the United States.[80]

The Red Sticks after Fort Mims were in a very vulnerable position. They lacked guns (probably two out of three were armed only with clubs and arrows) and could obtain only limited aid from their Spanish friends in Florida. Tecumseh's earlier promise that the Red Sticks would be given ample armaments at Pensacola proved ill-founded. They recruited very few allies from other tribes. Cherokees, Chickasaws, and Choctaw by contrast furnished significant numbers of warriors to fight against them. Their cause suffered a severe psychological blow in December when Claiborne's army attacked a town within the Holy Ground, an area near the present site of Montgomery, Alabama, which the prophet Francis had claimed was protected by a sacred barrier that would strike dead any white man who tried to enter. Claiborne burned that town, torched another eight miles away, and killed a number of Red Sticks including three of their prophets. Most of the defenders of the Holy Ground fled when they realized that their magic did not work. Only a small band led by William Weatherford stayed to fight.[81]

Elsewhere, the Georgia militia on November 29 had destroyed the Red Stick stronghold at Autosse, in Alabama near the juncture of the Tallapoosa River and Calabree Creek, and had driven away Red Stick warriors who had been besieging Coweta. The Georgians, however, did not have the supplies needed to continue their campaign, and withdrew. On January 27, 1814, at Calabree Creek, the Red

Sticks took the offensive, bloodied the Georgia militia, but through poor coordination failed to win a decisive victory. The decisive battle would occur at Horseshoe Bend on March 27, where they were attacked by a Tennessee army commanded by General Andrew Jackson consisting of 1,500 white volunteers supported by 500 Cherokee and 100 Creek warriors. Among the Cherokee fighters who joined Jackson were two future leaders of the nation, Major Ridge and John Ross, as well as Sequoyah, inventor of the Cherokee phonetic alphabet. Horseshoe Bend would end the Red Stick bid to control the Creek Nation.[82]

Andrew Jackson's early assessments of the threat posed by the Red Sticks were exaggerated and reflected his fundamental distrust of Indians and his belief that they were all too often willing tools of the foreign enemies of the United States. After he had received word of the battle at Burnt Creek and of his army's probable mobilization in late July 1813, he had advised Governor Willie Blount that "there can be no doubt but that the Creeks and the lower Choctaws are excited to hostilities by the influence of the British." He anticipated that "we will have to fight not only the whole Creek nation, but the greater part of the Choctaws." No reliance could be placed on any of the Creeks, in Jackson's estimation, as Indians always rallied to support other Indians whenever their territory was invaded. He feared that the government, not understanding that the entire Creek Nation must be occupied and subdued, would send only a limited force that would "barely make an incursion thro' their Towns, burn their houses, destroy their crops, hastily . . . return." Instead, he argued that there must now be a major sustained operation to "crush all opposition."[83]

When Old Hickory received news of the Fort Mims massacre, he was bedridden, recuperating from a bullet wound suffered in a most unseemly brawl with the Benton brothers over a petty personal insult.[84] But Jackson did not wait until he regained his strength but responded promptly to the call. On September 24, he issued his appeal for volunteers. "Brave Tennesseans! Your frontier is threatened with invasion by the savage foe! Already do they advance toward the frontier with their scalping knives unsheathed, to butcher your wives, your children, your helpless babes. Time is not to be lost. We must hasten to the frontier, or we will find it drenched with the blood of our fellow citizens." He assured them that "the health of your general is restored—he will command in person."[85]

But Jackson had not fully recovered. On September 29, he wrote to his close friend and fellow militia officer John Coffee to confess that "the pain in my arm" was so distracting that he found it hard to assess all of the rumors of hostile activity he was hearing. Some reports claimed the Creeks were rallying with the Spanish to attack Mobile, some that they were seen crossing the Mississippi, and others, most alarmingly, that they were about to strike Huntsville and then proceed to invade Tennessee. He appealed to Coffee to sort out the rumors and advise him as to where he could strike the Creeks. He still suspected that the whole nation was hostile.[86]

When Jackson arrived at Camp Blount in northern Alabama, he was gratified by the information he received from some of the Creeks he met there, and, based on their comments, now wrote Coffee to express doubt that Creeks were in fact planning to attack the Tennessee frontier. But he advised him to keep his ears open and "treat with great kindness all such spies from the Creek nation as may offer you any communication. Let them not be discharged until my arrival. We must have the truth. . . ." He ordered that Cherokees and other Indians wishing to fight for the United States "wear white plumes in their hair, or Deer's tails" so as "to make a distinction between our friends and our enemies."[87]

Jackson assured the Indians who remained at peace with the United States of his resolve to protect them, telling the anti–Red Stick Creek chief Chennubbee that "if one hair of your head is hurt, or of your family, or of any who are friendly to the whites, I will sacrifice a hundred lives to pay for it. Be of good heart, and tell your men they have nothing to fear."[88] Chief Pathkiller of the Cherokees received Jackson's guarantee that once he met up with "the hostile Creeks . . . it will be the last of their adventures," so the Cherokee could support his campaign with confidence. Pathkiller assured Jackson that "I have spys out constantly." He promised to keep the general informed of the movements of his enemies. He also informed him that "fifteen or sixteen of my people" had already arrived to assist Jackson's fighting force and that more would join the East Tennessee militia units.[89]

Although Andrew Jackson was a remarkably able commander of white militia men, he also needed the aid of chiefs like Chennubbee and Pathkiller and he knew how to court their support. As his army made its way into hostile country, Jackson reported to Governor Willie Blount that "old Chennubbee is now with me—having brought in as prisoners two of the hostile Creeks."[90] He relied on his Indian allies not only for desperately needed intelligence but also for fighters to augment the white militia. Appreciating the need for Cherokee support, Jackson protested vehemently when he learned from Pathkiller that a half-Cherokee planter had been abused and robbed by men under General Cocke's command, declaring that their action, which he feared would alienate the entire Cherokee Nation, constituted "an outrage to the rules of war, the law of nations, and of civil society."[91] Other commanders also relied on Indian allies. The federal Third Regiment operating in the Alabama River valley, for example, was joined by several hundred Choctaws and Chickasaws.[92]

Jackson's army's first major encounter with the Red Sticks occurred on the morning of November 3, 1813, when a mounted force of a thousand under the command of John Coffee struck the village of Tallushatchee and massacred most of its inhabitants. "We shot them like dogs," Davy Crockett recounted. Some who dodged the bullets were burned alive when the village was torched. One militia man wrote in his journal that "half consumed human bodies were seen amidst the smoking ruins. In some instances dogs had torn and feasted on the mangled bodies of their masters. Heart sick I turned from the revolting scene." Crockett recounted that at one burned outhouse, where 46 Red Sticks had been incinerated, soldiers found in the cellar a mound of sweet potatoes cooked in "the oil of the Indians we had burned up on the day before."[93] Jackson, who arrived after the battle, reported to the governor of Tennessee that Fort Mims had been avenged.[94]

He also wrote to Rachel, telling her that he had ordered General John Coffee "to destroy the Creek town . . . he has executed this order in elegant stile." At least 200 Red Sticks had been killed, and another 74 taken prisoner. Among the survivors was an Indian boy around a year old named Lyncoya. Lyncoya's immediate family had all died in the slaughter. He told Rachel that he was sending the child to her, to be a playmate for their adopted son Andrew.[95] On December 29, Jackson wrote about the Indian boy again, advising Rachel that she "keep Lyncoya in the house—he is a Savage." He claimed that the surviving Creek women at Tallushatchee had told him that the child should be killed as he had no surviving relations. But Jackson remembered that he too had been orphaned by war. "When I reflect that as to his relations he is so much as myself, I feel an unusual sympathy for him—tell my dear little Andrew to treat him well."[96] Lyncoya was not the only Indian child to live at the Hermitage. Another, named Theodore and also an infant, passed away in 1814.[97] Jackson, in a letter to Rachel, referred to Theodore as "a Pett" for young Andrew Donaldson.[98] Lyncoya survived, but little is known about his life with his new family, except that he did try to run away and rejoin the Creeks several times. Considering the fact that he had been separated from his people as an infant and educated under Jackson's instructions in the ways of Euro-Americans, his self-identification as Creek is striking. Despite Jackson's good intentions, the "savage" boy, it seems, never really felt at home at the Hermitage. After a brief time as a saddler's apprentice, Lyncoya died at age 15 of a respiratory illness.[99]

A few days after the battle of Tallushatchee, Jackson wrote to Rachel again, telling her that his men were hungry. "Last night," he related, "we had not one mouthful to give the wounded or the well . . . my mind for the lack of provisions is harassed." Although some supplies had arrived, they were far from adequate. "I hope for better times."[100] Jackson had complained for some weeks of lack of enough food to sustain his army. On November 9, the federal general Thomas Flournoy, then based near Mobile, responded by telling Jackson that he could not send any provisions at all, as "the distance up to that place [where Jackson was encamped], and the danger of sending up boats is so great, and withal the force under my command in this quarter of the district so small, it is impossible for me to give you that timely support, which my wishes & our necessity calls for." Perhaps Jackson could meet General Claiborne by moving 100 miles further south, to the "highest place, I think, he can penetrate with safety." Claiborne, he promised, would be given provisions for transfer to Jackson.[101]

Flournoy, a petty self-important man who was generally uncooperative with other commanders, later resigned his command in irritation over the War Department's decision to entrust coordination of the overall war effort to General Pinckney. Among Flournoy's plans for pursuing the war against the Red Sticks was an order, never implemented, to kill all the black slaves in areas threatened by the insurgents to prevent their enlistment in the war against the United States.[102]

Before he received the bad news from Flournoy, Jackson and his famished army went on the offensive once more, this time to counter a Red Stick attack on the village of Talladega which earlier had tried to make peace with the Americans. He received not only no provisions adequate for the task but no support from the East Tennessee militia. Jackson later accused its commander, General John Cocke, of undercutting his offensive and had him arrested on the charge of "enticing the soldiers to desert." Cocke's court-martial ended in his acquittal.[103]

Jackson did drive the Red Sticks from Talladega but did not win a decisive victory there, as some 700 enemy warriors escaped when one of Jackson's infantry units inexplicably retreated. After the battle Jackson marched north to Fort Stothers, hoping that his supplies had been sent there from Nashville. Nothing was available. His Tennessee contractors had failed him, as had General Flournoy earlier. As supply problems persisted, Jackson the following March informed General Pinckney of his "strong suspicions that there was a combination, to starve the army, and defeat the campaign." There were also, he complained, ongoing efforts to undermine his army's morale. Accordingly, he had given orders to arrest and confine "all and every description of persons, either officer, soldier, or citizen, that is guilty of exciting sedition, mutiny or desertion."[104] Pinckney, in reply, upheld Jackson's order, but warned him to respect established legal procedures in dealing with civilian offenders, lest he play into the hands of his "personal Enemies."[105]

Jackson's men, desperate with hunger, were close to mutiny after the battle of Talladega. Jackson faced down a group of militia determined to return home, but promised to lead them out of harm's way and back to Tennessee in two days if supplies did not arrive. When they did not, he exclaimed that he could not abandon his post and would stay even if only two others would remain with him. Over 100 agreed to do so. They set out to find the supply train. But after they found it and assuaged their hunger, a number of the militia men, including one entire brigade, defied the general and tried to return home anyway. He threatened to shoot them if they left camp. Historian Robert Remini calls this "the supreme challenge to his leadership." He faced them down and held his force together. It later turned out that the musket Old Hickory propped up on the sling that held his wounded arm and pointed at the would-be deserters was "too ancient a weapon to be fired." Jackson's fearless confrontation with the would-be deserters became a part of the Old Hickory legend.[106] But at the time, it inspired much resentment. A correspondent several weeks later told Jackson, "The Volunteers have been doing every thing in their power, since their return, to injure you."[107] Jackson then wrote Rachel to ask that "the calumnies" of "vile miscreants" not "disturb your mind," assuring her that "they cannot hurt me so long as I meet with the approbation of a peaceful conscience, and the full expression of approbation from my government, I smile with contempt upon those reptiles." He enclosed a copy of a letter from Secretary of War Armstrong conveying that approbation.[108]

In the weeks following the battle at Talladega, the supply problems which had bedeviled Jackson were partially resolved. But the manpower problem remained. Militia enlistments were for short term, with most expiring at or near the end of the calendar year 1813. His reputation as a charismatic leader notwithstanding, Jackson's efforts to persuade his men not to return home at the end of their period of service proved largely unavailing, as did his attempt to persuade Governor Blount to support a definition of the militia contracts which would have extended their enlistments by several months.[109]

The governor advised Jackson to leave Creek country, return to the Tennessee frontier, and wait for the federal government to take action. He claimed that as governor he could do nothing. Jackson replied on December 29 with a scorching letter accusing Blount of yielding through his inaction to "cowardly poltroons" who would "let thousands fall victim" rather than doing their duty. "Save yr. frontier from being drenched in blood," Jackson admonished, "and yourself for being damned for it." He refused to march back to Tennessee. It was essential, he told the governor, to "carry a campaign into the heart of the Creek nation and exterminate it."[110] A few days later, continuing his dispute with Blount over the terms of militia enlistment, Jackson asked, rhetorically, "is it sound policy to abandon a conquest thus far made, and deliver up to havoc, or add to the number of our enemies those friendly Creeks and Cherokees who relying upon our protection have espoused our cause and aided us with their arms? Is it good policy to turn loose upon our defenseless frontier 4000 exasperated savages to reek their hands, once more in the blood of our fellow citizens?"[111]

Jackson had reason to be worried. Despite the vehement determination to punish the Creeks for Fort Mims that had enflamed the states of the lower South in the summer of 1813, the outlook for victory over the Red Sticks at New Year 1814 was uncertain. The militia system was ill-suited to a protracted Indian war, and the regular army of the United States was of only limited help. The Mississippi forces commanded by General Claiborne were stripped of manpower as enlistments expired. Claiborne withdrew from the field. The Georgia militia, demoralized by the losses they had sustained, were no longer on the offensive. Jackson, realizing that he lacked the authority to force men whose enlistment terms had expired to remain, found himself virtually alone. There were only around 100 men with him at Fort Stother in early January.[112]

Governor Blount, however, finally did issue a new call for volunteers, and Old Hickory by mid-month had 800 new recruits, with more coming. He was also given command of the Thirty-Ninth Regiment of the federal army and placed in charge of offensive operations against the insurgents. Although delay would have been prudent, Jackson did not wait for his forces to be augmented to the point where he would have a clear advantage. As soon as the first reinforcements were in place, he mounted an offensive against the main Red Stick encampment at Tohopeka (better known in American history as the Horseshoe Bend) on the Tallapoosa River. His initial effort failed. On January 21, Red Sticks struck his 900 man force at Emuckfaw Creek, three miles from the insurgent stronghold. Jackson beat off the attackers, but finding he lacked the numbers needed to win a decisive victory, withdrew. As Jackson regrouped, he was hit again at Enitachopco Creek. Jackson and his militia, better armed than their foes, made the assailants pay dearly, killing some 200 Red Stick warriors. Only 20 of Jackson's men died at Enitachopco. In this action, notes Remini, "the Red Sticks had suffered a severe mauling, so severe in fact that they abandoned their aggressive policy and withdrew into their strongholds—especially the seemingly impregnable fortress at Horseshoe Bend."[113]

Jackson did not renew his offensive against Tohopeka until his army had reached its full strength. In camp at Fort Stother, he proved a tough disciplinarian, drilling his troops, browbeating those who wanted to go home at the end of their enlistment terms, and executing a young volunteer for insubordination.[114] He ordered the arrest and court-martial of several officers, including two generals, John Roberts and John Cocke, who questioned his authority.[115] In early February, the U.S. Army's Thirty-Ninth Regiment joined Jackson's forces at Fort Stother. In addition to a steady stream of new militia men from West Tennessee (including John Coffee's cavalry division) Jackson also now had at his command the 2,000 man East Tennessee army led before his removal by General Cocke. Also joining the war against the Red Sticks were 500 Cherokee warriors and 200 Creek. In all, Old Hickory's army numbered some 5,000 fighters. It greatly outnumbered the insurgents at the Horseshoe Bend, estimated at around 1,000 warriors. He deployed over 3,000 in his renewed campaign against the Red Sticks stronghold.[116]

The assault on Tohopeka began on March 27. The Red Stick position was well defended by a breastwork across the neck of the bend. Historian Frank Owsley Jr. explains: "The barrier, which ranged from five to eight feet high, was prepared with double rows of portholes arranged in such a way that an army could not approach without being exposed to a double crossfire. Because of the curvature of the breastwork, it could not have been raked by cannon, even if one flank of it had been taken. The engineering of the fort was excellent, according to all observers."[117] Jackson himself praised the skill the Red Sticks employed in its construction. "I endeavoured," he related, "to levell the works with my cannon, but in vain."[118] But while the breastwork protected the Red Stick position from a frontal attack, it could also serve to turn Tohopeka into a death trap. And that is exactly what happened. General John Coffee, in command of cavalry and of 600 Cherokee and Creek allies, marched some three miles below the bend in the river, then marched upstream in order, as he explained to Jackson, "to take possession of the bank of the river and prevent the enemy from crossing on the approach of your army." The Indians under Coffee's command then swam across the stream, destroyed the canoes that had been left there to provide for an escape should the fortifications be breached, and attacked the village from the rear. "Attempts to cross the river at all points in the bend was made by the enemy," Coffee reported, "but not one escaped, very few ever reached the bank, and that few was killed the instant they landed."[119]

Meanwhile, Jackson's forces, after bombarding the breastworks with artillery for two hours, broke through and began the slaughter of the defenders, who were now unable to escape. Forty-nine of Jackson's men were killed in the action. Of those, about half were Indians fighting on his side. Red Stick losses were staggering, numbering between 800 and 900. There were around 350 survivors, but almost all were women and children. Jackson reported to General Pinckney that "determining to exterminate them," he had left only "two or three" Red Stick warriors alive at the Horseshoe.[120] In the course of that extermination, Jackson's men sometimes slaughtered both the very young and the elderly. A soldier who killed a confused little Indian boy who had lost his way and wandered into the midst of the fighters from Tennessee justified his act by saying he had thereby saved white people from being murdered when the child grew up and became a warrior. The murderer of elderly, possibly senile male Creek noncombatant explained that he wanted to say, when he went home to Tennessee, that he had killed an Indian.[121]

After nightfall, to flush out the last of the enemy warriors, Jackson's men threw lighted torches into the woods near the battle site, setting them ablaze, and shooting down those who fled the conflagration.[122] "It was dark," Jackson wrote Rachel, "before we finished killing them."[123] The next day, after the slaughter of the few survivors his forces could locate, Jackson gazed upon the mutilated body of the Red Stick prophet Monahooee, whose jaw had been torn off by a blast of grapeshot. Writing to Governor Blount, Jackson mused that "heaven designed to chastise his impostures by a proper judgment."[124] Those who fought under Jackson's command showed their Creek adversaries little mercy, sometimes slaughtering women, children, and old men as well as warriors. Jackson himself boasted that he personally took and "preserved the scalps of my killed."[125] Historian Ronald Takaki notes, "his soldiers cut long strips of skin from the bodies of the dead Indians and used them as bridle reins: they also cut the tip of each dead Indian's nose to count the number of enemy bodies."[126]

After the mopping up at the Horseshoe, Jackson and his army burned a number of other Creek towns and villages. "We have," Jackson boasted to a correspondent, "enforced the *lex taliones*."[127] To his troops, he declared:

> the fiends of the Tallapoosa will no longer murder our women and children, or disturb the quiet of our borders. Their midnight flambeaux will no longer illumine their council-house or shine upon the victims of their infernal orgies . . . we have seen them flying from the flames of their own dwellings. We have seen the ravens and the vultures preying upon the carcasses of the slain unburied slain. Our vengeance has been glutted.[128]

The Indians at the Horseshoe gave Andrew Jackson a new name: Sharp Knife. It was not intended as a compliment.[129] While Jackson was now a hero to many of his white compatriots, the sentiment was not universal. Commenting on Jackson's conduct of the campaign, historian Henry Adams recalled that "Jackson's policy of extermination shocked many humane Americans, and would perhaps have seemed less repulsive had the Creeks shown more capacity for resistance."[130]

The entire Creek Nation, not just the inhabitants of the pro-Red Stick villages, endured great suffering during and after this war. To Rachel, Jackson wrote, after a negotiating session with the Creek chieftains who had been his allies: "Could you only see the misery and wretchedness of those creatures perishing from want of food and picking up the grains of corn scattered from the mouths of horses and trodden in the earth—I know your humanity would feel for them, notwithstanding all the causes you have to feel hatred and revenge."[131] Some weeks earlier, he had ordered rations distributed to relieve the sufferings of "the friendly Creeks" and of "a portion of the Cherokee who fought very valiantly with us."[132] The burnt earth tactics used by both sides in the conflict had taken a terrible toll.

A few of the surviving Red Sticks finally surrendered. Jackson ordered them to move north of Fort Williams, thereby cutting them off from contact with the Spanish or British. American authorities, speaking through the Indian agent Benjamin Hawkins, demanded that the Creeks hunt down and execute of all the remaining prophets.[133] Paddy Walsh was captured by General Gaines and hanged. William Weatherford surrendered to Jackson personally and promised to work to persuade other Red Stick leaders to lay down their arms. The general, said to be impressed by Weatherford's personal courage, granted him a pardon.[134] He resumed his career as an affluent planter. Other Red Stick leaders fled with around 1,000 followers to Spanish Florida. Jackson would later mount a war against those survivors that would lead to an unauthorized and controversial invasion of Spanish Territory. But that story belongs in a later chapter.

It is appropriate at this point to scrutinize Jackson's perceptions of his Indian adversaries and of his Indian allies during the Creek campaign for they provide important insights into the assumptions and convictions that drove his determination as president to secure total Indian removal. While Old Hickory never wrote anything that demonstrated much understanding of contemporary Indian life and culture, his letters from this period contain some very telling observations about his feelings, preconceptions, and prejudices. Surprisingly, given the invaluable military support he received from Cherokees, Choctaws, and Chickasaws, and from a number of Creeks, Jackson still harbored a deep distrust of all Indians, declaring them all potential future allies of the British and other enemies of the Republic. He justified treaties taking land from ostensibly friendly Indian tribes on grounds of national security.[135] Even more surprising, given the valiant performance of his Indian allies, Jackson qualified his expressions of appreciation for their individual courage with deprecation of their overall Indian military prowess, complaining "you cannot keep them in the field; as soon as they perform an excursion and take a scalp, they must go home and dance."[136] Indian warfare, he declared, was motivated only by the desire "to gather scalps." Correspondence from this period indicates that Jackson's basic assessment of Indian character was harsh, as he wrote repeatedly of their treachery and brutality. As noted earlier, in his call for troops to march against the Red Sticks, Jackson warned that "savages . . . with their scalping knives unsheathed" would soon, if not defeated, "butcher your wives, your children, and your helpless babes" and leave the Tennessee's frontier "drenched in the blood of our fellow citizens."[137] He told one correspondent that the Indian warrior who fights against the United States does not act to defend his homeland or avenging past wrongs but kills "only because he delights in blood."[138]

These statements were not simply a commander's battlefield rhetoric. Before, during, and after the war, Jackson constantly warned against half measures, insisting that it must be remembered that the enemy were "cannibals who reveled in the carnage of our inoffensive citizens." Recalling a lesson from Roman history, Old Hickory quoted, somewhat inaccurately, Cato's demand that Carthage be destroyed utterly. "Delenda est Cathago," he wrote General Armstrong, "or we shall never have peace with the Indians."[139] Moreover, in Jackson's estimation, such a peace even if secured by the most decisive of victories, could well prove ephemeral, as no Indians, not even those currently allied with the United States could really be trusted. Near the close of his career as an Indian fighter, he warned one correspondent that "the treachery of the Indian character . . . will never justify the reposing of confidence in their professions." Those who lived near Indians must therefore always be on their guard, "ready to inflict exemplary punishment on the offenders when necessary."[140] Essentially, Jackson did not believe in the possibility of long-term peace with independent Indian nations.

To place his view of Indians in broader perspective, it must be remembered that Andrew Jackson throughout his life lived in a country in which the white majority, with little dissent, regarded coexistence with "savage" Indian tribes as a temporary expedient at best. During the first Seminole War, *Niles Register*, the nation's premier political journal, declared Indians "natural enemies to a civilized state of society. . . . They resemble wolves, who would rather be exterminated than domesticated."[141] That view was not limited to the western frontier. John Quincy Adams, who in many respects had little in common with Jackson, declared early in his political career that the Indians had no right to complain when required to relinquish the vast lands over which they "accidentally ranged in quest of prey." To accept their claim to such domains would be to condemn to "everlasting barrenness . . . fields and valleys which a beneficent God has formed to teem with the life of innumerable multitudes." The savage, Adams believed, must now yield to the civilized.[142]

The issue for American policy makers was not whether the greater portion of the land holdings of the sovereign Indian tribes, being an obstacle to the expansion of the white population, would need to be taken from them. The question was how that could be accomplished? Was the physical elimination, through removal or war, the only way? The Washington administration as noted earlier hoped it could be accomplished through a voluntary process of assimilation and land relinquishment. Secretary of War Knox expressed on several occasions the view that "the Indians being the prior occupants possess the right to the soil. It cannot be taken from them unless by their free consent. . . . To dispossess them in any other principle would be a gross violation of the fundamental laws of nature and, and of that distributive justice which is the glory of the nation."[143] But that principle, endorsed by a federal government hoping for peace on the frontiers, seemed to many workable only if the Indians agreed to give up land. The negotiator of a treaty with the Choctaws in 1801 declared tellingly that if Indians did emulate whites, become farmers and surrender land rendered superfluous by their abandonment of the hunt "the United States may be spared the pain and expense of expelling or destroying them."[144]

President Thomas Jefferson shared that sentiment, warning that if Indians did not cooperate and make room for white expansion, "we shall be obliged to drive them, with the beasts of the forest, into the Stony [Rocky] mountains."[145] In correspondence with his secretary of war in 1807, he declared that if any Indian tribe tried to wage war against the United States, they would either be "exterminated or driven beyond the Mississippi. . . . In war they will kill some of us; we shall destroy all of them."[146] He hoped that would never be necessary. Thomas Jefferson often assured visiting Indian delegations that he looked forward to the time when "you will unite yourselves with us, join in our great councils and form one people with us, and we shall all be Americans, you will mix with us by marriage, your blood will run in our veins, and will spread with us over this great continent."[147] He assured Benjamin Hawkins, "in truth the ultimate point of rest and happiness for them [Native Americans] is to let our settlements and theirs meet and blend together, intermix and become one people."[148] But Jefferson knew that was visionary. He was well aware that white settlers in the West had little patience with the gradualist approach that had been championed by Washington and Knox and now endorsed in principle by Jefferson. They wanted two things: security from Indian attack and access to Indian land, objectives most believed could only be attained by Indian removal. Very few westerners were comfortable with the idea of "becoming one people" with Indians. In 1816, when Secretary of War Crawford recommended that the federal government undertake a program encouraging racial intermarriage in order to accelerate the process of "civilization" he stirred up a hornet's nest.

The most extreme response to Crawford's proposal came from South Carolina's Thomas Cooper who expressed outrage at the prospect of forcing "blooming, healthy, hard, active young whites" to take as wives "dirty, draggle tailed, blanketed, half human squaws. . . . You can no more turn an Indian into a civilized man than you can convert a negro into a white man."[149] White traders, of course, had been taking Indian women as mistresses and even wives ever since the founding of the first colonies, but they had not founded interracial communities within the states of the sort Crawford apparently envisioned. In the wake of Tecumseh's uprising and Indian alliances with the British in the War of 1812, coexistence seemed increasingly problematic. Accordingly, the removal alternative gained in popularity, and the civilization project lost favor, particularly in the South. By 1805, Jefferson privately had come to believe that the only alternative to Indian extermination was removal west of the Mississippi. Jefferson did not share Cooper's view of the Indian's incapacity for civilized behavior, but that hardly mattered. Too many other Americans did.[150]

Andrew Jackson's mentor William Blount had declared early in his career as territorial governor that there could be no lasting peace "while there is a tribe of Indians remaining on this side of the Mississippi."[151] From the outset, Jackson shared Blount's belief in the necessity of Indian dispossession, and denounced those who discounted the Indian threat. In 1812, Benjamin Hawkins's report that the Creek Nation as a whole was not hostile to the United States provoked his ire.[152] Several years earlier, Jackson had complained to President Jefferson that Hawkins's pro-Indian sympathies rendered him unsuitable for the task of persuading his charges that Indian lands must be ceded to the United States. The president assured him that his administration was committed to taking, through peaceful means, more territory from the Indians.[153] But for many frontier politicians, reliance on the efforts of federal negotiators was not sufficient. Blount's half-brother Willie, also a governor and Jackson ally, wrote to Old Hickory at the end of 1809 to enlist his help in persuading all Tennessee citizens that their best interests required that the state's Indian population be persuaded to relocate west of the Mississippi.[154]

Blount did not succeed in removing all of Tennessee's Indians during his governorship. But two decades later, as president, Andrew Jackson embarked on a comprehensive Indian removal program that covered the entire United States east of the Mississippi. Central to the rationale for that program was the denial that Indians were capable of sufficient improvement to warrant the inclusion of their communities in areas needed for the expansion of white settlement. In his fifth message to Congress as president, in 1833, Jackson would emphatically reject opposition claims that the Cherokee in Georgia had become a civilized people worthy of remaining on their homelands. The Cherokee, in common with other Indians, the president declared, had "neither the intelligence, the industry, the moral habits, nor the desire of improvement which are essential to any change in their condition. Established in the midst of another and a superior race, without appreciating the causes of their inferiority or seeking to control them, they must necessarily yield to the force of circumstances and ere long disappear."[155] As president, he would often defend the relocation of Indian peoples west of the Mississippi as a measure not only essential to the security of whites but imperative if the Indians themselves were to survive. Perhaps, if removed from immediate contact with the superior race, these inferior peoples could continue to exist as peoples and perhaps in time even achieve some degree of civilization. Indian removal, as President Jackson would come to portray it, was thus a humanitarian measure intended to save a vulnerable race from extinction.

Jackson on occasion expressed some kindly paternalistic feelings toward "savages" and counted some of his Indian allies as personal friends. Unlike a later Indian fighting general, he did not believe that "the only good Indian is a dead Indian." His instructions to Rachel about caring for the orphaned Creek boy Lyncoya are striking evidence of his capacity for compassion. But on balance, Jackson's letters from his Indian fighting years leave no doubt that concern for Indian well-being was not the major reason for his long-standing insistence on removal. One can make a stronger case that those letters disclose that Old Hickory *was* driven instead by fear and greed: fear of the Indians as treacherous enemies in our midst, and greed for the lands they still held, a greed rationalized by the claim that it was God's will that land be possessed only by the industrious, not by "savages."[156]

In the forging of the Old Hickory image that would one day propel Andrew Jackson into the presidency, his role as an Indian fighter shared billing with his stunning victory over the British at New Orleans. Two fellow Tennessee militia officers, John Reid and John Henry Eaton, with Jackson's encouragement and collaboration, published a biography of the general in 1817 that emphasized his exceptional role in protecting the frontier through killing Indians. With much exaggeration, the biographers claimed that from his earliest years of residence in the Cumberland Jackson led the way in punishing "Indian depredations." "Although young," they wrote, "no person was more distinguished than Andrew Jackson in defending the country against these predatory incursions of the savages. . . ." As noted earlier, contemporary source materials from the period assign no such role to Jackson. Although at the time of the Fort Mims massacre, Jackson, now a militia general, had still seen no action against Indians, Reid and Eaton declared him "the only man, known in the state, who was believed qualified to discharge the arduous duties" of putting down the Red Stick insurrection. In their account of the fighting, they gave little credit to any of the other commanders who also fought the Creek prophets and their followers. As they developed and embellished the Old Hickory image, Reid and Eaton stressed the cruelty and ferocity of Indian foe, the treachery of the British and Spanish in encouraging their atrocities, the shortsighted selfishness of politicians and of other commanders in failing to provide adequate support to the troops in the field who fought the enemy, the courage and vision of Andrew Jackson in facing adversity, and above all his fierce determination to defend the Republic from its enemies. He was, they declared, the ideal commander, "wholly unmoved by his own privations . . . filled with solicitude and concern for his army." His admirers believed that Old Hickory had saved the nation at Horseshoe Bend and at New Orleans.[157]

To the empire builders and Indian haters of the 19th century, Andrew Jackson was, as Reid and Eaton portrayed him, a larger-than-life hero. But Native Americans have had little reason to celebrate Sharp Knife's legacy. One Cherokee warrior who fought on Jackson's side at Horseshoe Bend said many years later that if he had foreseen the future, "he would have killed Old Hickory when he had the chance."[158] Many of Jackson's Indian allies as well as his enemies would soon come to share that sentiment. He did them the greatest damage not on the battlefield but at council fires and in the corridors of power in Washington, D.C. It is to that part of the story we must now turn.

Chapter 3

Empire Builder

Following the defeat of the Red Sticks, General Andrew Jackson imposed on the Creeks a treaty that, according to Henry Clay, exceeded any humiliation inflicted on any people during "the most haughty period of imperial Rome."[1] While one must make much allowance for Clay's political bias, and for his fondness for rhetorical hyperbole, the Treaty of Fort Jackson was remarkable. The penalty for the war was inflicted on Jackson's own Indian allies as well as on his enemies. It marked only the beginning of his drive for Indian dispossession. The land cessions Jackson would extort over the next few years from friendly Indian nations as well as adversaries would not only make well positioned land speculators very wealthy but, more importantly, would make possible the expansion of slave agriculture into a vast region of newly acquired land ideally suited to the large-scale cultivation of cotton. Within a few decades, the United States would dominate the world cotton market, generating through the exploitation of the enslaved the funding required for a large-scale capitalist economic transformation. The American southeastern frontier was no longer economically isolated or marginal but soon numbered among its white planter residents some of the wealthiest men in the world. Investors in the north and in England made immense profits through their dealings with the masters of the Cotton Kingdom.

The new order entailed a demographic revolution marked by phenomenal growth in the white population of the lower south, by the dispossession and deportation of most Indians, and by the importation of black slaves by the hundreds of thousands. In 1810, before the beginning of Andrew Jackson's career as an empire builder, the non-Indian population of the territories of Alabama and Mississippi stood at barely 16,000. By 1840, four years after his retirement from the presidency, it exceeded 965,000. Very few Native Americans remained, as the Cherokee, Creek, Seminole, Choctaw, and Chickasaw were induced or forced to move west of the Mississippi River. Slaves, however, were soon abundant. Some estimates hold that nearly half the white families in the Cotton Kingdom were slaveholders. But the non-slaveholding white majority found land prices inflated, and their opportunities for achieving economic independence accordingly diminished by the burgeoning influxes of new capital invested in the new cotton economy in the new plantation lands. Jefferson's dream of a republic of independent yeomen farmers including newly civilized Native Americas was hardly relevant to the new realities. To a far greater degree than is generally recognized, it was Andrew Jackson who subverted the Jeffersonian ideal through devising, during his years of service as a treaty negotiator and later as president, ways of undermining and subverting long-standing guarantees of Indian land rights and political autonomy. Without Sharp Knife's skill in intimidating and defrauding Indians, beginning with the Creeks, the Cotton Kingdom would have grown far more slowly and might have assumed a different character. "Jackson," writes Steve Inskeep, "more than any other single person, was responsible for the region we call the Deep South."[2]

The Madison administration did not initially intend to entrust peace negotiations with the Creeks to Andrew Jackson. Instead, the commanding federal General Thomas Pinckney and Indian agent Benjamin Hawkins were asked to handle the matter. That decision was not popular in the southwest. When word of the role assigned to Hawkins reached Tennessee, nine of her militia officers, led by Brigadier General George Doherty, protested to their Congressman against the use of "a man, whose interest and feelings . . . are too much identified with the enemy, and in whom the people of the West as well as many in the East, have long since ceased to retain any confidence."[3] Their fear was that, based on his past record as an advocate for his Indian charges, Hawkins would not treat the Creeks with sufficient severity or capitalize on the opportunity to take more of their land. Their complaint was echoed by Jackson's good friend General John Coffee who declared the exclusion of Tennessee officers "repugnant to the feelings of this army." He demanded that Andrew Jackson "be appointed from our state to act with Genl. Pinckney."[4]

After receiving instructions from Secretary of War Armstrong, Pinckney, now under orders to secure a quick end to hostilities, asked Hawkins to send word to the Red Sticks that those who were willing to capitulate would be well treated. Other Creek leaders were to be assured that those who had remained loyal to the United States would be rewarded, not harmed. In particular, Hawkins was to "inform them that the United States will not forget their fidelity . . . their claims will be respected" in the boundary readjustments that would be made to obtain land to defray the cost of the war.[5] As ordered, the agent conveyed those assurances to the Creek leaders who had fought against the Red Sticks.[6] In compliance with the spirit of his instructions, he also allowed some of them to return to their old homes. Based on his correspondence with Pinckney, Hawkins had assumed that the war settlement would leave those Creeks who had supported the United States in possession of most if not all of their former territory.

Andrew Jackson had a very different plan in mind. In a letter responding to an inquiry from Pinckney seeking advice concerning the amount of land the Creeks should be asked to cede, Jackson strenuously objected to Hawkins's conduct. "I am truly astonished that Colo. Hawkins is permitting the Indians to settle down on their former habitations, I did tell him the territory I had assigned them." Jackson advised Pinckney that the defeat of the Red Sticks should be seized upon as an opportunity to acquire extensive land cessions that would secure "the strength of the frontier of the union" by filling it with "thick and wealthy inhabitants, unmixed by Indians." He argued that the annexations of Creek land should not be limited to the amount needed to defray the cost of the war but should serve the broader needs of the United States. Other tribes should be asked to give up land as well. In particular, the Cherokee and the Chickasaw should be induced to relinquish their last claims in Tennessee. The United States, in Jackson's view, should take advantage of the recent military victory to create Indian-free regions that would provide barriers to their contact with America's European enemies in Florida and Canada. Resettled Indians should be hemmed in by white settlers. The ultimate objective of the government in these boundary adjustments should be to "extend our settlements to the Mississippi." To assure that the frontier would be defended by "a hardy race," Indian lands should be sold quickly at a reasonable price, with preference given to the veterans who had conquered it.[7]

General Pinckney played no role in the actual settlement with the Creeks. In April, he had requested reassignment to his old post in Charleston. His request was granted. In May, Jackson, having been awarded the rank of major general in the U.S. Army, was given command of the Seventh Military District, which included Louisiana, Tennessee, and Mississippi Territory. He was granted sole authority to negotiate a peace treaty with the Creeks. Hawkins was retained as a spokesman in negotiations but no longer had any authority or influence in the relocation of the Creeks. Jackson was well aware of the generous guidelines for Creek land settlement Pinckney and Hawkins had received from Washington, D.C. He had no intention of following them.

Jackson from his earliest days in Tennessee had looked forward to the time when the entire southwest would be white man's country, covered with prosperous farms and plantations. Jackson owed much of the personal fortune he would ultimately accumulate to speculation in lands taken from Indians. He was always acutely aware of the profits to be made from even minor territorial adjustments. To cite two early examples, during his term as a U.S. senator, he had written to his brother-in-law Robert Hays to inform him that the negotiations for a new land cession with the Cherokees could make property claims on the Duck River "very valuable" for he anticipated that the Tennessee River would "become the line" between white and Indian Territory. Hays should, therefore, "keep all you have and get what you can."[8] Seven years later, still anticipating the annexation of the Duck River region, Jackson himself tried to buy some 40,000 acres of land there, offering to pay $15,000.[9]

The Duck River venture failed, but Jackson remained on the lookout for new opportunities. We find in Jackson's papers a letter, written shortly after the Red Sticks defeat at Horseshoe Bend, in which he told one of his officers of his intention in the peace settlement to take territory from Indian allies as well as from hostiles. While explaining the reasons why national security required that land seizure, he added that he anticipated that "preference rights" in purchasing that "section of the union" would likely be given "to those who conquered it."[10] Jackson himself later expressed great personal interest in the Muscle Shoals area taken from the Cherokee, advising John Coffee that a settlement there would soon be "one of the largest towns in the western country . . . it will become the Nashville of the Tennessee."[11] Jackson and Coffee both invested at Muscle Shoals and elsewhere and profited greatly from their investments. "Andrew Jackson," notes historian Mark Cheathem, "used his knowledge of the lands he had seized from the southeastern Indians to benefit himself and his friends."[12] While such transactions might seem to us to be of questionable propriety, no such scruples disturbed men on the make in Jackson's day.

There was probably no single land cession in American history more lucrative to white occupiers and investors than the one Sharp Knife forced on Indian friends and enemies alike at Fort Jackson. "The ceded lands form one-third of the present-day Georgia and three-fifths of Alabama," as well as "a long, rich strip along the Florida line, from the Perdido River just west of Pensacola to the Pearl River—right through southern Choctaw country. No tribe was untouched by the seizure." The Cherokee, invaluable allies in the war against the Red Sticks, were forced to give up some four million acres. Even the isolated Seminoles of Florida, nonbelligerents in the recent war, lost land. The cessions were far more extensive than security concerns alone could justify.[13]

The document known to historians as "the Treaty of Fort Jackson," which granted this bonanza to the United States and to its land speculators, was actually entitled "An Agreement and Capitulation." It was not arrived at through negotiations with an adversary, but rather was imposed upon allies as well as enemies. It can hardly be considered a peace treaty, as the Red Stick leaders were not present and did not sign it. When Jackson informed Hawkins that he wished to meet with all of the Creek leaders, friendly and hostile alike, he added that they should be told that "destruction will attend a failure to comply with these orders."[14] The hostiles ignored his summons. His Indian friends would soon regret their cooperation.

Jackson's Creek and Cherokee comrades in arms did not at first realize what Old Hickory had in mind. Based on earlier promises from Hawkins and Pinckney, the Creek leaders who had supported the anti–Red Stick campaign had every reason to expect generous treatment. But when they met with Sharp Knife at Fort Jackson in August, they were stunned to learn he had no intention of honoring that promise. Indeed, when Big Warrior produced a copy of Pinckney's letter to Hawkins, Jackson declared he was not bound by it and denied that he was under any obligation to reward his Creek supporters with land grants. Instead, confronted with the complaint that meeting his territorial demands would destroy the friendly as well as the hostile part of the Creek Nation, Jackson denied that any Creeks had any legitimate territorial rights. To the chiefs' astonishment, he declared since they had once entertained Tecumseh and his followers without notifying the United States that its enemies were now in their villages, "the United States would have been justified by the Great Spirit had they taken all of the lands of the Nation . . . If my enemy goes into the house of my friend, and tells my friend he means to kill me—my friend become my enemy, if he does not at least tell me I am to be killed." Had the Creek chiefs acted properly, Jackson declared, "Tecumseh would have had no influence." He should have "been sent back to the British, or delivered to the United States as a prisoner, or shot." The Creek chiefs' failure to keep him from visiting their people, Jackson explained, warranted treating them as enemies, not with the indulgence he was now prepared to show them.[15]

The fact that, after his visit, many of the Creek chiefs and warriors had opposed Tecumseh and fought against the Red Sticks, in Jackson's mind, did not exonerate them. Instead, Jackson's official biographers, writing with his assistance the story of the war three years later, gave this matter a very strange twist. They declared Old Hickory's Creek allies dishonorable, charging that they had betrayed their kinsmen. Honor and duty, declared Reid and Eaton, required that they set aside their disagreements with the Red Sticks and rally to the defense of the Creek Nation when war broke out with the United States. Instead, they entered "the ranks of an invading army" and "fought for the extermination of their people, and the destruction of their nation." The curious logic behind that argument reflected Andrew Jackson's basic contempt for Indian character. The Creeks who fought for him, he believed, were not really steadfast allies, but "traitors to their country, deserving the severest punishment."[16]

Despite the objections of Big Warrior and other anti–Red Stick chiefs, the articles they were forced to sign in effect represented an admission of war guilt. Jackson insisted that they acknowledge not only that many of the nation's chiefs and warriors had just waged "an unprovoked, inhuman and sanguinary war" against the United States, but that in years past Creeks had been guilty of "numberless aggressions . . . committed against the peace, prosperity, and lives of the citizens of the United States." In addition to that admission of long-standing guilt, Jackson's capitulation document now required that the Creek chiefs surrender to the United States territories comprising half of the nation's remaining lands, including the fertile southern regions later to be an essential part of the South's "Cotton Kingdom."

The federal government's instructions to Pinckney had envisioned radical restrictions of Creek sovereignty. Jackson complied fully with those provisions. He forbade the Creeks with any future contact with "any British or Spanish post, garrison, or town." They could trade only with agents authorized by the president of the United States. They were to allow the United States to build roads, trading posts and military forts wherever the Creeks chose on their remaining lands. They were to restore all property seized by Red Sticks and apprehend and surrender any Red Stick who had not yet capitulated. Although this was essentially a surrender document, only one Red Stick was present at its signing. The other 35 signatories were Creek leaders who had supported the United States. Since many Creeks were now on the verge of starvation, the agreement offered a powerful incentive to sign, as Jackson held out the promise of food relief from the United States for those who cooperated.[17] In a letter to Big Warrior, Jackson also promised to delay the expulsion from the ceded lands of those Creeks who had crops to harvest until they had gathered in their corn. He would also to urge the federal government to provide payment for Creek warriors who had fought for the United States.[18] Some, at the discretion of the United States, might be allowed to keep a one-mile square area for so long as they or their descendants chose to occupy it. They would not, however, own that land in fee simple, and could not sell it. It would revert to the ownership of the United States when vacated. With a few exceptions, the capitulation agreement left the "friendly Creeks" far poorer in land and sustenance than they had been before they fought the Red Sticks.[19]

Although Benjamin Hawkins advised the chiefs not to resist, seeing no real alternative, he was privately appalled by the treaty. The chiefs had sent to him their objections to Jackson's terms.[20] He had responded by restating Jackson's arguments, but his heart was not in it. Excluded by Jackson from playing any role in formulating peace terms, he protested the mistreatment of the friendly Creeks in a letter to the secretary of war written a day after the signing, and in other correspondence.[21] From a summary of one of his letters that has survived, we know that a week later he recommended to Armstrong that Jackson no longer be used in Indian negotiations.[22] Hawkins's reasons for that recommendation, and his specific objections to the treaty and to Jackson's conduct in that letter and others, can be surmised, but not fully reconstructed, as most of his communications with the secretary of war on those matters have disappeared, "deliberately removed," in the judgment of one eminent historian of the Creek War. We have only summaries, not the text, of his dispatches.[23] But it is clear that Hawkins's misgivings were shared by others. Tennessee senator Jesse Wharton informed Jackson that, as the treaty initially faced "great opposition," his friends had waited until word had been received of the general's triumph at New Orleans before bringing it to the floor of the Senate. The treaty was ratified on February 15.[24]

Reservations about its provisions were well founded, and they did not simply involve questions of fairness and justice. Not only were some Red Sticks driven, by Jackson's severity, to continue the war, but many pro-American Creeks were now unwilling to fight for the United States. Jackson himself expected trouble. Several weeks before presenting the Creeks with his demands, he advised the secretary of war that once they learned what the new boundary lines would be, "the friendly Creeks" could well make "more difficulty . . . than the hostile party." He accordingly advised that the militia not be discharged but kept in readiness should new hostilities break out. The Creeks, he warned, no longer be relied upon for help in the event of trouble with the Choctaw and Chickasaw, who were also "wavering in their friendship with the United States," and might make common cause with the Seminoles and their British friends.[25] As Jackson predicted, hundreds of Red

Sticks, perhaps as many as 2,000, defied his capitulation demand and found refuge in Spanish Florida, where they regrouped to resume their struggle. They were welcomed by the Seminoles (former Creeks who had moved into Florida many years earlier), by Spanish authorities, and by British agents.[26]

Although Florida's Seminoles had not been directly involved in the Red Stick insurrection, they were not well disposed toward the United States. Two years earlier, Seminoles living on the Alachua plain in north central Florida had been caught up in the so-called Patriot War, a farcical quasi-revolution instigated by an American agent. George Matthews was an elderly former governor of Georgia who, with the equivocal encouragement of the Madison administration, plotted to detach the colony of East Florida from Spain. Matthews had earlier been involved in a failed effort to persuade the Spanish governor of West Florida to cede his territory to the United States. In East Florida, Matthews encouraged an insurrection. In March 1812, a ragtag armed band, numbering around 80, seized the Spanish town of Fernandina on Amelia Island and then, supported by some U.S. troops, moved south to besiege the Spanish provincial capital at St. Augustine. Most of the insurgents were Americans who had settled in Florida and sworn allegiance to the Spanish crown. Others, including their leader John McIntosh, were Georgia settlers eager to acquire Florida land and also to eliminate the colony's use as a refuge for runaway slaves. The U.S. government, for its part, feared Florida, only weakly controlled by Spain, would provide a base of operations for the British in the coming Anglo-American war that many regarded as inevitable.

Many southerners, Jackson included, wanted to take Florida by force. But Congress was not inclined to provoke a war with Spain. The Georgia militiamen and U.S. soldiers who crossed the international boundary in support of the Patriots expected to receive an order to seize St. Augustine. That order never came as the U.S. Senate refused, on two occasions (June 26, 1812, and February 2, 1813) to authorize the military occupation of East Florida. After much delay and many recriminations, Spanish authorities finally agreed to grant amnesty to the rebels. Accordingly, the American forces stationed near St. Augustine were withdrawn in March 1813. The Patriots continued to fight for a time thereafter, but without American intervention could not prevail.[27]

For several months prior to their withdrawal, both the Patriots and the American forces stationed near St. Augustine were harassed by Indians incited by the Spanish. The Seminoles living in on the fertile Alachua plain in north central Florida were at first disinclined to become involved in disputes between Spaniards and Americans. They were a comfortable and prosperous people, who had arrived at a workable but never entirely cordial accommodation with the Spanish. They engaged not only in hunting, horticulture, and the deerskin trade but also in horse and cattle breeding. Chief Payne, owner of 20 slaves, 400 horses, and 1,500 head of cattle, lived in a large European-style plantation house. His half-brother and successor Bowlegs marketed 1,000 head of cattle each year. Bowlegs, unlike Payne, from the outset counseled resistance to the Americans. He saw clearly that the intruders coveted the Seminole's rich plantation lands. Slavery was also at issue. Blacks serving as slaves with the Seminoles were relatively well treated and possessed rights denied to their counterparts in white territory, and also in some of the slave-holding Indian nations to the north.[28] Runaways from the lower south often found refuge in Seminole country, which also contained villages inhabited by Maroons, blacks who had escaped bondage and, after paying token tribute to the Seminoles, lived essentially as free men. To the slaveholders of the southern United States, they posed a serious threat to their "peculiar institution."[29] Governor Mitchell admitted that he hoped for a Seminole attack, as it would "afford desirable pretext to penetrate their country, and break up Negro Town, an important Evil growing under their patronage."[30] Elimination of free black communities in Florida was a high priority for American settlers in the lower south.

To encourage Indians to fight against the enemies of Spain, the governor of East Florida, Sebastian Kindelan y O'Regan offered the Seminoles not only scalp bounties (McIntosh's was valued at $1,000) but also weapons, various gifts, and the right to loot the properties of Patriot supporters. Payne and Bowlegs finally accepted, rejecting the counsel of General Matthews and other Patriot representatives who had urged that they remain neutral. The Seminoles had come to resent the Patriot blockade of St. Augustine, which interfered with their trade. More seriously, they were alarmed by several reports that the Americans supporting the Patriot cause had laid plans to seize and divide among themselves the Alachua lands. They also understood that, for many Americans living in Georgia and in Spanish Florida, capture and sale of blacks in Seminole country was an irresistible temptation. For their part, Spanish authorities did all that they could to encourage Seminole hostility toward the Americans. Benjamin Hawkins wrote from the Creek agency in Alabama to report to Governor Mitchell that he had been told the Spanish had sent a black slave to warn the Alachua Indians that the American invaders, having failed to take St. Augustine, were preparing to "turn their arms" against the Seminoles and against the "negro settlements" they protected, whereupon Payne immediately "set out all his Indians to war" against the Patriots.[31]

On July 23, 1812, Seminole war parties struck settlements on the St. Johns River, burning plantations and killing many of their inhabitants. On September 12, they attacked a party of U.S. marines outside St. Augustine. In retaliation, an American force led by Georgia militia Colonel Daniel Newman in September mounted a raid into Seminole country that resulted in mortally wounding 80-year-old Chief Payne and some other Seminoles (the exact number is unknown) but otherwise was inconclusive, as Newman was forced by inclement weather and fierce Indian opposition to withdraw before reaching the Seminole villages.[32]

After that raid, Chief Payne, who did not succumb to his wounds for several months, tried to raise a coalition of Florida Indian bands to fight the Americans. He failed as most other leaders, including his own close associates, preferred to seek peace. They appealed to the Creeks and to Indian agent Benjamin Hawkins to intercede to avert a renewed American attack on their villages. Hawkins sympathized, as did a few other peace advocates. The *Georgia Journal*, in an article later reprinted in the *Charleston Courier*, pointed out that the Seminoles "have offered to lay down their arms, and submit to any terms, even the most humiliating, which the United States might think proper to prescribe. Of this fact there can be no doubt. A more ardent desire for peace, we may venture to affirm, was never manifested by any people whatever. They propose to restore not only the property of the whites, but to deliver up all offenders against our laws. Could we ask—could they do more? Why then make war upon them? Why drive them from their homes and firesides, perhaps to utter ruin, a poor, defenseless, miserable race of beings, who are supplicating, as it were, upon their knees?"[33]

Hawkins reported the Seminole's desire for peace to President Madison and urged that there be negotiations. He asked the federal commander General Pinckney not to begin new hostilities. Pinckney replied that his orders were to punish the Seminoles for their crimes. But he agreed to wait to see if the president would revoke those orders in light of Hawkins's report.[34]

Hawkins had little support. Reports of Seminole atrocities, including their nailing to trees the severed heads some of Newman's men, inflamed the people of the frontier south. Colonel John Williams of the Tennessee militia captured their sentiments when he declared Florida's Indians "hell hounds fitted only for deeds of ferocity, who seek victory by the indiscriminate slaughter of all ages and sexes."[35] After waiting a few weeks for new instructions from Washington, D.C., and hearing nothing Pinckney, against his better judgment, authorized a new invasion of Florida. In February 1813, an American force comprised of militia from Tennessee and Georgia, augmented with U.S. Army troops from the command of General Thomas Flournoy, invaded the Alachua plain. They found it largely deserted, as the Alachua and Alligator Seminole bands, forewarned of the invasion, had fled. After killing some 20 Indians who had not gotten away, (most of them from towns not involved in the earlier hostilities) the Americans "burned 386 houses, consumed or destroyed from 1500 to 2000 bushels of corn, collected 300 horses and 400 cattle, and brought back or ruined 2000 deerskins."[36] But the campaign to "exterminate" the hostiles failed, as they and their leader Bowlegs had fled westward, where some joined Seminole bands on the Suwannee River, and others moved into the Tampa area.

With their rightful owners now absent, "the ragtag remnants of the Patriots," as one historian notes, "strutted into the Alachua lands to demand annexation by the United States." But, given congressional opposition, that was not a measure the Madison administration could implement, much as it wanted to do so.[37] While some of the negative votes in the Senate were motivated by personal quarrels with the administration, others reflected opposition to expansion and to war. Federalist senator William Hunter of Rhode Island spoke for his party when he declared both the proposed annexation of Florida and earlier American incursions there "not only an offensive but an unjust war . . . a wicked war . . . a robbery" justified only by the spurious "right of taking advantage of the troubles of our neighbors—of plundering weakness, of imposing on misfortune, of oppressing the oppressed."[38] The Senate, as we have noted, twice refused to authorize the occupation and annexation of East Florida. Secretary of State Monroe advised the remaining Patriot leaders that they could expect no support or relief from the United States. On the Alachua plain, the American invaders built a blockhouse and planted some crops. But "avenging Indians and Negroes" drove them back to Georgia.[39] Indian agent Hawkins, hoping to avert a war with the Seminoles, now assured them that "the intruders on the Seminole rights at Alachua are not people of the United States; that we will not protect or help them; those of them who did belong to our country, having left it and one into the territories of Spain, are subject to the Laws of Spain, and if the Spanish authorities or the Seminoles punish them, we have nothing to say on the subject."[40] His disavowal of American interest in the Patriot cause was, of course, somewhat disingenuous.

The British intervention in Florida that Andrew Jackson and a number of others predicted materialized in May 1814 when a British expeditionary force under the command of Captain Hugh Pigot, aided by marine Captain George Woodbine, landed and began construction of a fort at Prospect Bluff on the Apalachicola River near Pensacola in West Florida. Pigot's forces were soon placed under the command of Lieutenant Colonel Edward Nicolls, who brought two small warships, the *Hermes* and the *Carron*, some additional troops, and a supply of arms and ammunition for prospective Indian and black allies. Nicolls issued proclamations declaring that all slaves who left their masters to join the British force would be emancipated, and that all Indians who fought for him would have the lands the Americans had taken from them restored in perpetuity. The British intended to recruit Indians and blacks to assist in taking first Mobile and then Baton Rouge, thereby cutting off New Orleans from the interior and forcing its surrender.

To implement the plan to enlist the support of Florida's Indians in the campaign to drive the Americans from the Gulf, Nicolls distributed "a thousand pistols, a thousand carbines, five hundred rifles, and more than a million rounds of ammunition to an estimated four thousand Creek and Seminole warriors."[41] But the immediate results were disappointing. Only around 200 Indian warriors actually accompanied the British force which tried, and failed, in September to seize Mobile for use as a base of operations against New Orleans. The siege of Mobile was botched, but a number of other things went awry as well. The British were not able to provide much largess, other than arms, to their hungry new Indian allies. Food was in short supply at Prospect Bluff. The overbearing manner of the British officers, their penchant for not paying for the goods they requisitioned, and drunken looting by some of their poorly disciplined troops soon alienated the merchants at the nearby British-owned Forbes Company on whom they had expected to rely. Disaffected Forbes agents provided intelligence to the Americans. On August 14, Governor Manrique had welcomed Nicolls and his army to Pensacola. But Nicolls, an arrogant and sometimes brutal commander, soon antagonized his Spanish hosts, who not only resented the bad behavior of his men but also came to question their ability to counter an American invasion.[42] In early October, Andrew Jackson reported, with some amusement, that he had been told that Nicolls, in an effort "to convince the Governor of his power and prowess, paraded his savage force, marched it thro' the town, saluting his Excellency with the war whoop, and threatening to scalp all the inhabitants. Thus, we are informed, ended the strife."[43]

Jackson had picked up rumors of British activities in West Florida not long after their arrival. On June 27, he had written the secretary of war that he had received "a corroboration of the account that 300 British had landed and are fortifying the mouth of the Apalachicola, and are arming and exciting the Indians to acts of hostilities against the United States." He asked for authorization to rally the militia and invade the Spanish colony.[44] Jackson received no answer to his query for over six months, although a reply had been written but not posted shortly after his letter reached Washington, D.C., a reply which counseled caution but authorized Jackson to act if Spanish complicity were proven.[45] As historian Robert Remini notes, "had Jackson received this letter in July instead of the following January, he would have taken immediate action. His army would have slammed into Florida without another moment's delay."[46]

As it was, Jackson waited until November to invade West Florida. During the previous months, Jackson and other American authorities had received numerous reasonably authoritative reports of British activities in Florida and of Spanish acquiescence in their recruitment and arming of Creek and Seminole warriors and of blacks. Indian informants reporting to Benjamin Hawkins in particular provided ample early information indicating, as he reported to the governor of Georgia on June 15, that the British had delivered "a supply of the munitions of war . . . to the Red Clubs and the Seminoles at Pensacola and the mouth of Chattahochee."[47] In mid-August, he reported to the secretary of war that all the evidence of British activities in Florida indicated that they had armed "and are training the Indians and some Negroes for purposes hostile to us."[48]

Hearing comparable reports from a number of informants, Jackson had no doubts about the need to take action. His resolve was strengthened, indeed enflamed, by exaggerated stories about the size and composition of the British expeditionary force in West Florida. On August 27, Jackson concluded that 10,000 British marines were about to land at Pensacola. In a letter to John Reid, he predicted that they might soon to be augmented by Russian forces, as the Tsar "had offered England 50,000 troops to aid her & Spain to conquer and divide America . . . do not think this chimerical . . . there is no doubt that there are at least 35,000 British and Spanish troops on the coast and at Pensacola."[49] That was far from the case, but Governor Manrique of West Florida did nothing to reassure Jackson. The governor's responses to demands that the Spanish at Pensacola not aid America's enemies Jackson characterized, not inaccurately, as hostile, evasive, and mendacious.[50]

Despite the evidence of Spanish complicity in the British campaign, Secretary of War James Monroe in late October responded to copies of the stern and accusatory letters Jackson had sent to Manrique by writing the following to the general: "I hasten to communicate to you, the direction of the President, that you should at present take no measures, which would involve this Government in a contest with Spain."[51] But five days later, Jackson, who had not yet received those instructions, informed Monroe that he deemed the situation so grave that he felt it necessary to "act without the orders of Government."[52] On December 7, Monroe, still in the dark, wrote again.

> I hope that my letter to you of the 21st of October has reached you in time to prevent the attack which you then contemplated making on the British at Pensacola. As the conduct of the Spanish authorities there may justify the measure, the President desires that it may be avoided in the hope that the new effort which he is now making to obtain justice and preserve amity with that power may be successful. Should you have made the proposed attack, you will, on the receipt of this letter, withdraw your troops from Spanish territory, declaring that you had entered it, for the sole purpose of freeing it from British violation.[53]

Several weeks before Monroe wrote that letter, Jackson, with the help of over 700 Cherokee and Choctaw warriors, had in fact seized Pensacola. But he occupied it only for a few days, then returned it to the Spanish governor. With Jackson at the gates, Manrique had sought to distance himself from the British, claiming that they were unwelcome invaders who had seized the fort at San Carlos. He protested that Jackson had no right to enter his territory as Spain was not at war with the United States. Jackson, unimpressed, struck on November 7. Manrique surrendered the town after a brief skirmish. Facing Jackson's army, which numbered over 4,000, he had only about 500 ill-trained and poorly disciplined soldiers. Fourteen of the Spanish defenders were killed. Jackson lost only five. The British and their Indian and black allies, disavowed by their erstwhile Spanish friends, did not engage the Americans, but, after burning the fort and demolishing the harbor defenses on Santa Rosa Island, retreated. Jackson did not pursue them, as he had more pressing business elsewhere.

Without its fortifications Pensacola, a rustic frontier settlement with only two streets and a town square, was no longer of any military value. The British and their allies in West Florida retreated from Pensacola to Prospect Bluff. British military operations in the gulf now centered on New Orleans, the key to the Mississippi valley.[54] In his letter of December 7, directing Jackson not to attack Pensacola, Monroe had warned that "recent intelligence tends to confirm" earlier reports that "a strong force from Europe" would soon strike New Orleans. The secretary related that "much anxiety is felt" that Jackson would delay too long in marching his forces to the defense of the city, which he described as highly vulnerable to attack.[55]

Monroe's anxieties proved unwarranted. Jackson was there on time. Moreover, his victory over the British invaders at New Orleans would transform a relatively inexperienced frontier Indian fighter into a major American military figure and a national hero. Georgia congressman George Troup spoke for many when, on hearing news of Jackson's triumph, he declared it "almost incredible" that "the best disciplined and most veteran [troops] of Europe should be beaten by an undisciplined militia with the disproportionate loss of a hundred to one." Troup attributed the victory to General Jackson, for whose genius, he declared, no words of praise could suffice, and also to the valor and shooting skills of the plain farmers who left their ploughs to march through the wilderness to do battle with the invaders.[56]

Although the myth of Old Hickory and "the Hunters of Kentucky" singlehandedly saving New Orleans would be celebrated in songs, lithographs, and patriotic orations for many years thereafter, the truth was rather more prosaic. On his arrival at New Orleans, Jackson found the city's defensive preparations woefully inadequate and its population divided into squabbling ethnic and political factions. In putting together an armed force to fight the invader, he relied heavily on regular army units, local Creole forces, free blacks, Baratarian pirates led by the Lafitte brothers, and several hundred Choctaw warriors. The militia volunteers from Tennessee, Kentucky, Mississippi, and rural Louisiana who soon poured into the beleaguered city were a minority of the men who fought at Jackson's side. Contrary to later lore, the victory cannot be attributed to their shooting skills, which have been greatly exaggerated. Jackson's artillery killed far more redcoats. Moreover, despite a mythology that celebrates this battle as the triumph of the "Hunters of Kentucky" and other valorous white men, the contemporary record strongly suggests without the support given to Jackson by Creoles, blacks, and Indians, the city would have fallen.[57] These fighters received neither the recognition nor the recompense they deserved. The general had promised that black volunteers who fought on his side would each receive a 160-acre land grant. It was a promise he did nothing to keep. However, he did show "solicitude for the masters whose slaves had taken refuge with the enemy." After his victory, Jackson "repeatedly demanded that the departing British army return them." The British refused to comply, but "took two hundred self-emancipated people to poverty and freedom in Bermuda."[58]

After assessing potential invasion routes, Jackson erected breastworks, deployed his troops and artillery, and issued orders, not always carried out, that key bayous be blocked. He faced an invasion force that, it is estimated, numbered between 11,000 and 14,500 well-trained and disciplined troops. His army, diverse, inexperienced, and outnumbered, should have been no match for the conquerors of Napoleon. The American triumph at New Orleans has been celebrated and analyzed many times over during the nearly two centuries that has elapsed since General Sir Edward Michael Pakenham's defeat and death, and we will not refight the battle in detail here. A perusal of the rich primary and secondary historical sources indicates that, while Jackson deserves much of the credit he has received over the years for defeating the British, the blundering of General Keane, who was in command before Pakenham's landing, and of Sir Edward himself, several times threw away a victory that could have been achieved with a quick onslaught before Jackson was adequately deployed.

Early encounters were indecisive. The Americans suffered some reverses, most particularly the sinking of the warship *Carolina* which had been bombarding the

British position. However, when Pakenham finally mounted a full-scale attack on January 8, his columns, moving forward on the plains of Chalmette through an early morning fog, were decimated by artillery and musket fire from the entrenched defenders. In an engagement lasting only about 30 minutes, the British suffered some 2,037 casualties, including 291 killed, among them the ranking officers. Jackson's forces sustained only 13 casualties (6 killed and 7 wounded). Pakenham had been far too hasty that morning in mounting an attack before his troops were properly deployed on both sides of the river, and he paid the supreme price for his misjudgment, dying on the battlefield. Eyewitness accounts of the scene immediately after the battle described a field littered with horribly mangled bodies, some missing heads, some limbs, some still screaming in agony. One observer related that "you could have walked a quarter of a mile to the front on the bodies of the killed and the disabled." The surviving British officers, although still in command of a substantial force, never renewed their effort to take the city. Their late commander's "corpse, naked and disemboweled, was scrunched into a hogshead that was filled with rum. Thus preserved he was shipped home for burial and oblivion."[59]

Pakenham's brilliant career ended miserably because of a few miscalculations. Old Hickory's force of will and his skill as a commander (remarkable in a man who had not a single day of formal military training) were soon legendary, but they would not have sufficed had Lady Luck not been at his side. Jackson also made mistakes, one of which enabled the British to cross the Mississippi on the morning of the attack and rout the defenders there. As Jackson's leading biographer notes, "the defeat on the west bank of the Mississippi was as total as the victory on the east side. Jackson appeared oblivious to the needs and danger of his position across the river. He did not adequately reinforce it with his troops when he could have spared at least one of his regular regiments. Nor does it appear that he even visited the location during the sixteen-day period when the British were moving toward the city. Worse, he did not provide any boats for crossing the three-quarter-mile-wide river should reinforcements be necessary. The west bank defense—if it can be called that—was easily swept aside by the British once their offensive got under way."[60] It was Jackson's good fortune that the British, after the slaughter on the Plains of Chalmette that morning, were in no position to exploit their success. Old Hickory never conceded that he bore some responsibility for the west bank debacle, but instead blamed the commanders there for "the want of Discipline, the want of Order, a total disregard to Obedience, and a spirit of insubordination." He threatened to quit his command if the Kentucky militia commanders didn't cease their "inattention of duty." The Kentucky militia in fact did perform badly. It was ill equipped and poorly led. But Jackson's own leadership was partly at fault.[61]

There is another aspect of Jackson's time in New Orleans of great importance for our later analysis of his conduct of Indian affairs, as it expressed his determination not to allow legal obstacles to impede actions he deemed essential for the security of the Republic. Some months prior to arriving in New Orleans, Jackson had been warned by Louisiana state governor Claiborne that there was a pro-Spanish faction in the city "whose partiality for the English is not less observable than their dislike to the American government."[62] Although Claiborne assured Jackson that the vast majority were loyal to the United States, Old Hickory, ever distrustful of the English and the Spanish, replied that "we have more to dread from Spies, and traitors, than from open enemies."[63] While Jackson, after arriving in New Orleans on December 1, found the populace generally supportive of his efforts to prepare to defend the city, he was bothered by rumors of spies operating in the city. Moreover, the state legislature had refused to authorize the suspension of habeas corpus, a measure needed to legitimatize Jackson's proposed impressment of sailors to serve on the two American warships operating in the area. When Governor Claiborne asked that they adjourn and entrust to General Jackson and to him arrangements to counter the British invasion, the legislature refused. Jackson responded on December 16 by placing the city under the rule of marital law.[64]

That action was unprecedented. Never before, not even in the darkest days of the Revolution, had an American military commander imposed direct and total military control on an American city. There was no legal basis for subjecting civilians to marital law, which had hitherto been regarded as applying only to the conduct of men serving under arms. "Americans," writes historian Matthew Warshauer, "in their laws as well as in their military and legal treatises, failed to accord marital law any legitimacy except as a code for governing the military." But Jackson, undeterred by the reservations of his legal advisors, shut down the legislature, impressed men under 50 into military service, confiscated and in some cases destroyed property, and jailed those who criticized his actions. He suspended habeas corpus, even though a Supreme Court decision a few years earlier (*Ex parte Bollam and Swartwout*) had declared that only Congress had that power. Under Jackson's rules, a strict curfew was put in place, all street lamps were extinguished at 9:00 P.M., and anyone on the streets without a pass was arrested as a spy. Several dozen men, most if not all of them innocent, were imprisoned on suspicion of disloyalty. When state senator Louis Louaillier published anonymously a protest against these measures, Jackson forced the publisher to divulge his identity and then jailed the senator. When a military tribunal acquitted him, Jackson disregarded the verdict and kept Louaillier in prison. Jackson did not lift martial law after his victory on the plains of Chalmette, as a large British army remained in the region, one that was both larger and better equipped than his own. When federal judge Augustus Dominick Hall ruled in favor of the senator's application for a writ of habeas corpus, Jackson had the judge arrested as well. After holding him in jail for a short time, he expelled Hall from the city.[65]

When news that the war had been ended by the Treaty of Ghent reached New Orleans on March 13, Jackson finally ended marital law, released the prisoners, and reinstated the civilian government. Judge Hall returned to the city and charged Jackson with contempt of court, fining him $1,000. The Madison administration was well aware of the illegality of Jackson's action, but as Old Hickory was now a national hero, it declined to say so out loud. When Jackson traveled to Washington, D.C., later in the year to defend his conduct against critics, he found the cabinet and the president disinclined to pursue the matter.[66] In retirement many years later, Jackson insisted on vindication of his use of marital law at New Orleans. In 1841, a Congress controlled by the Democratic Party agreed and refunded his fine.[67]

In the negotiations at Ghent, the British delegation initially insisted that American cession of western territory to an Indian buffer state to be established under their protection was a non-negotiable condition for peace with the United States. But the British government, weary of war and hard pressed financially, abandoned that demand and accepted a settlement that essentially restored the status quo ante bellum. None of the belligerents would be required to give up land. Article IX of the agreement signed by the commissioners on December 24 provided that all territory seized from the tribes since 1811 be restored to them on condition that they cease warring against the United States. That article in effect nullified the Treaty of Fort Jackson. On May 26, Benjamin Hawkins sent Jackson a copy of a letter he had received from British colonel Nicolls in West Florida declaring that the Creek chiefs there had instructed him to inform the Americans that they were desisting from "hostilities of every kind, against the Citizens or subjects of the United States" and accordingly expected under the terms of the Ghent agreement to regain the territory taken in the now invalidated Treaty of Fort Jackson.[68] On June 12, President Madison sent word that he wanted General Jackson to "cooperate with all means in your power to conciliate the Indians, upon the principles of our agreement with Great Britain."[69] Jackson was willing to conciliate Indians in his own way, but he had no intention of returning any land, and he chose to ignore the president's order to restore old boundaries.

New reports from the frontier steeled his resolve. A week earlier, Old Hickory had learned from General Gaines that the Creek chiefs living at Fort Jackson had recently "received a message from the British Colonel Nicolls at Apalachicola, and the Indians with him, advising them to kill any American they find passing through their country, and not to permit any of the lands lately ceded to the United States to be taken possession of by us."[70] On July 17, Hawkins informed Jackson that Nicolls had promised the Indians that he would offer military support if they would resist by force any American effort to run a new boundary line that would deprive them of territory. In his reply to Hawkins, Jackson declared Colonel Nicolls guilty of "bare faced effrontery" that might necessitate military intervention.[71]

The agent agreed with Jackson. In a letter to General Edmund Gaines on June 14, he had described the colonel as a "blustering braggadocio" and recommended that if the British government did not recall him, the U.S. Army should remove him.[72] The month before, Hawkins had warned Nicolls to cease arming Indians in Spanish Florida, characterizing his actions as "an act of hostility which will require to be speedily met and speedily crushed." He added that he was certain that the colonel's actions lacked official sanction. Surely, he admonished, "the Sovereign of Great Britain could not from his love of justice in time of peace . . .

suffer any of his officers to go into a neutral country to disturb the peace." Nicolls's claim that he was acting on the authority of a "treaty of offensive and defensive alliance" he had entered into with the Creek Nation Hawkins dismissed as "a novelty," which could not possibly be supported by London as it violated the rights of Spain.[73]

But there was a more fundamental question. Quite apart from Nicolls's presumptions, did the Treaty of Ghent require the restoration of lands taken from various Indian nations by the Treaty of Fort Jackson? Jackson declared that it did not, on the grounds that the treaty, having been signed before the war's end, was not nullified by the peace agreement. The federal government decided to endorse that view, as its leaders had no desire to clash with the hero or with his many frontier supporters by restoring land to Indians. Agent Hawkins for his part knew full well that Jackson's claim was unsound, noting in a letter to acting secretary of war George Graham that when Jackson dictated his terms to the Creeks chiefs there "was but a single hostile one" present and that all who signed the document claimed to be allies of the United States.[74] But Hawkins, knowing he could not win in a confrontation with Old Hickory, tried to persuade the Creeks that the Treaty of Ghent contained "nothing that contradicted" the "one called Jackson's" as the Ghent negotiations did deal "with treaties between Indians and white people." The chiefs at Fort Jackson, he came to argue, had acted for the entire Creek Nation.[75] But that interpretation is not defensible. The Treaty of Fort Jackson could not fairly be considered binding on the Red Stick Creek faction as they did not sign it but regrouped in Florida to continue their resistance. The Treaty of Ghent was clear. It explicitly required that lands held by Indians in 1811 taken from them during the war be restored as soon as they made peace with the United States. Under that agreement between the United States and Great Britain the Creeks, hostile as well as friendly, were entitled to regain their lost territory when hostilities ended.

But entitlements even under international treaties are meaningless without the will and the power to enforce them. Colonel Nicolls still had a small force of men at Apalachicola, where he had entered into alliance with the prophet Francis and his surviving Red Sticks. The colonel continued to urge the tribes to resist American efforts to claim the lands ceded under the Fort Jackson treaty, and promised British aid, but he spoke only for himself. Accompanied by the prophet Francis and another Creek holy man, Nicolls sailed to London in the summer of 1815 to seek ratification of the alliance he had entered into with Red Sticks and Seminoles in Florida and to obtain the means to back it up. But the British government, weary of war, had no interest in further difficulties with the United States. Accordingly, it declined to challenge Washington's interpretation of the Ghent peace settlement and had no intention of supporting Nicolls's claim. Once again, the British abandoned their Indian allies. The colonel moved on to other ventures, finally retiring as a general in the British army half a century later.[76]

Although the Treaty of Fort Jackson was thus allowed to stand, the exact location of the boundaries of the land cession remained to be determined. Congress directed that three commissioners be appointed to run the line, and initially gave the job to former governor John Sevier, Indian agent Benjamin Hawkins, and William Barnett, a former Georgia congressman. Sevier and Hawkins were, for different reasons, both unacceptable to Old Hickory. Sevier conveniently died on September 14, 1815. General Edmund P. Gaines, a Jackson ally, took his place. Hawkins, in ill health, was dismissed at Jackson's insistence. The hero's close friend and colleague John Coffee was made the third commissioner. "The survey commission," notes one historian, "simply became an extension of Andrew Jackson's will."[77]

Control of the commission was crucial, as the task of drawing the boundary line was anything but routine. The southern boundary was the first to be surveyed. Jackson urged that it be done without delay, as some previously friendly chieftains, prompted in part by Nicolls, were now contesting the Fort Jackson cession, insisting that they had been coerced. At a meeting of Creeks, Cherokees, Chickasaws, Choctaws, and Creeks at Tuckabatchie, Big Warrior, the Creeks' principal negotiator at Fort Jackson, declared "it was no treaty" as "he was threatened and compelled to sign it."[78] In response, Jackson in early September met with the Creek leaders, concluding his speech to them with this declaration: "Listen! I now tell you that the line must and will be run." He promised that the least opposition would bring "instant destruction on the heads of the opposers."[79] Jackson's vehemence led one disillusioned chief, who had fought against the Red Sticks, to tell the Creek Council that he worried about Sharp Knife's "great power to destroy me."[80] In the intimidation of Indians, Jackson had few peers. But as we will see, his threats did not end Indian resistance.

As his surveyors mapped out the boundary line, General Gaines relied on both regular army men and Georgia militia to protect them from Creeks and Seminoles enraged by their impending dispossession. He began the process by meeting with the Creeks at the confluence of the Flint and Chattahoochee Rivers, accompanied by a substantial armed guard sent by Andrew Jackson. Old Hickory had earlier declared his intention "to instantly put down" any Indian opposition to running the southern boundary line.[81] His show of force, for a time, worked. Gaines's surveyors were not attacked. White squatters, who followed the surveyors into the newly opened lands, posed a more serious problem. Secretary of War Crawford demanded their removal, characterizing them as "the worst part of our citizens."[82] But the army was of little help. "The squatters raided into Florida to steal livestock and slaves, while soldiers winked or openly abetted them. The soldiers could be as odious when they put their minds to it. Survey Commissioner William Barnett was sickened by the violence, especially by one contemptible incident in which soldiers wantonly murdered a Creek woman."[83] Creek bitterness over such incidents was exacerbated by the failure of the federal government to honor its promise of food supplies and annuity payments to those Creeks who had supported Jackson and accepted his treaty. Some three years would pass before they would receive any satisfaction, despite Jackson's efforts on their behalf.[84]

With the southern line set through Gaines's prompt action, Jackson turned his attention to the northern and western borders, both of which remained ill-defined. At his insistence, Commissioner Coffee hastened to Fort Strother and waited impatiently for the two other commissioners to appear. After two weeks, he informed Jackson that since the other commissioners were still not present, he had "determined to act alone, believing it important to finish the business. I never experienced more anxiety than on account of this delay."[85] Jackson and Coffee had ample reason for their haste. They faced substantial opposition from their erstwhile Indian allies. Not only did the Fort Jackson treaty take some land from both the Choctaws and the Chickasaw, but Coffee, acting under Jackson's instructions, claimed as part of the Creek cession a 50-mile wide tract of land in northern Alabama running from the Coosa River to the Mississippi territorial border, an expanse that traditionally was not Creek at all but Cherokee and had been so recognized in a federal treaty ratified in 1806. Coffee tried to justify the taking of that huge track of land from an ally on the questionable ground that the Cherokee had loaned it to the Creeks who then ceded it to the United States. He collected a number of affidavits from white settlers and from a few compliant Indians to that effect, but the claim was shaky and he knew it.[86]

The Cherokee sent a delegation to Washington, D.C., to challenge the land grab. The administration instructed the commissioners to leave the issue alone until the Cherokee claim could be settled and attend instead to the drawing of the southern boundary. But when the other commissioners wrote to Coffee to remind him that they were not authorized to deal with the Cherokee and Chickasaw boundary issues, he simply ignored them and went on with his work.[87]

Part of that work involved disarming Cherokee opposition. Coffee tried several ruses, most notably exempting the village of Cherokee chief and Jackson ally Richard Brown from inclusion in the cession, thereby gaining that leader's silence. Jackson was pleased but feared that was not enough. Well aware of the possibility that Coffee's activities could place his surveyors and other whites in danger, he told his associate to proceed with his work but to be prepared to call in troops if needed to put down Indian resistance. Anticipating that the War Department might prove less than cooperative in that venture, Jackson instructed Coffee to act on his own authority and issue orders directly without consulting Washington, D.C. Jackson hoped, of course, that force would not be necessary. Perhaps threats would suffice. To Chickasaw chief George Colbert, whose people had challenged Coffee's claim that some of their land was included in the Fort Jackson cession, Old Hickory sent a letter warning that, regardless of their complaints, "the line will be run by Genl. Coffee and if yr, people attempt to interrupt him you will bring destruction on yourselves."[88]

In the nation's capital, Secretary of War William H. Crawford was initially unaware of Coffee's survey. In fact, he had not been informed that Coffee had joined the commission. In early March 1816, Crawford sent orders, addressed to the three original commissioners, that the survey of the northern and western border be delayed until settlement of the Cherokees' grievance. Soon thereafter, he signed an agreement with that tribe which recognized their land claim and also awarded them some $25,500 in damages for losses of crops and livestock suffered at the hands of the Tennessee militia, during the campaign against the Red Sticks. He wrote General Jackson to inform him that "the Cherokee delegation are now in the city, and feel much indisposed to the execution of the treaty with the Creeks proposed by our commissioners." The Cherokees, the secretary declared, were right. "An examination of the various conventions which we have held with the Cherokees, will not permit the United States to insist upon the line contended for by our Commissioners." Moreover, the "same obstacle" required that the western line be redrawn to recognize the land rights of the Choctaw and Chickasaws. "The President," Crawford told the general, "is determined to obtain no lands from either of those nations upon principles inconsistent with their idea of justice and right."[89]

Jackson was infuriated. But he responded in somewhat measured tones in his complaint to Secretary of State James Monroe. "The President," he informed the secretary, "has been badly advised on this subject." Jackson declared that he had reviewed all the relevant documents and, without citing particulars, assured Monroe that they offered "clear and conclusive" evidence that the territory in question was part of the Creek cession as Coffee had maintained. "The Cherokee," he asserted, "never had the least semblance of claim." In a statement expressive of his ongoing distrust of all Indians, Jackson argued that their continued occupancy in the contested area would endanger the security of the United States, as it permits "a free communication . . . between the northern and southern tribes of Indians" and thereby "again exposes our frontier to savage murders and depredations." For that reason, among others, Crawford's agreement with the Cherokee "is much regretted and deprecated in this quarter."

That was, if anything, an understatement. Mass meetings throughout the southwest in the spring of 1816 demanded its repudiation. Jackson, in letters more characteristic of his frame of mind, warned Crawford that if his concession to the Cherokees were not immediately withdrawn, the result would be "a civil war" that would lead to "the destruction of the whole Cherokee nation." "The people of the west," he declared, "will never suffer any Indian to inhabit this country again." The militia, he added, would refuse to protect Cherokees who tried to reoccupy the contested lands. The settlers, who were already settling "in considerable numbers on this land," would then wrack vengeance on the Indians. That would be tragic and unjust, as most Cherokees were not interested in pressing a claim that, according to Jackson, came not from their legitimate leaders but from "a few designing half-breeds and white men."[90]

Old Hickory found Crawford's award of damages to the Cherokees for their property losses during the late war against the Red Sticks offensive, construing them as an insult to the honor of Tennessee's militia. The claims themselves, he argued, were fraudulent proving "that no confidence is to be placed in the honesty or justice of an Indian." As to the endorsement of Cherokee requests for reimbursement by Indian agent Return J. Meigs, Old Hickory expressed astonishment that "a whiteman (holding an office under Gover'ment) should be found" taking such a position. It was illustrative of "the corruption of mankind, in colours too dark to dwell upon."⁹¹ We see here once again Jackson's deep prejudice against Indians and his disdain for whites who defended them. But, as Meigs's documentation revealed, the Cherokee damage claims were supported by a number of white observers who deplored what one officer at the time described as "plunder and wanton destruction" by militia who not only shot their cattle but even stole their clothing.⁹² Several years later, a governor of Tennessee, Joseph McMinn, freely admitted to the Cherokees that "Jackson's army" had indeed destroyed much of their property.⁹³ But Old Hickory never admitted that his men had in fact abused his Indian allies.

Under pressure, the federal government would soon withdraw its protection of Cherokees, Chickasaws, and Choctaws dispossessed by Jackson's treaty with the Creeks and by Coffee's survey. At first it appeared that the lands in question would be restored to the tribes. Crawford had emphasized in a letter to Jackson, dated May 20, 1816, that the general's argument defending the Creek cession of Cherokee lands had not "in any degree changed the opinion of the President upon that subject." Crawford insisted that the drawing of a boundary line that took from the Cherokee lands defined as theirs in the recently ratified federal treaty was not within the original commission's powers.⁹⁴

On July 24, he informed Jackson once again that "the Cherokee convention as well as every other which has been, or shall be ratified by the President, with the advice of the Senate, will be strictly executed." But that was bluster. The administration, understanding the political realities, was not prepared to defend Indian land rights against Jackson and his western supporters. All Crawford finally demanded was that negotiators reopen talks and persuade the tribes to accept new boundaries. In his July letter to Old Hickory, Crawford tellingly added to his statement about enforcing the most recent Cherokee treaty to the letter the following qualification: "unless the Cherokee and Chickasaw title to the lands in question, shall be extinguished by the Commissioners appointed to treat with the latter tribe."⁹⁵

Crawford thus gave Jackson, Coffee, and their associates a new opportunity to resume the work of dispossession through negotiation. While he instructed Coffee to suspend for the moment his land survey, Crawford also named him, along with Indian agent John McKee and Tennessee congressman John Rhea, to a commission charged with settling the relatively minor Choctaw land claims. To deal with the larger problem of Cherokee and Chickasaw land rights, the secretary called on Andrew Jackson, assisted by David Meriwether and Jesse Franklin. Crawford could not have doubted the outcome of those appointments. Jackson himself noted that had the government really been interested in upholding "this show of a treaty with the Cherokees," the commission would have had a different composition.⁹⁶ In his instructions to the commissioners, Crawford declared that the contested land was not to be taken from them by force, but added that justice to the tribe "does not require that the just rights and true interests of the nation should be impaired, much less sacrificed." Pointing to "the great value of the possessions of this tribe, compared to the smallness of its population," combined with its need for larger annuities, Crawford concluded that sale of the territory in question would serve "the true interests of both parties." That principle was to guide their dealings with the Indian nations. As to the Cherokee land question, Crawford advised Jackson that he was directing Indian agent Meigs "to effect through purchase" the acquisition not only of the 2.2 million acres south of the Tennessee River that had previously been restored to them by the 1816 treaty he had negotiated but also some 1.2 million acres north of the river as well.[97] But when the agent took that matter up with the Cherokee National Council, they proved uncooperative.[98]

The task of persuasion then fell to Andrew Jackson. Writing to John Coffee, he declared it imperative that the "hatefull instrument" that restored land to the Cherokees be set aside through new agreements with the tribes, as it was for the moment unfortunately the law of the land. He laid out a plan to accomplish that end. The Cherokees and other Indian claimants who opposed Coffee's boundaries should be reminded that they had no right to the contested territories as they had been ceded by their legitimate owners the Creeks to the United States under the Treaty of Fort Jackson. In effect, he advised Coffee and other negotiators to pretend that the national administration had not really recognized the legitimacy of their claim. Negotiators should stress the magnanimity of the United States emphasizing that even though Indians did not really have any right to the land in question, the government would nonetheless pay them for it, providing money that "will give them schools to educate their children, and money to buy negroes to work there [sic] land . . . by selling they will live in peace." That inducement should be accompanied by a warning. The Cherokees should be advised that if they refused to sell, they would face not only the opposition of whites already on the land but of Chickasaws who also claimed some of the territory in question. They needed to understand the hostility of the whites and the Chickasaws to their claims to that land would be unyielding. They would never be permitted to live in peace if they did not yield. Moreover, Jackson told Coffee, a recent change in federal policy was already helping disabuse the Cherokees of any notion that they might have about reclaiming their lost land. As commanding general of federal forces in the south, Jackson was no longer under orders to remove white squatters from the contested territory and would not be doing so. That development, he noted, "cannot fail to have a good effect upon their minds. They are a good deal alarmed, and not without cause."[99] In a later letter, he advised his friend to remember always that "an Indian is fickle" and must always be dealt with firmly, and without compromise.[100]

Jackson's tolerance and use of white squatters to force Cherokee land cessions was not exceptional. The federal government, represented in Cherokee Territory by agent Return J. Meigs, had proven unable and, some would argue, unwilling to stem the tide of white squatters who poured into the contested Cherokee country, seizing land and often killing the rightful occupants. Even before Jackson suspended all efforts to eject the invaders, those measures had been half-hearted. Virtually all of the illegal occupants soon returned to reoccupy their fields and rebuild the rude shanty-like cabins, which had sometimes been burned by the troops. They terrorized the Cherokee who tried to reclaim their property. White courts without exception refused to convict those who killed Indians, and federal negotiators were more than willing to exploit the plight of dispossessed Cherokees to gain new treaty concessions. While agent Meigs was well aware of, and complained about, the criminal behavior of many of the frontier ruffians who stole land and brutalized Indians, he was on balance not really very sympathetic with the victims. After supervising the temporary ejection of around 1,800 whites from Indian Territory in 1810, Meigs had written of his discomfort with the process. "These people bear the appellation of intruders, but they are Americans—our riches and our strength are derived from our citizens; in our country every man is an acquisition. We ought not to lose a single citizen from want of land to work on."[101] The Indians, Meigs believed, were sitting on more land than they could use, and whites would put that land to better use.

Let us turn now to the 1816 negotiations. Coffee's meetings with the Choctaws went very smoothly and have been characterized by one historian as "more like a friendly banquet than a meeting of opposing forces."[102] The outcome was the cession to the United States of a small tract of land east of the Tombigbee River. In a treaty signed on October 24, the tribe received some $120,000 payable in 20 annual installments and some $10,000 worth of merchandise.[103] Jackson's negotiations with the Chickasaw and with the Cherokee representatives present at the Chickasaw meeting proved more difficult, as much more was at stake. The delegates from the two nations insisted on conferring together privately before meeting with Jackson and his fellow commissioners. When the negotiations began on September 8, Jackson, resplendent in full military regalia, first assured his "red Brethren" of the friendship of the United States, then excoriated the Creeks anew as people who had "listened to the tongues of the lying prophets, and became crazy, and raised the hatchet, and stained it with the blood of our innocent women and children." By so doing, they had brought upon themselves a severe penalty. All the lands taken in the cessions of the Treaty of Fort Jackson, the general insisted, were Creek lands forfeited through their treachery. The other Indian nations must now affirm that action.[104]

The chiefs initially proved uncooperative. The Chickasaw produced a document signed by George Washington that confirmed their ownership of some of the land presumably ceded by the Creeks to the United States at Fort Jackson. The Cherokee, for their part, were also unmoved by Jackson's demand. Four days later, the commissioners produced drafts of two new treaties. For their acceptance of the proposed boundary, the Chickasaw were offered $100,000 payable over 10 years, sweetened with the promise of additional "liberal presents" to their leading men. The Cherokee were to receive $80,000, also over 10 years, with a comparable promise of "generous awards" for their chiefs. The commissioners advised the Cherokee that the land in question was no longer of any value to them, as it contained no game. If they tried to keep it, it would prove to be nothing more than "a fruitful source of Bloodshed and strife."[105]

Both Indian delegations initially balked at signing the new agreements. The Cherokee advised the commissioners that they did not have that authority but must take the matter back to the Cherokee National Council. The Chickasaw said that they needed to be sure just what was rightfully theirs before they could sign any agreement. Jackson's opening gambit had failed. Long having maintained that an Indian's "ruling passions" were "fear and avarice," he advised Secretary Crawford that since his instructions did not permit him to engage in outright intimidation, he must now resort to bribery. Crawford had no objection, having previously authorized the commissioners to spend public money to buy compliance. Key Chickasaw chiefs were given some $450,000, an amount equivalent to several million in today's currency. (In their report to Crawford, Jackson and his colleagues underscored the importance of keeping the identity of bribed chiefs secret. Otherwise, "the influence of the chiefs would be destroyed.") The corrupted headmen signed the treaty on September 20. They also swore, falsely, that the Cherokees had never occupied the contested lands, which they claimed had been Creeks' from time immemorial.[106]

The Cherokee proved more difficult. Controversy over past land cessions had only a few years earlier led to turmoil, social upheaval, and on occasion political assassinations, most notably the killing of chief Doublehead in 1807. The Cherokee leaders were under great pressure to resist Jackson's demands. The general met with the Cherokee National Council at Turkey Town on September 28. The chiefs were enraged by the Chickasaw claim that the land in question had never been theirs. They did not budge until Jackson and his fellow commissioners had made liberal use of bribe money, and it is not clear that the bribes really worked. Although Jackson claimed that the council ratified the treaty on October 4, a number of prominent Cherokee chiefs, including Principal Chief Pathkiller, later charged that Sharp Knife and his fellow commissioners had lied. They claimed that only a small minority of chiefs had actually voted for ratification and that "six or seven headmen present" had vehemently declared their opposition. Jackson's new treaty, they argued, was therefore invalid under Cherokee law. Predictably, Cherokee demands for an investigation were ignored by the administration. The "hatefull instrument" was now history.[107]

But Jackson and his colleagues were not satisfied. They had not yet acquired the remaining Cherokee lands in Tennessee. Their long-term objective was the elimination of all of the independent Indian nations east of the Mississippi. In pursuit of that goal, they secured passage in Congress of a resolution that revived a proposal, made by Thomas Jefferson to the Chickamauga some nine years earlier but later abandoned by his successor in the face of intense Cherokee opposition that proposed they cede some of their present tribal holdings to the United States in exchange for land grants in Arkansas. Andrew Jackson, added by Tennessee governor McMinn and by his old associate General David Meriwether, was directed to undertake new negotiations to induce the Cherokee to migrate.

As he had in the controversy over the boundaries set by the Fort Jackson treaty, Sharp Knife began by misrepresenting past history. He claimed that the Cherokee in 1809 had entered into an agreement with President Jefferson to allow those who wished to do so to exchange their eastern lands for Arkansas land grants but had not honored the agreement by appropriate land transfers, even though a number of Cherokees had taken up residence in the west. During some eight days of argument over the issue, the Cherokee chiefs offered ample testimony indicating that their council had never ratified any such agreement, had never authorized any of their people to move west, and in fact had declared those who did so no longer part of the Cherokee Nation. Jackson's response was to brand the chiefs liars and produce one of their number, Tochelar, who at first swore the general was right about what had transpired in the meeting with Jefferson eight years earlier. But Tochelar soon recanted. Undaunted, Jackson then forced other chiefs to recognize the legitimacy of the Arkansas migration and admit the representatives of the western Cherokee into their councils. They dare not, he thundered, give the president "the lie" by denying his version of the conference with Jefferson.[108]

Setting the tone for the negotiations that followed, Jackson proceeded to warn the Cherokee that if they persisted in their resistance to further land cessions, the United States would withdraw all protection from the invasion and pillage of their territories by white border ruffians, would cease payment of annuities, and would no longer assist in their efforts to develop a viable agricultural economy. The only alternative for those Cherokee who refused to move westward, he declared, was to give up tribal sovereignty east of the Mississippi, accept citizenship in the United States, subject themselves to the laws of the territory or state wherein they resided and pay taxes for the privilege. Those who chose that alternative would be allowed to remain on new land allocations of 640 acres for each head of family. Jackson represented this as a generous and attractive concession, indicative of the government's loving concern for his Indian children, but that was disingenuous. He did not explain that those who accepted would not actually have a personal title to their land with the right to sell and move elsewhere, but would legally only be tenants. Moreover, their citizenship would be that of free persons of color. Such second-class citizens were not allowed to vote, hold office, bear arms, intermarry with whites, or attend school with them. Nor could they serve on juries or testify in court against whites. Past experience indicated that an Indian could expect little justice in a state or territorial court. Whites who murdered Indians commonly went unpunished. Understandably, the Cherokee were not attracted to the prospect of becoming citizens of color in a racist republic that did not value their lives.[109]

The treaty drawn up at the close of Jackson's negotiations was opposed by a very large majority of the chiefs representing the eastern Cherokee, but by adding the signatures of the representatives of the western migrants, Jackson claimed it had in fact been ratified by the nation. He did not inform his superiors that both the Cherokee National Committee and Pathfinder, the nation's principal chief, vehemently opposed the treaty. The lands ceded were less extensive than Jackson wanted, as the United States gained only about 650,000 new acres in Tennessee and Georgia in exchange for a promise of a land grant in Arkansas. But Jackson believed that the principle it established, of exchange of eastern land for western territory, would lead very soon to their removal, as most Cherokee, being barbarians, would not wish to remain in the east under "a government of laws." In a letter to Coffee, he predicted that the whole Cherokee country would be given up "in less than two years." He was mistaken. Cherokee opposition to removal would drive their policy for the next two decades. But, despite a new land cession treaty, negotiated in Washington, D.C., in 1819, pressure to take their remaining eastern lands proved unremitting.[110]

Among the Cherokee leaders who defied Jackson was an affluent young merchant. Born in 1790 at his father's trading station on the Coosa River near the Cherokee village of Turkey Town in what would become Alabama, John Ross, the descendent of Scottish traders, was seven-eighths white. He spoke and wrote English fluently, but Cherokee only haltingly. (His childhood home contained many books in English, which Ross devoured but he never learned to read in the Cherokee alphabet invented by Sequoia.) A man of two worlds by both birth and rearing, light skinned and European in appearance, he considered himself a Cherokee first and foremost. Chosen a member of the national council in 1816, he soon, by virtue of his sure command of spoken and written English, became a prominent spokesman for his chosen people. He had served briefly with the Cherokee forces that fought the Red Sticks, but unlike some of the older chiefs, he was never close to Andrew Jackson and would soon come to loathe him. As one historian writes, as he listened to Old Hickory address the assembled Cherokees at a meeting of their national committee on June 28, 1817, "Ross was scarcely able to hide his disdain for Jackson's condescension and thinly veiled threats. . . . That day Ross formed an opinion of Andrew Jackson he would hold the rest of his life. That day, Jackson became his enemy."[111] On behalf of the Cherokee leadership, Ross wrote an eloquent affirmation of Cherokee sovereignty and restated their refusal to abandon their homeland.[112]

Indian agent Meigs, although a supporter of removal, recognized that Jackson's claims about the treaty were dishonest, and accordingly "refused to help enforce it." Jackson relied on Tennessee governor McMinn to carry on the work of persuasion through promises, bribery, and threats. An indeterminate number of Cherokee (probably a few thousand) were persuaded to move west. The majority refused McMinn's offers and ostracized those who cooperated with him. A pro-removal chief was expelled from the national committee. In the fall of 1818, Ross was elected president of the committee, a position which made him second-in-command to Principal Chief Pathkiller. He used the position to continue to fight removal, rejecting out of hand Governor McMinn's ongoing efforts to relocate the Cherokee. He demanded that the governor refrain from further interference in tribal affairs. In 1819, Ross led a delegation to Washington, D.C., to complain of the false claims and the underhanded tactics of both Jackson and McMinn. Secretary of War Calhoun found their story credible but, understanding the political realities, took no action on their behalf.[113] Instead, he advised the delegation that they would be required to make additional land cessions in the future, as they had more than they could use and the expanding white population, too little. If they could not yield up more land voluntarily and learn to embrace "the laws and manners of the whites," they would find they had only two choices: "migrate or become extinct as a people."[114]

Meanwhile, Jackson back at the Hermitage had turned his attention to planning for the sale and settlement of newly acquired lands. Ever sympathetic to the rights of those who invested money in land, he now ordered his troops to apprehend illegal white squatters and turn them over to the civil authorities. He no longer needed to use illegal white occupants of Indian land as a weapon with which to force acceptance of his definition of the Fort Jackson treaty boundaries. The notion that Andrew Jackson was an egalitarian champion of the economic interests of the common man would become a vital component of the Old Hickory myth. But the myth misrepresents the man. His correspondence from this period suggests that Jackson's struggles to acquire more and more Indian lands for white settlement were not motivated by the desire to accommodate poorer folk. Instead, he wrote most often of the new opportunities for wealth now available to those who could afford to purchase the land and develop it. Andrew Jackson was a self-made man, but he was not an egalitarian. Our review of his career to this point has revealed again and again that he was exceedingly sensitive about his place in the new propertied elite and guarded his status more carefully because of his acute awareness of his own lowly origins. Recall, for example, his prickly insistence that as a gentleman he could not fight duels with those who were beneath him. His own self-image was that of a benevolent but sometimes stern patriarch, master of a great plantation, and father figure to large extended family, often offering advice to promising younger men about the habits they must cultivate to succeed in a world of both opportunity and danger. To symbolize his own recently acquired high status, Jackson spent large sums on the acquisition of expensive furnishings for the small two-story frame house that was his first Hermitage, and far more to outfit the mansion he would later erect on that property. He had an acute sense of himself as both a commoner of humble birth and as a self-made man of property and power. It is in that biographical context that we must understand Andrew Jackson's attitudes and actions.

As we have noted in previous chapters, success in land speculation followed by ownership of slaves to work on lands acquired from Indians was the key to the acquisition of the wealth and status that placed a Tennessee gentleman in the ranks of the elite. Jackson was concerned that purchases of the new territory he had now wrested from "savages" prove profitable, so he devoted much attention to their development. Access was essential, so with Coffee's aid, he laid out plans for a military road running from Nashville to Madisonville near New Orleans, and then supervised its construction. (The road was completed in January 1819.) He encouraged Coffee to survey and lay out new townships. He advised his associate that once white settlers bought the land and occupied it, the legislature would incorporate towns and lay out counties. When that happened, land values would soar. Jackson himself purchased property in a newly ceded part of Alabama near the town of Florence.[115] The ultimate value of the newly acquired lands depended on their productivity. Indian dispossession in the old southwest coincided with the expansion westward of cotton cultivation and plantation slavery. The future states of Alabama and Mississippi, until recently Indian Territory, would soon be the heartland of the new Cotton Kingdom.

The lands now open for sale to enterprising whites provided the resource base for the emergence of a capitalist market economy on the southern frontier, an economy that would generate fabulous wealth and sustain a social order based on planter rule and slave exploitation. The foundation of the new order was cotton. Source of only 9 percent of the world's cotton production in 1801, by 1850 the United States "provided 68% of a total world production three times as large."[116] Between 1814 and 1816 alone, the market price for cotton doubled. Some lands acquired under the Treaty of Fort Jackson, initially offered at $2 an acre, were soon selling for between $20 and $40 an acre, a very substantial sum in the early 19th century.[117]

The overall magnitude of Jackson's accomplishment can be seen in federal land sale statistics. During the years immediately before the Creek War, those sales averaged around 350,000 acres. In 1815, as newly acquired Indian lands came to market, they exceeded 1,000,000 acres. Three years later, federal land sales totaled over 3,500,000 acres.[118] White occupation of former Indian Territory marked the coming of a new socioeconomic order in the southwest, one that offered great opportunities for well-placed, or lucky, whites. It also brought renewed and oppressive servitude for blacks shackled and marched westward in slave coffles, as well as exile and destitution for native peoples deprived of their homelands. It has rightly been said that the Cotton Kingdom rose on the backs of black slaves. But it is equally true that it was raised on lands stolen from Indians. If the worldwide industrial revolution was made possible by the profits of the cotton trade, as Eric Hobsbawm and others have argued, then it should also be noted that modern industrial capitalism owes much to the frontier general who so skillfully opened up vast ranges of Indian land to plantation agriculture.[119] During Jackson's lifetime, around 1,000,000 black slaves were marched "by force into the vast territories that were seized—also by force—from their native American inhabitants."[120]

Jackson's land transactions made him a very wealthy man. There were some who suspected he abused his military position to gain access to the choicest of Indian lands. In late 1815, Jackson's business partner and close friend John Coffee warned that they were both victims of rumors about "fraud" in recent land transactions. Jackson responded with characteristic, accusing his critics of "wanton wickedness and depravity of heart." He had, he declared, risked his life to protect the interests of "such monsters." Jackson's friends confronted and intimidated the accusers, who denied responsibility, engaged in some finger-pointing blaming others and, thereafter, remained silent. Many Jackson apologists over the years have minimized or, in some cases, whitewashed Jackson's more questionable business practices.[121] But Jackson's involvement in the personal acquisition of some of the lands he took at the point of a bayonet from Indians both hostile and friendly is clearly documented in records that expose Jackson's involvement not only in the purchase and sale of some of that land but in planning for transportation improvements that would enhance its value.

As historian Steve Inskeep explains, "what must have made the rumor especially galling was that it was true . . . Andrew Jackson was about to participate in the biggest land deal in the history of the nation."[122] An example of the assistance Jackson's friends extended to him may be found in a letter marked "private," which Jackson received in the late summer of 1817. Its author, federal land agent Arthur Hayne, after thanking the general for the hospitality he had been shown at the Hermitage, advised the general that "we have succeeded in acquiring an accurate Knowledge of all the sections of good Lands to be sold at the present sales." He drew Sharp Knife's attention to four particular sections that "would establish a most desirable establishment for yr. old age."[123] Hayne was only one of many advisers and business associates who assisted Andrew Jackson in his quest for wealth through purchase of land made available directly or indirectly through his Indian wars and subsequent Indian negotiations. Sharp Knife's most valued adviser was his close friend and partner John Coffee, who was particularly well situated to identify "the best land to buy," as he had earlier "had it surveyed at federal expense." One close student of Jackson's land transactions reports that, while no definitive account can now be rendered as "many real estate records from the past have been lost," those that have survived bear signatures that indicate that Jackson and his associates acquired at least 45,000 acres in northern Alabama alone.[124]

Michael Paul Rogin writes that "primitive accumulation is the heroic stage of capitalism, and it found its hero in Jackson."[125] In the encounters of colonizers and indigenous peoples, the process of primitive accumulation is one of land seizure and dispossession, sometimes through war, sometimes through the pretense of voluntary agreement and sale. On the American frontier, the thefts were partly concealed by the fig leaf of the treaty process. Jackson, more candid than most negotiators, freely acknowledged that his treaties were obtained through coercion and bribery. He recommended to President Monroe that the federal government no longer negotiate with Indians at all but treat them as inferior conquered peoples with no right to the land. They should, he declared, be redefined legally as tenants at will, subject to eviction and relocation whenever the superior race had need of the territories they occupied. "I have long viewed treaties with the Indians an absurdity not to be reconciled to the principles of our Government."[126] But Monroe did not agree, nor did Congress. In 1818, the House Committee on Public Lands explicitly rejected Jackson's recommendation that the United States invoke the power of eminent domain to dispossess Indians whenever their lands were needed by white settlers. Indians, the committee advised, must continue to be dealt with through the treaty-making process. Monroe, and his successor John Quincy Adams, were both sympathetic to removal but also insisted it could not legally be done by force. Congress rejected their proposals to fund voluntary

Indian relocation, insisting that the policy of the federal government remain focused on their "civilization."[127]

Andrew Jackson was never able to persuade that government to abandon treaty-making rituals, but as president, as we will see, he did obtain the funding for removal that had been denied to his predecessors and, in defiance of guarantees of Indian rights contained in the removal law, would find new ways to abuse and on occasion bypass or undercut the treaty-making process. It is neither inaccurate nor inappropriate to think of him, as Rogin has, as the quintessential hero of Marx's Primitive Accumulation, or, as followers of a more recent school might put it, as the great agent of American Settler Colonialism.

Chapter 4

A Backwoods Napoleon?

During the winter and early spring of 1818, Andrew Jackson invaded the Spanish colony of West Florida, burned several Seminole villages, killed a number of Indians, captured and executed two Red Stick leaders as well as two British subjects, and deposed the governor. The Spanish, shocked and indignant, complained that Old Hickory was acting like "a backwoods Napoleon." At home, Jackson's actions were not universally applauded, but prompted a congressional investigation, unprecedented in its length and acrimony, into his alleged abuse of authority. President James Madison, in a message to Congress on March 25, tried to justify military intervention in Florida by pointing to the Seminoles' presumed unrelenting hostility against the United States and by the failure of the Spanish government to keep them under control. He also insisted that the army's commanders were under strict orders to "respect the Spanish authority wherever that authority is maintained."[1] Given Jackson's treatment of Spanish officials and citizens during his occupation of Florida, many found the president's explanation less than persuasive.[2]

An American armed incursion over a year before had failed to resolve concerns about Florida. Before leaving Spanish Territory, Colonel Nicolls had encouraged both Indians and blacks to occupy the very well-armed fort the British had built at Prospect Bluff. General Edmund P. Gaines in the spring of 1816 had sent Jackson the following description of their stronghold. The fort, he wrote,

> stands upon the left Bank of the Apalachicola, about 50 miles below the mouth of the Flint River. The ramparts and parapets built of hewn timber filled in with earth, mounting 9 to 12 pieces of cannon, several of which very large, with some Mortars and Howitzers. It has a very deep ditch intended to be filled up

with water, but was dry when last seen by my informants, two or three months ago. The wall is nearly square, and extends over near ten acres of ground, has comfortable barracks and large stone houses inside. It is rendered inaccessible by land excepting a narrow pass near the margin of the river, by reason of an impenetrable swamp in the rear and extending to the river above. The negroes are attempting to raise corn, and some are reported to have gone to St. Marks [site of a Spanish fort]. The number at or near the fort is stated to be upward of three hundred men. They have Red Coats and are supplied with a large quantity of British muskets, Powder and other supplies.[3]

Jackson, Gaines, and their superiors in Washington, D.C., had received several rather alarming reports of Red Stick activities in Florida. Some came from Indian agent Hawkins who warned that Florida's Seminoles also posed a serious danger, as they had sent messengers to urge "negroes in the Creek nation and frontiers of Georgia to come down and be free."[4] On April 23, 1816, Jackson, acting under instructions from Secretary of War Crawford, wrote to Mauricio de Zuniga, governor of West Florida, to complain that "upward of two hundred and fifty negroes, many of whom have been enticed from the Service of their Masters, Citizens of the United States" had gathered at "the Negroe fort." Invoking the "principle of good faith," he asked that the governor act immediately "to destroy or remove from our frontier these Banditti" and "return to our citizens and the friendly Indians inhabiting our Territory those Negroes now in the said fort which had been stolen and enticed from them." He warned that if the Spanish authority did not comply with that request, the United States would be compelled "in Self Defense to destroy them." He ended his letter with another demand. The governor was to state whether the fort originally had been built "by the government of Spain" and whether that government considered its inhabitants their subjects.[5] The governor in his reply a month later denied any Spanish involvement in the construction of the fort or the support of those who had gathered there. He agreed with Jackson that it should be destroyed, but maintained he could take no action until he had received supplies and instructions from Havana.[6]

Crawford had advised Jackson that in the event the Spanish did not act swiftly to eliminate the Negro fort, he was to await further orders, as "it will be incumbent on the Executive to determine what course shall be adopted in relation to this banditti."[7] That directive was ignored. Generals Jackson and Gaines had their own plans. To deal with the Florida problem, they first undertook a frontier fortification project that included the building of an outpost on the Apalachicola River near the Spanish border. Then, in late July, a U.S. naval flotilla entered Spanish waters and made its way up river to provision the new fort. The expedition stopped at Prospect Point, emplaced artillery, and bombarded the Negro fort. A shot struck the fort's powder magazine. The explosion was heard in Pensacola a hundred miles away. Of the fort's 320 inhabitants, 270 were killed in the blast, many literally blown apart.[8] The commander of that action, Colonel Duncan Clinch, later related that:

> the explosion was awful, and the scene horrible beyond description. In an instant lifeless bodies were stretched upon the plain, buried in sand and rubbish, suspended upon the tips of the surrounding pines. Here lay an innocent babe, there a helpless mother, on one side a sturdy warrior, on the other a bleeding squaw.

Clinch estimated that about three out of every four dead was a woman or child.[9] They were, notes one recent historian of Florida, members of a multiracial "emergent community of free subsistence farmers."[10] But to Andrew Jackson, they were nothing more than "villains" intent on "rapine and plunder." They had not been left without the means to defend themselves. Rummaging through the gruesome ruins, the Americans found among the corpses a huge arsenal left behind by the British. There were 2,500 muskets, 500 carbines, 500 swords, and 400 casks of gunpowder. The weapons were found in their original packing cases, which should have raised doubts about Jackson's claim that the people of Prospect Bluff were planning to engage "rapine and plunder" against the United States. His assertion that many were renegade American slaves who should be returned to their masters was belied by the fact that there is no evidence that any of the survivors actually fit that category. The blacks captured in the area for the most part spoke Spanish, not English. But they were turned over to slave dealers anyway. It was later argued that while they may not be runaways themselves, they were no doubt descendants of slaves who had been, and therefore were not entitled to freedom. One crucial point was overlooked. As the blacks were seized on Spanish soil, their transportation into the United States violated the 1807 federal law against participation in international slave trading. Two of the captives, one an Indian and the other a mulatto, were identified as commandants at the fort. They were not enslaved. Instead, Clinch paid some anti–Red Stick Creeks $50 to put them to death by torture.[11]

Some of the Negro fort's survivors made their way to Fowltown, a Seminole village in southwestern Georgia. Concern over activities at Fowltown and other Seminole settlements soon replaced anxiety about the Negro fort. The first blow in what would come to be known as the first Seminole War was struck at Fowltown in late November 1817. Acting under orders from General Gaines, American troops led by Colonel Matthew Arbuckle attacked and burned it to the ground. Five or six of its inhabitants died during that raid, but most fled into the neighboring swampland. Located in southwestern Georgia on the banks of the Flint River some 15 miles from a newly established American military outpost (Fort Scott), Fowltown had remained neutral during the Red Stick War. Its chief Neamathla and his people were Mikasuckis, one of the groups comprising the so-called Seminole tribe. They were related to the Creek but were not part of the Creek confederacy.

Even though they had not fought against the United States nor been represented at the meeting that led to the promulgation of the Treaty of Fort Jackson, the United States now claimed under terms of that treaty those Seminole lands that lie within the boundaries it defined. Matters remained in abeyance for a time as work proceeded with land surveys and plans for land auctions. But in the fall of 1817, the secretary of war directed General Gaines to proceed with arrangements for the removal of Seminoles from the ceded lands, so they could be relocated on the territory that had been left to the Creeks under the Fort Jackson treaty. Accordingly, Neamathla's village was to be dismantled and his people moved to the reserve. But the chief refused to recognize the treaty and defiantly asserted his independence by ordering American troops stationed at Fort Scott not to intrude on his side of the river. He would not even allow the soldiers to cut wood on his territory.[12] Gaines summoned Neamathla to Fort Scott to discuss various matters of concern, including the recent killing by Indians of some whites in Georgia. The chief refused the summons. To the consternation of the local Indian agent, former Georgia governor David Mitchell, Gaines made no further effort to reach a peaceful accommodation with Neamathla but ordered that he be apprehended and Fowltown destroyed.[13]

Nine days after the burning of Fowltown, Seminole warriors struck back, ambushing a supply boat on the river near the smoldering remains of the town, they killed over 40 whites, including some women and children. Gaines reported to Jackson that while a few friendly Indians in the area offered him aid after the Scott massacre, most were preparing to mount another attack. "Hostile warriors of every town upon the Chattahoochee," he told Old Hickory, "set about preparing canoes and moving off down river to join the Seminoles as soon as accounts of my movement . . . reached them." An all-out war with the Florida Indians, he believed, was imminent.[14]

Prior to General Gaines's action against Fowltown, Indian agent Mitchell had hoped that peace could be maintained on the Florida frontier. (The agent's motives were not entirely altruistic. He personally profited from peace, and after years of controversy over his conduct was finally dismissed from his post in 1821 for engaging in illegal slave trading across the Spanish border.[15]) Although there had been a few instances of interracial killing, the period following the ratification of the Fort Jackson Treaty had been fairly quiet. But rumors of violence, real and impending, had persisted, having been actively fostered by southern political and military leaders. Informing Andrew Jackson of an earlier Indian attack that took the lives of Mrs. Obediah Garrett and two of her children, Gaines had declaimed that "another outrage of uncommon cruelty and barbarism has recently been perpetrated on the southern frontier of Georgia."[16] But Gaines had no other recent examples of frontier families assaulted by Indians. The only other recent white casualties were a few itinerants who had been kidnapped or killed on the trails that transverse Indian territories. It is worth noting that his main complaint against Fowltown prior to ordering its destruction was not that its people were murdering whites but that they were engaged in cattle rustling.[17] Prior to the burning of that village, the death total on the Gulf frontier since the end of the Red Stick war stood at 10 Indians slain by lawless white intruders and seven dead whites including the members of the Garrett family.

Mitchell had advised the secretary of war that the Garrett killings "were easily accounted for on the Indian principle of retaliation . . . I should expect no further bad consequences from it."[18] He had this to say during the congressional inquiry into the origin of the Seminole War: "the first outrage committed on the frontier of Georgia, after the Treaty of Ft. Jackson was by . . . [white] banditti who plundered a party of the Seminole Indians, on their way to Georgia for the purpose of trade, and killed one of them. This produced retaliation on the part of the Indians, and hence the killing of Mrs. Garrett and her child."[19] But while Mitchell saw little immediate danger, few on the frontier agreed with his assessment. A correspondent reported to Gaines in late February 1817 that "the defenseless inhabitants of our frontier have been thrown into a distressing state of alarm" by news of the killing, as "on this open extensive and entirely unprotected frontier, the poor and innocent inhabitants have ever been exposed to these calamities."[20] They demanded military protection. But despite all the hysterical talk, there were no further massacres there prior to Gaines's assault on Fowltown.

Mitchell was correct in his assertion that violence on the southeastern frontier in the years immediately after the Red Stick War had been set off not by Indian raiders but by white squatters. As noted earlier, Secretary of War Crawford among others described them as "the worst part of our citizens."[21] But the authorities did next to nothing to protect Indians from the criminal behavior of whites intruding on their lands. In a letter to General Gaines, dated September 11, 1817, 10 Seminole village chiefs reported that when they asked that action be taken to deter or punish whites who had stolen their cattle and killed some of their people, they received no satisfaction but were told simply that those were the deeds of "outlaws" whom the Indians themselves should kill. Tellingly, the chiefs, not understanding white concepts of justice, explained and justified the Garrett killings as retribution for the murder by whites of several of their young men. "The white people," they declared, "killed our people first; the Indians then took satisfaction." Consistent with their conception of the means to be used to restore balance and harmony between contending peoples after a homicide, they believed that peace had been made possible through their retaliation, which roughly evened the score. Accordingly, they promised henceforth "to stay at home, and meddle with no person." The letter confirms Mitchell's explanation of the Seminole's understanding of the Garrett killings. It also suggests a desire on the part of the Seminoles to avoid further hostilities.[22] But Neamathla and the other Seminole chiefs in the area were not willing to capture and surrender to American justice tribesmen accused of killing whites, nor would they return the cattle and other property they had allegedly stolen.[23]

Their recalcitrance deepened suspicion of their intentions and fed the rumor mill. Stories about Red Sticks and British adventurers in the Seminole villages had been circulating for several months and gave credence to rumors of a conspiracy to wipe out American settlements.²⁴ And there were other disturbing reports from the frontier. In February, an Indian informant told an American officer that a friend who had recently visited Fowltown told him that the Indians there "speak in the most contemptuous manner of the Americans" and plot a reprisal for the recent destruction of the Negro fort. "There is," he added, "another of my acquaintance returned immediately from the Seminole towns" where he "saw the Negroes on parade; he counted about six hundred that bore arms. They have chosen officers of every description, and endeavor to keep up a regular discipline." They were supported by the same number of Indian warriors. Together, they intended to wage a new war against the whites and against the anti–Red Stick Creeks led by McIntosh. "They have chosen Bowlegs for their head," the informant reported, "and nominate him King, and pay him all kinds of monarchial respect, even to idolatry."²⁵ This highly inaccurate report resonated with the American fears of a race war.

General Gaines for his part forwarded to the War Department in early April an even more fanciful story that claimed that Indian hostilities had made it impossible for settlers on the Georgia frontier to plant crops, all their livestock having been stolen and their houses occupied by hostiles.²⁶ There was no concrete evidence justifying the frontier panic Gaines promoted. Seminole chief King Hatchy responded to Gaines's characterization of Seminoles as "a bad people" by declaring "you charge me with killing your people, stealing your cattle, and burning your houses. It is I who have cause to complain. While one American has been justly killed in the act of stealing cattle, more than four Indians [from this village] have been killed by lawless freebooters."²⁷

As rumors proliferated on both sides of the cultural divide, tensions mounted. In early November, the general reported he had been told that nearly 3,000 Seminole warriors had assembled south of the Spanish border and were preparing to invade Georgia. He believed the numbers might be exaggerated but agreed that an attack was imminent.²⁸ The discovery after the attack on Fowltown of the uniform of a British officer in chief Neamathla's house underscored for Gaines and others the urgency of swift action.²⁹

Gaines's instructions initially forbade sending troops into Spanish Florida.³⁰ The difficulties with Neamathla, however, prompted newly appointed secretary of war Calhoun to modify those orders, permitting the crossing of the border in pursuit of hostiles. When word of the Scott massacre reached the nation's capital, the secretary issued new orders, directing Gaines to invade Florida and put an end to the Seminole menace. The general was not, however, to preempt, let alone fight, the Spanish authorities there, but instead should seek their cooperation.³¹ Gaines was not able to act on that order, as he was conducting a campaign against pirates on Amelia Island in East Florida when he received Calhoun's message. The task then fell to Gaines's superior, Andrew Jackson, the commander of the Southern Division of the U.S. Army. Calhoun forwarded to Jackson his orders to Gaines forbidding any hostile action against the Spanish in Florida. He intended that Jackson should understand that he was to respect Spain's sovereignty in the colony.³²

Jackson did not correspond with Calhoun regarding that restriction but instead wrote directly to President Monroe offering to seize "the whole of East Florida," which could then be "held as an indemnity for the outrages of Spain upon the property of our citizens." Such an action, he argued, would protect the United States from the threat posed by hostile Indians, British conspirators, and "their Spanish friends." He assured the president that "this can be done without implicating the Government; let it be signified to me through any channel (say Mr. J. Rhea) that the possession of the Floridas would be desirable to the United States and in sixty days it is accomplished." Jackson warned that failure to put down "all opposition" in Florida would expose the United States to "defeat and massacre."[33]

Monroe's response to that letter has been a matter of much controversy over the years. Jackson claimed that Congressman John Rhea of Tennessee told him Monroe approved his proposal. But Monroe insisted he did no such thing, adding that he had not even read Jackson's letter prior to the Florida invasion. (Monroe was in fact ill at the time it was received at the White House.) Rhea for his part also failed to confirm Jackson's story, assuring Monroe in 1819 that he had not given the general any reason to believe that he had authorization to attack the Spanish. Old Hickory rather belatedly insisted in 1827 that he had received a letter from Rhea conveying Monroe's authorization in writing. Most authorities on this phase of Jackson's career conclude that he was either lying about that letter, or chose to interpret Monroe's silence as consent.[34] The current editor of Jackson's papers, however, has found evidence that suggests Jackson did receive some correspondence from Rhea, which has been lost, and conjectures, quite plausibly, that he may have misconstrued Rhea's remarks about Monroe's overall confidence in him as a green light for his Florida plan.[35] But Monroe was not in fact in favor of the seizure of Florida at that time. On January 30, he directed Calhoun to specifically instruct Jackson "not to attack any post occupied by Spanish troops."[36] Inexplicably, Calhoun sent no further instructions to the general, probably believing that his earlier orders sufficed. He was unaware of Jackson's backdoor efforts to gain approval of his proposed seizure of Florida. But since he was well aware of the difficulties faced by those who sought to restrain Andrew Jackson, his oversight is puzzling.

Jackson arrived at Fort Scott in southern Georgia early in March, accompanied by 500 regular army troops, by about 1,000 Tennessee volunteers, and a number of Georgia militiamen. He was also supported by 1,400 anti–Red Stick Creek warriors led by William McIntosh. McIntosh and his Creek fighters, as we have seen, provided invaluable assistance to Jackson during the battle of Horseshoe Bend and would do so again during the Florida campaign. Old Hickory called McIntosh "the bravest man I ever knew." His career reflected the conflicts and contradictions that plagued the Creek Nation in the early 19th century. Of mixed blood, William McIntosh was the son of a British loyalist from Savannah who had taken refuge in Creek country during the American Revolution. His mother, Senoya, was Creek, a member of the powerful Wind Clan. He was raised as a Creek, but from his father gained a fluent command of the English language and a sure knowledge of white commercial culture. He prospered as a trader, an inn keeper, and a slave-holding planter. By virtue of his ability to operate in two worlds, McIntosh quickly gained political prominence but used his connections with Indian agent Benjamin Hawkins and his successor David Mitchell to enrich himself. Among other things, he gained control of federal annuity payments and later enjoyed a monopoly of the deerskin trade.

For McIntosh, fighting under the command of Andrew Jackson was a very profitable proposition. During the first Seminole War, McIntosh seized and sold into slavery scores of blacks and sambas (persons of mixed Indian and black ancestry) as well as cattle found in Seminole villages. Although he later refused to support Jackson's removal proposals, he was hardly a defender of his people's land rights. Some years after the war, in 1825, McIntosh engineered without the consent of the Creek National Council the Treaty of Indian Springs, yet another Creek land cession. But in doing so, he violated Creek law, and along with several of his supporters was put to death by the tribal law menders. It was said that a posse of some 400 warriors accompanied the executioners. McIntosh and an associate were shot down as they fled his burning house. Both the Creeks and the U.S. government rejected his treaty as fraudulent. The agreement was revised (in the Treaty of Washington in 1826) to restore to the Creeks some 3 million acres in Alabama that McIntosh had ceded. Indian Springs was not McIntosh's first questionable sale of Creek land. It was, however, his last.[37]

Returning to the Florida campaign of 1818, McIntosh's warriors struck the first blow, capturing three Red Sticks early in their march into the Spanish colony. After the American commander at Fort Gaines (a post erected on the site of the demolished Negro Fort) refused to keep the prisoners, McIntosh had put them to death, and then overran the town of Red Ground, taking some 238 Seminoles captive, including 53 warriors. McIntosh then pressed on to link up with Jackson's forces at the Ochlockonee River. Jackson arrived first, and after transporting his army across the river in canoes, sent a detachment under Major David Twiggs to the Mikasucki village called Tallahassee. It was deserted. Twiggs and his men burned it to the ground and soon thereafter were joined by Jackson's main force. Once his army was augmented by the arrival of McIntosh's warriors, Jackson mounted an attack on the main Mikasucki town. It did not go well, as some of the white militia mistook McIntosh's Indians for the enemy, and opened fire. In the confusion that ensued, most of the Mikasuckis escaped. But Jackson proudly explained to the Spanish commandant at St. Marks that he had "reduced . . . to ashes" the Mikasucki settlements in the area. He reported that he had found in their principal town horrifying evidence of the "hostile spirit" of the Seminoles. "On a red pole in the Center of the Council houses," he related, "more than fifty scalps of all ages from the infant to the aged matron were suspended. In addition to this upwards of three hundred old scalps were found in the dwellings of the different Chiefs."[38] As the taking of scalps was a regular feature of Indian warfare, this finding was hardly surprising. Jackson had no actual evidence that those scalps had in fact been taken during attacks on white settlements north of the border of Spanish Florida. Curiously, although under orders to deal with the Seminole threat to the Georgia frontier, Jackson "never mounted a systematic search for the large number of Seminoles who had evacuated the towns but obviously remained in the area."[39] Instead, leaving McIntosh to deal with the aftermath of their raids, Jackson marched with his main force to the Spanish fort at St. Marks. He advised Calhoun that he was convinced that "a portion of the hostiles had fled to St. Marks" and that the Spanish there might be giving them active support.[40] But he had no hard evidence to support that supposition.

Jackson, we must remember, was under orders to respect Spanish authority where it was still intact in Florida. His conduct at St. Marks clearly violated that order. In a letter to the fort's commandant Francisco Caso y Luengo, Jackson demanded that he immediately surrender control to the American forces. Basing his claim on rumors, he charged that "Hostile Indians and Negroes" had not only been welcomed and given shelter at St. Marks but had "obtained their supply of ammunition" there. In the light of Spanish "incompetency" in the colony, Jackson continued, it would be in the best interests of the King of Spain to enable Jackson to "chastise these lawless & inhuman savages." Insisting that he acted as a friend and ally of Spain, Old Hickory promised to observe and protect "the property and rights of Spanish subjects."[41]

Replying to Jackson's letter, the commandant at once denied the charge of supplying the hostiles, promised to cooperate with the Americans in fighting hostile Indians, but stated he could not surrender the fort without the consent of his superiors. He promised to apply promptly for permission to relinquish command to Jackson.[42] Jackson, unwilling to wait, informed Calhoun that Luengo's delay proved that he was "of a disposition to favour the Indians," and had in fact "taken an active part in aiding and abetting them in this war." Jackson proceeded to march through the fort's open gates. His men disarmed the tiny Spanish garrison which, surprised by the Americans' sudden appearance, tried but failed to man their cannon. Jackson then personally lowered the Spanish flag, handed it to the humiliated and protesting Luengo, and then raised the Stars and Stripes over Fort St. Marks. He transported the commandant and his men to Pensacola, at their request, after making a careful inventory of their property.[43]

Jackson's conviction that the Spanish were provoking and arming the Seminoles were confirmed, in his mind, by his discovery that the elderly Scots trader Alexander Arbuthnot had been residing at St. Marks as a guest at Luengo's residence. A year earlier, Gaines had complained to Jackson about Arbuthnot's activities, characterizing him as "one of the *self-styled Philanthropists* who have long infested neighboring Indian villages, in the character of British Agents—fomenting a spirit of discord."[44] Jackson, after finding the trader at St. Marks, declared that he probably was "one of the instigators of the savage war." He reported to Calhoun that he had ordered Arbuthnot's confinement "until evidence of his guilt can be collected."[45] While Jackson soon concluded that the evidence that was produced was sufficient to justify the elderly trader's hanging, more dispassionate assessments over the years have agreed that in fact it only established that the accused had been a friend and advocate for Florida's Indians. Seventy years old at the time of his capture, Arbuthnot had been in Florida since the spring of the previous year and had quickly established both a lucrative trade with Seminoles and Creeks and a warm personal relationship with some of their leaders, who had chosen him to serve as their spokesman. Granted their power of attorney, he had written to both American and British officials appealing for their intercession to protect his clients' rights. In August 1817, he had reported to Colonel Edward Nicolls that local newspapers in Georgia were claiming that "the Seminole Indians are continually committing murders on the borders, and making incursions into the state." Those stories, he declared, were "fabrications" intended to provoke the American government to take action "against the poor Indians." During the months, he had lived with the Seminoles, the only American they killed had been caught trying to steal chief Bowlegs's cattle. By contrast, American cattle thieves not only killed several unoffending Indians but also scalped a young boy. Not only did American cattle rustlers prey on the Seminoles, but "a considerable number" had also occupied their land and driven off its rightful owners.[46] In a letter to the British minister to the United States in January protesting the killing and robbing of Indians, Arbuthnot had written, "I am in hopes that these aggressions of Americans are not countenanced by the American government, but originate with men devoid of principle, who set laws and instructions at defiance, and stick at cruelty and oppression to obtain their ends." He doubted that the president of the United States knew anything about such outrages.[47]

One of the pieces of evidence seized on Arbuthnot's trading ship the *Chance* that Jackson scrutinized in his determination of the trader's guilt exemplifies the trader's activities on behalf of his clients. On January 19, 1818, Arbuthnot had written Indian agent Mitchell to appeal, at the request of "Kenheggee, chief of the Lower Creeks" for protection against "the cruel and oppressive conduct of the American people living on the border of the Indian nation." "Your known philanthropy and good will toward the Indians in general," Arbuthnot advised, "induce the chiefs to hope that you will lose no time in using your influence to put an end to those invasions of their lands and paternal birthright." He deplored the fact that Indians had been forced to take up arms, predicted that war would be "their ruin," and urged that "as they were not the aggressors, if in their rage, they committed any excesses," they should be excused as the expression of "an indignant spirit against an invading foe."[48]

Jackson on reading that letter was, predictably, outraged by the trader's claim that the Florida Indians were acting in self-defense. Giving no credence to the argument that they might have real grievances, the general in his report to Calhoun wrote that "on the commencement of my operation I was strongly impressed with the belief that the Indian War had been excited by some unprincipled Foreign or Private agents." Both the refugee Red Sticks and the Seminoles, he reasoned, "were too weak in numbers to believe they could possibly alone maintain a war with even partial success against the United States." It was the assurance of foreign aid, allegedly conveyed by Arbuthnot and by a former British officer named

Ambrister (whom Jackson also captured) that emboldened the Florida Indians and unleashed a savage war. In his justification of his decision to put both to death, Jackson recognized that there was no written evidence that either one was empowered to act on behalf of Great Britain. But since the British government was undoubtedly aware of their activities, "the execution of these two unprincipled villains will provide an awful example to the world, and convince the Government of Great Britain as well as her subjects that certain, if slow, retribution awaits those unchristian wretches who by false promises delude & excite an Indian to all the horrid deeds of savage war."[49]

Was Alexander Arbuthnot guilty of encouraging the Indians to wage "savage war" against the United States? There is no evidence in his correspondence that he was. Quite the contrary. Jackson's most sympathetic modern biographer, after a careful review of the documentation, concludes that Arbuthnot had consistently "urged them to keep the peace and avoid the provocations that lead to war."[50] But Andrew Jackson all too often equated recognition of Indian grievances with the instigation of "savage war." Arbuthnot's trial by a military panel of army and militia officers handpicked by Jackson was a travesty of justice. To support the charge that he was guilty of "exciting and stirring up the Creek Indians to war against the United States and its citizens," the prosecution produced a witness who claimed to have seen a letter written by Arbuthnot to the lower Creek leader Little Prince urging resistance to the enforcement of the Treaty of Fort Jackson and advising that he appeal to the Prince Regent of Great Britain for help in reclaiming his lost territory. Arbuthnot denied writing such a letter. It was never found. The witness, a middle-aged man named John Winslett, was a Georgia militiaman of humble background but some ambition. He appears in later records as a slave trader among the Creeks and as army interpreter in the Second Seminole War. The court in its haste in 1818 made no effort to locate other witnesses who could confirm, or deny his story.[51] The evidence provided in other documents confirms that Arbuthnot regarded the Fort Jackson Treaty as invalid, given the guarantees of Indian rights at Ghent, and that he so advised his Indian clients. But there is no evidence that he ever tried to incite the Creeks and Seminoles to wage an offensive war. The trader placed his reliance on appeals to American and British authority to secure justice for the Indians. He never entertained the view that the answer was an all-out war. As to Jackson's conviction that he was an agent of the British government, the fact is that his letters urging that Britain exert pressure on the United States on behalf of his clients were ignored. The British, as we noted earlier, after Ghent had no interest in a conflict with the United States over Indian rights. Arbthunot was neither a warmonger nor a British agent.[52]

The tribunal also charged Arbuthnot with spying on Jackson's army on behalf of the enemy and with supplying the Indians with munitions. Their evidence of spying: a letter written to his son John asking that the Seminole chief Bowlegs be warned of the approaching American army and urged to flee. "Tell my friend Bowleck [Bowlegs]," he wrote, "that it is throwing away his people to attempt to resist so powerful a force." He conjectured that Jackson's main objective was to destroy the Negro settlements on the Suwannee. The American invaders, he predicted, would probably "be well satisfied" once that was accomplished and could be expected to leave Florida after a few weeks. Meanwhile, the Seminoles should move out their way, then hide and wait.[53] Nothing in his letter to his son, or in any other documents placed before the court, supported the charge that Arbuthnot was working to provoke a "savage war." He was, however, clearly determined to help his Indian friends and trading partners to protect themselves against what he regarded as American aggression.

Also found in Arbuthnot's papers, and brought forth in evidence against him, was an unsigned enumeration, written on the back of a copy of a letter to the British minister, of the number of warriors who could fight against "those who have made inroads into their territory" and of the military supplies they currently needed. Even if this document did come from the hand of Arbuthnot, it hardly proved he was encouraging an Indian attack on American soil.[54] There were other letters which the court also construed as incriminating. One which Arbuthnot had sent to the governor of the Bahamas contained a request from Bowlegs asking for ammunition to enable his warriors to counter "the predatory incursions of the black Georgians, who enter his territory and drive away his cattle." Another from Bowlegs asked for assistance in resisting Jackson's invasion of his territory.[55] Those letters offered no proof whatsoever of the charge that Arbuthnot was inciting a "savage war" against the United States. But his solicitation of British intervention in American Indian affairs was deeply offensive to Andrew Jackson and his officers. They were infuriated by his charge that they were the aggressors.

The military tribunal also relied upon the testimony of several witnesses who testified about the trader's assistance to his Indian clients. Among them was Peter Cook, a former employee whom Arbuthnot had discharged. Cook claimed Arbuthnot had obtained and given the Indians "a large quantity of powder and lead." But he was a man of questionable character, having also been fired from an earlier position in the Bahamas for theft. Arbuthnot's claim that the gunpowder he sold Indians was of limited quantity and intended only for use in hunting is reasonably credible.[56] The most damning prosecution witness was a business rival, William Hambly, who had a long-standing feud with the Scots trader. Hambly charged that the accused had given the Seminoles 10 kegs of gunpowder to use against the Americans, had requisitioned from the Spanish two more kegs for the use of the Red Stick prophet Francis, had written several letters for the chiefs appealing to the British for additional aid, and had assured them that Great Britain would indeed intervene to protect them from the Americans. He also alleged that Arbuthnot had ordered the Seminoles to capture and rob a rival trader, Peter Doyle, and had then conspired with them to kill both Hambly and Doyle. Hambly's testimony by his own admission was for the most part based on hearsay, but the court denied the defendant's motion to exclude it. His most damning claim was that he had been told by Indians that the defendant "had advised them to go to war with the United States, if they did not surrender them the land that had been taken from them, and that the British government would back them in it."

Interestingly, in one letter in the possession of the court, Arbuthnot had accused Hambly of colluding with Jackson and Gaines to provoke a needless war that would end in further seizures of Indian land. That allegation is more credible than Hambly's claim that Arbuthnot encouraged Indians to attack the Americans, but of course it only further incensed the court. Claiming lack of jurisdiction, the court dropped the charge that Arbuthnot had plotted the death of his rivals. But it gave full weight to their testimony regarding the other alleged activities of the accused in Florida.[57]

In his defense, Arbuthnot pointed out to the court that there was nothing in his actual correspondence of "an inflammatory nature," nothing supporting in any way the charge that "I was prompting the Indians to war." He once again reminded the judges that Hambly's testimony was "hearsay evidence" whose use to condemn him would be "without precedent." He closed by asking that if the court nonetheless found some reason for "censure," it "lean to the side of mercy."[58] It was to no avail. The tribunal condemned the elderly Scots trader to death. To Jackson's great satisfaction, he was hanged from the yardarm of his trading ship the *Chance* on April 29, 1818.[59]

A codefendant was also executed, in his case by firing squad, on the same day. Robert Ambrister was a former British lieutenant in the Royal Marines cashiered for dueling who had hoped to revive his career by joining with two other British freebooters caught up in a fantastic "dream of a personal Florida empire protected by black and Seminole warriors."[60] He knew and traveled with Arbuthnot, but despised him as "a weak and feckless man" who feared armed conflict.[61] Ambrister harbored no such fears. Accused of encouraging and assisting Creeks and Seminoles hostile to the United States, and with spying, he offered no real defense but restricted himself to a rather ineffective cross-examination of witnesses. In fact, he was guilty. Wearing an old and soiled British officer's uniform, falsely representing himself as a British agent empowered to promise British aid, he had encouraged Indians to take the warpath. At the trial's close, he did not contest the charges, but threw himself on the mercy of the court. The judges initially voted that he be put to death by firing squad, then, swayed by his youth (he was 20 years old), relented and ordered that he "receive fifty stripes on his bare back, and be confined to labor for twelve calendar months." Andrew Jackson overruled the tribunal and ordered Ambrister's execution.[62] The order was carried out the following day. One historian charges that Jackson rushed both executions "so there would be no chance for appeal. A former Justice of the Tennessee Supreme Court, he must have known the sentences would not stand up to appellate scrutiny."[63] As we will see, many of Jackson's contemporary critics, including the members of two congressional committees, regarded the proceedings against Arbuthnot and Ambrister as travesties of justice.

Jackson, shortly after his arrival at St. Marks, had also ordered the hanging of the Red Stick prophet Francis and the war chief Homathlenico. Both had been taken prisoner when they boarded a ship near St. Marks. The ship was flying the British flag. The prophet hoped it had come to offer belated assistance to his cause. He had earlier met Arbuthnot and felt reassured by the Scots trader's concern for Indian welfare. But at St. Marks he was the victim of a deception. The ship was in fact American. Her captain turned his prisoners over to Jackson shortly after Jackson's seizure of the Spanish fort. Francis asked to meet with Old Hickory. Jackson refused. He then asked to die by firing squad. That request was also refused. Both men were hanged the following day.[64]

Jackson also hoped to capture and kill Peter McQueen. He never did so. On April 11, Jackson's army, on its way to confront Bowlegs at his settlement 100 miles southeast of St. Marks, stumbled upon a Red Stick refuge village on the Ecofina River. McIntosh and his Creeks led the charge, killing 40 warriors and capturing some women and children. The invaders seized several hundred cattle and a large cache of corn, at the cost of only three dead. McQueen and 200 or so of his warriors escaped into the swamp, made their way further south, and regrouped near Tampa. Their wanderings were not over, but McQueen was never captured. The date and place of his death are unknown.[65]

Jackson's efforts to defeat the Seminole chief Bowlegs and his warriors were also thwarted. Warned, as noted earlier, by a message from Arbuthnot, Bowlegs and his people had fled southward, leaving their villages on the west bank of the Suwannee deserted. Jackson's army burned the now empty dwellings, pillaged corn fields, and confiscated cattle. Writing to Rachel, Jackson related that he was sending her a cow as "a present." He rejoiced that his army, hitherto short of supplies had "been fed like the Israelites of old in the wilderness." He also boasted that through the intervention of "the hand of heaven," every prominent Indian enemy "has been killed or taken."[66] That was not true. Not only was McQueen still at large, but Bowlegs and most of his people had fled into the swamp lands of central Florida. Jackson chose not to pursue them, complaining in a dispatch to Secretary of War Calhoun that "the depth of the swamps added to the want of forage occasioned the horses to give out in great numbers." As to his infantry men, they were "wet to the middle." He told the secretary that since the adversary had fled, the Indian War was really over. He now intended to return to Nashville.[67]

Despite his claim to have enjoyed support from "the hand of heaven," Andrew Jackson's first Seminole War thus far had not gone smoothly. At first, he faced supply problems reminiscent of those he had faced during the early stages of the Creek War.[68] He also found local authorities often less than appreciative of his efforts. Throughout the campaign, the governors of Georgia and Alabama complained that his Florida adventure placed their frontiers in danger by stirring up Indians and taking away militia needed for help at home.[69] A few isolated Indian attacks fed persistent rumors of impending large-scale massacres. Those rumors set the stage for a senseless preemptive action against Indians rumored to be hostile mounted by the remnants of the Georgia militia left behind when Jackson invaded the Spanish colony. On his return to his Florida base at Fort Gadsden (site of the demolished "Negro Fort") after his pursuit of Bowlegs, Jackson received word that a ragtag force under the command of Captain Obed Wright had attacked a friendly Creek village at Chehaw, killing at least 10 innocent inhabitants, including the

Tiger King, an aged chief who had greeted them bearing a white flag. Earlier, the Chehaws had furnished not only food but some 40 warriors for Jackson's army. Their murdered chief was William McIntosh's uncle. They had no reason to expect to be attacked, and with most of their men away fighting on the American side in Florida, they were essentially defenseless.[70]

Angered by the unprovoked killing of tribesmen who were his allies, Old Hickory was further enraged when Georgia's governor William Rabun denied his authority as the commanding federal general to try the offender, and then somehow failed to prevent Wright's flight from the country. Jackson characterized Wright as "a cowardly monster in human Shape" who had led a "base, cowardly, and inhuman attack" on elderly members of "an Indian tribe in perfect peace and under the protection of the U. States." He damned the governor for his failure to punish the perpetrators of "an act which will to the last ages fix a Stain on the character of Georgia." Rabun for his part had hoped to try Wright in a Georgia court, but in the face of strong anti-Indian sentiment at home, found it expedient to look the other way when the captain was set free and made his way to Havana. The federal authorities in Washington, D.C., found it equally expedient to ignore the governor's claim that Jackson had violated Georgia's state rights by sending Georgia militia into Florida without the state's consent. Nor did they chose to deal with Jackson's claim that Wright as a militia member called into federal service was subject to his personal jurisdiction as his commanding officer. They simply did not wish to be involved in the quarrel.[71]

Adding to Jackson's discomfort was his conviction that British agents in Florida aided by the Spanish were still somehow using Indians to plan war against the United States. On May 5, he warned Calhoun that:

> the Moment the American army retires from Florida, The War Hatchet will again be raised, and the same scenes of indiscriminate murder with which our frontier settlers have been visited will be repeated so long as Indians within the territory of Spain are exposed to the delusions of false prophets and the poison of foreign intrigue.

He predicted that "so long as they can receive ammunition, munitions of war, etc., from pretended traders or Spanish commanders, it will be impossible to restrain their outrages." He made clear once again his conviction that nothing less than American annexation of all of Florida could bring peace and security on the frontier.[72] In evidence, he pointed to his earlier correspondence with Jose Masot, governor of West Florida over the issues of granting the Americans free access to the Escambia River in order to resupply Fort Crawford. The governor had replied that, while he had granted that privilege on one previous occasion, in the future he would have to insist that shipments be made through Pensacola in a Spanish ship and the usual duties paid until such time as he received contrary orders from a higher authority. That answer, Jackson raged, "cannot but be viewed as evincing a hostile attitude."[73]

More serious were persistent rumors of ongoing Spanish complicity with the Seminoles that, in Jackson's mind, made it imperative that he abandon his previously announced intention to demobilize his forces and return to Nashville. He accordingly told the secretary that he must resume the war he had declared ended two weeks earlier. He had information "from the most unquestionable authority" that confirmed that:

> the Indians at war with the United States have free access into Pensacola; That they are kept advised from that quarter of all our movements; that they are supplied from thence with ammunition and munitions of war, and that they are now collecting in large bodies in the amount of 4 or 400 warriors in that city; That inroads from thence have latterly been made on the Alabama, in one of which 18 settlers fell by the Tomahawk.

These statements from his informants, Jackson advised Calhoun, "compel me to make a movement to the West . . . Pensacola must be occupied by with an American force."[74]

In justification of that action, he wrote the Spanish governor of West Florida to declare that "there is too much ground to believe that the Indians have been encouraged, aided and abetted by the officers of Spain in this cruel war against the United States. Proof positive exists that the Indians were supplied with ammunition by the late commandant of St. Marks." Throughout the conflict, he charged, the Spanish had provided sanctuary and aid to the "Indian foe." He pointed to what he regarded as physical proof of Spanish complicity with savages, their possession of some garments once worn by Americans. "The clothing found on board a vessel in the employ of the Government of Spain, sailing from Pensacola directly for this port, compels me to call on you for a statement in what manner you came in possession of said clothing." Jackson believed it came from the victims of the Scott massacre and thus offered proof of Spanish collusion with the enemy.[75]

Governor Masot tried hard to placate Jackson. He assured him that there was no assemblage of hostile Indians in West Florida. "Your Excellency," he advised, "assuredly has been misinformed." There were in fact only a very few Indians in the area. "The greater part of them were women and children who procured a subsistence by furnishing the inhabitants with wood, fish, and other trifling objects, and were here before the present war with the Seminoles." The governor himself, in response to a request from the Alabama militia conveyed earlier by U.S. Army Major William Young, had taken a census of all Indians in the Pensacola area and found that they "all together, amounted to eighty seven." Assuredly, "these few unarmed and miserable men were not hostile to the United States." In proof, he pointed to the fact that Americans had been traveling through his territory "alone and unarmed . . . without being, at any time, insulted or molested in their persons or property." Jackson therefore had no reason for concern, no need to intervene.

The governor promised Jackson that he would fully cooperate with the Americans on all matters, including the previously contested issue of free use of the Escambia River route. As to the very awkward question of the American clothing found on the Spanish ship bound for Pensacola, he explained, somewhat improbably, that those items had been purchased at New Orleans and Havana and had not been obtained directly from the Seminoles. Finally, responding to the charge that the commandant at St. Marks had aided Indians at war with the United States, Masot assured Jackson that he would investigate the matter and if Luengo were demonstrated to be guilty, he would be "punished with all the severity his transgressions deserve."[76]

Given Masot's response, Jackson, under the orders that authorized the Florida intervention, should have tried to work with the Spanish authorities. He did not do so. Instead, he informed the governor that he found his explanations about the clothing unacceptable and for that reason intended to occupy and hold Pensacola, "until Spain has the power or will to maintain her neutrality."[77] Masot protested and ordered Jackson to leave Florida, calling his continued presence an act of aggression. Jackson, undeterred, marched on Pensacola, arriving there, after some 12 days lost in poorly mapped country, on May 24. Hearing rumors of Spanish plans to block his supply line from the gulf, Jackson at one point had threatened to "put to death every man found in arms." But the Spanish in fact offered little resistance. As Jackson approached, Governor Masot fled to Fort Carlos de Barrancas outside the city, then after a very brief artillery duel, surrendered with his 300-man garrison to the invader. Jackson allowed the governor and the garrison to leave the area, which was now placed under American military rule.

Old Hickory justified his occupation, in a proclamation to the people of Pensacola, on the grounds that the Spanish colonial authorities had proven themselves unable to control hostile Indians. He claimed, disingenuously, that he came as an ally of the Spanish, sent by a friendly government to rescue them from the Indian menace. He assured the inhabitants that he had no intention of remaining in West Florida permanently.[78] In fact, as we have seen, he had long advocated American annexation of all of Florida. On June 2, he advised the president that Florida should be occupied and held "for as long as we are a republic."[79] After taking West Florida, Jackson hoped to mount a military expedition against St. Augustine and occupy East Florida as well. Two months after the Pensacola occupation, without consulting Washington, D.C., he sent orders to Gaines directing him to seize the East Florida capital should he find any evidence that the Spaniards were providing Indians with arms. Informed after the fact, Secretary of War Calhoun quickly countermanded that order.[80] Jackson responded by warning the secretary that the Indians with Spanish support would soon renew the war and asking for authorization to mount a new preemptive strike that would end by "finally crushing Savage hostilities in the South."[81] The secretary, who was now skeptical of exaggerated reports of Indian hordes about to devastate the frontier, declined to support a continuation of Jackson's war against Seminoles and Spaniards.[82]

It must be emphasized that Jackson's claim that American security required the immediate removal of Spanish authority in Florida was never supported by real evidence, only by rumors. Gaines's recent report that several thousand hostile Seminoles were massing on the St. Johns River in East Florida was patently false.[83] The stories Jackson heard about enemy activity in West Florida were no more accurate. Earlier, Masot had told the truth when he protested that there were no hostile Seminole forces near Pensacola. Equally valid was his denial that he had deliberately armed Indians hostile to the United States.

Jackson's efforts after the war to provide proof that some 500 enemy warriors armed with Spanish rifles and munitions really had been based in West Florida were unpersuasive. To gather evidence in support of his claim that he had to seize Pensacola, Jackson sent Major Young back to the city in September 1818. The major looked for eyewitnesses who could verify his suspicion that Governor Masot had provided Seminoles with arms. He could find none. Some informants did testify that the governor had on occasion given some food to hungry Indians who were traveling through the area. They differed as to numbers, ranging from around 50 to 200 or so. But none had seen or heard anything that would give credence to the notion that 500 Spanish-supported Seminole warriors had been poised to assault the American frontier. Quite simply, there was no hard evidence before or after the seizure of Pensacola supporting Jackson's characterization of Masot as an enemy of the United States. Even so, Jackson expressed regret, after the governor's restoration, that he had not hanged him.[84]

Once he arrived in the Pensacola area, Jackson made no effort to send out patrols to locate hostile Indians in the area but instead deployed his forces to eliminate Spanish authority. Despite his protestations to the contrary, the evidence suggests his main reason for marching on the Spanish colonial capital was not to deal with renegade Seminoles, however many or few they might be. He had a greater goal in mind. Jackson, as we have noted, stressed on many occasions the need to counter the continuing danger to America's present security and future growth posed by a European presence below the southern boundaries of Georgia, Alabama, and Mississippi Territory. His actions in 1818 were driven in large measure by his abiding distrust of the Spanish, the British and their Indian allies, a distrust which inspired in him a fierce determination to settle the Florida question once and for all.

But that is not the whole story. Underlying Jackson's defiance of his instructions to respect Spanish authority many perceived a continuing indeed insatiable hunger for the acquisition of yet more land for settlement and exploitation by white Americans. A few of his political enemies whispered that the Florida invasion was nothing more than a scheme to profit from land speculation. Jackson, it was alleged, was a silent partner in a company that had been investing in Pensacola real estate, property which would appreciate in value greatly were Florida annexed. Calhoun believed and spread the rumor, as did some of Jackson's other critics. Secretary of State Adams hoped it wasn't true.[85] There is no evidence that Jackson and his friends had actually bought any Pensacola lands at the time of the invasion. But that does not mean that the rumor was without foundation. Jackson was a major investor in Cyprus Land Company, an enterprise committed to the acquisition of newly acquired Indian land. He generally relied on associates to handle his various land acquisitions, thereby concealing his personal role. His correspondence over the years reflects a keen interest in the economic potential of Florida. It is telling that, in connection with his demand for the seizure of St. Augustine, Jackson forwarded to his superiors a report that spoke of the "magnificent farmland in north Florida."[86] In Nashville, a number of his close friends and relatives in December 1817 had formed a new land company for the specific purpose of "purchasing lots in the town of Pensacola" and had obtained from the general a letter of introduction to the Spanish governor there. In a deposition intended to counter rumors that Jackson was profiteering from his Florida invasion, one of the partners in 1820 declared "I do not believe that Gen. Jackson is or ever has been either directly or indirectly interested in said speculation, or that he is or ever was directly or indirectly to receive any profit or advantage from said speculation."[87] That may be true. But there is ample evidence of Jackson's ongoing encouragement of Florida land speculators, and of his behind-the-scenes involvement and participation in land deals elsewhere made possible by military action against Native Americans.

Whatever his reasons for seizing Pensacola, Jackson's actions in Florida were controversial. The British government raised questions about his execution of two of their citizens, but hoping for peaceful relations and profitable trade, did not really press the matter despite extensive expressions of public outrage at home. The Spanish, who derisively called Jackson "the Napoleon of the Woods," protested the deposing of their governor but were too weak to do more than complain. (They were neither the first nor the last to compare the headstrong American general to France's self-anointed former emperor.) Monroe's cabinet pondered ways of dealing with the diplomatic embarrassment and political difficulties Jackson's invasion had occasioned. Secretary of War Calhoun's demand that Old Hickory be tried by a military court for gross subordination frightened most other cabinet officers intimidated by Jackson's great popularity. Secretary of State Adams for his part appreciated Old Hickory's rough treatment of the Spanish, thinking it might well serve to hasten the day when Spain would decide to relinquish a colony it could not control or defend. The secretary proceeded to inform the Spanish envoy to the United States that no action would be taken against Jackson, warning that if Spain could not find a way to establish real control over Florida, she should cede it to the United States, as the present situation was an "annoyance" that would not be tolerated.[88]

Calhoun and Crawford remained privately critical of Jackson but decided not to press the matter publically or officially. The cabinet discussions provided President Monroe, who hated controversy, with a facile if evasive solution. He denied authorizing Jackson's seizure of West Florida, ordered the restoration to office the Spanish officials whom Jackson had exiled from St. Marks and Pensacola but placated the voters at home (while sending a message to foreign adversaries) by refusing to reprimand the general. In his annual address to Congress, delivered on November 17, Monroe justified Old Hickory's invasion of West Florida on the grounds that the colony, not adequately policed by the Spanish, had become the refuge of "every species of lawless adventurer." Accepting Jackson's word, the president declared that the commandant at St. Marks and the governor at Pensacola had actively aided the Seminoles. He had returned the colony to them only because he did not have the authority to annex new territory. Only Congress could do that.[89] Monroe did not acknowledge that while he had restored St. Marks and Pensacola to the Spanish, American troops remained in Florida. Fort Gadsden, built on Spanish Territory at the site of the demolished Indian fort, was not evacuated but remained under the army's command, available should a new offensive prove necessary.

The administration's critics and enemies in Congress and elsewhere were not satisfied and demanded that Jackson be held accountable for the excesses of the Florida campaign. On January 19, 1819, a select committee of the House of Representatives, investigating the executions of Arbuthnot and Ambrister, declared that the general had acted illegally in subjecting them to a court marital. "We can find no law of the United States authorizing a trial before a court martial for offensives such as are alleged" against the defendants, the committee's report concluded. The committee professed astonishment at Jackson's claim that Arbuthnot and Ambrister could legally be treated as outlaws and pirates simply because of their relationships with Indians reputed to be hostile to the United States. It found no basis in international law for such action. The trials themselves the committee declared not only illegal but unfairly conducted. The accused were not granted full due process. Nor were the penalties appropriate.

> In vain has your committee sought, among the documents on the Seminole War, for a shadow of necessity for the death of the persons arraigned before the court. The war was at an end, to all intents and purposes! The enemy's strongholds had been destroyed, many of them killed or taken prisoner, and the remainder a feeble band, dispersed and scattered in every duration.[90]

Those findings were not unanimous. Richard M. Johnson of Tennessee, a former Indian fighter and future vice president who claimed to be the killer of Tecumseh, submitted a minority report that concluded, while his overruling of the court's decision not to execute Ambrister was questionable, overall Jackson's actions in Florida were justified by what Johnson termed "the laws of retaliation." In support of that conclusion, he referred to the bloody past history of Indian massacres of whites and of European complicity in those atrocities.[91]

Johnson's claim did not persuade Jackson's detractors. On the floor of the House, Congressman Thomas Cobb of Georgia argued that the majority report did not go far enough in its censure of Jackson. By his brutal and illegal conduct in Florida, the general, Cobb declared, had disgraced the nation, causing it to lose in the eyes of the world that reputation "for justice and mercy" which had previously been its glory. He accordingly asked that Congress also censure Jackson for his seizure of St. Marks and Pensacola. To prevent future abuses, Cobb called on Congress to pass laws requiring congressional approval for any military action outside the nation's boundaries and forbidding the execution of captives without presidential consent.[92]

Congressman John Holmes of Massachusetts responded with a lengthy review of the recent history of Florida, which defended Jackson's actions in invading the colony on grounds that the colony was, as Jackson believed, a center of conspiracy against the security of the United States. As to Jackson's killing of Indians and his execution of Arbuthnot and Ambrister, Holmes declared the Britons "volunteers in the service of a lawless tribe of savages, whose mode of warfare is indiscriminate massacre of all ages and sexes. It is right, it is merciful to inflict on these savages these cruelties which they practice and inculcate." Arbuthnot and Ambrister were even more culpable and less worthy of mercy than the Indians, as they were not savages but "had been taught in the school of humanity, and understood the distress which their conduct would inflict." Accepting fully and uncritically Andrew Jackson's characterization of their activities in Florida, Holmes concluded that "they were worse than Indians; they were the exciters and instigators of the war; they deserved death."[93] Holmes was the first of several speakers who repeated and in some cases embellished Old Hickory's argument. Jackson himself, hearing that his conduct was under question, hastened to Washington, D.C., to rally his supporters. His vehement comments behind the scenes so intimidated several congressmen that they started carrying firearms. Among other things, he reportedly threatened to cut off the ears of Pennsylvania senator Abner Laycock, who chaired the Select Committee investigating his conduct in Florida. Laycock, not easily intimidated, assured his colleagues that although he often crossed paths with Jackson, "I still have my ears."[94]

The Seminole debates were lengthy and at times acrimonious. As Cobb had hoped, it was not restricted to the court marital question but covered a wide range of questions about the origins and conduct of the Seminole War. The high point, in terms of public interest, was reached on January 20 when the Speaker of the House relinquished the chair and walked into the pit to deliver, after professing no personal disrespect for the general, an excoriation of Jackson's conduct remarkable in its scope and vehemence. As most history books relate, Henry Clay described the general as a would-be military dictator whose defiance of lawful authority was reminiscent of Alexander, Caesar, Cromwell, and Napoleon and no less dangerous to republican liberty. But he did not limit himself to Jackson's insubordination, or to his violation of international law. Clay condemned his inhumane treatment of Indians. Jackson's demand at the close of the Creek War that Red Stick prophets either be killed or turned over to the Americans for execution Clay found particularly repugnant. Even Rome at its most tyrannical, he declaimed, respected "the altars and gods of those whom she subjugated." Jackson, by contrast, subjected "even their religion" to "open and cruel violence." By subjecting the Creeks to "harsh and unconscionable terms, extorted by the power of the sword, and the right of conquest," Jackson had provoked an unnecessary new Indian war in Florida (the Seminoles, Clay believed, were never a major threat), a war he then conducted without respect for either civil authority or the rule of law. Clay deplored not only by the executions of Ambrister and Arbuthnot but also by the hanging of the two Red Stick leaders captured deceitfully by flying a false flag. He professed horror at Jackson's assertion of the right to subject Indian prisoners of war to summary execution. In his summation, Clay declared that failure to censure Jackson for his misconduct during his Indian Wars would be "a triumph of the principle of insubordination—a triumph of the military over civil authority—a triumph over the powers of this house—a triumph over the constitution of this land" and might ultimately also prove to be "a triumph over the liberties of the people."[95]

Clay's speech, several hours in length, delivered with all the skill of a master orator, thrilled the audience in the gallery, which greeted his peroration with "a fearful burst of noise. Cheers, groans, shouts, applause, bedlam."[96] But despite the Speaker's eloquence, the House of Representatives was not convinced. When a vote on the censure motion was finally called, on February 8, it lost by a vote of 63 in favor, 107 opposed. Congressman Cobb's proposed restrictions on future "military chieftains" were also decisively defeated.[97]

The Senate's deliberations were less conclusive. The select committee on the war, after reviewing documentation relating to Jackson's overall conduct in Florida, found that he had acted illegally not only in the executions, which it labeled "an unnecessary act of severity," but also in taking command of state militias and using them to mount an invasion without the consent of Congress. The actual circumstances in Florida, it found, did not warrant such actions. After receiving a copy of the committee's report, Jackson responded at length, contesting its findings item by item. But the Senate as a whole declined to take action. The report was permanently tabled when that body adjourned for the year.[98] The effect of congressional inaction was to uphold Old Hickory's belief that "nonwhite people inside and along the American territory could be treated as outside the protective umbrella of law."[99]

Jackson was gratified by the outcome, advising a confidant even before Congress adjourned that the efforts of Clay, Crawford, and their associates to use an attack on him as a means to "crush" Monroe had misfired. They would now in consequence, Jackson predicted, face "political ruin," as this issue "must become the Touchstone of the election of the next President."[100] Jackson exaggerated, but he was not entirely wrong. Criticism of his conduct in Florida was not politically wise. His many defenders, inside and outside political life, were hardly troubled by the excesses that concerned the more scrupulous members of Congress. Far from it. They wholeheartedly supported Old Hickory's call for the termination of the Spanish presence south of the border and were not bothered by the means he used to affect that end.

Jackson's vision of an expanding white republic required not only the immediate elimination of Florida as a refuge for hostile Indians, runaway slaves, and conniving British agents but also acquisition of the vast tracks of land in Georgia, Alabama, and Mississippi still guaranteed to Indian nations by solemn and presumably perpetual treaties. Jackson, as we have noted, never believed in the legitimacy of those treaties. They were, in his view, nothing more than convenient expedients, to be set aside whenever whites needed more space. At the close of the Seminole War, Jackson was called upon to undertake a new land cession negotiations with the Chickasaw Indians. He wrote fellow commissioner General Isaac Shelby that Indians "must be taught to know that they do not Possess sovereignty" or "the right of domain" over the lands they currently claimed and occupied.[101] That was the principle that would continue to inspire his Indian policy, even though expediency would often require less candor.

The Chickasaw, whose homelands extended from northern Mississippi and Alabama through portions of western Tennessee and Kentucky, had been close allies and trading partners of the British throughout the colonial era. Under leadership of the mixed blood descendants of James Logan Colbert, a Scots trader who had settled in Chickasaw country in the mid-18th century, they soon established close ties with the newly independent United States, signing the Treaty of Hopewell of 1786. The Chickasaw, true to their vows of friendship, refused to support the pan-Indian Northern Confederation and sent warriors to join Mad Anthony Wayne's campaign against the Shawnee and their allies in 1794. William Colbert was one of a number of Chickasaw warriors who served in Andrew Jackson's army during the Creek War. Other Chickasaws joined William Henry Harrison's forces in the north and fought against Tecumseh in Canada in 1813.[102]

In his letter of instruction to Jackson and Shelby, Secretary of War Calhoun had conveyed President Monroe's hope that the Chickasaw might be persuaded to relinquish all of their land east of the Mississippi River and accept in exchange territories "to the west."[103] That objective, however dear to Jackson's heart, was not one that could be achieved in 1818. Having relinquished substantial land already in treaty negotiations two years earlier, the Colberts at first refused Jackson's invitation to come to a new treaty meeting in Nashville by declaring that "they would lose every drop of blood in the veins before they would yield to the United States another acre of land."[104] But Jackson in a letter to James Colbert in late July warned that it was in the best interest of the Chickasaws to cooperate. He explained that "all the lands claimed by your nation within the state of Tennessee had been sold by North Carolina thirty odd years ago . . . to discharge the debt occasioned by the revolutionary war." Now the purchasers were "pressing your father the President for possession of the land" they had paid for. The president in concern for the well-being of the Chickasaw had sent Generals Jackson and Kerby to arrange for fair compensation. Should it be necessary for whites to take the land without their consent, they could expect Congress to accord them much less generous treatment. Reconsidering the matter, the Chickasaw leaders decided they would indeed find out just what Jackson and his fellow commissioner had to say and offer.[105]

After some weeks delay occasioned by the government's failure to deliver annuity payments due under previous agreements, Chickasaw chiefs and warriors met with the commissioners on October 12. After expressing his concern for the well beings of his Chickasaw children, particularly for the poorest among them, Jackson bluntly declared that they had no choice. They must now surrender more land to white settlers. They had two alternatives: they could accept a generous land exchange and move all their nation west of the Mississippi, or sell more of their present domain to the federal government for cash. They must understand that Congress and the president would not allow them to retain all of their present holdings. He explained their father the president had allowed the Chickasaw to remain on land north of the Tennessee border for many years, even though it was not really theirs, but now since the game was gone they had no need or excuse to hold on to it. Jackson added he was well aware that some Chickasaws had threatened to kill chiefs who gave up land. Should they carry out that threat, he warned, "your father the President will put them to death." Should the Chickasaw not accept one of the offers he was now extending to them, white settlers, with the blessing of Congress and the president, would take the land anyway. They must act now, while Jackson could protect their interests. Should they refuse, the president would be deeply offended by their "acts of ill will and ingratitude."[106]

For three days the Chickasaw leaders, meeting at George Colbert's home, argued over Jackson's proposals. They were unwilling to accept either a land exchange that would mean total abandonment of their traditional homeland or a new land sale that would open up more of it to white settlement. They feared that any new concession "would result in the death of many chiefs" at the hands of their countrymen, as few of the Chickasaw favored further land concessions.[107] It was soon apparent to Jackson and Shelby that the Chickasaw leaders must once again be bribed. There was a problem, however. The appropriation provided by Secretary of War Calhoun for the expenses of negotiating new Chickasaw treaty (some $10,000) did not include enough money to adequately feed "the avarice of the chiefs." Jackson found a way around that obstacle by a secret agreement to raise more money (some $20,000) through granting a new fee simple deed on the reservations set aside for George and Levi Colbert in the 1816 treaty, then leasing and issuing a bond on the chiefs' land. He later boasted to Tennessee governor Joseph McMinn that "we created funds out of the property of the Indians that obtained the cession."[108] But when the treaty was submitted to the Senate for ratification, there was some criticism of the granting of land in fee simple to the Colberts, criticism that reflected only in part squeamishness over Jackson's methods. The notion of allowing the Colberts any permanent inheritance rights did not sit well with many senators who feared the precedent. It had been a policy to limit land concessions in territories surrendered by treaty to the lifetime of the favored Indians. Also controversial was the granting of a valuable salt lick concession in Chickasaw Territory to a close Jackson associate. Mississippi senator John Williams challenged the grant and his allegations of cronyism and corruption led to the striking of that clause of the treaty before its ratification.[109]

Jackson did not get what he really wanted from the Chickasaws. Despite the bribes and the generous land grant to the Colberts, the chiefs could not be persuaded to move across the Mississippi. But after several days of blandishments and threats, they did agree in exchange for a modest annual annuity ($10,000 initially for 14 years) to sell all of their holdings in Tennessee and Kentucky. The land they lost far exceeded in extent the dubious North Carolina post-revolutionary land grants. They retained their fairly sizeable territory in northeast Mississippi and a much smaller tract in northwestern Alabama.

This new treaty, like so many others Jackson negotiated, was, as historian Robert Remini notes, "dishonorable." Among other things, "the journal of the proceedings was kept secret to protect the lives of the chiefs who had been bribed." Moreover, Jackson, who early in the negotiations withheld a desperately needed past due annuity payment, at one point at the end even tried to disavow a verbal agreement to extend the annuity payments for an additional, 15th year. "In later years the Chickasaws felt anger, bitterness and frustration over what had been done to them by the American government and by their own chiefs."[110] But Sharp Knife felt they had no reason to complain, assuring them that their remaining land was "more than you can cultivate for six hundred years."[111] (As president a dozen years later, he arranged through the Indian Removal Act for the acquisition of remaining Chickasaw Territory.) Back home in Nashville, Jackson's fellow citizens, as he related, "gave myself and staff a Ball in celebration of the chickesaw treaty." He informed General Shelby that he personally marked what he characterized as his retirement "from all Public appointment" by buying at a very low cost a large tract of land on south of the Tennessee River. No one had bid against him. He related that his solitary and winning bid was "hailed by the unanimous shouts of a numerous and mixed multitude."[112]

Jackson did not in fact retire from the Indian negotiation business after the 1818 Chickasaw acquisition. A year later, he was called upon to take over negotiations with the Choctaw, a large and once-powerful Indian federation that occupied a vast track of land in Mississippi south of the Chickasaw homeland.[113] The Choctaw, like the Chickasaw to whom they were closely related, had long been friends and allies of the United States. They had provided scouts to American armies in the early years of independence. Their three principal chiefs had turned a deaf ear to Tecumseh when he visited them in 1811 to enlist support for a pan-Indian alliance. They had assisted the Mississippi militia in the campaign against the Red Sticks in 1813 and had stood with Andrew Jackson in the defense of New Orleans in 1815. They had also already sold much of their territory to the new republic in treaties negotiated in 1801, 1802, 1805, and 1816. But with the expansion of the Cotton Kingdom into Mississippi and the state's admission to the federal union, land-hungry white settlers wanted all the rest and clamored for total Indian removal.

At the end of the first decade of the 19th century, despite earlier treaty concessions, roughly two-thirds of Mississippi remained in tribal hands. Many, perhaps most, white emigrants, who now outnumbered Indians in the new state by around five to one, for reasons that compounded fear, bigotry, need, and greed, found that intolerable.[114] The *Mississippi Star Gazette* declared their continued presence "to the great detriment of this state."[115] Although the Choctaws were in fact a fairly prosperous and peaceful people whose fields and stockyards were among the most productive on the continent, most white Mississippians, troubled by old frontier atrocity stories, and alarmed anew by occasional Choctaw altercations with white squatters or settlers in the ill-defined borderland areas, regarded them as lazy, drunken, shiftless thieves, and murderers. Few would have quarreled territorial governor Claiborne's characterization of Choctaws as "with few exceptions, very worthless characters."[116] From the perspective of most whites, the land would not be safe for decent God-fearing folk until they were gone. By their toleration of periodic intrusions on Indian treaty lands, and by their repeated failure to call to account whites who terrorized, robbed, and murdered Choctaws, Mississippi officials did their best to undermined Choctaw society. For his part, federal Indian agent William Ward made it clear that he had no interest in investigating complaints against whites. State courts offered no relief, as both Mississippi and Alabama passed statures denying Indians the right to sue or to testify in court in any cases that might be brought on their behalf.[117]

Many white Mississippians in the early 1820s were not satisfied with the federal government's Indian policy. Governor George Poindexter early in 1820 demanded that Congress force the Choctaw to sell their holdings in the state "for a small consideration" and accept a federal land grant west of the Mississippi.[118] The Monroe administration and the Mississippians agreed that Indians should not remain within the state permanently. Not only was the surrender of their land essential to the expansion of the Cotton Kingdom, but it was also presumably in the Indians' best interest. White hostility combined their own weaknesses and presumed character flaws, it was believed, in time would result in their total extinction were they not removed to sanctuaries where under federal protection they could progress on the road to "civilization." But administration was committed to a gradualist approach to removal, hoping that a noncoercive policy of persuasion coupled with appropriate generosity to those who agreed to relocate would make it possible to acquire the Indians' remaining lands east of the Mississippi without resorting to the sort of intimidation or violence that might prove not only politically embarrassing but prohibitively expensive to a nation without a substantial standing army. Thus, when Calhoun sent Commissioners John McKee and David Burnet to the Choctaws in 1818 to discuss a possible land sale that might involve resettlement in the west, he advised them to explain the advantages of that option but not press the matter if the Choctaws objected. They did object, vehemently, so the commissioners departed without gaining any new land cession. They advised that steps be taken to win the trust of the Choctaw before there was any further talk of land sales.[119]

Although personally willing to be patient, Secretary Calhoun was soon under great pressure from Mississippians eager to acquire more Choctaw land as quickly as possible. So he appointed a new negotiating commission in March 1819. The previous December, Calhoun had received a letter from Andrew Jackson relating that James Pitchlynn, the mixed-blood son of an interpreter, had advised him that contrary to the report of the 1818 commission, there was in fact considerable support within the Choctaw Nation for relocation on "lands west of the Mississippi river." Jackson enclosed a letter from Pitchlynn that attributed the failure of the previous negotiation to the personal ineptness of the commissioners and to the opposition of "the half breeds" and of the "Chiefs who have the most valuable farms and stocks" in Mississippi. If adequate provision were made for their reimbursement and future support, a removal treaty, he insisted, could be obtained. Jackson agreed with Pitchlynn's assessment and urged that the matter be reopened.[120] Calhoun in response appointed Jackson to a new commission to deal with the Choctaw land issue but urged caution. "It is the wish of the government," he advised Old Hickory, "that a treaty not be held, unless there is a strong probability of success."[121]

Jackson had no intention of not holding a treaty. Nor did he intend to honor a promise he made to Calhoun when he accepted the appointment, a promise not to resort to any sort of intimidation.[122] Sharp Knife immediately set to work devising ways of forcing the Choctaw to accept removal as their only real option. He was initially intrigued by the possibilities suggested by a bill unsuccessfully introduced in Congress by George Poindexter two years earlier, which would have forced those Choctaws who had already settled west of the Mississippi or sometimes hunted there to return to the east unless all the nation agreed to join them. He suggested to McKee that the Choctaw be warned that Congress would pass that law in its next session and that the result would be that they would no longer have hunting reserves there. He advised that the Choctaw should also be told that if they did not act promptly to accept the government's offer of relocation in Arkansas, all the land there would soon be occupied by white settlers. With insufficient game in the east to meet their needs, the tribe would then face disaster. Choctaw men, Jackson asserted, were lazy; "a vast portion of them will not labor and cannot support [themselves] East of the River by hunting." Choctaw leaders, he added, must now also be warned that continued encroachments of white settlers would soon make it impossible for many of their towns to "exist where they now are . . . necessity will compel them to separate and some join one tribe, and some another, and become extinct, and lost as a Nation."[123]

Jackson's analysis of the Choctaws' political situation was not entirely accurate. While there were members of Congress who favored radical changes in Indian policy, most still supported a gradualist approach to Indian relocation. Jackson's threat that the Choctaw would be denied access to hunting grounds in the west if they did not agree to his terms was a bluff. Congress had no intention of reconsidering Poindexter's bill. As to his assessment of the present economic status of the Choctaw, Jackson's claim that a "vast portion" of the Choctaw Nation was unwilling to do anything but hunt and if forbidden to cross the Mississippi would then go hungry was simply wrong. Choctaw farms produced large surpluses of corn which, in addition to feeding the nation and providing a valuable trade commodity, supported sizeable herds of horses and cattle. They also raised great numbers of chickens and pigs, which being considered unclean and therefore unfit for

Choctaw consumption, were sold to whites. By 1820, "farming and stock raising had become the means of subsistence" for the Choctaw.[124]

In the previous century, Choctaws, like other Indian peoples of the region, through involvement in the peltry trade, had depleted the game animal populations in their homeland and had sent hunting parties as well as some settlers across the Mississippi. But by the end of the 18th century, most Choctaw leaders recognized that the nation could no longer rely upon hunting as a major means of support. The deer skin trade in the past had left the Choctaw hungry, poor, and demoralized. It was directly responsible not only for debts that had to be discharged through land cessions but also for rampant alcoholism. Although early in the century, Pushmataha and other Choctaw chiefs had led war parties against the Caddos and other indigenous tribes in order to secure continued access to the trans-Mississippi regions, and, perhaps more importantly, to win credentials as warriors, they no longer believed preservation of the horticultural/commercial hunting economy of the colonial era possible or even desirable. Mushulatubbee, principal chief of one of the three autonomous Choctaw regions, in 1820 stated the obvious: "we cannot expect to live any longer by hunting. Our game is gone."[125] The Choctaws by that time had developed in their old homeland a new and diverse agricultural economy that blended traditional modes of exchange and reciprocity with a marketplace entailing substantial trade with whites who bought both foodstuffs and handicrafts produced by Choctaw women and livestock herded by Choctaw men. Cotton, grown on Choctaw farms and spun in their households, was among the products the women brought to market. A handful of Choctaw leaders, Mushulatubbee included, used black slaves on their cotton plantations. While Choctaw women sometimes were hired as cotton pickers on white-owned farms and plantations, Choctaw men generally refused to work as field hands. But the new economy did involve redefinition of gender roles, as males "adapted by incorporating cattle herding into their warfare and hunting traditions."[126] Although alcohol abuse among male Choctaws was a serious problem, the former warrior/hunters were by no means as lazy or unproductive as Sharp Knife imagined. As he did throughout his career, Jackson misunderstood, perhaps willfully, the nature of the Native American societies in the southeast, portraying them as backward and static.

Jackson's negotiating strategy did not succeed in 1819. Accompanied by fellow commissioners McKee and Burnet, he met with the Choctaw leaders at a site on the Yazoo River. There he "lectured, threatened and cajoled for three days—but to no avail."[127] At the end of the negotiations, the two principal chiefs present sent messages to President Monroe. Mushulatubbee complained that the land offered in Arkansas was "not as good as the one we live in." Pushmataha concurred, "I am well acquainted with the country contemplated for us. I have had my feet sorely bruised by the roughness of its surface." As to the Choctaws already there, the chief was unimpressed by the threat to expel them and give that land to whites. In fact, he asked that the federal government do just that. The Choctaws who lived there should be removed. "They have no houses or places of residence, they are like wolves, it is the wish of the [Choctaw] council that the president direct his agents in the west to order these stragglers home." As to the sale of additional Choctaw lands in Mississippi, Pushmataha declared that they had already with good grace given up every bit of land they could spare. He appealed to President Monroe to act as a father and protect the Choctaw "from danger."[128]

Jackson, infuriated by his failure, blamed his fellow commissioner John McKee for undercutting his efforts, complaining to Calhoun that McKee had been overly sympathetic to the Choctaws and had refused to employ means he regarded as "inconsistent" with their best interests. He also once again condemned the treaty-making process itself. "It is high time," he wrote, "the legislature should control the Indian tribes." Congress, in other words, should simply take their land as needed.[129] As one historian notes, "the vicious implications of this letter foreshadowed what the future would hold for the Indians when the quick-tempered western general won a prominent place in the government."[130]

In the fall of 1820, the Monroe administration resumed its efforts to relocate the Choctaw. Jackson as principal negotiator was now assisted by Mississippi militia general Thomas Hinds. He was angered by the efforts of the Choctaw factor Mr. John Hersey, who tried to advise the Choctaws in their negotiations, and labeled Hersey "one of those itinerant Yankees who are endeavouring to poison the minds of our slaves as well as the Indians." He refused Hersey's request that a letter he had written the chiefs be read to them, telling Calhoun that people like Hersey "ought never to be entrusted with an office in a southern climate."[131]

Still taken with the erroneous notion that opposition to removal came only from some "half breeds," a few profiteering chiefs, and some meddling whites, Jackson advised the secretary that he would appeal to "the real Indian chiefs" whose prime concern was "to perpetuate their existence as a nation." Jackson claimed that the Choctaws at present "are scattered and wandering over a great space of country." He asked that he be permitted to offer them a specific, well-delineated region west of the Mississippi. He proposed to "point to the land, and prescribe its bounds" explaining that it was there that "their father the President of the United States meant to settle his red children, concentrate and perpetuate them as a nation, and thereby make his people happy."[132] Calhoun quickly agreed that the commissioners could indeed delineate such a homeland "anywhere in the Quapaw purchase [in Arkansas] . . . the further to the south and west the better."[133]

Despite Jackson's belief that a large number of "real" Choctaws were eager to move to a new western homeland, the chiefs and the warriors who responded reluctantly and slowly to the summons to assemble at a place on the Yazoo called Doak's Stand (named after a white trader who ran a nearby tavern) initially refused to accept the provisions that Jackson offered them, on the grounds that they had been instructed not to enter into any discussions about new land cessions. Chief Puckshenubbe explained that as "it was not his intention to grant anything that might be asked by his father the president . . . he did not wish to subject him to any expense."[134] Only after the commissioners warned the Choctaw that the president would be gravely offended if they did not hear his message, did the Choctaw agree to listen.

Andrew Jackson opened the negotiations by announcing that "your father the President of the United States" had learned that many of "the chiefs and warriors of your nation are anxious to remove" and take possession of "a new country" west of the Mississippi. The president understood that "a large portion of his Choctaw children are in a distressed condition, and require his friendly assistance. They live upon poor land, and are not willing to cultivate it. The game is destroyed, and many of them are often reduced almost to starvation . . . Many have become beggars and drunkards. Humanity requires that something be done about it." The commissioners accordingly were empowered to offer those willing to relinquish some land in Mississippi a bountiful new homeland where "they may live and be happy." There they could farm, or "hunt the deer, the bear and the buffalo." They must understand that holding on to all of their present homeland was not an option. Within Mississippi, they had more land than they needed for farming but no good hunting territory. The whites there had only a third as much land as the Choctaw but five times as many people. They lacked enough territory to defend themselves from foreign enemies. The president's offer of an exchange of "a small part of land" in the state of Mississippi for a new homeland across the river must be accepted immediately. It might never be repeated. If they refused it, the president would be unable to defend his Choctaw children from white Mississippians. But if they accepted, his protection would be extended to all his Choctaw brothers on both sides of the river.

Jackson ended with a warning against those who advised against a new land cession. These "few designing whites and half breeds," he declared, were enemies of the majority of Choctaw. Some had gained their wealth by virtue of their occupation of "some of the valuable stands on the main roads" and hoped to keep all the Choctaw in place in order to gain further wealth through exploitation of the poor. If the Choctaw listened to them, "you will be advised by your enemies instead of your friends." Should their bad advice prevail, most Choctaw would suffer, and the nation as a whole would perish, abandoned by its friend the president.[135]

The Choctaw chiefs responded to Jackson's speech by requesting that the commissioners provide a written statement of the president's proposal. They received that statement on October 13. In it, Jackson and Hinds assured them that "your father the President of the United States . . . for securing the happiness and protection of all his Choctaw children . . . proposes to give you a large country west of the Mississippi. It will be laid off adjoining your Cherokee brothers, so that each can protect and befriend the other. The limits will extend from the Arkansas river, where the Cherokee line begins, south to the Red river, and west to the source of the Arkansas river." Those who chose to take up the president's offer would receive guns and ammunition, "sufficient for hunting and defense," and a year's supply of corn, paid for by the proceeds of some of the land they would cede in Mississippi. Provision would also be made for a school, a blacksmith, and a federal trading post to supply their needs. Those who emigrated would receive payment for whatever "improvements" they had made on their former Mississippi lands. In closing, the commissioners emphasized again the president's benevolence and stressed in particular that the plan offered a means of caring for those Choctaw "who will not work," that is, give up hunting and become farmers.[136]

Although Jackson assured them that the president now wanted only a "small" cession grant of land to whites, the land cession whose boundaries he now specified, although smaller in extent than the Arkansas grant, in fact took nearly half of the Choctaws' remaining territories. Jackson might well think they had much more land than they needed, but the chiefs could not be expected to agree, and as noted initially refused to discuss the matter. As Jackson was not provided with funds adequate for the large-scale bribery of chiefs he had previously found so useful in Indian treaty making, he now needed to rely primarily on his powers of persuasion, on time-tested techniques of threat and enticement. Jackson was correct in perceiving that some biracial chiefs who profited from the status quo would oppose him. But he was wrong in assuming that there was a large body of traditionalist Choctaw who were eager to move west but were being held back by selfish, exploitive "half breeds." The politics of Choctaw removal was far more complex than that.

The Choctaw people for many years had been divided into three autonomous districts, each led by a "mingo" or principal chief, supported by local village chiefs and war leaders. A unified Choctaw government would not be established until 1826. Although Jackson and McKee believed that one particular biracial local chief, Robert Coles, was the ringleader of "half breed" opposition to removal, Choctaw political dynamics cannot be understood as a conflict between biracial and full-blooded factions.[137] Historian James Carson argues persuasively that it is best understood in terms of differences over the means to be used to maintain Choctaw independence and cultural integrity, with a "primordialist" group less eager than the "cosmopolitans" to embrace change. The latter adhered to an "ideology that reached to outside rather than inside sources of power and that reflected an abiding need to build a new society posed somewhere between what the primordialists viewed as their ideal and what the Americans held out as 'civilization.'" Although they differed over issues such as political structure and education, with the cosmopolitans advocating changes and accommodations not favored by their foes, both groups included both biracial and full-blooded Choctaws. As the chronicles of the 1819 and 1820 negotiations indicate, neither initially favored removal. But chiefs of both persuasions finally agreed under pressure to relinquish land, heeding Andrew Jackson's warning that rejection of the treaty would be followed by the withdrawal of the favor and protection of the president of the United States, a loss that could well "prove fatal to your nation."[138] But they also worried about reprisals from Choctaws determined to yield no land. Hence, both the commissioners and the chiefs emphasized that resettlement in the Arkansas lands was voluntary.

Jackson gave his solemn word that those who chose to go there would be protected and provisioned by the federal government. But as he gave those assurances, he was well aware that the government had failed to keep its promises to some 5,000 Cherokee who, under the 1817 treaty he had negotiated, were already settled in Arkansas. Several months before, Jackson had received a letter, written by the English husband of a Cherokee woman, advising that the food promised for the first year of resettlement had never been delivered. "The sufferings and privations we had to contend with in consequence of this failure are better felt than described—hunger, sickness, and in some cases death had been the fatal consequence." Moreover, the local federal agent, contrary to the treaty promises, refused to remove the white intruders who were laying claim to land promised to the Cherokee. Jackson forwarded the letter to the administration, asking for redress.[139] But he knew from past experience that Washington could not be relied upon to keep promises to Indians. He had complained many times about problems with annuity payments.

Few Choctaw in 1820 chose to move west of the Mississippi. Those who did found some of their supposed new homeland already occupied by white settlers. The Treaty of Doak's Stand had to be replaced by a new one in 1824 compensating the Choctaw for some of the Arkansas lands they had been promised but were now unavailable.[140] Advocates of Indian removal in Mississippi were not satisfied with those treaties. In 1826, Governor Gerard Brandon repeated the state's demand for the total forcible removal of all Indians remaining in the state. At his biding, the legislature's House of Representatives initially passed an expulsion bill, but recognizing that it lacked the authority to overrule the federal government on matters relating to Indians, reconsidered and dropped the whole matter.[141] But the Choctaw in Mississippi were far from secure. Few southerners believed coexistence of Indian and white communities within states desirable or even possible.

One of Andrew Jackson's duties as commanding general of the federal army in the south was the enforcement of various laws and treaties protecting Indian rights. He made a number of efforts to remove squatters from Indian land but soon found he lacked the manpower to do the job. The intruders, he noted, "are of the worst characters," lawless riffraff who "treated the Indians badly." He issued proclamations and warnings, seized property, drove off livestock, burned down cabins, to no avail. Reporting on just one of several areas where whites had invaded Indian Territory, he wrote Calhoun that "three times, I had the stock of the intruders driven from the Cherokee land North of the Tennessee river, their houses and improvements destroyed. But this availed nothing. The troops would no sooner leave the country, than the intruders would return." Calhoun advised that Jackson should continue to use federal forces to protect Indian rights but added that white squatters should always be treated leniently.[142] Neither the Napoleon of the Woods nor his administrative superior and critic felt any inclination to resort to more punitive measures in such cases, as both believed that removal, not protection of "savages," was the only possible long-term solution to the Indian problem.

Chapter 5

Candidate

Andrew Jackson's seizure of Pensacola, by dramatizing Spanish weakness, set the stage for a renewed American diplomatic offensive intended to secure the annexation not only of the Floridas but of extensive Spanish Territory north and west of Louisiana. The Transcontinental Treaty, negotiated by Secretary of State Adams in 1819 and finally ratified in 1821, although acclaimed as a triumph at the time, was later severely criticized by southerners for failing to add Texas to the American Union. Although he would vehemently deny it in later years, Andrew Jackson in fact advised Adams that first priority must be given to the acquisition of Florida.[1] To demand Texas as well might delay both Spanish acceptance of a cession of lands and Senate ratification of a treaty. As it was, the negotiations were marked by Spanish delay and obstructionism, and might well have failed had it not been for fear of a new American invasion. Although Jackson's First Seminole War has often been passed over as a minor episode in the history of America expansionism, a recent reassessment of its immediate impact and long-term consequences argues persuasively that it played a very important role in the establishment of the United States as a new imperial power to be reckoned with in the region.[2]

In poor health, afflicted by a wracking cough, recurrent pain from bullet wounds, and attacks of dysentery and malaria, Jackson, now in his fifties, frequently spoke of resigning his military commission and retiring to the Hermitage to pursue full time the life of a gentleman planter. But as Spain delayed ratification of the Adams–Onís treaty, Jackson came to believe that his services might yet be needed in a full-scale war against "the dons." He wrote President Monroe that he had "no doubt but that Spain will attempt . . . to paralyze the nation by threats of foreign alliance." He hoped Congress would deal firmly with "the insult offered to us by the perfidy of Spain."[3] The administration, concerned with Spain's delay, asked the general to draw up a new plan for the invasion of Florida. He provided that plan, accompanied with a detailed analysis of the strengths and weaknesses of Spain's fortified settlements. Jackson now described all of them as fairly formidable. He declared St. Augustine as "one of the strongest Fortress in the World." He anticipated that, in addition to the garrison there, "300 Negroes and as many Indians as can be seduced by Spanish bribes and persuasions" would rally to its defense. In contrast to his boast in 1818 that he could easily seize East Florida as well as West Florida in a matter of weeks, Jackson now anticipated a tough campaign and emphasized the need for more troops and artillery.[4] Calhoun responded that the president found his plan "very judicious," but added that, given the time needed to prepare the troops, action would need to be delayed until the fall in order to avoid "the sickly season" that plagued Florida throughout the spring and summer.[5]

Jackson would not be called upon to lead a new invasion of Florida. Instead, he was scheduled to be retired from the federal army on June 1, 1821, under the cost-cutting measures recently mandated by Congress. Although Jackson disagreed vehemently, the lawmakers believed that there is no longer any need for augmented military forces. The anticipated crisis with Spain had not materialized. On February 21, President Monroe announced that the treaty had finally been ratified.

Earlier, the president had asked Jackson to accept appointment as governor of the new territory.[6] Jackson was reluctant to do so, advising his personal physician that, among other things, his wife Rachel found the prospect "repugnant." He added, however, that the annexation would prove profitable to American investors, suggesting in particular that "with a small fund . . . a great spec[ulation] might be made" by trafficking in negroes left behind by departing Spaniards. He advised the doctor "I name this to you that you may look and see."[7] On the same day that he wrote that letter, Jackson reconsidered, and informed Monroe that he would accept. He had been persuaded, he wrote, by concerned citizens who argued that his governorship of the former Spanish colony "would tend to draw to that country a respectable population." He stipulated, however, that he would serve only for the short time it would take to organize a new government there and put it "in full operation." He protested that "my means are not competent to bear the expenses necessary to execute the Government of that Territory for any length of time. My fortune and constitution have already been much impaired in the service of my country."[8]

Jackson resigned the governorship of Florida after four months. Residence in Pensacola did nothing to improve Rachel's feelings about the former Spanish colony. Her first impression, she wrote a friend, was of a place where "the Sabbath [was] profanely kept; a great deal of noise and swearing in the streets; shops kept open; trade going on." In deference to her feelings, the general soon imposed "Great Order . . . the doors kept shut; the gambling houses demolished; fiddling and dancing not heard any more on the Lord's day, cursing not to be heard." But, she added, despite the new rules for conduct on Sunday "still I think the Lord has a controversy with them. They were living far from God." The "worst people here," Rachel added, were "the cast out Americans and negroes."⁹ For his part, Jackson detested both the town's hot humid weather and its Spanish-speaking citizenry. During his governorship, "the Spaniards knew nothing but the contempt, fury, and near-manic behavior of the long suffering, ill, and frustrated Jackson."¹⁰ He had a particularly contentious relationship with the outgoing Spanish governor, Colonel Jose Callava, at one point jailing him in a dispute over access to some documents needed to settle a lawsuit over an inheritance brought by Mercedes Vidal, the illegitimate quadroon daughter of a wealthy deceased Spanish landowner. He also feuded with Eligius Fromentin, the federal judge Monroe had appointed for West Florida, finding the judge in league with Callava and with British merchants. In his disputes with them, Jackson saw himself as the defender of the poor and the humble against the powerful and the privileged. "Just laws," he declared in reference to the Vidal matter, "can make no distinction of privilege between rich and poor . . . In general the great can protect themselves, but the poor and humble require the arm and shield of the law."¹¹

Despite his frustrations, Jackson nonetheless accomplished much during his short time in Florida, establishing a new administrative and legal system consistent with American practice, including, for white males, universal suffrage. He deeply resented Monroe's refusal to give him complete control of all appointments, with some posts going to supporters of his adversary William H. Crawford. Nonetheless, Jackson did put in place a number of office holders who would play a major role in Florida's future.¹² But in one crucial area, he failed to achieve his objective: Indian removal.

Before Jackson's arrival in Florida, unscrupulous American land speculators and slave dealers spread the word that Sharp Knife was coming with a 2,000 man army that he would immediately use against the Indians in the colony. Many Seminoles, terrified by that rumor, sold their herds and their slaves at rock-bottom prices and fled into the interior.¹³ The impact of the 1818 invasion and the new panic on Seminole life was devastating. One of their chiefs, speaking to an American visitor, declared "When I walk about these woods, now so desolate, and remember the numerous herds that once ranged through them, and the former prosperity of our nation, the tears come into my eyes."¹⁴ The demoralized Seminoles were not only hungry, some were actually starving to death.¹⁵

Andrew Jackson did not in fact return to Florida in 1821 with a large military force. The American army's presence in the former Spanish colony was minimal. However, Jackson, although he had neither the means nor the authority to carry it out, was persuaded that the security and prosperity of an Americanized Florida required that all Indians be removed from the territory. He denied that the Seminoles had any legitimate land rights in Florida, as most of them were renegade Creeks not indigenous to the territory. He argued that their removal should be accomplished not through treaty making but through a direct non-negotiable assertion of government authority backed up by military power.¹⁶ Secretary of War Calhoun was sympathetic but advised Jackson that the immediate forced deportation he advocated was politically impossible. Another solution must be found. Jackson, soon finding that he lacked the forces needed to round up and deport the Seminoles in any case, reluctantly agreed. He suggested concentrating them on a small reserve near the Apalachicola River, a solution soon opposed by whites who coveted that land.[17]

Soon after assuming office, the newly appointed governor summoned chiefs representing both Red Stick Creeks who had taken refuge in Florida and Seminoles who had been there for half a century or more and advised them that their past offenses against the United States were forgiven. They would now enjoy the benevolent protection of the president of the United States. But they could no longer be permitted "to settle all over the Floridas and on her Sea Coast." Instead, Jackson promised, they would be given a reservation and would be expected to stay within its limits. He believed his "talk" had been well received.[18] In the weeks and months that followed, the Seminoles, demoralized and impoverished, remained peaceful, cautiously hoping for the best.

The reservation of which Jackson spoke was not established during his brief governorship, nor was it located near the Apalachicola. Two years after he left Pensacola, Seminole leaders were finally summoned to a site near St. Augustine. There, in the words of one eminent Florida historian, "American commissioners bribed and intimidated the Seminoles into the Treaty of Moultrie Creek."[19] The chief commissioner, Jackson protégé James Gadsden, had assured his mentor that his colleagues clearly understood that "we have only to dictate and the Indians must and will no doubt agree." There would be no recognition at Moultrie Creek of "the right of their refusing."[20] Gadsden and his colleagues had no intention of following the recommendations of the select congressional committee which, after investigating the situation in Florida, had recommended that the Seminoles be granted full citizenship, as required under the terms of the Adams–Onís transfer treaty, and given individual family land grants and other assistance to enable them to live harmoniously with their new white neighbors.[21] To the negotiators, citizenship was out of the question, and good land was not to be wasted on Indians. The reservation the commissioners now mapped out for the Seminoles was described by Jackson's successor, Governor William P. Duval, as "by far the poorest and most miserable region I have ever beheld."[22] Covering swampy marshlands and expanses of sandy soil ill-suited for horticulture, its boundaries ran from a point slightly above present-day Ocala on the north to the latitude of Tampa Bay on the south. Its eastern and western limits were drawn to prohibit any Seminole settlement within 20 miles of the Atlantic or 15 miles of the Gulf of Mexico, lest Indians continue their contacts with Spanish traders from Cuba or British agents from the Bahamas.

Chiefs familiar with the area begged the commissioners not to send them there. To co-opt the most influential sources of opposition, six of the most prominent Seminole leaders—Neamathla, Emathlochee, Blunt, Mulatto King, and Tusli Hajo—were personally exempted from relocation and granted the right to remain in the Apalachicola River region in north Florida. The rest were forced not only to resettle on the reservation in central Florida and deed over the rest of the territory to the United States but were also ordered to discontinue their prior practice of granting refuge to runaway Negroes. All Seminoles were now obligated by treaty to capture and turn over to white authorities any blacks who might seek their help. In exchange for giving up all claims to any other part of Florida, the Seminoles were promised some compensation (never fully paid) and a food subsidy. They were also to be provided with a school and with the services of a blacksmith and gunsmith. The total cost to the government is estimated at $221,000, less than a cent an acre. The treaty did not achieve its objectives, as only about 1,000 Seminoles out of a population estimated at around 5,000 actually resettled on the new reservation.[23]

The Florida territorial legislative council nine years after its ratification formally recognized, in a petition to Congress for funding, that the Treaty of Fort Moultrie had relegated Indians to a wilderness without adequate food resources, where they were "left with the wretched alternative of Starving within their limits or roaming among the whites, to prey upon their cattle." But rather than seeking an enlargement of Seminole Territory, the Council in 1827 had passed legislation allowing any white settler troubled by Indian intruders to seize the offenders and turn them over to justices of the peace empowered to administer "no more than thirty-nine lashes." It followed that up with a call for the removal of all Indians from Florida.[24] As president, Andrew Jackson would respond to that demand some years later, and trigger the longest, and arguably most controversial, Indian wars in the nation's history.

After leaving the Florida governorship in November 1821, Jackson's political future was obscure. His various aliments left him, for a time, bedridden at the Hermitage. As he convalesced, he devoured current newspapers and ploughed through his voluminous correspondence. He was now embittered against Monroe, whose support during his governorship he found lacking. The president, among other slights, had brushed off his complaints against Judge Fromentin. Moreover, Jackson was deeply alarmed by the prospect that William H. Crawford, a man he regarded as both untrustworthy and corrupt, and as a personal enemy, might well be Monroe's successor. Agreeing that a Crawford presidency would be a disaster for the nation, he assured one correspondent "I would support the Devil first."[25] But Crawford was hardly the nation's only politician whose alleged misdeeds upset the retired general. As he sat in his study at the Hermitage, Jackson scribbled notes to himself referring to news items about various scandals which he intermixed with angry comments about unfair criticism, in the press and elsewhere, of his own past conduct at New Orleans and in the Seminole campaign. Old Hickory in the waning days of 1821 was "a gloomy and morose convalescent."[26]

But he was not a forgotten man. Numerous correspondents and some visitors told him that only his own presidential candidacy could guarantee Crawford's defeat. Some also suggested that only a Jackson presidency could truly secure the nation's safety by restoring republican values. The general, both flattered and deeply touched, listened carefully. After at first disavowing any interest in succeeding Monroe, Jackson by the spring of 1822 was telling supporters that while he would not seek the office, he would respond to the people's call if it came. Duty, he declared, required that he not say no.[27] On July 27, 1822, the Tennessee legislature's lower house nominated Jackson for the presidency of the United States. On August 3, the Tennessee Senate added its endorsement. (Not all who voted for the nomination were genuine Jackson supporters. Some were Clay partisans who hoped to outflank Crawford.[28]) In October, the legislature, in a divided vote, elected him to the United States Senate. After an absence of over two decades, Andrew Jackson would once again serve in Congress. And he was now a candidate for the nation's highest office.

Jackson did not welcome his new role as a federal senator. Memories of past national legislative service were not happy ones. He deferred to the judgment of friends and supporters who felt it essential that their presidential candidate now be a presence in Washington, D.C. But he soon wrote Rachel, who remained at the Hermitage, to complain about the empty time-consuming social rituals he once again had to observe.[29] But he carried them out with skill and grace, noting wryly that those who expected he would confront them with a scalping knife in one hand and a tomahawk in the other were soon disappointed.[30] Uncharacteristically, he went to some pains to reconcile with certain old adversaries, including Winfield Scott, who was relieved not to be challenged to a duel, and Missouri's senator Thomas Hart Benton, who had left Jackson severely wounded after a barroom brawl in Nashville a decade earlier.[31] Despite his passionate and often irascible nature, and well-known disinclination to suffer those he considered fools gladly, Jackson understood that politics is personal, and that he needed to turn some old enemies into friends and to neutralize some others. The old warrior even dined several times with his arch enemy Henry Clay. Despite his well-cultivated public image as a nonpolitician, as the original outsider, Old Hickory was in fact a skillful master of the politician's art. As his biographer Jon Meacham notes, while Jackson could "lapse into alarming violence . . . he also had a capacity for political grace and conciliation when the spirit moved him."[32] During the 1823–1824 Senate term, it was that capacity that was on full display. Mrs. Daniel Webster, writing to her brother, reported that Jackson was not the "perfect savage" she had expected to meet. He was winning over polite society with his "very mild and gentlemanly" manners. She added, "It is only for him to be seen to make him the most favorite candidate."[33]

Jackson complained that the Senate transacted very little real business. His first vote as a senator concerned the ratification of the Treaty of Moultrie Creek. Jackson predictably voted for ratification but opposed the tenth article of the treaty, which expressed the chiefs' appreciation of Indian agent Gad Humphreys and awarded him a one-mile square land grant near Tallahassee. He supported a change in the language of the treaty, replacing "Seminole tribe" with "Florida tribes." The Congress did not address overall Indian policy issues during Jackson's tenure as a senator. But some of the measures that it did consider were of interest to those who hoped to extend Mr. Jefferson's "Empire of Liberty." Jackson voted in favor of several federal expenditures for roads that, in his view, would enhance national defense and promote territorial expansion. His most controversial vote was in support of the Tariff of 1824, an act he justified to critics as essential to national security. He consistently opposed amendments that would have lowered duties. Jackson supported abolition of imprisonment for debt and a two-term limit for future presidents, measures that failed to win majority support. Generally, however, he voted with the majority. As a legislator, he did not stand out. Jackson restricted his few public comments to brief factual reports from the Military Affairs Committee, which he chaired.[34]

In the run up to the presidential election, three of the candidates—Clay, Adams, and Calhoun—were understood to be supporters of a nationalist, essentially neo-Hamiltonian program ultimately termed "the American System," a program that envisioned the use of federal power to promote national economic growth. Initially, its sponsors called on the federal government to finance internal improvements, with particular emphasis on road construction. A moderate and selective federal protective tariff would raise funds for those ventures and also encourage industrial development. Later, support for the nationally chartered national bank and the orderly development of the west through a conservative land sale policy that would generate revenue to fund internal improvements became part of the program. Implicit in the American System from the outset was the acceptance of a loose constructionist reading of the Constitution. A fourth candidate, Secretary of the Treasury William Crawford, considered the front-runner, was regarded as a foe of such activism. Crawford, it was believed, stood for states' rights and strict construction. He was supported by the Richmond Junto, led by Thomas Ritchie of Virginia, and by Marin Van Buren's Albany Regency. Those four aspirants were all well connected and well entrenched in the Washington establishment.

The fifth candidate, General Andrew Jackson, although now a national celebrity, was an outsider. His candidacy initially was not taken very seriously by some of those in power. But he soon proved, by virtue of his heroic public image and popular appeal, a formidable contender. Supporters of his rivals quickly mounted a propaganda campaign describing Jackson as a crude, ignorant, uneducated, intemperate, and brutal "military chieftain" unfit for high office. To cite two examples of many, one pamphleteer, purporting to review Jackson's military record, concluded, "His only delight is in scenes of blood and carnage."[35] Another declared him "the notorious violator of every law of God and man."[36] But it was soon apparent that defamation of the hero would not be effective. He was winning support in surprising places. John C. Calhoun, who had counted on support from Pennsylvania, dropped out of the presidential race when Jackson won the endorsement of party leaders in the Keystone state. The South Carolinian ran for the vice presidency instead, teaming up with Jackson in most states and with Adams in some others.

Jackson's campaign did not address specific questions about the proper limits on the role of the federal government or offer a legislative agenda. Instead, his supporters mounted an all-out frontal attack on those who were currently governing. The tone was set by the appearance in Philadelphia early in 1824 of a slender volume titled *The Letters of Wyoming, to the People of the United States, on the Presidential Election, and in Favor of Andrew Jackson* Anonymously authored by Jackson's military aide and future secretary of war John Henry Eaton, its 12 letters had previously been published in the *Columbian Observer*. Those letters argued that of all the candidates only Andrew Jackson was a man of "virtue" in touch with the country's "honest yeomanry." The rest were dishonest schemers seeking to enrich themselves at public expense. Jackson alone had shed his own blood and risked his own life in the cause of freedom, first in the Revolution, then repeatedly in a long, honorable career. He was a second Washington.[37] Other Jackson spokesmen struck the same note, representing Old Hickory's mission as nothing less than the restoration of honesty and integrity in government. The movement historians came to call "Jacksonian Democracy" had many facets and was not without its inconsistencies and contradictions, but one theme dominated its rhetoric from the beginning: the deliverance of the Republic from the grasp of a designing, selfish, and corrupt would be aristocracy of privilege, power, and wealth.

The national scene in 1824 lent itself to allegations of corruption and conspiracy. The so-called Era of Good Feelings was imagined to be a time free of partisan rancor. But the demise of the Federalist Party did not in fact bring political tranquility but vicious infighting as cabinet officers vied for the succession and freely employed patronage, nepotism, and sweetheart government contracts in their quest.[38] The two-party system was dead, but the surviving party could no longer make a binding presidential nomination. When Crawford's supporters endeavored to deliver the Republican Party's nomination to him through use of the traditional congressional caucus, legislators committed to other candidates cried foul and boycotted the proceedings. Jackson declared in a letter to Rachel reporting on events in the nation's capital that it was his mission to "save the nation from the rule of Demagogus, who by intrigue are and have attempted to cheat the people out of their constitutional rights, by a caucus of congressional members."[39] To his ward and aide Andrew Jackson Donaldson, Old Hickory observed astutely that "such is the feelings of the nation that a recommendation by a congressional caucus would politically Damn any name put forth by it."[40]

Crawford's candidacy was damaged not only by the caucus controversy but by a catastrophic health crisis. A stroke left him paralyzed, mute, and partially blind. While physicians correctly predicted that Crawford would ultimately recover, he was in no condition to serve as president. But his backers persisted in their efforts to secure his election. In 1824, seven states—Vermont, New York, Delaware, Georgia, New York, South Carolina, and Louisiana—still entrusted the task of selecting their presidential electors to the legislature. In the remaining states, 17 in number, electors were now chosen by a vote of the people. Jackson ran a strong race in every section of the country except New England and dominated the vote in the South. But he fell short of an absolute majority in the Electoral College.

He led the field, winning 99 votes, 31 short of the number needed for election. He also led in the popular vote, with 152,901 votes against 114,023 for Adams, 47,217 for Clay, and 46,979 for Crawford, but here too he lacked a majority. But he had every reason to expect to be elevated to the presidential chair. Under the Constitution, the election would now be decided by the House of Representatives, with each delegation casting one vote. Only the top three candidates in the electoral vote were eligible for election. Clay, although third in the popular vote, was disqualified, as a combination of pro-Adams and pro-Jackson legislators had deprived him of a needed electoral vote in Louisiana. Jackson had carried 11 states and expected support of their congressional representatives. He needed two more states. The legislature of Henry Clay's home state of Kentucky, a state Clay had won, instructed its representatives to vote for Jackson. In other states Clay had carried, Jackson had been a close second choice.

Jackson's supporters appealed to their congressmen to respect the popular will. In early January, however, Jackson heard that "a coalition is about to be formed . . . of Crawford, Clay and Adams . . . for the purpose of defeating my election."[41] Washington was soon awash in rumors of conspiracies and sell-outs. Jackson, not certain what to believe, reported to a close friend that it seemed that the whole cabinet might be working against him. He declared that he personally would not engage in "unions, combinations, or intrigue" to win the presidency.[42] One story held that Adams had agreed to name Clay secretary of state in exchange for his support for the presidency. That rumor was widely believed, as Henry Clay, unable to advance his own personal cause, was in fact now using his very substantial influence in Congress and elsewhere on Adams's behalf.

Adams had won only seven states in the Electoral College. But, primarily because of Clay's prodding, delegates of six states Adams had not carried (including four whose popular vote had actually been won by Jackson) voted in Congress to make the New Englander president. He won the office with a bare majority of 13 votes on February 9. Jackson's supporters would soon charge that the election had been "stolen" from the people, and historians over the years have echoed that charge. It is an essential part of the myth of "Jacksonian Democracy."[43] But while Jackson had won a plurality of the popular vote in 1824, it must be remembered that several states (most notably New York) did not hold a popular election but selected electors by legislative caucus. Historian Donald Ratcliffe calculates the probable popular vote had direct elections of electors been held in those states and estimates that Jackson would have outpolled Adams in those states by a count of 92,228 to 34,313 and thereby gained a comfortable popular plurality nationwide. His argument is persuasive, despite the skepticism inspired by such exact hypothetical numbers, as Jackson had very little support in New York, and had not yet won over the conservative southerners who supported Crawford.[44]

A few days after his election, the president-elect announced that he would indeed name Clay secretary of state, an appointment considered by many a stepping stone to the presidency itself. Washington was stunned. General Jackson maintained his composure in public, but privately he was enraged. On hearing the news he had exclaimed "the Judas of the West has closed the contract and will receive his thirty pieces of silver—his end will be the same. Was there ever witnessed such a bare faced corruption in any country before?"[45] Jackson returned to the Hermitage with his conviction that the country faced disaster at the hands of a venal office-holding gang confirmed and deepened. Under Jackson's guidance, his supporters would raise the cry "Corrupt Bargain" over and over again in the years to come. Those words would damage Adams's presidency irreparably. They would permanently blight Clay's persistent efforts to win that office. For Andrew Jackson, they were a political godsend.[46]

While Indian policy issues played no direct role in the election of 1824, there is no doubt that Jackson's reputation as the nation's preeminent Indian fighter, and as a tough treaty negotiator committed to Indian removal, enhanced his appeal to voters in the south and west. Controversies over President Adams's handling of Indian affairs would strengthen Jackson's hold on those voters in 1828. The first controversy developed in the early months of the Adams administration. Three days before Adams was inaugurated, the Senate voted to endorse the Treaty of Indian Springs. The treaty stipulated that the Creeks would give up all their lands within the state of Georgia and also cede extensive tracts in Alabama. The treaty included special favors for certain compliant Creek leaders. Adams at first saw nothing objectionable in the agreement, so he endorsed its ratification. Under the compact of 1802, there was a long-standing agreement between Georgia and the United States that in exchange for Georgia's abandonment of its claims to the western lands that would soon become Alabama and Mississippi, the federal government would seek through negotiation the removal of all of Georgia's Indians. But two decades later Indians still occupied large parts of Georgia. In exasperation, the state legislature in December 1823 had sent President Monroe a memorial complaining that the federal government's failure to remove all of the state's Indians exposed the frontier "to the predatory incursions of the Savages, and the lives of her citizens who dwell there, to their subtle and relentless vengeance." The legislators demanded that "the soil of Georgia . . . no longer be imprinted with the footstep of the savage."[47] For the incoming president, ratification and enforcement of this new treaty would solve a very troublesome political problem.

Although he was, as we have repeatedly noted, an eager advocate of removal, Andrew Jackson had not voted on the Indian Springs treaty, explaining to a correspondent that on the day it came before the Senate, he was "confined to my room by the severe indisposition of Mrs. Jackson." But had he been there, he continued, he would have suspected immediately that the treaty was fraudulent, as it contained "none of the old chiefs names but McIntosh." The other so-called chiefs who signed the document, Jackson declared, were "self created" to give the impression of tribal support for a "fictitious treaty." Had he had the opportunity, Jackson continued, "I should have moved its postponement and called for information from the President."[48]

The president was soon in possession of ample information about the Treaty of Indian Springs, information that would lead him to take the unprecedented step of calling on Congress to revoke its ratification on grounds that the constituted authorities of the Creek Nation refused to recognize the treaty's legitimacy. The circumstances of the treaty's negotiation were indeed questionable. During the previous year, Adams's predecessor James Monroe had sent two commissioners to the Creeks, with instructions to secure, if possible, their removal to lands yet to be designated west of the Mississippi. The Creek chiefs, in meetings beginning on December 7, 1824, made it clear that they would not agree to such a proposition. The commissioners, Duncan Campbell and James Meriwether, responded in a singularly high-handed and inept manner, telling the assembled Creek chiefs that they had no right to any of the Georgia lands they then occupied. The Creek, the commissioners asserted, were not natives but invaders, having migrated from the west and displaced the original inhabitants some years earlier. They, therefore, could not claim the land by ancestral right. Nor could they claim ownership by virtue of current occupancy, as the Americans by winning the Revolutionary War owned it by right of conquest. Indians were merely tenants on lands, which now belonged to the United States. But their tenancy could not continue, as their removal from Georgia had been mandated by the federal government's 1802 Compact with that state.[49]

The commissioners' assumption that the Creeks were so ill-informed as to accept those specious arguments is laughable. The chiefs knew very well that the Compact did not mandate forced removal but only committed the United States to negotiate relocation "peacefully and on reasonable terms." The notion that the Creeks were not regarded by the United States as landowners was belied by a long series of treaties beginning with the Treaty of New York in 1790. As for the present, the Creek representatives made it clear that they did not wish to enter into any more land cession agreements. They had too little land left. Accordingly, their national council had renewed a law that stipulated that any Creek who agreed to a new land sale should be put to death. The chiefs had no choice, declaring that "we must positively decline the proposal of a removal beyond the Mississippi, or the sale of any more of our territory."[50]

That should have ended the matter, for the time being anyway. But it did not. Campbell and Meriwether proceeded to launch "a gigantic fraud" by passing out bribes "with a startlingly generous hand" to anyone, Creek or white, who might be of help in securing a removal treaty. Although there were many recipients of their largess, Andrew Jackson's old associate Chief William McIntosh "was the object of the commissioners' special attention." Their plan was to negotiate with McIntosh the cession of all the Creeks land in Georgia, land occupied by about 10,000 Creeks, half of the population of the nation. For his efforts, and in payment for land reserves he had been given in an earlier cession, the chief would receive $40,000, a huge sum in 1825. But there was a problem. The commissioners' orders from Monroe directed them to deal with the Creek National Council, not with McIntosh alone. But the council as a whole was not bribable. Accordingly, they now asked to be allowed to negotiate with the chiefs in Georgia, rather than with the council, which essentially meant dealing only with McIntosh and a few of his hirelings.[51]

Monroe wisely turned down that request, but the commissioners took advantage of an ambiguity in their instructions and went ahead anyway. McIntosh for his part was well aware that his activities were punishable by death under Creek law. To conceal his new involvement with the Americans, McIntosh continued to oppose in public any land concessions. Afraid for his life, he met with the commissioners only under cover of darkness.[52] He appealed to the president of the United States for special protection, claiming that those Creeks like himself who were friendly to the United States and agreeable to land negotiations now found their lives endangered by a new Red Stick conspiracy.[53] While his talk of a Red Stick revival was fanciful, McIntosh nonetheless had much reason for anxiety, as he was already an object of suspicion because of his involvement with Campbell, a year earlier, in a scheme to obtain through bribery the consent of Cherokee leaders to their removal from Georgia. McIntosh made the mistake of trying to bribe John Ross, and compounded his error by putting the offer in writing. Ross summoned the tribal leadership and read them McIntosh's letter. The Cherokee National Council, which had previously accepted the Creek general as a trusted friend and adviser, promptly expelled him from their territory and warned his Creek countrymen of his treachery. The Creek chiefs, now uncertain about his reliability, then removed McIntosh as speaker of the council. McIntosh's efforts to explain away the Cherokee affair were supported by the American negotiators, who lied about his role, but were not entirely convincing. His continued loud public endorsements of the Creek law providing the death penalty for those who sold land to whites disarmed some but by no means all of his critics. They would soon discover that their doubts were well founded.[54]

Abandoning the designated treaty grounds at Broken Arrow within the Creek Nation, the commissioners reconvened on February 10 at the tavern owned by McIntosh at Indian Springs in central Georgia. They were joined by McIntosh, by a number of his followers, and some independent headmen who were opposed to removal. The pro-removal chiefs in league with McIntosh represented only eight of the fifty-six towns that made up the Creek confederacy. Only one of them—McIntosh himself—was a member of the Creek National Council. But at Indian Springs that minority ratified and signed a treaty, previously drawn up in secret by McIntosh and the commissioners, that not only gave up all of the Creek lands in Georgia but sold some two-thirds of their holdings in Alabama as well. Under the treaty's provisions, the Creeks were to receive in exchange lands west of the Mississippi and payment for the improved lands they were giving up. (The lion's share of those funds was specifically earmarked for McIntosh and a handful of his followers.) Campbell and Meriwether, in presenting the treaty for ratification, assured the federal authorities that "the opposition was feeble," with most of the chiefs now assenting to removal.[55]

That, as Adams and others would soon discover, was a lie. Even at Indian Springs, most of the Creek headmen present refused to sign the treaty. The commissioners had not acted independently to represent the interests of the United States in securing a treaty that would be acceptable to the Creeks but had been in collusion with Georgia officials from the outset and had represented only their interests. As to the Creek negotiators, it must be noted that Chief William McIntosh was a cousin of Georgia's governor George M. Troup. Neither John Crowell, the local federal Indian agent, nor the members of the Creek National Council had been present at the secret meetings at which McIntosh and the commissioners drew up Treaty of Indian Springs. Crowell had written to the secretary of war the day after the treaty was signed to warn that it was not supported by the real Creek leadership.[56] The national council, assisted by Indian agent Crowell, sent representatives to Washington, D.C., to expose the treaty fraud. Their claims were initially ignored. The national council, hoping that the fraudulent treaty would not be ratified, delayed in ordering McIntosh's execution for violation of the law against land sales. But McIntosh, against his better judgment, then agreed to Governor Troup's demand that the surveying of Creek land for reassignment to whites through a state lottery begin at once, in violation of a treaty provision giving the Creeks several months' time to prepare for removal. Outraged, the council, having declared him guilty of a capital crime, dispatched law menders to put him to death. On April 30, 1825, a band said to number around 150 warriors surrounded McIntosh's plantation, set its buildings on fire, and shot McIntosh and one of his supporters. Two others were executed elsewhere later in the day. The council made clear that the Creeks would not recognize the legitimacy of the Treaty of Indians Springs.[57]

President Adams supported Indian removal at this stage in his career. His administration initially hoped that the Creeks could be persuaded to keep the peace and accept the treaty despite the controversy over its origins. He later assured Congress that he had done his best to secure their acquiescence. But General Edmund Gaines, entrusted with the task of dealing directly with the Creeks in Georgia, found that while the frantic warnings of an imminent Indian attack emanating from the state's governor were without any foundation, his informants did believe that most of the Creek were willing to accept death passively "rather than sell or leave" their land. As to the treaty itself, the general's aide-de-camp summed up the situation as follows: "Such a mass of corruption and bribery as has been elicited in the course of the investigation and will be exposed in the next session of Congress, has never been presented to the world." A special agent, Major T. P. Andrews, also dispatched to Georgia to look into the matter, reached essentially the same conclusion.[58]

President Adams, after receiving those reports concluded that the Treaty of Indian Springs needed to be renegotiated. He ordered the state of Georgia to suspend its lottery survey of Creek lands. Governor Troup, in language so extreme some questioned his sanity, damned agent Crowell and General Gaines, demanded the execution of the Creeks who had killed McIntosh, and threatened civil war if the federal government interfered with the enforcement of the original treaty. The Georgia militia, he proclaimed, would protect the state's sovereign right to take the Creek lands. The Adams administration responded that federal troops would be used to uphold the "the faith of the nation" by blocking the implementation of the Indian Springs fraud. After much bluster, Troup backed off and allowed the Adams administration to resolve the conflict by negotiating a new agreement with the Creeks. The Treaty of Washington of 1826 restored their Alabama lands and a very narrow strip of territory in northwest Georgia (territory they would give up in a new agreement a year later) but overall it was not very favorable to the Creeks. They were required, on very short notice, to evacuate almost all of their Georgia holdings and relocate the major part of their population. The chiefs did not want to leave Georgia, but learning from their meetings with federal officials that the national government ultimately would not protect them against the white Georgians, they came to realize they had no real choice. The president warned that if a new treaty satisfactory to Georgia were not negotiated, Congress would insist on the enforcement of the Indian Springs document and he would have no choice but to comply.

Although Adams secured for Georgia almost all of the Creek lands within the state, the controversy won Andrew Jackson new supporters. Adams's respect for the rights of the Creek National Council, implying his endorsement of the sovereignty of an Indian nation, was offensive to many southerners. In the presidential election of 1828, Adams received not a single vote in Georgia, as he was excluded from the ballot. He fared poorly elsewhere in the south and west.[59] The irony is that Adams during his presidency was not in fact particularly pro-Indian. In diary, he noted his agreement with Henry Clay who, despite his public excoriation of Jackson's cruelty to Indians, advised the cabinet that Native Americans were an inferior race whose extinction was inevitable.[60] Adams did, however, note privately that despite Americans' claims to be a benevolent people, "none of that benevolence is felt when the rights of the Indian come into collision with the interests of the white man."[61] Later, as a member of Congress, Adams would emerge as one of the most vociferous of the critics of removal.

Jackson, as noted earlier, recognized that the Treaty of Indian Springs was fraudulent. He was unimpressed by Troup's defiance of federal authority, declaring that "his whole conduct of late has offered evidence of derangement."[62] But he also found Georgia's harassment of her Indian inhabitants useful in disabusing Indians of the idea that they could obtain any security by selling part of their eastern holdings and remaining on the remainder. In a letter to a recently appointed commissioner charged with negotiating new land cessions with the Chickasaws, Jackson wrote of the great importance of "concentrating our Southern tribes of Indians to a point west of the Mississippi, thereby strengthening our southern border with a white population that will occupy the lands." He advised the commissioner to cite "the case of Georgia" in his talks with the Chickasaw, so that they would come to understand that "situated where they are . . . they will always be exposed to encroachments from the white people." Partial land sales would not improve their lot. They must give up all their holdings east of the river.[63]

Jackson's followers in Congress did nothing to support Adams's efforts to correct the Indian Springs fraud. A Senate investigating committee chaired by Thomas Hart Benton commended Governor Troup and condemned the president for infringing upon Georgia's states' rights. Benton and seven other senators voted against ratification of the new treaty, on grounds that the Treaty of Indian Springs should have been enforced so that all the lands in Alabama and Georgia it specified could be taken from the Creek.[64]

For white Georgians in the Jacksonian era, the Indian territories within their borders were a promised land. Georgia alone among the states did not offer ceded Indian land for sale but awarded it free to the winners of a state lottery. A popular ballad of the day reflected their hope of a good life to come through Indian dispossession proclaiming:

> All I want in this creation
> Is a pretty little wife and a big plantation
> Away up yonder in the Cherokee Nation.[65]

The federal Indian agent entrusted with relations with the Cherokee in the years after the 1802 agreement with Georgia was Colonel Return J. Meigs, who served from 1801 until his death in 1823.[66] Born in Connecticut, he had served as a militia officer during the Revolutionary War and soon thereafter was one of the founders of Marietta Ohio. Although Andrew Jackson felt that Meigs, born a Yankee, was too sympathetic to his Cherokee charges, the agent in fact believed that the Cherokee were occupying far too much territory, and accordingly worked assiduously and successfully to persuade their chiefs to agree to several new treaties ceding vast tracts of land to the United States. His ultimate goal, like Jackson's, was total Indian removal. The Cherokee for their own well-being and security, he believed, should ultimately abandon all their eastern holdings and move west of the Mississippi. Although he followed the conventional practice of negotiating land cession treaties, Meigs did not believe that Indians had any ongoing right to all the lands they occupied. Not only were they a conquered people declining in numbers, but they were "savages" who did not make proper use of the soil. Indians, he believed, had no right to refuse to give up territory needed by an expanding and civilized white population. Like Jackson and other men of the frontier south, Meigs held that they were only "tenants at will," not real landowners. Although more tactful and, one might say, more honorable than Jackson in his dealings with the Cherokee, Meigs shared Old Hickory's vision of a Republic free of independent Indians.

To achieve his objectives, which involved both the acquisition of Cherokee land and the transformation (some would say elimination) their culture through the "civilization" program, the agent meddled extensively in Cherokee political and economic life, supporting pliable chiefs with bribes and favors, while seeking to marginalize the less cooperative. Those particularly favored by Meigs received special land grants, cash awards, and in some cases lucrative commercial concessions to operate ferries and taverns. Befriended by the agent, enriched by his patronage, they often lived in the style of wealthy slave-holding white planters. Meigs defended the largess he bestowed upon them by arguing that the example of their affluence would inspire their more backward fellow tribesmen to abandon the old ways and cooperate with those who sought to bring them "civilization." But Meigs success in creating a new elite class of affluent tribal leaders, many of them the mixed-blood descendants of Anglo-American traders, undercut his case for removal. Those Cherokee leaders who were prospering had strong incentives to remain on their land.

In 1807, after the assassination of Meigs's corrupt and brutal ally Chief Doublehead, the agent found it harder to control an increasingly suspicious and recalcitrant Cherokee leadership. They could no longer be easily won over through favors and bribes. Paradoxically, the political changes, educational advances, and economic innovations encouraged by Meigs were instrumental in the emergence, not of a generation of compliant and subservient admirers of the United States, but of a new and defiantly independent Cherokee Nation, with a unified national council replacing the decentralized village-based Upper Creek and Lower Creek polities.

That council was firmly opposed to removal. No longer could Meigs control the Cherokee through manipulation of a divided leadership. On the eve of the War of 1812, Meigs's superiors ordered him to suspend efforts to persuade the Cherokee to move west, lest the British be given opportunity to exploit Cherokee disaffection. As we have noted in an earlier chapter, Andrew Jackson's postwar effort to force the Cherokee to concede that they had entered into a removal agreement with President Thomas Jefferson ended in failure. While several thousand Cherokee did relocate west of the Mississippi during the early years of the 19th century, continuing efforts to persuade the remainder of the nation to join them had been unavailing. Most recently, as you will recall, agents Campbell and Meriwether had tried and failed to obtain Cherokee removal through bribery and coercion. In 1822, Cherokee chief Charles Hicks spoke for his generation when he advised Georgia governor John Clark, "I wish you Sir to understand distinctly that we are unwilling to sell one foot of our circumscribed country, although we are reduced to a handful and you are becoming as the trees of the forest."[67]

Throughout Adams's administration, Georgia's governor and her congressional delegation demanded that the federal government make good on its 1802 promise to secure the removal of all Indians, including Cherokee, from the state. Federal efforts to secure a new land cession and removal treaty once again led nowhere. Adams, while sharing Georgia's exasperation with the Cherokee, refused to resort to coercion. Nor would he permit Georgia to do so, rejecting Troup's claim that the federal government had no right to protect Indians from state action as the state was "sovereign upon her own soil."[68] (States' rights, in this view, trumped federal treaty guarantees.) The issue came to a head with the adoption by the Cherokees in 1827 of a national constitution, which formed a governing structure closely modeled on that of the United States. In defiance of Georgia, the Cherokee Nation had proclaimed its sovereignty and, abandoning its traditional tribal structure, had created a Euro-American model state. Governor Troup immediately demanded that President Adams declare the Cherokee constitution illegal. Adams, though displeased by the Cherokees' actions, did nothing. As the controversy progressed,

Adams had privately developed some grave doubts about the wisdom and justice of removal. "My own opinion," he told the pro-removal Baptist missionary Isaac McCoy, "is that the most benevolent course towards them would be to give them the rights and subject them to the duties of citizens, as part of our own people." He noted regretfully that the "people of the States within which they are situated" would not permit "that humane solution."[69]

In his annual message to Congress, on February 5, 1827, Adams, troubled by reports from Georgia of plans to invade the Cherokee Nation, warned the state that he would use military force, if necessary, to protect "the territories secured by solemn treaty to the Indians."[70] Presidential candidate Andrew Jackson, solidly on the side of the state, greeted that threat with scorn, writing to his future secretary of war that Adams's "declaration of War against Geo[rgia]" was "too preposterous and absurd for belief." The president's "little army of 6,000" would hardly be equal to the task, Jackson opined, and the militias of the southern and western states clearly would "never arm in such a cause."[71] Nor would Jackson. His views on the matter were well known. It was generally understood that Adams's defeat at the polls would close the door to any moderate solution to the Cherokee-Georgia conflict. Shortly after Jackson's electoral victory, word spread in Georgia that the president-elect had responded to a congressman's question about hastening Cherokee removal by advising Georgians to "build a fire under them. When it gets hot enough, they'll move."[72] The recently established Cherokee newspaper, the *Phoenix*, on December 10, 1828, predicted that under the newly elected Jackson administration, "republican tyranny" would lead to their expulsion from their homeland.[73] Those words were prophetic.

Andrew Jackson's renewed campaign for the presidency had begun shortly after Adams's inauguration and was coordinated from the Hermitage by Jackson himself. He forged new political alliances, first with Vice President John C. Calhoun, then with Martin Van Buren, and other former Crawford supporters that not only advanced his presidential prospects but provided the core of what would emerge in a few years as a new political party. The theme of reform in government, of the restoration and preservation of a republic grounded in respect for the will of the people, of deliverance from a would-be aristocracy, continued to be the major motif of Jackson's crusade. To those whose passions were moved by the Jacksonian appeal, the movement's objective was nothing less than the salvation of the country. Editorial writers and stump speakers for Jackson declaimed that corruption, venality, and contempt for the rule of people characterized the administration in power. Jackson's supporters, reviewing the country's recent history, declared that Adams, Clay, and the political opportunists with whom they allied themselves had profaned the Temple of Republican virtue. Through their arrogance and venality they had betrayed the most sacred precepts of the founders and placed the nation in jeopardy. But once again the Old Hero, the Victor of New Orleans, and of Horseshoe Bend and Pensacola, like Cincinnatus and like George Washington, had responded to the Republic's call to leave his plough and save the nation. This was, of course, claptrap. But it worked. Daniel Webster, no fan of Old

Hickory, testified to the effectiveness of Jacksonian campaign propaganda when he remarked, at the 1829 presidential inauguration, that the people "really seem to think that the country is rescued from some dreadful danger."[74]

During his presidency, Adams faced unremitting opposition from Jackson's supporters in Congress. His ambitious internal improvement proposals, which included founding both a national university and a national astronomical observatory, were not only ridiculed but characterized as dangerous to the freedom of the Republic. Adams, who had little sense of political realities of popular politics, had admonished members of the Congress as the nation's leaders they ought not be "palsied by the will of our constituents" but should follow a bold course of national "improvement." Clear evidence, the Jacksonians cried, of his monarchial aspirations. Adams supporters lost control of both houses of Congress in 1826. The one major piece of legislation that was passed during his administration, the Tariff of 1828 (soon to be known as the "tariff of abominations") had been cleverly framed, by Martin Van Buren, to accommodate certain partisan and sectional economic interests and injure others, with the areas hostile to Jackson receiving the least benefit. It was, the acerbic John Randolph quipped, really not for manufacturing but for the "manufacture of a president." Some felt that Adams should have vetoed it. Whatever the case, hostility in Congress to his administration seemingly knew no bounds. An innocuous proposal to send delegates to a conference of Latin American states in Panama ran into such vehement opposition from Jacksonians that by the time congressional approval was granted it was too late. One delegate died en route. The others arrived after the conference had adjourned.

Few if any of the men elected to the White House have matched John Quincy Adams in learning or experience, and few have been less successful is using the influence, and the powers, of the office to attain his objectives. In part, his political failures reflected personal shortcomings. "I am," he confided to his diary in 1819, "a man of reserved, cold, austere, and forbidding manners. My political adversaries say, a gloomy misanthrope, and my personal enemies, an unsocial savage. With a knowledge of the actual defect in my character. I have not the pliability to reform it."[75] He was not mistaken in that assessment. An English acquaintance, who knew Adams as a diplomat in Russia, described him as "dogged and systematically repulsive . . . he sat in the frivolous assemblies of St. Petersburg like a bull dog among spaniels."[76] Adams clearly lacked the common touch, and he seemed curiously lacking in personal warmth. Moreover, he came to the presidency, notes one historian, at a time "of abandonment of the standards of brilliance in public life established by the Founders of the Republic. The derision heaped on John Quincy Adams by the Jacksonians in 1828 established a pattern in American politics, warning aspiring politicians to conceal their intellect rather than proclaim it."[77] But we must not make too much of Adams's temperament, personal style, or intellectual elitism in explaining the failure of his reelection bid, let alone the emergence of an opposition political party during his presidency. Underlying personal aspirations and rivalries were conflicting sectional interests that led to sharp disagreements over a host of policy issues. As we shall see, Indian policy, for a time, was one of those issues.

The election that put Andrew Jackson in the White House was one of the dirtiest in American history. Jackson partisans portrayed Adams not only as a power mad, extravagant would-be monarch contemptuous of the people but also as an amoral opportunist who, while serving in Russia, had forced a young and innocent American girl to prostitute herself to the Czar. Jackson's opponents were no less vicious, reviving on a far larger scale the libels of 1824 and adding some new ones. Some charged Jackson with sexual immorality, claiming that years earlier he had persuaded Rachel to dishonor her marriage vows and desert Lewis Robards, her lawful husband. Anti-Jackson scandalmongers also painted Rachel Jackson, a plain spun country lady not only respected but truly beloved by her Tennessee neighbors for her kindness and her piety, as a woman of loose morals guilty of bigamy at the very least. Anti-Jackson pamphlets called her a "profligate woman," "whore," and in one case "a black wench."[78] One writer also alleged that Jackson's mother had been a prostitute. Another questioned Jackson's own racial identity, claiming that his mother was a mulatto.[79]

The Adams campaign emphasized Jackson's lack of education, his presumed ignorance of the larger world, and his famous inability to control his passions. The "Coffin Handbill" reminded voters of his execution of deserters during the Creek War. Adams's supporters once again dismissed Jackson as nothing more than a "military chieftain," unqualified to be chief magistrate by reason of his "ignorance of our laws," and often expressed "contempt" for civilian authority. A pamphlet published by pro-Adams *National Intelligencer* found in Jackson's governorship of Florida an ominous foretaste of things to come should the violent old general win the White House. No tyrant had ever before "assumed power so despotic" or "issued ordinances more odious, rapacious, or repressive." Never before had an American official created "so hideous a despotism in the midst of freedom, striking terror into those around him . . . displaying a continued violation of humanity and law." Should this man of "violent, arbitrary, and rapacious disposition" win the election, he would "put a price on the head" of all who dared resist his imperious will, and would soon decree "the proscription of all who side with freedom."[80] John Binns, the Philadelphia editor responsible for the "Coffin Handbill," asked voters to "mark the perfect indifference with which Gen. Jackson shoots, hangs or stabs his fellow beings, with or without trial, and the more than callous, aye, even exulting composure, with which he details his horrid and bloody deeds."[81] Other writers had visions of gibbets and guillotines on the White House lawn during a Jackson presidency.

A majority of the voters were not impressed by those dire predictions. Jackson easily defeated Adams by an electoral vote of 178 to 83, prevailing in every section of the country except New England. The popular vote stood at 647,276 for Jackson to 508,064 for Adams. But the man who now assumed the office of president of the United States was a man in deep sorrow, for his beloved wife Rachel had died on December 22, 1828. He believed that the vicious stories about his marriage circulated, or at least tolerated, by Adams, Clay, and other political enemies, had caused her death. During the election campaign, Rachel had lamented that "the enemies of the General have dipped their arrows in wormwood and gall and sped them at me. Almighty God, was there ever anything equal to it?"[82] At her funeral, Jackson declared, "I can forgive all who have wronged me, but will have fervently to pray that I may have grace to enable me to forget or forgive any enemy who has ever maligned that blessed one who is now safe from all suffering and sorrow, whom they tried to put to shame for my sake!"[83] But Andrew Jackson could not forget, nor did he forgive.

CHAPTER 6

President

Reflecting on Andrew Jackson's presidency some years after his own retirement from politics, Martin Van Buren remarked on the exceptionally high priority Old Hickory gave to Indian removal. "There was no measure, in the whole course of his administration, of which he was more exclusively the author than this."[1] Ironically, historians of Jacksonian America for over a century after Jackson's death either ignored or downplayed the Indian question in their assessments of the partisan battles of the day. Prior to the late 20th century, detailed and critical analyses of the controversy were to be found only in the works of a few specialists who wrote about Native Americans.[2] A Pulitzer Prize–winning study of "the Age of Jackson" published in 1945 contained no discussion of Indian removal.[3] Textbooks at all levels generally spent little or no time on this issue. But Jackson's contemporaries were well aware of "the trail of tears." Van Buren's own niece was so upset by what she perceived as its cruel injustice that she told her uncle that she hoped that he and Jackson would be defeated in the 1832 presidential election.[4] A study of voting patterns in Congress during the 1830s reveals sharp partisan and sectional divisions over Jackson's Indian policies. One recent analysis concludes that no issue was more divisive.[5]

Although hostility to Indian removal commanded its greatest support in the northeast, and is most commonly associated with evangelical reformers, it was more broadly based than is generally realized. There were some surprises. To cite just one example at this point, General Edmund Gaines, who had played a major role with Jackson in the First Seminole War and would command federal forces during part of the Second, consistently advised against removal, arguing that the civilization and assimilation of the Indian tribes was best accomplished by "leaving them in their present homes or villages." In 1827, in an official report on the affairs of the Western Department of the federal army, Gaines declared that mass resettlement of Indians in the trans-Mississippi west was not a humane option. "If we put them into the wide expanse of western prairie, we thereby assume the responsibility . . . of contributing in part to their annihilation."[6] After the removal program was well underway, Gaines wrote to a friend, "for my own part I would just as soon seek for fame by an attempt to remove the Shakers, or the Quakers, as to break up the Indians, take their land and throw together twenty tribes speaking different languages where the most ferocious savages will cut the throat of the most civilize and orderly."[7]

President James Monroe in his second inaugural address, in 1821, anticipated some of the changes in Indian policy Andrew Jackson would undertake a decade later. Monroe, responding in part to advice from Jackson, recommended that the federal government no longer recognize Indian nations as sovereign entities rightfully possessed of "vast territories." Indian surplus land, he argued, should be taken from them. But the Native Americans were not to be left either landless or destitute. Monroe proposed that the federal government provide, from the old Indian territories, land grants "in competent portions . . . guaranteed in perpetuity" to each Indian head of household and "his posterity." He called on Congress to establish a permanent fund "for the support of civil government over them, and for the education of their children, for their instruction in the arts of husbandry, and to provide subsistence for them until they could provide for themselves." Congress declined to do so.[8]

Initially, Monroe did not anticipate the elimination of Indian communities in the United States east of the Mississippi, just their reorganization. But he came to question the possibility of peaceful coexistence, given the mounting pressure from whites who were not inclined to share space with "savages." In his final address to Congress in 1825, he moved away from the "civilization" program he had previously endorsed and advised that comprehensive Indian relocation west of the Mississippi was essential to save them from destruction. He insisted, however, that removal must be voluntary.[9] Congress again took no action on his recommendations regarding Indian policy.

Andrew Jackson had never been comfortable with the prospect of continued coexistence with semi-sovereign Indian communities within the states. You will recall that in several treaty negotiations after the Creek War, he had agreed to allow Indian nations (Creek, Cherokee, Choctaw, and Chickasaw) to retain large tracts of land east of the Mississippi. But he did so because at the time he had no choice. With a very few personal exceptions, Sharp Knife did not regard Indians as acceptable neighbors. From his earliest days as a Tennessee pioneer, he had looked forward to their total removal.[10]

One very prominent southern political leader had a very different vision of future Indian policy. Anticipating Monroe's proposal five years later, Secretary of War William Crawford, in a report to Congress in March 1816, recommended that the federal government assist Indians in their progress toward "civilization," by setting aside in future treaty purchases land for Indians wishing to farm within their own eastern homelands. Their individual plots, each one-mile square, "should become a fee simple estate after the expiration of a certain number of years and actual residence upon and cultivation of it." In addition to promoting agriculture and individual land ownership, the government, Crawford declared, should also encourage intermarriage. "It will redound . . . to the national honor," Crawford declared, "to incorporate by humane and benevolent policy the natives of our forests in the great American family of freemen."[11]

Andrew Jackson, predictably, had no interest in incorporating "natives." Writing to Crawford several months later about a land dispute with the Cherokee, he advised the secretary that "the people of the west will never suffer any Indian to inhibit this country again." In explanation, Jackson invoked memories of past Indian massacres of women and children on the contested land and hinted that federal favoritism toward Indians in land disputes might well provoke a violent response from white settlers.[12] Thirteen years later, as president, he drafted a memorandum concerning the acquisition of Texas through negotiations with Mexico. Texas, he reflected, would provide "additional territory" that could be used for "concentrating the Indians" and hereby "relieving the states of the inconveniences which the residue within the states presently afford."[13] Throughout his eight years in the White House, Jackson not only consistently but incessantly, advised "the residue" of Indians remaining in the United States that, regardless of their progress toward "civilization," they could not comfortably continue to live within state boundaries. To cite but one typical example, in a letter to the Creeks living in Alabama in March 1829, Jackson warned "where you are now, you and my white children are too near to each other to live in harmony and peace."[14]

Even a superficial reading of Jackson's speeches, memoranda, and letters both public and private leaves us no doubt that Jackson's Indian removal policy was ideologically grounded in his unquestioned belief in inherent Indian intellectual and moral inferiority. But he was not an Indian hater in the model of Melville's Colonel Moredock, or of the folk hero Tom Quick who devoted their lives to their slaughter. Andrew Jackson did not kill Indians for sport. Unlike a later frontier general, he did not claim that the "only good Indian is a dead Indian." On the contrary, he was fond of portraying himself as the Indians' savior, as a humanitarian who sought through western relocation of Indian nations to remove a vulnerable people from harm's way and give them a chance to survive. But it must be emphasized again that Andrew Jackson never shared Jefferson's vision of racial amalgamation, nor was he persuaded by Monroe's earlier cautious optimism about the "civilization" program. A continuing Indian presence within the states was unacceptable to Jackson for several reasons. While he granted that there were some exceptions, he believed that Native Americans as individuals were generally untrustworthy. He repeatedly warned treaty negotiators that the word of an Indian cannot be trusted. He saw their presence in frontier areas as a serious threat to American security, believing that they were all too prone to make common cause with America's European enemies, or to tolerate other Indians who did so. You will recall he deemed the Creeks' failure to kill Tecumseh in 1811 justification for treating them all as enemies in the treaty negotiations following the defeat of the Red Sticks.

Old Hickory saw Indian communities not only as security risks but also as obstacles to the economic progress and long-term prosperity of the Republic, occupying and, in his view, misusing rich lands needed by worthy white farmers and plantation owners. For Jackson, as for other white men of his region and generation, it was an article of faith, held in defiance of evidence to the contrary, that Indian males with very few exceptions were by nature lazy, improvident, and often drunken, unwilling to earn their bread by the sweat of their brows, unwilling to adjust to changing circumstances. Removal to the unsettled areas west of the Mississippi where game was still plentiful offered the only reasonable hope of survival for a backward people who, Jackson argued (erroneously), were not willing to give up hunting and embrace a civilized mode of living.[15] As to their long-term prospects, Jackson sometimes conjectured that in western isolation Indians, removed from contact with the worst of the white race, might slowly learn civilized ways and even someday qualify for statehood, but on balance he did not consider that very likely. In Andrew Jackson's overall vision of the American Republic's providential destiny, Indians were a people whose immediate future remained somewhat unsure but who, given their character faults and innate inferiority, were clearly not entitled to a continuing place on their ancestral lands east of the Mississippi. In one message to Congress, he conjectured that Indians were providentially destined for extinction. He declared that "true philanthropists" would not lament their passing, for they would be replaced by a more industrious people who would build cities, cultivate farms and plantations, advance the arts and sciences, and prosper.[16] In his rejection of coexistence of whites and Indians within the states, Jackson mirrored the sentiment of his region. It is telling that in 1824, southerners in Congress tried unsuccessfully to eliminate all federal appropriations for the Indian Civilization Fund.[17]

As president, Jackson was obligated to enforce the Trade and Intercourse laws that regulated relations with Indians and that guaranteed that their landholdings as specified by treaties would be protected from white incursions.[18] But the new president did not accept the fundamental premise upon which those laws were based: federal jurisdiction over Indian affairs within the states. All of his predecessors had maintained that under the federal constitution of 1789, state sovereignty did not extend over Indian Territory. Jackson expressed his opposition to that limitation on state power many times, but never more frankly than in an undated memorandum found in his presidential papers wherein he argued that the states must be conceded the right to take Indian land whenever it was needed by white settlers without interference from the federal government. He noted that many of the early land grants given to white settlers in the upper southwest had never sanctioned by treaties. They were based instead on the right of conquest. To claim now that Indian land was under federal protection would in effect declare those grants "void." That, he wrote, was "a doctrine that would not be well received in the west." The states, he concluded, possessed full jurisdiction over all territory within their borders. Indians could remain on the land only at the sufferance of its true owners.[19]

That Jackson held such views was well understood. Emboldened by his election to the presidency, the Georgia legislature in late 1828 claimed jurisdiction over all Cherokee lands within the state borders and added them to its northwestern counties. Alabama and Mississippi soon followed suit. Long-standing federal treaty guarantees were set aside unilaterally by the states, which not only denied Indians their right to self-government but also their ownership of the land they currently occupied. Georgia declared all laws passed by the Cherokees invalid as of June 1, 1830. Cherokee officials were threatened with four-year imprisonment should they try to continue to govern their own people. The legislature specified that while all Indians were henceforth to be subject to the jurisdiction of Georgia law and her courts, "no Indian or the descendent of any Indian . . . shall be deemed a competent witness in any court in this state to which a white person may be a party."[20] Under this law, "a white man might rob or murder a Cherokee, in the presence of many Indians and descendants of Indians" yet be immune from prosecution.[21] The state also passed legislation specifying that a contract made by an Indian would be valid only if verified by two white men. As one writer notes, "this, in effect, cancelled out almost all debts owed to Indians in Georgia." Moreover, when "whites came into Indian country in large numbers, seized Indian property, and dispossessed them, resulting cases against the whites were then dismissed because Indians could not testify in court."[22] The Jacksonian administration's support of state jurisdiction over Indian residents, as Grant Foreman noted, "also led to new opportunities for "whiskey peddlers" who now "plied their trade" in defiance of the laws of the United States. The result, for the Indian, was often "utter demoralization" with many tribesmen becoming "so impoverished that they were compelled to live on roots, or starve."[23]

In a move aimed at eliminating interference from missionaries and other potential "Yankee troublemakers," Georgia banned whites lacking a state license from living in Cherokee country. New restrictions were placed on the Cherokees themselves, including a prohibition from engaging in the mining of the gold newly discovered in Cherokee country. Cherokee families were granted temporary permission to remain in Georgia on 160-acre tracts of land to be surveyed and made available by the state but were not given fee simple deeds to those plots but were instead declared tenants at will and as such subject to future eviction. Cherokee land deemed surplus was to be distributed to whites by lottery. Another legislative enactment declared that Indians could not sell livestock for cash but must grant credit to white purchasers, who of course could not be sued for payment as the courts could not legally hear Indian testimony.[24] Criminal penalties were imposed on Cherokees who sought to impede emigration, countering a Cherokee statute that imposed a fine of "not less than a thousand dollars" and a public whipping of "one hundred lashes" on those who chose to cooperate with removal.

The Jackson administration responded to the Cherokees' appeals for restitution of their treaty rights by declaring that the federal government could not legally interfere on their behalf, as the states were fully sovereign within their own borders. In April 1829, Secretary of War John Henry Eaton, at Jackson's direction, reminded the Cherokee that they had supported the British during the War for Independence and had not made peace with the United States until 1791. They were thus a defeated people, not a sovereign nation. While they had been granted by the victors various "compacts" permitting them to remain on their former lands and enjoy hunting privileges, "it is not thence to be inferred that this was any thing more than a permission." Those "compacts" (Eaton declined to call them treaties) did not in any way abridge the sovereignty of the state of Georgia or grant the Cherokee any permanent land rights. Since the federal government could offer the Cherokee no help in their quarrel with Georgia, their wisest course of action, Eaton advised, would be to leave the state and accept "a removal beyond the Mississippi." Removal alone could assure them "protection and peace."[25] Some months later, Attorney General John M. Berrien on behalf of the administration advised Congress that the Cherokees had been allowed to remain in Georgia not because it was their right under the treaties they signed with the United States but by the "mere grace of the conqueror."[26]

Combined with Jackson's long-standing belief that the government should not negotiate with Indians, but dictate to them as a conquered people, his administration's denial of federal protection would appear to herald the radical transformation in Indian relations the *Cherokee Phoenix* foresaw in its prediction of a "republican tyranny" that would drive them from their homelands. And so it did. But the process was a bit more subtle than the *Phoenix* may have anticipated. Although long deplored by Jackson, the treaty-making process continued. Politically, the new president was in no position to secure congressional approval for a clear-cut and unequivocal repudiation of past practices. Nor could he win congressional support for federal legislation mandating forced deportation of all Indians to lands west of the Mississippi. Contrary to the impression of some later historians, he neither sought nor gained approval of any such law.[27] Jackson was well aware that, while mandatory removal might be supported by large numbers of whites in the south, the rest of the country was deeply divided on the question. Early in his presidency, in a letter to his close friend John Overton, Jackson declared that "the course pursued by Georgia is well calculated to involve her and the United States in great difficulty," which could be averted only by persuading the Indians to remove themselves voluntarily from state jurisdiction by relocating west of the Mississippi.[28]

Shortly after his inauguration, Jackson, in a letter to the Creeks, warned them that "your white brothers have always claimed the land" they currently occupied and, given the whites' present needs, Indians could not continue to live there "in harmony and peace." He urged that they move "beyond the great river Mississippi . . . There your white brothers will not trouble you; they will have no claim to the land, and you can live upon it, you and all your children, as long as the grass grows or the waters run, in peace and plenty . . . In that country, your father the President, now promises to protect you to feed you, and to shield you from all encroachment."[29] A subsequent appeal from the Creeks for protection against Alabama's violation of their treaty rights was unavailing.[30] Jackson dispatched two close associates, Tennessee militia generals John Coffee and William Carroll, to Georgia and Alabama with instructions to convey a message to the Indians there. The generals, speaking for the president, warned that only through agreeing to a removal treaty could they avert "destruction upon their race." But their mission failed, as Indian leaders reiterated their determination to remain on their tribal lands.[31]

In his inaugural address, Jackson had promised to "observe towards the Indian tribes within our limits a just and liberal policy, and to give that humane and considerate attention to their rights and their wants which is consistent with the habits of our government and the feelings of our people."[32] The question of which Indian "rights" and "needs" would be deemed "consistent" with government "habits" and popular "feelings" Jackson left unspecified. But a letter written several months after his inauguration to James Gadsden in Florida is more revelatory. Therein, Jackson declared, "you may rest assured that I shall adhere to the just and humane policy towards the Indians which I have commenced. In this spirit I have recommended them to quit their possessions on this side of the Mississippi and go to a country in the west where there is every probability they will always be free from the mercenary influence of white men, and undisturbed by the local authority of the states: under such circumstances the General Government can exercise a parental control over their interests and possibly perpetuate their race."[33]

In his first annual message to Congress, delivered on December 8, 1829, Jackson sought to counter criticism of his call for Indian removal by stressing that the program he envisioned would "be voluntary, for it would be as cruel as unjust to compel the aborigines to abandon the graves of their fathers, and seek a home in a distant land." He granted that Indians in the past had not been treated fairly, noting the contradiction inherent in policies which on the one hand encouraged Indians to embrace "the arts of civilization, in the hope of gradually reclaiming them from a wandering life" but on the other "lost no opportunity to purchase their lands and thrust them farther into the wilderness. By this means they have not only been kept in a wandering state, but been led to look upon us as unjust and indifferent to their fate." The continued expansion of white settlement "by destroying the resources of the savage doom him to weakness and decay . . . Humanity and national honor demand that every effort should be made to avert so great a calamity." But rather than calling for protection of Native American communities through enforcement of treaty guarantees, Jackson reminded the Congress that he had "informed the Indians inhabiting parts of Georgia and Alabama that their attempt to establish an independent government would not be countenanced by the Executive of the United States, and advised them to emigrate beyond the Mississippi or submit to the law of those states." Resettlement in the west offered the means to secure their survival. "There," Jackson declared, "the benevolent may endeavor to teach them the arts of civilization, and by promoting union and harmony among them, to raise up an interesting commonwealth, destined to perpetuate the race and to attest the humanity and justice of this government."

While Jackson promised that those Indians who did not wish to emigrate would be allowed to remain within the states, where under state authority they "will no doubt be protected in the enjoyment of those possessions which they have improved by their industry," he added a very important caveat. Whatever their choice, Indians in the future must not expect to remain in possession of all the tribal lands still allocated to them in various treaties. They had, in his view, no legitimate claims "on tracts of country on which they have neither dwelt nor made improvements, merely because they have seen them from the mountain or passed them in the chase."[34] To justify their dispossession, Jackson thus evoked again the myth that Indians were by nature savage, nomadic hunters. His repeated characterization of Indians as living "in a wandering state" struck his critics as blatantly dishonest. It was generally known the Indians Georgia sought to evict had cultivated the soil and lived in populous villages for some centuries before the arrival of the first whites.

Even before the beginning of Jackson's presidency, critics of removal mounted an aggressive campaign to mobilize support for the protection of the Indian land rights Jackson questioned. Opposition to Jackson's removal program, although strongest in New England, was present in all areas and constituted a clear-cut minority only in the South. It claimed support not only from male Christian missionaries intent on bringing both civilization and salvation to Indians but also from reform-minded women who within a very few years would also commit their fervid moral passion and not inconsiderable organizational gifts to the crusade against slavery.[35] Jackson's removal bill was very nearly defeated in Congress despite numerous assurances from the president and his congressional supporters that the program would be strictly voluntary.

The campaign against Jackson's plan began sometime before his proposal was placed before the Congress. In 1829, the pro-Adams *National Intelligencer* began publication of the *William Penn Essays*, a widely circulated series of articles that set the tone and defined the major themes of the struggle against removal. It is estimated that around 100 newspapers reprinted the essays. They were soon republished in book form. Their author was Jeremiah Evarts, a deeply religious man inspired by the vision of a world transformed by the gospel of Christ. Born in Vermont, educated at Yale, Evarts's poor health had led him to abandon plans to enter the ministry. Admitted to the bar, he practiced law for a few years after graduation. In 1810, however, Evarts abandoned that profession to accept the editorship of the *Panoplist*, a religious journal which under his leadership would be devoted to the promotion of missionary outreach. He also became an officer in the newly founded American Board of Commissioners for Foreign Missions, editing its journal the *Missionary Herald* and finally serving as its corresponding secretary from 1821 until his death in 1831. His work with the Board of Commissioners brought him into contact with both missionaries who worked in the southern Indian nations and with some of their converts. He soon became their most passionate advocate, visiting their missions and pleading their cause.[36] "If any man ever held an absolutely sure position," comments one historian, "it was Jeremiah

Evarts in regards to the rights of the Cherokee Indians to stay where they were in Georgia, and the obligation of the federal government to protect those rights without delay or equivocation."[37]

During the Adams administration, Evarts spent much time in Washington, D.C., lobbying against Indian removal. Although initially sympathetic to a program of voluntary relocation, he came to distrust the motives and intentions of removal advocates. He tried unsuccessfully to secure the defeat of a congressional appropriation to fund a survey of trans-Mississippi territories suitable for Indian emigrants. He worked assiduously to counter the arguments of men like Indian commissioner Thomas McKenney and Baptist missionary Isaac McCoy who agreed with Jackson that Indian removal offered the only means by which a backward and vulnerable people might be saved from extinction.

Evarts's case against removal rested on four premises. The first was that federal treaty obligations could not be set aside unilaterally, either by states or by the federal government itself. The land boundaries they guaranteed were inviolable and could be changed only with the consent of the Indian nations acting individually. While it was true that those treaties circumscribed their rights to trade or enter into diplomatic relations with any government except the United States, they had not forfeited their sovereignty but should be regarded as comparable to weaker European nations protected by a stronger power. He noted that "it has been said . . . that the Indians, being an uncivilized people, are not to be ranked among nations . . . There is as little reason as truth in the objection. Has not God endowed every community with some rights? And are these rights not be regarded by every honest man and by every fair-minded and honorable ruler?"[38] They had certainly been so regarded by the government of the United States in years past, as Indian treaties invariably included guarantees of their right to their own territories and to domestic self-government.

Evarts's second premise was that removal, even if voluntarily agreed to, would disrupt the Indian nations' progress on the road to civilization. Those who portrayed all Indians as backward savages ignored recent history. Evarts saw in the example of the Cherokee experience proof of the errors of those like Jackson who saw only Indian backwardness. Having adopted Euro-American agricultural practices, they "now derive their support from the soil, as truly and entirely as do the inhabitants of Pennsylvania or Virginia. For many years they have had their herds, and their large cultivated fields. They now have, in addition, their schools, a regular civil government, and places of regular Christian worship. They earn their bread by the labor of their own hands, applied to the tillage of their own farms; and they clothe themselves with fabrics made at their own looms, from cotton grown in their own fields."[39] Expulsion from their homelands, and resettlement in territories alien to them, he argued, might well undo much of that progress.

The third premise in Evarts's argument, perhaps the most prophetic, was that removal would bring "much suffering" to Indian peoples. He foresaw "much exposure, sickness, hunger, nakedness, either on the journey, or after arrival." The new lands on which they would be settled would not only be unfamiliar, but might well also prove unsuitable for cultivation. "The crowding together of different tribes speaking languages entirely unintelligible to one another, and accustomed to different habits" would no doubt lead to conflicts. Evarts expressed grave doubt about the ability, or willingness, of federal agents to provide effective assistance and protection. "Judging from all prior experience," Evarts wrote, "some of them would be profane, licentious, and overbearing, and a majority would be selfish, looking principally at the emoluments of office, and caring little for the Indians."[40]

Finally, should such a cruel and unjust program be implemented, the United States would not only be dishonored in the eyes of the world, but, Evarts warned, might well also incur the wrath of heaven. "The Great Arbiter of Nations," he wrote, "never fails to take cognizance of national delinquencies . . . we should humble ourselves before God and the world that we have done so much to destroy the Indians and so little to save them." Removal would advertise to the world that Americans respect only "bayonets and cannons," have no fear of God, and can be overawed only "by physical force."[41] Such rash disregard for the will of the Almighty would invite disaster.

Others joined in Evarts's crusade. Employing language more extreme than Evarts, some publicists argued that removal would end in extermination, as the land to which Indians were to be consigned was said to be a barren, lifeless desert. George Cheever, who had never actually been west of the Mississippi, declared "the curse of perpetual desolation rests upon the greater portion of the country to which they are to be driven. There, hardly a flower grows, or a brook runs, or a tree strikes its roots into the soil or lifts its branches to the sunlight . . . [there] human existence cannot be sustained."[42] Others shared his anxiety about Indian survival under Jacksonian rule. Among the numerous memorials and petitions prompted by Jackson's address was one that warned "the Benevolent Ladies of the United States" that "measures are fast ripening, which, if put in execution, are to exterminate the Indians."[43] Mass meetings in all of the large cities of the northeast, and in some of the smaller ones, protested Jackson's call for removal, generally using rhetoric only slightly less vehement. Thousands of citizens signed petitions to Congress. Evarts and American Board of Commissioners for Foreign Missions worked assiduously to maintain and intensify the outcry against Jackson's Indian policy. They were not alone. Native American leaders also protested against removal. The Cherokee and several other Indian nations sent petitions and in some cases delegations to Congress. Pro-removal southern politicians charged that Yankee missionary agitators had organized those protests. Georgia, as we have noted, responded by enacting legislation barring missionaries unlicensed by the state from living in Indian country.

Removal advocates also launched publicity campaigns designed to sway Congress and the public. While the veteran federal superintendent of Indian Affairs Thomas McKenney worked assiduously to argue for the new administration's removal plan, the most widely noted defense of Jackson's position was published anonymously in the very influential *North American Review* in January 1830. Its author was Lewis Cass, territorial governor of Michigan and self-styled Indian expert. Although he had previously been a fervent supporter of the "civilization" program, Cass now warned that there was "some insurmountable obstacle in the habits or temperament of Indians" that seemingly made it impossible for them to overcome their savagery.[44] Throughout the North American continent, he reported, they remained as they had been found centuries earlier by the first white settlers: "a rude and barbarous people . . . a people whose only business was war and hunting; who acted from impulse more than from reason; whose customs required blood for blood, injury for injury . . . who had no governments to guide or control them, no laws to restrain them, no officers to punish them; who had no permanent, settled residence where they could be found, nor any property to defend; whose institutions irresistibly impelled them to war; whose young men were despised until they had shed the blood of an enemy; and whose old men were disregarded when too feeble to pursue that enemy; who, in all their intercourse with the whites, seem to be actuated only by the fear of consequences or the hope of obtaining some advantage." They had no understanding of "principles." To the argument advanced by Evarts and others that the Cherokee and other southern Indian nations had made great progress in recent years, Cass replied that only the mixed bloods in their midst, and a few of their close associates, had actually embraced change and thereby prospered. Clinging to the myth of the wandering savage hunter, he also falsely dismissed traditional Native American horticulture as only a minor source of nutriment. The great majority of Indians, he insisted, remained, despite the best efforts of white missionaries and educators, ignorant, violent, lazy, impoverished, and often drunk. Contact with whites had done them very little good, but much harm. Their only hope for survival, Cass concluded, was to migrate to the federal territories across the Mississippi where they could enjoy the protection and guidance of the United States.[45]

Cass quoted extensively from a pamphlet published in 1827 by a disillusioned Baptist missionary, Isaac McCoy, who also argued that contact with whites had thus far done little to elevate the Indians. McCoy was one of a small handful of clergymen who publicly supported Jackson's Indian policy. Unlike Cass, McCoy did not believe that Indians were racially inferior to whites. He fervently believed that in time, if given proper assistance, they could be prepared for full membership in the American community. But there was a serious problem. Judging from his experiences in the northwest, McCoy concluded, that in their present state "Indians do not thrive among whites . . . they often become profligate and wretched, or wander back into the forest, and mingle with their barbarous kindred." For their own good, therefore, they must not be left in close proximity to the superior race until they had gained the skills and work habits needed to survive and ultimately prosper in the new order. Relocation west of the Mississippi, McCoy argued, offered their best hope for their immediate preservation. Recognizing the progress already made by the Cherokee and other southeastern nations in becoming "civilized," he initially exempted them from his plans for Indian removal. But McCoy soon realized that the federal government under Jackson would not protect them from the state, and accordingly joined with his friend Georgia congressman Wilson Lumkin and others in supporting Jackson's program.[46]

The argument that removal was essential to the physical preservation of Indians in the present and to their ultimate civilization in the future would be central to the administration's case, often emphasized even more heavily than the related argument that Indians residing within the states were an obstacle to progress. It was an argument most southerners found not only persuasive but comforting, and one that won substantial consent in the old Northwest. But as the debates and votes in Congress would soon demonstrate, throughout the North skepticism about Jackson's motives was rampant.

In an effort to build a broader base of support for removal, Superintendent McKenney in 1829 organized an "Indian Board for the Emigration, Preservation and Improvement of the Aborigines of America." Based in New York, drawing some support from the Dutch Reform Church and from Episcopalians, the board never enjoyed anything like the sort of influence Evarts and his American Board of Commissioners for Foreign Missions commanded. The organization met only once, disappearing soon after McKenney's dismissal from office in August 1830. However, several clergymen, of whom McCoy was the most active, continued to work for removal.[47]

In the spring of 1830, Congress undertook the task of responding to President Jackson's call for an Indian removal bill. An early version of the report on removal drafted by Jackson's friends on the House Committee on Indian Affairs echoed his old assertion that the custom of negotiating treaties with Indians was nothing more than an "empty gesture" or "stately form of discourse" intended to sooth Indian "vanity" and gain peaceful consent to land cessions.[48] That language did not appear in the removal bill that passed Congress, which by contrast included a clause guaranteeing that "nothing in this act shall be construed as authorizing or directing the violation of any existing treaty between the United States and any of the Indian tribes."[49] But some removal advocates during the debates in Congress continued to deny that Indian treaties were legally binding on the United States, and thereby fed some very dark rumors about the administration's real intentions. In both houses of Congress, critics warned that Andrew Jackson could not be trusted to deal fairly with Indians. Their suspicions were confirmed when War Department correspondence advising that removal treaties might be obtained despite tribal opposition by bribing and intimidating key leaders fell into the hands of Jackson's opposition. Senator Theodore Frelinghuysen of New Jersey, a close friend of Evarts and like him a devout Christian, quoted extensively from those instructions, which had been sent on May 20, 1829, to Generals Carroll and Coffee to guide their conversations with the Cherokee in Georgia. Frelinghuysen characterized them as a disgraceful blend of terror and bribery. The Cherokee leaders were to be threatened with withdrawal of all federal protection, which would "entail destruction upon their race," if they did not cooperate with removal and were to be rewarded with land grants if they did. Those instructions, Frelinghuysen declaimed, should lead all men "to blush with honest shame."[50]

Anti-removal congressmen for the most part echoed Evarts's earlier themes in their speeches against the bill, with particular emphasis on the need to uphold national honor by respecting the land rights enshrined in Indian treaties. But they also now stressed the duplicity of Andrew Jackson and his pro-removal supporters. Old Hickory's spokesmen worked hard to counter the charge that the administration had no intention of keeping its promise that Indian relocation would be both voluntary and humane. To cite several examples out of many, Congressman James Buchanan of Pennsylvania assured the House that Andrew Jackson had never considered "using the power of the government to drive that unfortunate race across the Mississippi," while Robert Adams of Mississippi denied that the president would ever force the unwilling from "their present abode." Georgia's Congressman Wilson Lumpkin, in previous sessions one of the most vehement advocates of forced removal, now declared that "no man entertains kinder feelings towards Indians than Andrew Jackson." Secretary of War Eaton added his assurance that no thought had ever been given to "compulsory removal." Concerned about the administration's credibility, Eaton some months earlier had sent a confidential letter to the governor of Georgia urging that the state be patient for a time and avoid "the appearance of harshness towards the Indians" as Congress debated the matter.[51]

Jackson's congressional critics were not reassured and demanded more explicit guarantees that the administration would be required to respect Indian rights. In the Senate, Frelinghuysen offered two amendments that, by affirming that federal treaties were indeed the law of the land beyond the reach of state authority, would have provided continued federal protection for those "tribes and nations" that chose not to emigrate. One specified that, in the absence of a new treaty authorizing removal, Indian "tribes and nations . . . shall be protected in their present possessions, and in the enjoyment of all their rights of territory and government as heretofore exercised and enjoyed, from all interruptions and encroachments." The second declared that changes in their status could be made only through the negotiation of a new federal treaties, thereby explicitly denying the Jacksonian doctrine that Indian "tribes and nations" were subject to the authority of the states. Despite substantial support, the determined opposition of southern senators defeated both amendments. Jackson's opponents in the House and the Senate introduced several other amendments that would have explicitly guaranteed federal protection of the property rights of both Indians who accepted removal and those who were left behind. They were also voted down.[52]

One amendment, introduced by a Jacksonian congressman from Pennsylvania fearful of anti-removal sentiment at home, almost passed the House. Reflecting the concerns of his Quaker constituents, Joseph Hemphill's amendment called for the appointment of "three disinterested commissioners" charged both with ascertaining the sentiments of the various Indian tribes and with certifying the suitability of the western lands earmarked for their relocation. The commissioners were to be given a year's time to complete their work and submit their report. Congress was forbidden to take any action on removal until that report had been received and reviewed. The vote on the Hemphill amendment ended in a tie, 98 in favor, 98 opposed. The Speaker of the House, Andrew Stevenson of Virginia, a Jackson loyalist, broke the tie, and the amendment was defeated, as was a similar resolution in the Senate.[53]

The refusal of Jackson's supporters in Congress to vote for amendments, which would have reinforced their verbal guarantees about the voluntary nature of the proposed removal program confirmed the suspicions of the opposition. The Indian Removal Act of 1830 passed the Senate by a vote of 28 in favor and 19 opposed but almost failed in the House. It passed only because Old Hickory, alarmed by the near passage of the Hemphill amendment, "pressured and bullied" the recalcitrant.[54] In the end, the House voted for removal by the narrow margin of 102 to 97.

The vote reflected a deep sectional division: Members of Congress from states north of the Mason Dixon line opposed the bill, by a vote of 96 to 69. In the northeast, the margin was not even close: 79 against the bill, 42 in favor. The Old Northwest was divided, but pro-removal by a margin of 27 to 17. In the South, there was little dissent: 60 in favor, 15 opposed. Although the vote on removal is usually represented as a partisan vote, a number of northern Jacksonians broke with Old Hickory on this issue, despite substantial pressure from the White House. Some others, fearful of both their constituents and their president, as Van Buren recalled, "felt themselves compelled to shoot the pit" and were absent on the day of the vote.[55] Overall, some 40 congressmen considered to be Jackson supporters voted against him on this issue. Of those congressmen considered to be among his political opponents, only 8 supported removal, and 7 of those were southerners. The North/South division on Indian removal is pronounced and significant.[56]

Three months after its passage, Jackson explained to the Choctaw interpreter John Pitchlynn that the Indian Removal Act was

> a measure I had much at heart and sought to effect because I was satisfied that the Indians could not possibly live under the laws of the States. If now they shall refuse to accept the liberal terms offered, they only must be liable for whatever evils and difficulties may arise. I feel conscious of having done my duty to my red children and if any failure of my good intentions arises, it will be attributable to their want of duty to themselves, not to me.[57]

In this letter and in numerous later statements, Jackson made it clear that he did not consider remaining within the states a viable option for Native Americans. Their continued presence in the states, he suggested, would lead only to "evils and difficulties." Jackson's earlier promise to Congress that Indians who chose to remain behind would "be protected in their persons and property" was disingenuous. Jackson did not really believe that the states would protect Indian rights and he had made it clear he had no intention of using his authority as president to do so.

Despite the emphasis on the presumably voluntary nature of removal in his message to Congress, it is very important to note that Jackson's own first draft of this document did not hold out the promise that Indians could choose to remain in their homelands if they were willing to acknowledge and obey state laws, but instead emphasized their ongoing backwardness and unsuitability for citizenship. In that draft Jackson described Indians as generally "erratic in their habits and wanting in those endowments" necessary for self-government. He argued that since most efforts "to open to them the ways of civilization" while they lived near whites had failed, their removal beyond the Mississippi clearly offered the only possible means of doing "something to better their condition."[58] In his own first version of the speech Jackson did not speak of removal as voluntary. It is in revisions and additions, some of them prepared by his advisers, that we find Indian submission to state authority offered as an alternative.[59]

It is also telling that Jackson's draft did not include the eloquent acknowledgement, contained in the final version delivered to Congress, that forced relocation of Indians would be an act of cruelty that would reflect adversely on our national character. It is doubtful that those were really Jackson's sentiments. A year later, in his second message to Congress, Jackson took a very different position. After acknowledging again that it was "painful for them to leave the graves of their forefathers," he then minimized their distress and suffering. "What," he asked, "do they do more than our ancestors did, or our children are now doing?" Jackson then proceeded to propound an essentially racist view of historical evolution which justified the displacement of backward and inferior races. "True philanthropists," the president declared, did not lament the disappearance of backward peoples unable to meet the demands of the present and of the future. "The tribes which occupied the countries now constituting the Eastern States," Jackson reminded Congress, "were annihilated or have melted away to make room for the whites." If one "took a comprehensive view of the general interests of the human race," one finds "nothing to be regretted." His removal program, Jackson argued, was simply a more humane continuation of an old policy.[60] As historian Steven Salaita notes, "Native loss of life during the removal years was terrible. To Jackson, the deaths were neither immoral nor preventable. In his more reflective moments they may have been unfortunate or even tragic—not because of any problem with the philosophies of settlement, but because of the tragic misfortune of the stagnating Native."[61]

In implementing the Indian Removal Act, Jackson and his associates from the very beginning sought, in their dealings with Native American negotiators, to counter the impression they themselves had given Congress and the public that this was to be a voluntary program. At this point, they could not simply set the law aside and march all Indians westward at the point of a bayonet, although later they would do just that in dealing with the Creek and the Seminole. But they could threaten to withdraw federal protection from those who did not understand immediately the dangers of attempting to remain within the states. They could also offer the government's special protection to those leaders who agreed to sign a removal treaty, and extend to them its largess. Federal bribery of cooperative chiefs was a time-honored practice, as was the ouster of the uncooperative. Such measures continued to play essential role in the conduct of Indian policy.

Under the law, tribal relocation could be achieved only through the negotiation of a removal treaty with each of the separate Indian tribes and nations. During Jackson's presidency, dozens of removal treaties were ratified. His administration's approach to those negotiations was formulaic. Its spokesmen would begin with assurances that their Great Father the president truly loves his "red children" and had only their welfare in mind in urging their migration to new lands west of the Mississippi. Jackson himself, addressing the Chickasaw in 1830, invoked that theme: "Your father has the frost of many years upon his head. From his early youth he has lived near to his red children. He has slept with them—hunted with them—and fought with them—towards them he has always entertained feelings of strong regard and will not fail to be their friend, if they shall permit it and repose their confidence in him."[62] But while the Great Father and the federal government were benevolent, negotiators warned that the states and their white inhabitants were not. While the federal law did not compel Indian to move, they must understand that they did not have any real option. Should they attempt to remain where they were, they would be fully subject to the authority of the states and denied any federal protection whatsoever. They could continue to receive that protection, and be truly safe from the predations of hostile whites, only on federal lands west of the Mississippi. At this point in the negotiations, Jackson's representatives spoke of prospective Indian "annihilation" or "extinction" should they attempt to remain on their tribal lands within the states. Those words were used in two ways in "talks" with the Indian nations: factually, to speak of the recent termination of their tribal governments and mark the decline of their traditional way of life, and more ambiguously, to suggest the possibility of their physical extermination.

Shortly after Congress passed the removal act, Jackson personally summoned Indian leaders from the southern states to meet with him at Franklin, Tennessee, to discuss the terms of their emigration. When a number of them declined to do so and sought legal assistance in resisting removal, Jackson railed against their attorney, former attorney general William Wirt and other unnamed white advocates of Indian rights. Their advice, he predicted, "will lead to the destruction of the poor ignorant Indians. I have used all the persuasive means in my power, I have exonerated the national character from all imputations, and now leave the poor deluded Creeks and Cherokees to their fate, and to their annihilation, which their wicked advisers has [sic] induced."[63]

The Creek and Cherokee Nations had refused to meet with Jackson at Franklin. Nonetheless, he expected to talk there with the Choctaw and the Chickasaw, but the Choctaw, who had drawn up their own removal treaty, did not appear either. (On Jackson's recommendation, the Senate subsequently rejected their treaty proposal as too expensive.) The Chickasaws who did respond to the invitation to meet with "the Great Father" were not eager to discuss removal, but instead used the occasion to appeal to him for the restoration of their rights of tribal self-government in Mississippi, which had recently been taken from them by the state legislature, and for protection against white depredations.[64] Jackson told them bluntly he could not grant their wish. Within Mississippi they were subject, he explained, to state law, not federal authority. They must understand that while he hoped they would "be perpetuated and preserved as a nation," that could be accomplished only if they agreed "to remove to a country beyond the Mississippi." He warned that "where you are, it is not possible for you to be contented and happy."[65]

The 21 assembled Chickasaw chiefs prepared a written response to Jackson's "talk" in which they pleaded to be allowed to keep the small remnant of their "immemorial" homeland that they had not yet sold "to our white brothers." It was, they said, "barely sufficient to subsist on while living and to bury our bones when we are dead," but sparse as it was "we cannot consent to exchange the country where we now live for one we have never seen." In his response, Jackson reiterated his warning that their salvation as an independent people depended upon migration. In the west, they would endure "as long as the grass grows or the waters run," but in Mississippi "you must disappear and be forgotten." He warned the leadership of the nation, old chiefs and young warriors alike, that if they refused the offer he had made, "call not on your Great Father to hereafter to relieve you of your troubles." Jackson then withdrew, leaving Secretary Eaton and General Coffee to complete the removal negotiations.[66]

Several days later, the president was called back to receive a new communication from the Chickasaw. They now advised him that "we have listened—and your words have sunk deep in our hearts . . . we are now ready to enter into any treaty based upon the principles communicated to us by major Eaton and gen. Coffee." Jackson was pleased and invoked the blessing of the "Great Spirit" on his Chickasaw children.[67] Jackson had assured the Chickasaw that "your great father does not desire to place you in a country, where you will not find the soil and climate equal to the one you have. He will never consent to place you where you would be in a worse situation; his great desire is to make your condition better, not worse."[68] Not entirely convinced, despite their gracious words in their last communication with the Great Father, the Indian negotiators asked for and were granted a treaty provision that stipulated that there would be no migration of Chickasaws until the nation's leaders had inspected and approved an appropriate new homeland west of the Mississippi. The agreement Eaton and Coffee negotiated, known as the Treaty of Franklin, would be voided if they did not.

The treaty was never ratified. An ill-conceived government plan to merge the Chickasaws in the proposed new western nation with their longtime enemies the Choctaw was firmly rejected by both tribes. Chickasaw notables who toured other possible sites for their new homeland within the federal lands west of the Mississippi found them all unacceptable. A proposal to settle on Spanish lands in Texas also led nowhere. Andrew Jackson's first effort as president to achieve his objective through diplomacy had failed.

Despite the removal law's characterization of western migration as voluntary, Jackson was not willing to accept the Chickasaws' decision. He ordered Coffee to obtain a new Chickasaw removal treaty. The task proved difficult. Quarrels within the Chickasaw Nation over eligibility for land allotments and over reserves to be set aside for prominent leaders plagued Coffee and the federal negotiators for over two years. But they finally obtained the Treaty of Pontotoc in 1832 by forging of Chief Levi Colbert's name to the document and then forcing other leaders to sign it. As historian Arrell Gibson put it, Coffee "drove a treaty down their throats."[69] The Treaty of Pontotoc provided for the survey of Chickasaw lands and the allotment of individual plots to heads of families. Those plots could then be sold to white settlers and thereby raise funds for the relocation to the west of that substantial majority of Chickasaw who, now deprived of their own government, would not wish to remain under the jurisdiction of Mississippi and Alabama. Despite protests from a number of people, white and Chickasaw, who had interests of various sorts in the matter, and reasons to expose the fraud, the Senate ratified the treaty in early 1833 by a vote of 34 to 4.[70]

Andrew Jackson immediately urged Coffee to "have the best part of the chickasaw country in market this fall so that a sufficient fund may be raised to meet all the wants of the chickasaws."[71] Those "wants" included the need to buy land in the west from the Choctaw, as the administration's plan to merge the two nations had fallen through. Jackson and Coffee refused the Chickasaw request that they be allowed to control the funding raised by their land sales. The president also continued to turn a deaf ear to Chickasaw pleas for federal protection, now needed to control the hordes of whites who, in defiance of treaties, laws, and decrees, ignored the land sale process and simply took what they could.[72]

Coffee's tactics in negotiating the Treaty of Pontotoc were not exceptional. Most if not all of the 70 some removal treaties negotiated during Jackson's presidency and thereafter were not really voluntary agreements but were generally obtained through various combinations of false promises, threats, bribery, and personal intimidation. Withholding or manipulating annuity funds owed Indians for prior land sales was a measure often employed to create hardships for those who resisted removal. Coffee at one point threatened to withhold funds badly needed to buy food, giving the Chickasaw the choice of compliance or hunger. Corruption in the payments of those annuities, in the allocation of removal expense appropriations, and in the assignment of land "reserves" not only to favored Indians but to some whites involved in the process was also commonplace. Cooperation with the demands of the negotiators could bring wealth to key chiefs. Resistance could lead to destitution or worse. These tactics were not Jacksonian inventions but had long characterized the processes through which Indians were persuaded to give up land. But the threat of the total withdrawal of federal protection and the prediction that Indians would soon face "annihilation" when placed in the hands of the states set the Jackson administration's bargaining strategy apart from earlier practices.

In their continued denial of responsibility for Indian well-being within the states, Jackson and his agents violated not only the Indian Trade and Intercourse

Act, and the guarantees contained in numerous still valid treaties, but also broke promises contained in new treaties they had negotiated under their own federal Indian Removal Act. Jackson may have really believed that his removal program was not only humane but beneficent. His scholarly defenders have on occasion not only stressed his good intentions but even portrayed him as the savior of the Indians.[73] But debates about intentions are all too often not only inconclusive but also of limited value in the assessment of outcomes. There is a more important question we must ask. It concerns not his motivation but his conduct. When problems and abuses in the removal process were brought to Jackson's attention, how did he respond? Was he willing to use his power and influence to protect his "red children?"

The record does not reflect favorably on Sharp Knife. The U.S. Senate in 1834–1835 published five very large volumes of correspondence from and to various federal officers charged with implementing removal. Those letters reveal great concern on the part of Andrew Jackson and his administration that removal be carried out not only quickly but cheaply. Removal agents and the contractors with whom they worked were repeatedly required to explain delays and justify irregular expenditures. But we find in the thousands of pages that make up that massive correspondence very little indication that Jackson was personally willing to intervene to ameliorate the many hardships Indians were enduring on their long marches westward. In the spring of 1832, to cite one example from many, the removal agent in Lebanon, Ohio, reported to his superiors that the emigrants were not being given adequate food and asked that the matter be brought to the attention of the president. Jackson dismissed the complaint and directed the commissary general to tell the agent that "the ration provided by the regulations" was "sufficient."[74] In fact, the ration often was not sufficient. For one thing, there were disputes over who was eligible to be fed. Agents were instructed to deny food to family members who had been late in registering for removal. The Ohio agent who asked that provision be made for all of the emigrants was told that the president had made it clear that "the idea of enlarging the muster roll cannot . . . be entertained."[75] Elsewhere, slaves accompanying Indian masters were also sometimes denied rations, as were some white "countrymen" accompanying Indian relatives. The worst abuses, however, stemmed from the practice of awarding contracts to private suppliers who submitted the lowest bids but then augmented their profits by providing the Indians with skimpy or spoiled portions. In one notorious case, the meat supply the contractors distributed came from a cache of old salt pork at Fort Gibson that had been declared unfit for human consumption five years earlier.[76]

Further south, in Louisiana, former senator Joseph Kerr, an eyewitness bystander to one chapter in the Choctaw removal, complained to secretary of war that the contractors hired to feed the Indians were not only not delivering the supplies they promised on schedule but were also cheating on the quantities allowed each family. "Their object," Kerr charged, "is to make money without the least feeling for the sufferings of their unfortunate people." Kerr recounted that on their march from Vicksburg, Mississippi, to Lake Providence, Louisiana, a distance of 68 miles, the Choctaws had been given only "scanty" rations, and received even less "to do them for the next leg of their migration which took them eighty miles through uninhabited country, fifty miles of which is an overflowed swamp . . . They were forced to ford nearly impassable streams . . . during the worst time of weather I have ever seen in any country—a heavy sleet having broken and bowed down all the small and much of the large timber. And all this was to be performed under pressure of hunger by old women and young children, without any covering for their feet, legs and body except an under-dress generally." Kerr asked the secretary of war to appeal to President Jackson to see to it that food was provided "for these long marches" even when the Indians fell behind schedule. He also suggested that instead of supplying to "each family, a blanket for each individual would not be too much . . . I would go further. I would give each at least a pair of shoes or moccasins and two pairs of short stockings." Appalled by the conditions he witnessed, Kerr declared the whites sent to oversee removal were "the most unprincipled of the human family." As a loyal Jacksonian, the former senator trusted Cass and Jackson who, he assumed, were honorable men unaware of the facts. He expected them to take action to ameliorate the sufferings of the Choctaws once they learned of their situation.[77]

Kerr heard nothing for two months, then received a letter from Commissary General George Gibson informing him that the federal government was not responsible for the Choctaws' plight, as they had chosen not to accept removal by steamboat, as proposed by government agents, but chose rather to go by land. The commissary general did not acknowledge that the Choctaw had good reason to fear steamboat travel as the boats were overcrowded, filthy, and disease ridden. He also failed to acknowledge that the Choctaws had been abused and cheated by the contractors they, of necessity, had to employ to supply the migrant parties. Kerr, for good reason, was not satisfied with Gibson's excuses but continued to question the actions of the contractors who supplied the migrants and the government agents who tolerated their abuses.[78]

Concerned primarily with "speed and economy," the administration did little to assure the food and other necessities with which emigrants were supplied met minimum standards.[79] Letters of appointment of white agents to direct and oversee the removals always included advice to deal with Indians in a "civil" and "humane" way, but in those thousands of pages of correspondence published by order of Congress we find very little evidence that those who ignored that counsel were disciplined. Overall, there was little real oversight. Jackson and his successors, as historian Ronald Satz notes, never developed a systematic set of guidelines for removal but "were willing to allow subordinates a considerable amount of decision-making power, including authority to exploit the economic naivete of the Indians and tribal rivalries in order to expedite Indian removal."[80] But in one respect the agents were closely supervised. Expenditures for funding of emergency needs, such as tents to shelter the sick and elderly in inclement weather, or medical care to some of those hundreds of migrants who were stricken with illness aboard steamboats or during the march westward, were often denied in the name of economy.

As a primary source providing insights into the effect of removal on Native American life and culture, these letters are disappointing. They were clearly written by bureaucrats preoccupied with regulations and ledger sheets. But in a few of the exchanges between agents and their superiors are we given glimpses of the conditions inflicted upon the human beings who were the subjects of this enterprise. We have, for example, the report of Special Indian Agent William S. Colquhoun from Vicksburg, Mississippi, dated December 10, 1831. He described the arrival of a band of Choctaws who marched "through sleet and snow, barefoot . . . they are generally very naked, and few moccasins are seen among them." He wished he could give them shoes. "The situation is distressing, and must get worse." In the months that follow, Colquhoun reported that Choctaw emigrants were packed onto filthy dilapidated steamboats infected with cholera and bubonic plague. They were forced, by the crowding, to travel standing in their own excrement. The agent found his budget woefully inadequate, and on occasion supplemented it with his own funds. In his reports, he continued to document and protest the deplorable conditions inflicted on his Choctaw charges.

In 1832, Colquhoun was demoted, and finally fired, ostensibly for drunkenness, mismanagement, insubordination, and assault. (At one point, he was accused of trying to pistol whip his superior officer during an argument about Indian supplies.)[81] After a careful review of the evidence, Native American historian Barbara Mann concludes that Colquhoun lost his job and his reputation, not because of his job performance, but because of his continued complaints about the "cruelties" of his superior, Major Francis W. Armstrong, complaints that became particularly vehement "when Armstrong refused blankets to the sick, wet, and dying Choctaws he had ordered back to disease in Vicksburg for transportation to the Land of Death."[82] Colquhoun was not the only removal agent whose career suffered in consequence of his advocacy for his charges. James B. Gardiner, the special commissioner of Ohio Removal, objected too vigorously to President Jackson's initial insistence that all Choctaws be transported by steamship. As a result, Mann concludes, Gardiner also lost his post and "his reputation was trashed at the highest level of government."[83] Those who hoped for preferment during Old Hickory's presidency had to keep their concern for Indians under careful control.

The Choctaw removal was the first migration negotiated and implemented under Jackson's Indian Removal Act. Assessing its first phase in 1831–1832, the program's director congratulated his agents for presumably having "effected a delicate task in a manner highly credible to themselves and to the government."[84] But Jackson and his close advisers were less satisfied, not because of the reports of Choctaw suffering (which they chose for the most part not to acknowledge) but by the cost, which had exceeded budget by over 200 percent. In 1832, Lewis Cass replaced John Eaton as secretary of war. Cass placed the management of the removal program in the hands of the army and undertook a series of measures designed to economize. Despite reports of hunger and on occasion near starvation, Cass ordered a reduction in food rations. Then, he issued guidelines which were to be followed "regardless of the circumstances." The secretary stipulated that special agents were to "determine the mode of transportation. If they traveled by land, all of the Indians would remove on foot except for the young and the infirm. The emigrants would be allowed only 1500 pounds of luggage for every fifty persons, no wooden or heavy utensils, and only one wagon for every fifty persons. If they traveled by water the special agent would rent steamboats, if government boats were unavailable." Cass's guidelines required that all supplies "were to be acquired by contract" but left it to the agents to determine if the contract terms were fulfilled in a satisfactory manner, thus opening the door to fraud. Finally, Cass added that "the United States government was not responsible for any accidents that occurred along the route."[85]

The Jackson administration regarded second phase of the Choctaw removal, conducted in 1832 under Cass's guidelines with the supervision of army, "much more successful than the first." But historian Arthur DeRosier, writing from the perspective of 1970, declared it "as much a failure as the previous effort. More Indians had been removed, but more had died of cholera and exposure, the government had saved money by making Indians walk more than five hundred miles and by cutting their rations, but the saving had been made at the sacrifice of Indian life and strength."[86] What was the cost in life? It is hard to calculate with any precision, but scholars generally agree that at least 6,000 Choctaw perished as a result of the removals.[87]

During his two terms in office, Andrew Jackson met on a few occasions with tribal leaders distressed by the conditions they found in their new homelands. To cite an example, a delegation of Chippewa, Potawatomi, and Ottawa chiefs, called on Jackson at the White House in 1835 to complain that "we have been deceived." Assured by Jackson's agent "that the country assigned to us west of the Mississippi was equally good as the lands in Illinois" they had been persuaded to give up, they found that "there is scarce timber enough to build our Wigwams, and some of that land is too poor for snakes to live upon." Old Hickory, they recalled, "listened . . . but did not hear."[88] He offered them no help. He knew very little about conditions in the areas west of the Mississippi where the tribes he uprooted were now to be resettled, and he was not much interested in learning more.[89] He generally ignored letters from disaffected Indians. For example, an elderly chief wrote to Jackson in the spring of 1831 to complain that while federal soldiers looked the other way when whites stole from Indians, they hunted down and shot Indians who resisted the thieves "as if . . . they had been so many wild dogs."[90] Jackson ignored the chief's appeal for protection and issued no new orders to the army.

Although he carefully reviewed their provisions, Jackson generally did not personally negotiate the treaties or preside directly over their enforcement. He relied not only on negotiators but on Indian agents. The agents played a key role. It should be remembered that earlier in his career, Jackson had been highly critical of agents he considered too sympathetic to their Indian charges. You will recall from earlier chapters his vendetta against Silas Dinsmore, his efforts to secure the dismissal of Benjamin Hawkins, and his fierce denunciation of Return J. Meigs. It is therefore not surprising that during his first term, Jackson fired half of the agents and subagents in the field and replaced them with his own handpicked appointees. Those appointees, as we will see, were not always men of exemplary behavior. One of his nominees, William Rector, was unable to serve, having been twice denied confirmation by the Senate. Rector had been convicted in Arkansas of attempted murder and had fled the jurisdiction. The senators did not find Jackson's efforts to attest to his good character persuasive.[91]

Jackson tolerated no criticism of his removal policy from whites living in Indian country and took steps to silence them. Indian agents were not his only target. A directive from the Indian Affairs office advised that all opponents of government Indian policy were to be excluded from the territories.[92] When Choctaw agent William Ward wrote Jackson to complain that Presbyterian missionary Louring S. Williams had urged the Choctaws to resist removal, the president ordered Williams's arrest.[93] During the negotiation of the Choctaw removal treaty at Dancing Rabbit Creek in September 1830, missionaries were excluded, by order of the secretary of war, from the treaty grounds, although "the worst elements of white society" were welcomed. "Gamblers, saloonkeepers, frontier rowdies, and prostitutes, all interested in separating the Indians from their meager possessions, established themselves on one side of the treaty ground and plied their trade under the assumed protection of the United States government." Among their number were "two noted desperadoes, Red-headed Bill and Black-headed McGrews."[94]

Jackson was well aware of the misdeeds committed or tolerated by his Indian agents. Shortly after leaving the White House, he told his friend and ally Francis Blair that "dealing with the Indian office was the most arduous part of my duty, and I watched over it with great vigilance, and could hardly keep it under proper restraint, and free from abuse and injury to the administration."[95] But his claim about "proper restraint" cannot be accepted at face value. While Jackson removed some corrupt agents and contractors who were defrauding either the government or white investors, an examination of the record fails to provide us with instances in which he intervened to protect or reimburse any of the thousands of the Indians abused, defrauded, or robbed during the removal process, sometimes with the help of the very officials charged by law with their protection. The Benjamin Smith case exemplifies Jackson's failure. Smith, a friend and supporter of the president, was the Chickasaw Indian agent. He not only defrauded his Indian charges by paying removal claims in depreciated rag money but stole outright thousands of dollars of tribal funds. With the exposure of Smith's embezzlements, he was forced to resign. But there was no further penalty. Despite the administration's awareness of the substantial evidence against him, Smith was never prosecuted and was instead allowed to keep his ill-gotten wealth. His Chickasaw victims got nothing.[96] Jackson was also forced to remove John Phagan, his agent in Florida. But Phagan was dismissed not for his notorious abuse of the Seminoles, which helped provoke a major Indian war, but for embezzling public funds.[97]

When Senator Ewing of Ohio complained that yet another of Jackson agents was guilty of "frauds, deceptions, and treacheries," the president's response was that even if those charges were proven, it "would in no manner affect the validity" of the removal treaty he had negotiated.[98] Jackson consistently told Indian supplicants that they could find safety only on the federal lands in the west. Jackson's old Seminole War colleague General Edmund Gaines privately deplored the administration's failure to protect Indians "from the clutches of those hordes of swindlers, who have been hovering about them, in violation of our laws, and preying, like so many vultures upon the vitals of these ill fated tribes." Those comments did not set well with Sharp Knife.[99]

For a prime example of Jackson's toleration of the abuse of Indians, we have only to look at the record of William Ward, agent to the Choctaws. Under the terms of the Treaty of Dancing Rabbit Creek, the federal government was obligated to provide, from the Mississippi lands now ceded by the Choctaw, individual allotments which the recipients could either occupy under state jurisdiction or sell to finance their removal to the west. But agent Ward, an alcoholic, was seldom available to Indians seeking to claim their allotments. When he did visit the land registration office, he erased many of the entries recording Indian claims. Ward informed Washington, D.C., that only 69 Choctaw had qualified for allotments. He conceded that that many more had tried to do so but explained that he had denied them land grants on the grounds that they had probably been influenced by "designing men" who opposed the removal program. When the Choctaws brought Ward's outrageous and illegal behavior to the president's attention, Jackson refused to do anything, claiming he had no jurisdiction. Perhaps, he suggested, the Choctaws rendered homeless and destitute by Ward's refusal to honor their claims should look to Congress for relief. Despite ample evidence of his malfeasance, agent Ward was not removed but on the contrary continued to enjoy Jackson's confidence. When he informed the president that the Choctaws had no objection to whites taking up residence in their territory prior to the September 1833 transfer date set in the treaty, Jackson believed him and revoked his earlier order to remove white intruders.[100] Secretary of War Cass assured Mississippi congressman Franklin Plummer that "the president is happy . . . that he is not called upon to execute those . . . provisions of the treaty" that forbade immediate white occupation of Choctaw land.[101]

Despite his earlier disavowal of jurisdiction, Jackson finally did order an investigation of the Choctaw land claims. His discovery of his power to do so was prompted by the complaints from several prominent Mississippi Democrats who had hoped to profit from the purchase and resale of Choctaw allotments. At the urging of his good friend William Gwin, a federal marshal, attorney, and land speculator currently serving as Mississippi's registrar of public lands, Jackson authorized an investigation which led, among other things, to the confirmation of around a thousand Indian land grants Ward had tried to suppress. The Mississippi allotment fraud investigations took nearly a decade and pitted white settlers and speculators against one another. It is a complicated and sordid story.[102] Jackson denounced the speculators but continued to regard Indian removal as the sole means of protecting Choctaws and other Indians from the unprincipled and the corrupt. In those cases where claims commissioners found evidence of the illegal dispossession of Choctaws, the victims did not receive the land allotments to which they were entitled, but rather were to be given in compensation paper script. But half of the script the Choctaw were supposed to receive was never issued. Much of the rest fell into the hands of speculators. As to the Choctaws left destitute through various shady land transactions, Jackson's secretary of war Lewis Cass declared that the Indians themselves were to blame because their own poor judgment and "improvident habits" had led them to make bad decisions.[103]

The Choctaws were not an exception. The Jackson administration consistently failed to honor promises to Indians contained in the removal treaties it negotiated with Indian tribes and nations. The controversies that developed over the allocation of Creek land allotments offers additional examples of Jackson's disregard of his responsibilities to his "Indian children." In 1826, as you will recall, the Adams administration repudiated the fraudulent Treaty of Indian Springs, which had taken from the Creeks all of their holdings in Georgia and "the northern two thirds of the national domain in Alabama."[104] But while Adams refused to accept the Indian Springs travesty, or endorse Georgia's claim of the right to pre-empt Indian land without their consent, he was eager to avoid a conflict with the state over this issue. Accordingly, Creek leaders were persuaded to accept a new treaty that required that they leave Georgia and resettle some 7,000 people on their restored territory in Alabama. But their Alabama holdings, as redefined by the new treaty, were "of low quality," having very little good soil. They were far from adequate to support that many refugee Creeks.[105] Alabama's state government had no interest in making provision for several thousand new Indian residents. They knew full well that the lands to be assigned to the displaced Creeks could not really support them.

Reports from Alabama in 1827 and 1828 were grim. One report, addressed to Secretary of War Barbour, declared that the Creeks arriving in Alabama "were in the most miserable and wretched condition it is possible to conceive. Many of them skeletons and their bones almost worn through the skin."[106] A British visitor, Captain Basil Hall, declared in shock "great numbers of them actually perished from want."[107] In order to survive, many of the Creek emigrants from Georgia trying to find a place in Alabama were forced by hunger to sell the land claim certificates they had been given for their "improvements" on the land they had relinquished in Georgia. They were left destitute. They were frequently victimized by price-gouging merchants, land speculators, and other white operators of questionable character, and occasionally by opportunistic fellow Indians as well. Merchants sold liquor and other commodities on credit to needy Creeks, then laid claim to annuity funds and land allotment titles in satisfaction of those new debts. One scholar notes that "by 1833 it was estimated that there were almost four hundred whiskey shops in the Creek country."[108] White traders, often in collusion with corrupt local officials, seized Indian lands and property in satisfaction of past debts real or imaginary.

Early in Andrew Jackson's administration, Creek leaders appealed to "our father the president" to remove "the white people" who, in violation of prior treaty guarantees, were settling on their land and stealing "our Negroes and our horses." Alabama courts, they complained, would not hear their testimony about "the thefts."[109] Jackson did not honor their request that he take action to "protect the rights guaranteed to us by the U.S. government." His representatives, however, suggested that they would be protected if they agreed to transfer their Alabama holdings to the federal government. Under the term of the 1832 Treaty of Cusseta, the Creeks ceded to the federal government the 5,200,000 acres they held in Alabama and were to receive in return individual land allotments in Alabama totaling 2,157,000 acres. They could either live on those allotments or sell them and use the money from the sales to resettle west of the Mississippi where a band of Creeks loyal to the late Chief McIntosh had lived for some years. Those who remained in Alabama and cultivated their allotment lands for five years were to be given title to that land and state citizenship.[110]

For number of years, the federal government had sought, and failed, to persuade the Creek leadership to agree to removal west of the Mississippi. Chief McIntosh had been executed in punishment for his involvement in the removal negotiations of 1825. Over the years, the chiefs from time to time had threatened the lives of other advocates of relocation. Although several bands of Creeks did join the McIntosh settlement in the Indian Territory, it is estimated that around 90 percent of the nation opposed their enterprise. It is, therefore, important to note that the Creek leaders who signed at Cusseta believed that they had negotiated a secure alternative to removal for those who wished to remain. They were wrong.

Although the Alabama legislature did not delay the extension of Alabama sovereignty over the Creek country, the state took no action to protect the personal and property rights of the Creek. The plea sent by the chiefs to the Great Father in 1830 remained unanswered. The Creek governing council once again begged the Jackson administration to enforce the treaty and remove intruders, telling Secretary of War Cass "we are surrounded . . . our lives are in jeopardy, we are daily threatened."[111] The local federal marshal confirmed the chiefs' complaint, reporting that white squatters "had not only taken the Indians' land from them and burnt and destroyed their houses and corn, but used violence to their persons."[112] Frontier "roughs" did not bother with contrived legalities but took what they could, stealing cattle, horses, food supplies, tools, whatever they could carry away. At the other end of the white social scale Columbus, Georgia, a new town planted across the border from Creek Territory became a center for wealthy and avaricious land speculators who preyed on Indians.[113]

Creeks thrown off their land by intruders or defrauded by speculators received little help from federal agents or from the investigators the administration dispatched to Alabama. While more than willing to investigate and provide federal adjudication of the conflicting claims of whites who had cheated one another in the purchase of Creek lands, Jacksonian officials were not particularly concerned about their Creek victims. The president for his part was worried that white settlers of limited means would be displaced by voracious speculators in the rush to lay claim to the lands the Creeks gave up at Cusseta and profit from their sale and resale. But as one federal agent put it, "the interest of the Indian is not much at hart [sic]" in Alabama land fraud investigations.[114] Another reported that nowhere in the world could one find "a greater mass of corruption . . . than has been engendered by the Creek treaty."[115] While the Creek Indian agent, John Crowell, unlike his Choctaw counterpart, encouraged Indian land claims, the leading historian of this sorry episode concludes that his main interest was in profiting personally through the acquisition of Creek land when allotments were sold at bargain prices.[116] As to the condition of Crowell's charges, a federal official writing in early 1833, warned that many faced starvation. "How the Indians are going to subsist the present year I can't imagine. Some of them are sustaining themselves upon roots. They have, apparently, very little corn, and scarcely any flock. The game is gone, and what they are to do, God only knows."[117]

Andrew Jackson had expressed the hope that the Creeks would be treated fairly as the treaty was implemented. But he was not willing to make use of his powers as president to secure that end. Jackson was obligated, by federal legislation and by the terms of the Treaty of Cusseta, to eject whites who occupied Creek land before it had been surveyed and allocated. By his order, federal agents initially made some efforts to do so. But when the governor of Alabama John Gayle threatened civil war in a dispute over jurisdiction triggered by the killing of a squatter by federal soldiers, the president suspended the removals and dispatched Francis Scott Key, a Maryland lawyer and amateur poet (author of the lyrics to the "Star-Spangled Banner") to Alabama to negotiate a settlement with the defiant governor. Key's proposed settlement essentially protected white squatters who would no longer be removed from the land they had illegally occupied. If they had settled on an allotment already awarded to the Creeks, the new agreement with the governor specified that they could either buy the land in question at a low price or accept an allocation from the Creek land taken from them under the Cusseta agreement. The president heeded Key's advice and essentially nullified that portion of the treaty that appeared to protect Creek ownership of their remaining Alabama lands.[118]

Key recognized that the Creeks "were in deplorable condition," having been victimized by both frontier ruffians and gentlemanly speculators and so informed the administration. Other reports established that the vast majority of the land allotments approved under the Cusseta Treaty deprived the rightful Indian owners of their land. One federal agent estimated that "nineteen out of twenty contracts he certified were fraudulent."[119] The Creeks who were the victims of those frauds were not only left without the lands in Alabama they had been promised, but lacked the means to emigrate, or pay their debts to white merchants and liquor dealers. Some became laborers on white farms, living in a state of debt peonage. Others were reduced to wandering the countryside, selling the few goods they had, or resorting to theft, to survive. White "roughs" on occasion joined with landless Indians to steal horses and raid farms. But most of the dispossessed Creeks had no means of support whatsoever. A petition from a number of white settlers in Columbus, Georgia, to President Andrew Jackson asked that he intercede to save Indian lives, as "large bodies" were "in a state of actual starvation ... if they are not speedily relieved by some general and systematic plan, great numbers of them must inevitably perish." The administration refused to help, declaring its unwillingness to promote Indian "idleness," or give them any reason to believe that they could continue to live among the Americans.[120]

In the summer of 1832, as tensions mounted after attacks on white settlers, a confrontation between the Georgia militia and a band of dispossessed Creeks in the Chattahoochee Valley in May turned violent. In the weeks that followed, hostile Creek warriors, sometimes accompanied by lawless whites, robbed stage coaches, murdered settlers on isolated homesteads, and burned several small settlements.

Jackson's response was to suspend the investigation of land frauds and order the forced deportation of virtually all of the Alabama Creeks. This order applied not only to Creeks who had attacked whites, but also to those who had not. Most had not been involved in this affair at all. Some had actually fought on the side of the United States in the previous Creek War and in this uprising. There was no justification in federal law for their dispossession. Nonetheless, some 10,000 troops commanded by federal generals Winfield Scott and Thomas Jessup not only fought and defeated Creek insurgents but rounded up and transported to Indian Territory nearly 20,000 Creek men, women, and children, "some of them handcuffed and in chains," the vast majority innocent of any offense. The process extended over two years. Some traditionalist Creeks, believing that the west was a region of misery filled with the ghosts of the dead, committed suicide in the relocation holding camps.[121] Exempted from deportation were a handful of wealthy Creek planters and slaveholders, many of them of mixed blood, who had fought for Jackson against the Red Sticks in the First Creek War. Several hundred other Creeks evaded capture and removal. Some hid out in remote areas of Alabama. Others joined the Seminoles in Florida.[122] While white Alabamans generally regarded the removal of the Creeks as essential both to their own prosperity and Indian well-being, a number of prominent citizens and several newspapers were outspoken in their condemnation of land speculators, merchants, and grog shop operators for provoking a Second Creek War through their abuse of the Indians.[123]

The most controversial and contentious removal negotiations involved the Cherokee residing in Georgia. Unlike the Choctaw and the Creek in Mississippi and Alabama, the Cherokee were not given the option of remaining within the state as citizens subject to its laws. Georgia officials had long demanded their total removal, and Andrew Jackson, after first holding out the prospect of Indian citizenship under state jurisdiction, soon yielded to Georgia's insistence that no Indian be allowed to remain within the state. In 1833, he advised Congress that the Cherokees themselves were to blame for this situation. For too long they had lived "in the midst of a superior race without appreciating the causes of their inferiority or seeking to control them." Given their lack of progress in transcending their essential backwardness and savagery, the Cherokee had no choice. They must "yield to the force of circumstance and ere long disappear."[124] Two years later, Georgia's governor Wilson Lumpkin commended Jackson for his "general plans and policies for relieving the states from their remnant Indian population." The governor reiterated the state's determination that no Indian would be allowed to own land in Georgia.[125]

The Cherokee leaders, you will recall, had declined Jackson's invitation to meet with him at Franklin in the fall of 1830. They had petitioned both Jackson and the Congress for protection against the aggression of the state of Georgia and of lawless individuals the state had refused to control.[126] Those appeals failed. Neither the president nor Congress would take steps to uphold long-standing treaty guarantees to the Cherokee. But Principal Chief John Ross and his associates believed that they would receive a more sympathetic hearing from the federal Supreme Court. Encouraged by Jeremiah Evarts and other white allies, the nation engaged William Wirt, the former attorney general of the United States, as their attorney. Wirt was assisted by John Sergeant, who would serve as Henry Clay's running mate in the 1832 presidential election. The Cherokee recourse to litigation was not surprising, as they had incorporated many features of Anglo-American jurisprudence into their own political and legal structure, and had worked hard to blend Cherokee traditions and modern innovations. The 1827 constitution of the Cherokee Republic was modeled after the federal and state constitutions of the United States. But it also was rooted in certain fundamental Cherokee values and underscored the importance of communalism. Private ownership and sale of land was forbidden, as Article 1, section 2 declared all Cherokee territories "are, and shall remain, the common property of the nation."[127] While the adoption of some Anglo-American concepts and practices provoked traditionalist opposition (led for a time by the dissident chief White Path), the Cherokee had no intention of gratifying white well-wishers who hoped for their elimination as a nation. Their leaders sought through litigation to protect the nation's land base, its political autonomy, and its cultural integrity.

Previous federal court rulings on the status of Native Americans had been somewhat uneven and inconclusive, but they did offer reasons for hope. In *Fletcher v. Peck*, a controversy over purchases of Indian land decided in 1816, Chief Justice John Marshall added to his lengthy commentary on the sanctity of contracts a brief statement regarding Indian land titles. Indians, he declared, did not possess full legal title in fee simple as they were uncivilized and "merely roamed over and hunted on the land . . . It is a mere occupancy for the purpose of hunting. It is not like our own tenures idea of a title to the land itself." But Marshall significantly invented a new category, "Indian title," which was "a right of occupancy" that could be "extinguished" only through the federal treaty-making process. In the absence of a voluntary land cession, Indians could not be dispossessed.[128] In *Johnson v. McIntosh*, decided in 1823, the court invoked the doctrine of discovery, which conferred sovereign rights on European colonizers. Since the United States had gained through conquest the "discovery rights" previously enjoyed by Great Britain, it followed, the Marshall court declared, that no Indian nation could sell any of their land or engage in any commerce except with the consent of the federal government. While the doctrine of discovery denied to Indian nations full sovereignty, it did not strip them of the rights to internal self-government guaranteed in treaties, or of what Marshall had defined as a "right of occupancy" conferred by "Indian title." The Cherokee thus had ample precedent to ask for federal court intervention to block Georgia's efforts to take from them both their independence and their land.

The first case the Cherokee and their supporters brought to the court dealt with the kidnapping and trial by Georgia of one George Tassel, a Cherokee, who had killed a fellow tribesman on Cherokee land. Responding to a challenge to the state's action, the Georgia Supreme Court ruled that Georgia, under the doctrine of discovery, possessed full jurisdiction over all territory within its boundaries. It declared that any "compacts, misnamed treaties" that the federal government might have entered into with Indian tribes that limited state action were "simply void." The Cherokee, through their attorney William Wirt, appealed to the U.S. Supreme Court. Chief Justice Marshall issued a writ of error. Georgia officials, called upon to show cause why their action in the Tassel's case should not be set aside, refused to answer Marshall's summons. The state legislature, after declaring that the federal court had no right to interfere in Georgia's internal affairs, ordered Tassel's immediate execution, and on December 24, 1830, he was hung.[129]

The outcome of the second case was also disappointing. In 1831, in *Cherokee Nation v. Georgia*, the court declared that it was unable to hear a Cherokee suit, which challenged the legality of Georgia's denial of their right to self-government. Chief Justice Marshall expressed personal sympathy for their cause but led the court in ruling that the Cherokee tribe was not a foreign nation entitled under the Constitution to sue in federal court but was rather, in Chief Justice Marshall's words, a "domestic dependent nation . . . in a state of pupilage" to the United States. Marshall's creation of a unique new category of statehood, unrecognized in international law, has often been characterized as a facile way out of a very difficult political position. It was not, however, the chief justice's last word on the matter.[130]

Georgia, angered by the sympathy for the Cherokee cause expressed by a number of Protestant missionaries, in 1831 passed a law denying whites the right to live in Cherokee country without a license from the state. Georgia authorities then arrested eleven missionaries, nine of whom accepted pardons from the governor and promised to respect Georgia laws. But two others—Samuel Worcester and Elizer Butler—denied Georgia's right to ban them from Cherokee country and accordingly refused to accept pardons. They were convicted and sentenced to four years at hard labor in the state penitentiary. As the missionaries, being American citizens, did have standing to sue in federal court, their case (*Worcester v. Georgia*) was heard. Writing for the court's majority, Marshall declared unequivocally that "Indian nations have always been considered as distinct, independent political communities, retaining their original natural rights, as the undisputed possessors of the soil." The fact that they lived under the special protection of the United States and lacked full sovereignty did not strip them "of the right to self government." To the contrary, treaties and federal laws placed them outside the authority of the state of Georgia. In convicting the missionaries, and in its other violations of Cherokee rights, the state had acted illegally. The court ordered the release of Butler and Worcester. Georgia, which had once again refused to appear before the court, at first ignored the order. Governor Lumpkin declared he would hang Butler and Worcester rather than submit to "this decision of a few superannuated life estate Judges." But representatives of the Jackson administration, hoping in the midst of the Nullification controversy to avoid any further agitation over states' rights, urged the governor to reconsider. On further reflection, Lumpkin decided to release the missionaries on the condition that they ask for pardons and agree to make no further appeals to the Supreme Court. They were set free in January 1833.[131]

It was once widely believed that Andrew Jackson, on receiving word of the Supreme Court ruling, quipped, "John Marshall has made his decision. Now let him enforce it!" But there is no contemporary evidence to support that claim, which is now generally regarded as apocryphal.[132] Jackson did, however, note in a letter to his good friend John Coffee that the "the decision of the Supreme Court has fallen still born . . . it cannot coerce Georgia to yield to its mandate." He added that even if he were inclined to use military force to implement the court's ruling, "not one regiment of militia" were to obey his command. The end result of efforts to force the state to respect Cherokee rights would be disastrous, as "the arm of the government is not sufficiently strong to preserve them from destruction."[133]

Jackson's observation about the court's weakness was correct. In 1832, the Supreme Court did not possess the power to coerce but had to rely upon Georgia to honor its decision, which the state refused to do. Moreover, state court rulings held that the federal government had no jurisdiction over Indians living within state boundaries. The tribes were not sovereign nations under federal protection but were totally subject to state authority. The leading authority on those cases declares that their decisions in *Georgia v. Tassals*, 1830, *Caldwell v. Alabama*, 1831, and *Tennessee v. Foreman*, 1833, were "backed by legal rationale as duplicitous and fallacious as any in American legal history."[134] But Andrew Jackson agreed with the state courts. Moreover, he denied that Marshall's court had any exclusive right to determine questions of constitutionality. In the 1830s, federal judiciary quite simply did not have the means to protect Native Americans from state power or presidential malfeasance. John Marshall could not in fact enforce his decision.

Following the court's earlier decision in *Cherokee Nation v. Georgia*, a Cherokee delegation paid a courtesy call on President Jackson and used the occasion to inquire if he would now intervene to protect the rights that Marshall had affirmed were theirs. As John Ridge recalled the conversation in a letter printed in the *Cherokee Phoenix*, the president gently reproached his guests for allowing "your lawyers to fleece you." He assured his visitors of his continuing affection for the Cherokee people. They had "freely shed their blood with the blood of my soldiers in defending the United States . . . how could I be otherwise than their friend?" But Jackson emphasized that by denying that the Cherokees were fully sovereign "the court has sustained my view with regard to your nation . . . you can live on your lands in Georgia if you choose, but I cannot interfere with the laws of that state to protect you." To illustrate the dangers of remaining in territories "surrounded by white people," Jackson told an ugly story about the deterioration of the Catawba who in their heyday sometimes, in demonstration of their power, took Cherokee warriors, "threw them in the fire and, when their intestines were barbequed, ate them." The Catawba were no longer feared, Jackson declared, but were now "poor, miserable, reduced in numbers."[135] In his many conversations with Indian leaders over his two terms as president, Jackson continued to predict suffering and destitution for those Indians who persisted in living close to the superior race.

After the Supreme Court in *Worcester v. Georgia* issued a more clear-cut decision that upheld the Cherokees' right to internal self-government, Ridge met with Jackson again and urged him to enforce the new decision and thereby protect the Cherokee Nation. His expectations were low. "The old chicken snake General Jackson," Ridge remarked a few days before the meeting, "has time to crawl and hide in the luxuriant grass of his nefarious hypocrisy."[136] Ridge and his two fellow delegates to the U.S. government had received from Ross formal instructions to demand that Jackson finally take steps to honor past treaties with Cherokee and protect them from Georgia's aggression. They were also to advise him that "the Cherokee will never consentingly abandon this country to move west of the Mississippi River."[137] Responding to those points, the president once again refused to offer any federal protection for those Indians who lived within state boundaries, declaring that he had no constitutional power do so. He advised Ridge "most earnestly" to go home and persuade his people to accept relocation in the west.

After the meeting, Jackson told his friend John Coffee that he believed he had made his point. In fact, he had. Reflecting on his conversation with the president after leaving the White House, a deeply discouraged John Ridge reluctantly concluded that the "old chicken snake" was telling the truth when he warned that the survival of the Cherokee as a people now required that they abandon their homeland.[138] While in Washington, Ridge had conversed with a number of white leaders who had supported the Cherokee appeal. Their assessments of the political situation were not reassuring. Jackson, they now believed, would inevitably prevail. Back home in the Cherokee Nation, John Ridge now advised there was no real alternative to removal. He persuaded his father Major Ridge, a chief of great influence, as well as his cousin Elias Boudinot, editor of the *Phoenix*, and a handful of other prominent Cherokee leaders that further resistance was futile. Ridge called on Principal Chief John Ross to undertake a search for a new homeland. "We all know," he wrote Ross, "that we can't be a nation here. I hope we shall attempt to establish it somewhere else!"[139] Ross, however, was still unwilling to consider removal and used his power as principal chief to block public debate on this issue. The Ridges and Boudinot in response formed a rival faction that came to be known as the "Treaty Party." Their conflict with Ross would soon turn not only acrimonious but violent.

Andrew Jackson had no respect for John Ross. He privately described the leader of the Cherokee Nation as "a great villain," seeing him as a prime example of the affluent, mixed-blood opportunist who lacked the integrity and spirit of the true Indian warrior. People like Ross, he believed, were selfish and greedy and cared nothing for the good of their people. Ross, who had been chosen principal chief in 1828, was indeed a very affluent merchant and planter of predominantly white ancestry, the descendant of two generations of traders who had fared very well in Cherokee country. At the time of his selection as head of the nation, Ross owned 19 slaves and a plantation of some 175 acres. His establishment included not only a commodious and well-appointed two-story house but a number of other buildings, including stables, a wagon house, a blacksmith shop, and several workshops. His very comfortable income came not only from fields and orchards but also from a store and a ferry he ran on the Coosa River. His unwavering opposition to removal was hardly opportunistic, as it would soon place at risk not only his fortune but his life.

Although Ross was a passionate defender of Cherokee sovereignty and land rights, he was not an unconditional defender of traditional Cherokee culture. In a letter to President-Elect John Quincy Adams in 1825, Ross had expressed the hope that as the Cherokees continued to give up their "aboriginal ways" and embrace "civilization" they would win acceptance as good neighbors to white Americans.[140] In his annual address to the Cherokee Nation in 1831, he predicted that in time his people would be incorporated into "the great family of the American republic" as a new state in the union. Ross was confident that they would win that status through abandoning their past "savagery."[141]

Cherokee spokesmen in their quest for allies in the fight against removal commonly sought to refute the Jacksonian argument that they were still living like "savages." Elias Boudinot, the future editor of the *Cherokee Phoenix*, in a series of speeches delivered a fund-raising trip through New England in 1826, assured his hearers that he understood the fear and loathing of Indians prompted by past recollections of the horrors of "savage warfare" of "the yells pronounced over the mangled bodies of women and children." He prayed that his audience would come to understand that the Cherokee were now "bursting the fetters of ignorance," abandoning the "vices of heathenism," and, with white help, would transform themselves into an "intelligent and virtuous people." He enumerated the "savage" customs the Cherokee were now setting aside: polygamy, promiscuity, idolatry, clan blood vengeance, and "the practice of putting aged people to death for witchcraft." With proper nurture and assistance from whites other Indian peoples could also be saved.[142]

Several years later, John Ridge (before his change of heart on the removal question) struck a more aggressive note during speaking engagements in New York and Philadelphia. "You asked us to throw off the hunter and warrior state. We did so. You asked us to form a republican government: we did so—adapting your own as our model. You asked us to cultivate the earth and learn the mechanic arts. We did so. You asked us to learn to read. We did so. You asked us to cast away our idols and worship your God. We did so." The conclusion was obvious. Georgia and Jackson had no right now to declare the Cherokee, savages unworthy of remaining on their homelands.[143] But John Ridge failed to understand that "the factor that most antagonized the Georgia state government was not actually the recalcitrant savagery of which Indians were routinely accused, but the Cherokee's unmistakable aptitude for civilization."[144] As historian Sean Michael O'Brien notes, "the self made Cherokee entrepreneur was really what white Georgians feared. Their biggest obstacle to acquiring Cherokee lands was the cultivator's plow and the overseer's whip—not the war club, bow, and scalping knife."[145] Andrew Jackson commonly argued that opposition to his removal plan came primarily not from "real" Indians but from prosperous mixed-race farmers, ranchers, slaveholders, tavern keepers, and others who profited from the status quo. That statement was not at all accurate, but it did expose if not the hypocrisy then at minimum the ambivalence in Jacksonian attitudes about civilization and savagery. Savagery, however imaginary, could be politically useful.

At the outset, Ross and his colleagues in resistance won the support of some very prominent anti-Jacksonian politicians. Former president John Quincy Adams, now serving in Congress, presented to the House an anti-removal petition that was some 47 yards long.[146] Henry Clay, the Whig presidential candidate in 1832, was no admirer of Indian character, but he had long deplored Jackson's "cruel violence" toward those unfortunate albeit inferior people.[147] Declaring the Removal Act "a foul and lasting stain upon the good faith, humanity and character of the nation," Clay determined to rally the emerging anti-Jackson opposition party to prevent the laws' enforcement.[148] The strategy to be employed was to block appropriation bills in the House and refuse to ratify removal treaties in the Senate. Although opposition Congressman, acting from a variety of motives ranging from political opportunism to sincere concern for Native American well-being, made obstruction of removal one of their objectives, they were never able to stop the removal process. No appropriation bills were defeated. Only the New York Iroquois succeeded in negotiating the right to retain some of their tribal lands in the east.[149] Sporadic efforts to repeal the Indian Removal Act failed. Although the steady stream of anti-removal petitions received by Congress gave evidence of popular outrage, those petitions predictably came largely from the northeast. Opinion in the West remained somewhat divided, with a majority of western congressmen supporting Jackson. In the South, while opposition to removal was not absent, it was muted, and Southerners controlled the Senate. Even so, Clay believed that he could win the presidency by coupling an attack on Jackson's "barbarous and cruel" Indian policy with a call for repudiation of his banking policy and a repetition of the previous decade's attack on his character, temperament, and intellectual fitness for office. He was wrong. Even though Van Buren believed, perhaps correctly, that the Indian issue cost him several thousand votes in New York, Jackson easily won reelection. With the nullification/tariff revision issues foremost in early 1833, Webster, Clay, and some other opposition leaders came to regard the Cherokees and their missionary allies as an "embarrassment." Nothing, in their view, should be done to incite further agitation over states' rights.[150]

With the Cherokee judicial campaign "still born," to use Jackson's phrase, and Jackson himself reelected, the "friends of the Indians" in Congress advised the Cherokees and other Indian nations that their cause was lost. They should now seek from Jackson the best terms they could secure.[151] Their missionary allies agreed. Early in 1833, Ross received a letter from the American Board advising that "it would conduce to the best good of the Cherokees for them to accept terms proposed to them by the Government of the United States and remove to the Country west of the Mississippi." The board would no longer send missionaries to the Cherokee settlements east of that river.[152]

Despite the severe reservations about their prospects now voiced by erstwhile white supporters, Ross and a solid majority of the citizens of the Cherokee Nation persisted in their refusal to agree to a removal treaty. At the beginning of the process, Jackson had predicted that the only substantial Indian opposition to his program would come from privileged and wealthy tribal leaders of mixed blood who profiteered from the status quo. "I have no doubt," he wrote Secretary of War Eaton in 1830, "but that the common Indians, seeing that their chiefs have become wealthy by the course pursued by them, whilst the common Indians have been reduced to beggary, will soon burst their bonds of slavery, and compel their chiefs to propose terms for their removal."[153] Jackson cherished a fantasy image of the true full-blooded Indian male as an unreconstructed hunter/warriors who would be grateful for his efforts to protect traditional ways of life through removal to the west. But the uprising of "common Indians" angry at their presumed exploitation by a mixed-race elite never materialized. Analysis of the background and status of those who led the so-called Treaty Party indicates that, apart from the Ridges, they came neither from the wealthy elite nor from the ranks of the impoverished. They were generally "better off economically than the vast majority of Cherokees" but found "avenues of wealth blocked by the aristocracy" that controlled the Cherokee government. Removal, writes Theda Purdue, enjoyed the support only of a "small, dissatisfied and ambitious middle class."[154]

As we noted earlier, removal treaties across the country were the product of negotiations between Jackson's agents and tribal leaders. In those cases where legitimate leaders could not be persuaded through reason, bribery or coercion, other members of the nation were located who would sign. In the case of the Cherokee, Jackson from the outset sought to undermine the government elected under the 1827 constitution by refusing to continue the long-standing practice of paying annuities owed for previous land cessions directly to the tribal leaders. Instead, the money was paid in small amounts to individual Cherokee. Ross was forced to cover some of the costs of the Cherokee government out of his own pocket. Jackson also, as we have noted, refused to honor previous treaty provisions extending federal protection to the tribe and made clear his intention to disregard the Supreme Court's decision upholding the Cherokees' right to self-government. Georgia had declared that government illegal and threatened to imprison Cherokees who tried to carry out its functions. In addition to the punitive legislation passed by the state, Cherokees were harassed by white ruffians who invaded their territory, stole horses, despoiled crops, burned houses, and sometimes assaulted and killed their owners. Neither Georgia nor the federal government offered the Cherokee any real protection. As Indians could not testify against whites in Georgia courts, they were essentially defenseless.[155]

Although he remained opposed to removal, Ross came to realize that the Supreme Court decision would not be enforced and that neither the president nor Congress would intervene to protect the Cherokee from the Georgians. He reluctantly accepted the need to make some concessions. He had previously refused Jackson's invitation to come to the Hermitage to discuss a removal treaty. But Ross now proposed to Jackson a compromise that would provide whites with a very substantial new land cession but retain parts of the homeland for those Cherokee who chose not to move across the Mississippi. He offered to abandon the nation's land holdings in Georgia if the Cherokee Nation were allowed to keep and reside on a reserve of land in the border regions of Alabama, Mississippi, Tennessee, and North Carolina. He also asked that Cherokees who chose to do so be allowed to become citizens of the United States and remain in Georgia subject to the state's jurisdiction.[156] Jackson rejected those proposals out of hand and demanded that all of the Cherokee agree to move west. Ross then tried to negotiate a good price, asking, in light of the recent gold strike in Cherokee country, some $20,000,000. Jackson declared that preposterous. Both men then agreed to defer to the Senate, which suggested $5,000,000, a sum Jackson considered generous but Ross found far too low.[157]

Ross did not trust Jackson. He was convinced that the western lands Jackson touted as the Cherokees' salvation were nothing more than "a prairie badly watered" with few trees, already claimed by "fifteen or twenty different tribes." He foresaw a bleak future of deprivation and conflict in that "barren and inhospitable region," and predicted that removal would mean "degradation, dispersion, and the ultimate extinction of our race."[158] In 1831, in a letter to Congressman Davy Crockett, Ross had declared Jackson's policy regarding Indians "unrelenting and its effect ruinous to their best interests and happiness."[159] His dealings with Jackson three years later did nothing to change his mind.

In the late summer of 1834, Jackson heard rumors suggesting that Ross and his council were responsible for death threats made against those who supported removal. Enraged, he ordered his agents to warn of severe federal reprisals should those threats be carried out. He would hold Ross personally responsible. Ross, deeply offended, declared the allegation "a malicious and slanderous falsehood."[160] But while Ross himself was not guilty of inciting violence against members of the pro-removal "Treaty Party," the story about death threats was not a "falsehood." There were politically motivated killings in the Cherokee Nation, which continued after removal. The most important victims after relocation were the leaders of the Treaty Party Elias Boudinot and the Ridges. Although he did not approve of the assassinations, Ross did not tolerate opposition, feeling that Cherokee survival depended on unity. The Cherokee Nation's constitution was suspended during the Removal controversy, and the new elections for principal chief and for the two legislative councils scheduled for 1832 were not held. The Ridges were expelled from the governing council, and Boudinot forced out as editor of the *Phoenix*. Ross henceforth controlled the paper's editorial policy and blocked the publication of materials unfavorable to his Nationalist Party's position.[161]

The removal faction leaders were willing to bypass Ross and his government and deal directly with the Jackson administration. But their first effort to obtain a treaty ended in an embarrassing fiasco. A small clique of opportunists, led by John Ross's inept and embittered brother Andrew, went to Washington and negotiated a deal wherein the government would receive all Cherokee land east of the Mississippi in exchange for a 25 year annuity of some $25,000. "It was," writes historian Brian Hicks, "a pitiful deal, far less than the government had offered John Ross, but it included $1000 for Andrew."[162] Jackson was suspicious from the outset and asked if the key Cherokee chiefs would sign such a treaty. Without their endorsement, he warned, the Senate would never ratify it. Andrew Ross assured him he could get at least 1,800 signatures. But in fact he could produce only three, none of them prominent chiefs. The Ridges and most others in the Treaty Party were appalled at the low price Andrew Ross and his cohorts proposed to accept for the Cherokee homeland. The anti-Removal majority considered their actions treasonous. The U.S. Senate, as Old Hickory predicted, refused to ratify the treaty.[163]

Encouraged by reports of dissension within the Cherokee Nation, Jackson in early spring of 1835 met with a group of Cherokees and warned them once again that only through accepting removal could disaster be averted. "Most of your people," Jackson lectured, "are uneducated and are liable to be brought into collision at all times with your white neighbors. Your young men are acquiring the habits of intoxication . . . they are frequently driven to excesses which must eventually terminate in their ruin." "Stay in the midst of whites," he warned, "and your condition will become worse and worse, and you will ultimately disappear."[164] Over the protests of the Ross government, Jackson instructed his representatives in Cherokee country to begin the removal process by arranging the transportation westward of those Cherokees who hoped to escape the disasters that the Old Hickory predicted for those who tried to remain in white man's country. Although the Jacksonians claimed removal was voluntary, as the law required, it was, in fact, as one scholar notes, "anything but that: Cherokees were threatened with the confiscation of their property if they would not consent to go; firewater was used by some agents as a means of persuasion. Indians made drunk discovered when they sobered up that they had committed themselves and their families to emigration." It is believed that perhaps a third of the nation agreed to migrate, although some subsequently refused to go. For those who did, their departures strengthened Ross's hand, as those most opposed to his policy of resistance were the ones who were most likely to accept the agents' offers.[165]

To gain uncontested title to all the lands Georgia coveted and claimed, a federal treaty was still necessary under the terms of the Indian Removal Act. The Andrew Ross fiasco had been embarrassing, but it did not put an end the administration's efforts to obtain a federal removal treaty through bypassing the uncooperative principal chief and his supporters. The Jackson administration and the Georgia state government sought to force the assent and obtain the signatures of members of the affluent elite that controlled the Cherokee national government through both harassment and bribery. In direct defiance of the rulings of the U.S. Supreme Court, and of the federal Indian Removal Act itself, the state legislature with Jackson's tacit consent had passed laws that denied Cherokee ownership of the lands they occupied within Georgia, declaring them all tenants at will. The first of those resolutions had been passed in 1827, and declared that since "Indians are tenants at will . . . the state of Georgia may at any time she pleases" end "that tenancy by taking possession." The governor was directed to inform all parties that "the lands in question belong to Georgia. She must have them and will have them."[166]

Georgia thus set the stage for the seizure of Cherokee lands and their subsequent reassignment to the winners of land lotteries open only to whites. Under the new Georgia laws, federal treaties notwithstanding, there would no longer be any protection of Cherokee holdings. In 1831, former congressman Wilson Lumpkin was elected governor after a campaign in which he pledged that he would secure total Indian removal.[167] Under some prodding from Jackson, the confiscations were delayed in the hope that the president could secure an appropriate removal treaty, but by 1832 some Georgia's political leaders were no longer willing to wait. Jackson responded to prodding from the newly elected Governor Wilson Lumpkin, by asking that the governor disregard rumors that his support for Georgia's position was wavering. But he added, in explanation of those rumors, that "my great desire was that you should do no act which would give the Federal court a legal jurisdiction over a case that might arise with the Cherokees." He expressed surprise that "those so much in my confidence and so well acquainted with my views on the Indian question, as you were" should question his commitment to their program.[168]

Georgia proceeded with its offensive against the Cherokees. The state had initially promised that the "improvements" Cherokees had made to the lands they had occupied—houses, barns, shops, cultivated fields—would be exempt from the lottery, but the process of obtaining exemptions was made so difficult and expensive that few could avail themselves of it.[169] Where the plots of land in question were held by prominent members of the anti-removal National Party, state officials, or white ruffians acting on their own, often simply evicted the Cherokee with no pretension of due process. In a petition to Congress submitted in 1836, Cherokee spokesmen described the dispossession of their principal chief. "He was in Washington city on the business of the nation," the petition related, "When he returned, he traveled till about 10 o'clock at night, to reach his family; rode up to the gate, saw a servant, believed that it was his own; dismounted, ordered his horse taken, went in, and to his utter astonishment, found himself a stranger in his own house, his family having been some days before, driven out to seek a new home." Ross was reduced to paying the new owner rent to stay the night. He finally located his wife and family in a rude two room cabin across the Tennessee line.

To cite another example of land seizure, Joseph Vann, described as the wealthiest man in the nation, lost his estate to trumped-up charges of having hired a white man to work on his plantation. (Vann in fact had rescinded a job offer made to a prospective white overseer when he learned of the law against such employment.) Unlike Vance, most of the prominent members of the emerging treaty party were given special consideration. Governor Lumpkin asked the federal agents who were enrolling Cherokees to give special protection to those who were pro-removal.[170] He personally intervened to secure favorable treatment for the now cooperative Ridge family. The Ridges were able to obtain a good price for their Georgia holdings and made an orderly and comfortable move to their new lands in the west.[171]

The vast majority of Cherokees, however, enjoyed no such privileges. Under Georgia law, the lands reassigned by lottery to white farmers and speculators had to be vacated by November 11, 1836. Most of the Cherokee who had not as yet migrated refused to yield, remaining observant of the Cherokee laws that defined land sale and removal without the consent of the nation as criminal acts. Georgia and Jackson, in response, both threatened reprisals against anyone who interfered with the removal process. One Georgia law prescribed a four-year prison term at hard labor for any Cherokee who tried by persuasion or threat to dissuade a fellow Cherokee from accepting removal. The same penalty was prescribed for anyone who tried to act as an officer or legislator of the now outlawed Cherokee Nation.[172]

But the nation continued to function. Forbidden by law to assemble in Georgia, Ross in the years before removal regularly summoned the national legislature to various sites in Tennessee and Alabama. To undercut Ross and his party, Jackson sent various agents in 1835 to those sessions relying particularly on the efforts of John F. Schermerhorn, a retired Dutch Reform preacher of questionable character, whom he named a special commissioner with orders to negotiate a removal treaty.[173] The general outlines of such a treaty had been given to several Cherokee representatives in Washington, D.C., by Secretary of War Cass in April 1832, but quickly rejected by the Ross administration. Understanding past practice in such matters, Schermerhorn asked for funds to bribe the tribal leaders. But Jackson doubted that bribes would be necessary. Repeated warnings about the dangers of remaining in Georgia should suffice. Insisting on his right to address the nation at its gatherings, the reverend, who excelled in fire-and-brimstone preaching, on one occasion alone harangued some 2,500 Cherokee for over three-and-a-half hours, without much effect. During his six months residence in the Cherokee Nation, he did command the support and cooperation of the minority Treaty Party faction, gaining in the winter of 1835 their approval of a removal treaty expected to be acceptable to Andrew Jackson.[174]

In December, Schermerhorn summoned the nation to meet at the old capital at New Echota to draft and ratify that agreement. Ross's supporters, estimated to total at least 90 percent of the Cherokee remaining in the east, boycotted the meeting. Schermerhorn, however, declared that those who did not appear to vote on the treaty would be counted as favoring it. Only 86 Cherokee appeared at New Echota on December 28, the day designated for ratification; 79 voted to approve. It is said the most prominent treaty supporter, Major Ridge, at the close of the proceedings, muttered, "I have signed my death warrant." That remark was prophetic, as both supporters and opponents of the treaty would fall victim to assassins in the years to come. Schermerhorn, transmitting the document on to Washington, D.C., for the approval of President Jackson and the Senate, claimed it had been ratified by the nation.

No one really believed that. Captain W. W. Davis, assigned the task of enrolling Cherokees agreeing to migration, advised Secretary of War Cass to tell the president that the delegates carrying Schermerhorn's treaty to the capital "had no more authority to make a treaty than any other dozen Cherokees accidentally picked up for the purpose." He estimated that 95 percent of the Cherokee opposed the agreement. Efforts to enforce it, he warned, "would bring trouble on this government and eventually destroy this [the Cherokee] Nation. The Cherokee are a peaceful, harmless people but you may drive them to desperation."[175] The recently elected governor of Georgia William Schley agreed, warning Jackson directly that the so-called Treaty of New Echota "was not made with the sanction of their leaders."[176] The president nonetheless sent that treaty on to the U.S. Senate for ratification.

In the early months of 1836, the leaders of the Treaty Party tried hard to win John Ross's endorsement of their work at New Echota. The treaty, they argued, provided the resources needed to preserve the Cherokee Nation: ample land west of the Mississippi on which to settle, as well as some $5,000,000 to be used to pay for the improvements they would leave behind in the east, settle debts owed by them and to them, and provide money for the support of schools and the relief of the needy. They were to be given fee simple ownership of their new homeland and enjoy the protection of the United States. The federal government would pay both the cost of moving west and provide for their subsistence for a year after removal. They were to be given two years to prepare for removal. Ross, then residing in Washington, D.C., responded by asking his assistant chief George Lowry to prepare a petition against the treaty. He soon had in hand a document bearing over 14,000 names. Ross hoped that show of opposition to the work of the Treaty Party would persuade Jackson to agree to better terms. But Sharp Knife was not moved. Although he treated Ross with courtesy in their final meeting in the White House, he made it clear that he would not engage in any further negotiations.[177]

In early 1835, Edward Everett and Henry Clay, both hitherto vehement opponents of Jacksonian Indian removal, had presented to the two houses of Congress a memorial asking for help in securing generous terms for Cherokee relocation in the west. Its author was John Ridge. Its signatories, some 57 members of the Treaty Party. Everett and Clay, along with most of their fellow Whigs in Congress, were now convinced that the battle against Cherokee removal could not be won. Everett, echoing Jackson, advised Congress that their condition, should they not remove, would soon be "but little if at all better than slavery."[178] The Ridge delegation in Washington, D.C., notes one scholar, "now found themselves courted and flattered in contrast to the cool reception accorded to the Ross delegation."[179] Principal Chief Ross's appeal to Congress for an appropriation to purchase land in Georgia that could then be granted in fee simple to Cherokees wishing to remain in their homeland fell on deaf ears.[180] Instead, as noted earlier, the Senate, called upon to mediate a disagreement between Jackson and Ross over the purchase price of Cherokee Territory, recommended a payment ($5,000,000) Ross deemed far too low. But the blundering of Schermerhorn in trying to claim against clear-cut evidence to the contrary that the New Echota agreement had the support of the Cherokee Nation reignited Whig opposition to removal. After an acrimonious week-long debate, the Senate ratified the treaty by a one vote margin. Daniel Webster, outraged by the defection of Whig senator Robert Goldsborough of Maryland, railed against "the shame and sin of the treaty." John Quincy Adams called it "an eternal disgrace upon the country."[181] Virginia Whig Henry Wise wryly noted that treaties generally require the approval of both parties. In response to such criticism, Georgia's Wilson Lumpkin declared that 19 out of 20 Cherokees were too dumb to understand the issues at stake, so the treaty's approval by the intelligent part of the tribe made it valid.[182] The argument was absurd, but the Jacksonians nonetheless had the votes, albeit barely.

Principal Chief Ross, still enjoying the support of at least 90 percent of the Cherokees remaining in the east, declared the treaty a fraud. As he continued to his efforts to negotiate better terms, Ross asked his people to ignore the claim that they were bound by 1838 removal deadline. But neither Georgia nor the federal government were willing to recognize his authority. A very troubling incident late in 1835 underscored his vulnerability. Ross and a guest, John Howard Payne, the author of the popular song "Home, Sweet Home," were at work in his cabin in Tennessee on a history of the Cherokee Nation when a detachment of Georgia Guard burst in and arrested both of them. They were shackled, marched back into Georgia, and thrown in prison. After 10 days, the men were released without any explanation beyond some vague allegations about their presumed interference with land surveys and collaboration with abolitionists. No formal charges were ever filed against them, but the point had been made.[183]

Andrew Jackson left office before the beginning of the forced removal of the Cherokee in 1838, but watched the proceedings with great care, persuading his successor to grant the Cherokee no extra time to prepare and railing against General Scott and Secretary of War Poinsett for their willingness to involve Ross in the planning and execution of the last stages of the process. "Why," Sharp Knife complained, "is that scamp Ross not banished from the notice of the administration?" He demanded his arrest.[184] Van Buren for his part, refused to meet with Ross.

Although federal authorities promised the Cherokee that they would be well provided for on their trip westward, they had every reason not to trust those assurances. Although the Cherokee "Trail of Tears" is the best known of the removal tragedies, it was neither the first nor the last, and the stories they heard of suffering and death during earlier migrations were anything but reassuring. As to the Cherokee death rate, the pioneering ethnologist James Mooney in 1900 noted the difficulty of arriving at a precise figure, as in addition to the hundreds who did not survive the trail many of the victims died in internment camps before the marches began or perished "soon after arrival in Indian territory, from sickness and exposure on the journey." Mooney believed there were around 4,000 Cherokee deaths.[185] But recent authorities suspect that figure is much too low. Some contemporary commentators believed that half of the Cherokee population in Indian Territory died during the first year after removal.[186] More recently, demographer Russell Thornton, applying more sophisticated methodology than his predecessors, calculates a death rate twice as high as Mooney's estimate. While the evidence does not permit a precise count, a case can be made for a 50 percent mortality rate.[187]

Death statistics however grim cannot convey a full sense of the human tragedy of removal. From varied written sources—letters, journals, official reports—we can draw a vivid and troubling picture of conditions on the "Trails of Tears." We have already related eyewitness testimony from the first and second Choctaw removals of 1830–1831. The pattern of deprivation and abuse set there persisted. The missionary Daniel Butrick who accompanied the Cherokees on their forced march westward in 1838, after their confinement in filthy, crowded, and disease-ridden internment stockades, wrote in his journal that "from their first arrest they were obligated to live very much like brute beasts, and during their travels at night were obliged to lie down on the naked ground, in the open air, exposed to wind and rain, and herd together, men, women, and children, like droves of hogs, and in this way many are hastening to an early grave." Virtually no Cherokee infants under one year of age and very few adults over sixty survived the ordeal. It would have averted "a vast amount of suffering," Burdick noted bitterly, "if they had just been killed directly." Overall, for the victims of whatever age, removal "was a most expensive and painful way of putting the poor people to death." To his account of the general hardships of trail, Burdick added individual reports of abuse, beatings, robberies, rapes, and even murders sometimes committed by whites along the line of march and sometimes by the soldiers who were under orders to protect their Indian "prisoners." Later in his journal, he asked "for what crime was this nation condemned to perpetual death? This almost unheard of suffering?" His answer: because they dared affirm their right not to be made "houseless and homeless" by the actions of a few corrupt men. "The year past," Burdick wrote, "has been a year of spiritual darkness."[188]

Burdick was not a disinterested observer. His commitment to the Cherokee cause was passionate. But his account was confirmed by other eyewitnesses. A Georgia soldier, John G. Burnett recorded that:

children were often separated from parents and driven onto the stockades with the sky for a blanket and the earth for a pillow. And often the old and the infirm were prodded with bayonets to hasten them to the stockade. In one home, death had come during the night. A little sad faced girl had died and was lying on a bear skin couch and some women were preparing the little body for burial. All were arrested and driven out leaving the child in the cabin. I do not know who buried the body.[189]

Another eyewitness writes that "in many cases, on turning for one last look as they crossed the ridge, they saw their homes in flames, fired by the lawless rabble that followed on the heels of the soldiers to loot and pillage."[190] Many years later, a Georgia militia volunteer, who later served as a colonel in the Confederate army, recalled: "I fought through the war between the states and I have seen many men shot to pieces and slaughtered by the thousands, but the Cherokee removal was the cruelest work I ever knew."[191]

Despite the hardships and the occasional atrocities of the removal process, senior Indian leaders almost always rejected the counsel of those who called for armed resistance. They were well aware that the time was long since past when even a pan-Indian alliance could hope to win a war with the United States. To reinforce that understanding, Jackson administration regularly hosted tours of the cities of the eastern seaboard, so that prominent chiefs would be awed and intimidated by the power and might of their prospective adversary. Generally, the chiefs were persuaded that they had no real choice but to make and keep peace. But sometimes that ploy failed. Jackson's removal program was not entirely peaceful. We have already made note of the violent episodes often now referred to as Second Creek War, a conflict provoked in large measure by the administration's failure to provide even minimal assistance to defrauded and dispossessed Indians facing starvation. Another violent interlude, which claimed far more national attention, was the Black Hawk War of 1832, a war aptly described by future president Zachary Taylor as "that disgraceful affair," disgraceful not only because of the inept conduct of the militia that fired the first shots, but because the war itself could easily have been avoided had political leaders chosen conciliation rather than confrontation.[192]

The origins of the conflict can be traced in part to a controversy over a land cession treaty several minor chiefs of the Sac tribe of Indians had allegedly accepted some 28 years earlier. The trouble began in the early fall of 1804, several months after the transfer of Louisiana from France to the United States. Four young Sac warriors struck a tiny settlement on the Cuivre River, a few miles north of St. Louis, scalping and killing "in a most barbarous manner" three Americans. The Sac raiders had been angered not only by white incursions on lands they considered their own but by the favoritism U.S. officials were seemingly showing to their old enemies, the Osage. To avert an escalation of hostilities, the Americans had recently "turned back a three hundred man war party headed for the Osage country. Sauk and Mesqualike warriors seethed with rage." While wiser and more experienced heads counseled caution, some of their younger kinsmen clamored for action. When the four raiders returned from the Cuivre, "they threw their grisly trophies on the ground in front of the chiefs, and taunted them to go cry with the whites."[193]

The Sac leaders refused to be provoked by that insult. They knew full well that given the old animosities and current divisions among the neighboring Indian nations, an all-out war against the Americans would be risky in the extreme.[194] Their interests would be better served by establishing and maintaining friendly relations, and lucrative trade ties, with the newcomers. In keeping with long-time tradition, they tried to restore peace and harmony by offering to compensate the families of the victims, thereby "covering the blood." But the Americans refused their offer. In accord with their understanding of justice, U.S. spokesmen demanded that the killers be apprehended and surrendered to them for trial and possible punishment. At this juncture, the newly appointed governor of the territory of Louisiana came on the scene. William Henry Harrison would soon win a reputation as a skilled, devious, greedy, and rather ruthless negotiator of Indian land acquisition treaties.

The Sacs sent two minor chiefs to St. Louis to meet with the new governor. Their instructions restricted them to discussions about "covering the blood." They hoped that, through the payment of compensation for the killings, the envoys could secure the lives and freedom of their kinsmen. Harrison had much broader objectives in mind, and demanded that they sell, at low price, all of the Sauk and Fox lands east of the Mississippi River. As Harrison kept no journal of his "talks" with these chiefs, we do not know what he said to them, we do not know what points they made, or just what it was they believed they had given up, or what they were to receive. The sources, such as they are, can best be described as murky. But three things are fairly clear: (1) The Sac negotiators did not have authorization to sell Sac land, let alone give up territory occupied by their allied tribe, the Fox (sometimes referred to as the Mesquakie). (2) They did not understand that the document they signed required that they abandon their present homeland and resettle west of the Mississippi. The treaty was poorly written and included the statement: "as long as the lands which are now ceded to the United States remain their property, the Indians belonging to the said tribes, shall enjoy the privilege of living and hunting upon them." That language apparently led the Sac to assume that they were merely recognizing the political sovereignty of the United States over that territory. They denied that they had "sold" the land in question and expected to continue to enjoy occupancy rights under the authority of the United States. (3) Governor Harrison made little if any effort to assure that the chiefs fully understood the contents and implications of the document they signed. Reliable sources indicate that he kept the chiefs drunk throughout the conference. Drunk or sober, they no doubt were confused by the language in the treaty. Native speakers of English had problems, then and now, understanding exactly what the passage quoted above really meant. Sac and Fox Indian leaders generally believed the American claim that they had agreed to evacuate their lands east of the Mississippi in the 1804 treaty was a lie. Those who had negotiated with Harrison in 1804 were adamant in their denials. Nonetheless, they were forced, in a new treaty in 1817, to affirm the cession of lands east of the Mississippi. But most of the chiefs believed the matter wasn't worth risking a war with the United States and with those traditionally hostile rival Indian nations who would no doubt support the whites, as they would probably lose. Since the United States for some years made no effort to sell the land in question to white settlers, there was no immediate reason for concern.

Nonetheless, the 1804 treaty, as Harrison and his successors interpreted it, included land occupied by the principal Sauk summer village. "Saukenuk," writes historian William T. Hagan, "was the wonder of all who visited it. Occupied by a majority of the Sac Nation, in 1817 it contained probably one hundred lodges, and its chiefs could muster one thousand warriors. The location, on a point of land between Rick River and the Mississippi, was an enviable one." Its fields and orchards, cultivated by the women of the tribe in the spring and summer, produced bountiful surpluses of corn, pumpkins, beans, and squash, and in the surrounding countryside berries, apples, plums, and nuts were available in abundance.[195]

For about a quarter of a century after Harrison's 1804 treaty laid claim to their territory on the east bank of the Mississippi, the Sac continued each spring to return to Saukenuk and were left undisturbed. (During cold months they lived in winter hunting camps.) But in 1829, the United States served notice that it would survey and sell Sac lands on the east bank, including Saukenuk. The Sacs were told that they must now remain west of the Mississippi after their winter hunt. Most of their leaders were willing to swallow their anger and comply. But an aging warrior named Black Hawk was defiant. In 1831, he led a band back to Saukenuk. He was intercepted by General Edmund P. Gaines, who commanded a small detachment of federal troops supported by the Illinois militia. Forced to capitulate, Black Hawk signed an agreement to remain west of the Mississippi. He did not keep that agreement, but crossed the river again in 1832 accompanied by about 1,000 Sac men, women, and children. He was not planning to wage war but had been led to believe, by his ally the Winnebago prophet, that the United States would take no action if he resettled Saukenuk, as the terms of the Treaty of Ghent obligated the Americans to restore territory occupied by Indians at the beginning of the War of 1812. He had also been told by one of his followers that the British had given word that they would come to his aid should a conflict ensue over ownership of the land in question. Black Hawk had been misinformed on both points.

Since Black Hawk's party included women, children, and the aged, it should have been clear to the Illinois governor and other whites that there was no need for panic. But recently there had been a number of rather ugly frontier incidents, including a very nasty low-level war with the Winnebago in 1827. With Black Hawk leading some sort of invasion of his old homeland, Illinois politicians and militia officers vied with one another in sounding the alarm. On May 14, at Stillman's Run near Saukenuk (and the modern city of Rockford), the Illinois militia attacked Black Hawk's band. The outcome of the Battle of Stillman's Run was, for the Illinois forces, a disaster. Poorly commanded, and in many cases roaring drunk, they soon lost control of the situation and succeeded only in igniting a very nasty Indian war. As historian Patrick J. Jung observes, "Black Hawk felt compelled to fight in order to avenge his warriors' deaths at Stillman Run. Federal officials and their white constituents on the other hand believed that if Black Hawk and his followers were not thoroughly defeated, their disaffection might spread to the Potawatomies, Winnebagos, Sante Sioux, and other tribes."[196] At the White House, President Andrew Jackson, angered by reports of "depredations and murders" committed by Black Hawk's band, demanded that they be "chastised" in order to "deter others."[197] Thus, no effort was made to negotiate a peaceful settlement with Black Hawk.

In the following weeks, the militia and the U.S. Army commanded by General Henry Atkinson, although outfoxed and sometimes bloodied in early engagements, finally managed to kill about 300 Sac and Fox in the Battle of Bad Axe, and secure Black Hawk's surrender. A new treaty confirmed their removal and imposed an indemnity to pay the costs of the war. The vanquished chief was made a prisoner, held for a time at Jefferson barracks, St. Louis, and then sent to Washington, D.C., to receive the chastisement of the Great Father. Jackson administered a tongue lashing to Black Hawk for "drenching the frontier in mindless violence."[198] He refused to listen to the old chief's explanation of the wrongs suffered by his people but ordered him imprisoned at Fortress Monroe. After about a month, Black Hawk was deemed sufficiently contrite and reformed to be released and allowed to return to his people. But first Jackson sent him on a tour of several cities, so he would clearly understand the power and might of the United States. Before his departure, the president and Black Hawk attended the theater together. Many white Americans, to Old Hickory's irritation, came to lionize the old Indian chief as the epitome of the noble but doomed savage warrior.

Andrew Jackson's dealings with the Seminoles of Florida were of a very different nature, although his conflict with them also produced in Osceola another popular Indian hero. The Seminoles were not a single unified people but included descendants of some who had migrated into Florida beginning in the early 18th century and others of Red Stick persuasion displaced by the Creek War. They did not have a common language. Some spoke Hitchiti dialects, others Muskogee, a few Yuchi. They lacked a cohesive governing structure, and although often of Creek background, did not acknowledge the jurisdiction of the Creek governing council. They were ethnically diverse, including in their communities many of mixed-racial heritage. A number of residents of Seminole villages were black. Many were escaped slaves who had fled the plantations and farms of the lower South. Some blacks were owned as slaves by the Seminoles, held in a form of bondage much more lenient than that imposed by both whites and Indians north of Florida's border. Others were free. Some black villages established by refugees from the southern states maintained close ties with their Seminole neighbors, in some cases paying tribute. In other instances (in the case of the interpreter Abraham, advisor to the Alachua chief Micanopy most notably), blacks held prominent positions within Seminole villages. The main Seminole population centers were in the Apalachicola region of west Florida and the Alachua plain in the north central area.[199]

The reservation assigned to the Seminole in the Treaty of Moultrie Creek, as noted earlier, could not provide adequate subsistence for even a small population. The Seminoles were not able to live comfortably on either the sparse and sometimes unhealthy rations provided by the United States under the treaty or on what they could themselves raise or catch. Thus, they often broke the territorial law that banned them from leaving their reservation lands and in their hunger and anger raided white farms. Enraged by the loss of livestock and crops, fearful of continued Indian attacks on isolated homesteads, white Floridians clamored for their total removal.

The Jackson administration in Washington, D.C., regarding the Seminoles as a minor problem, at first procrastinated, then, despite warnings to the contrary, assumed the Seminoles would offer little if any resistance to relocation west of the Mississippi. Instead, efforts to enforce a removal treaty triggered the longest, and arguably both the dirtiest and most controversial Indian war in the nation's history. To understand this tragedy, we must begin by looking carefully at the often inept behavior of the Indian agents Jackson charged with carrying out his directives, as well as at Jackson's own failure to understand that a purely military response to Seminole insurgency could not yield a quick solution.

As we have often noted, Jackson was exceedingly suspicious of Indian agents reputed to be at all sympathetic to the land claims and other demands of their charges. A number of experienced and skillful old Indian hands—Dinsmore, Meigs, Hawkins—had at one time or another provoked his wrath. In Florida, local settlers, and the territorial governor William Duval, at the time of Jackson's election to the presidency, were clamoring for the dismissal of Indian agent Gad Humphreys whom they regarded as far too sympathetic to the Seminoles. Humphreys, who served from 1822 until 1830, offended in several ways. When drought led to food shortages and near starvation in Seminole settlements, Humphreys defied the governor and supplied the hungry with additional rations beyond the quantity specified in the Treaty of Moultrie Creek. He also declared the reservation set aside for the Seminoles under that treaty woefully inadequate for their needs and accordingly was lenient in dealing with Seminoles found outside its boundaries. He thus offended white Floridians who demanded that all Indians be kept away from their farms and plantations and expected strict enforcement of territorial laws punishing those who strayed onto the lands they no longer owned.

There was another issue that to some Floridians was even more serious. While Humphreys, in obedience to his instructions, sought Seminole compliance with treaty provisions concerning the return of runaway slaves belonging to white Americans, he insisted, despite pressure from the governor and other prominent planters, in following due process in determining ownership through hearings presided over by a judge appointed for that purpose. He was under pressure from Duval and others to turn over, without further inquiry, certain Black Seminoles who were probably either free members of maroon communities or slaves legally owned by Seminoles. He resisted those pressures and also generally refused to allow whites to buy slaves from Indians, as he realized such sales all too often were characterized by fraud or intimidation. He also opposed the governor's plan to force the Seminoles to apprehend and surrender runaways alleged to be living in Seminole country by suspending the annuity payments promised by treaty.

Although Humphreys was charged with various offenses—including personal involvement in the slave trade—an investigation ordered by President John Quincy Adams failed to find any credible evidence against him. But it did not matter. Adams lost his bid for reelection, and the new president, as we have seen previously, had little use for agents who were deemed too sympathetic to Indians. Humphreys was fired. Old Hickory appointed to his place John Phagan, a man not bothered by the sort of scruples that brought down Humphreys. The former agent remained in Florida Territory, where he established a private trading post and advised the Seminoles not to agree to removal.[200]

On January 30, 1830, Jackson's close friend James Gadsden, architect of the Treaty of Moultrie Creek, received from the War Department a commission to go to Florida to negotiate a new agreement. His instructions, drawn up after consultation with Andrew Jackson, stipulated that the Seminoles were to be persuaded to move west of the Mississippi where they would be merged with their presumed former kinsmen the Creeks.[201] This demand for the merger of the Seminole and the Creek was exceedingly unwise. As the leading historian of the Seminole War has noted, and as Andrew Jackson well knew, "the only sentiment the Seminoles felt toward the Creeks was hatred."[202] The negotiations Gadsden conducted at a remote location near the present-day town of Ocala, which ended with the promulgation of the Treaty of Payne's Landing, were irregular in a number of ways. Contrary to long-established practice, Gadsden kept and submitted no notes on his negotiations. It was widely believed that those negotiations were characterized by misrepresentation, fraud, and coercion. In his later recollections, Gadsden declared that he warned the chiefs that henceforth, if they remained in Florida, they would receive from the U.S. government neither the food nor the protection from white depredations promised in the earlier agreement. Essentially, Gadsden admitted that he had unilaterally abrogated the guarantees contained in the Treaty of Moultrie Creek, which he had negotiated nine years earlier. It is not clear how many Seminole leaders actually signed the Treaty of Payne's Landing that set aside the earlier agreement. Some, including Micanopy, leader of the powerful Alachua band, insisted their signatures or marks were forged, in some cases by younger tribesmen impersonating their elders. Whatever the truth of those charges, and they are hard to prove but nonetheless very plausible, there were in fact fewer names on the new treaty than on the Moultrie Creek agreement, so we have every reason to believe that many Seminole were far from content with Gadsden's conduct.[203]

The document the Seminole leaders may or may not have signed at Payne's Landing stated that the treaty would go into effect only after representatives of the Seminole had inspected and approved their new homeland, but, through vagueness of language, left it unclear as to whether the chiefs who were to travel to Indian Territory had the power to bind all the Seminoles to removal, or were obligated to report back to their people and ask for ratification of their recommendation. The Seminole leaders maintained that the people as a whole had to approve removal. Specifically, the first article stated that "should they be satisfied with the character of that country, and of the favorable disposition of the Creeks to reunite with Seminoles as one people" the Seminole removal treaty would go into effect. But to whom did the pronoun "they" refer? The Seminole chiefs insisted that it referred to "the Seminole Nation" and that they thus were not empowered to act unilaterally. After traveling with agent Phagan to the territory aside for them in Creek reservation in the west, the chiefs signed an agreement at Fort Gibson, on February 14, 1833, which, the Jackson administration maintained, effectively committed all Seminoles to leave Florida within three years.

But on their return to Florida, four of the chiefs charged that Agent Phagan had resorted to coercion and fraud in obtaining their signatures. Three others argued that Phagan lied, insisting they had never signed any agreement whatsoever. In addition to the controversy over signatures, the Seminoles challenged new language that Phagan inserted in his draft of the agreement which gave the visiting chiefs the power to bind the entire Seminole people, who under the new document were to be merged with the Creek Nation but given a separate section of the Creek reservation. The chiefs denied that they had ever claimed any such authority. While the stories about what transpired at Fort Gibson are contradictory, it must be noted that one very credible observer, Major Ethan Allen Hitchcock, claimed that Phagan obtained the signatures by threatening to leave the chiefs stranded in the west. Another equally reliable authority, Captain John H. Sprague, author of a remarkably well-documented contemporary history of the Second Seminole War, characterized Phagan as "totally unqualified both by education and morals" to serve as an Indian agent. The man, in Sprague's judgment, had been "brutal" in his treatment of Indians, and personally bore much responsibility for the "protracted and sanguinary war" which broke out when the Jackson administration tried to implement the new Seminole treaties. Phagan was personally corrupt and embezzled funds entrusted to his care. Acting governor James D. Westcott, Jr., after investigating numerous charges of "fraud and improper conduct," asked for and obtained Phagan's dismissal.[204]

As to the status of treaty negotiations with the Seminoles, Secretary of War Cass initially believed that the chiefs did not in fact have the power to make the final decision about removal, informing Jackson in December 1832, that after the Seminole delegation visited and approved their proposed new homeland, it would still require the consent of the whole tribe to make removal "mandatory."[205] But Jackson did not accept Cass's conclusion about the need for tribal approval of the removal documents. Insisting that the chiefs had been empowered to accept the land offered them in the west, and had done so, Jackson submitted the Seminole removal treaties to the Senate, which ratified them by unanimous vote on April 8, 1834. The secretary did not pursue his reservations, and the president made it clear that there would be no further negotiations.[206]

Jackson had replaced agent Phagan with Wiley Thompson, a former Georgia congressman and militia general who had served with him in the Creek War. Gadsden, in addition to his work at Payne's Landing, had secured a separate agreement with the Seminoles living in the Apalachicola area of west Florida. The Apalachicola chiefs, for the most part, had been cooperative. But a few were not. Their passive resistance to relocation delayed the final removal of the western Seminoles until 1838.[207] The response of the Seminole peoples living in the eastern part of the territory, particularly on the Alachua plain, proved far more problematic. Wiley Thompson's instructions called for the immediate implementation of the Payne's Landing and Fort Gibson treaties. To his surprise and anger, eastern Seminole leaders informed their new agent that the treaties negotiated by Gadsden and Phagan were obtained by fraud and intimidation and were therefore invalid. Moreover, they claimed that the 20-year guarantee of their right to land in Florida contained in the earlier Treaty of Moultrie Creek, remained in place. Thus, they argued, they were under no obligation to move for another seven years. Underlying their opposition to removal was not only anxiety about the suitability of their proposed new homeland and their resentment to being placed on a reservation with the despised Creeks but also concern about the future status of Black Seminoles both slave and free. Some blacks, most notably Micanopy's interpreter Abraham, had gained considerable influence in tribal councils, where they argued passionately against removal. The blacks and Seminoles both feared that they would be victimized by both white and Creek slave hunters if they left their Florida haven. Their anxieties were well founded, as conflicts over the status of Black Seminoles, as we have noted previously, had complicated relations with white Americans and with Creeks allied with Jackson since before the First Seminole War two decade earlier.[208]

Bound by his instruction, Thompson refused to acknowledge Seminole concerns. Instead, he demanded that they honor the new agreement signed at Fort Gibson, declaring "you solemnly bound yourselves to remove within three years of the ratification of that treaty, and the whole delegation that went west confirmed that promise by entering into a final agreement to do so, by which the whole nation is bound. You know you were not forced to do so."[209] Upon reporting to Washington, D.C., his problems with the chiefs, he was given a letter from Andrew Jackson to read to the Seminole leaders. Sharp Knife told the Seminoles they had no choice but to migrate. If they tried to resist, he would order the army to remove them by force. In order to alleviate some of their anxieties about the status of Black Seminoles, Thompson and Jackson decided to restrict the activities of some of the white slave traders. They were now not to be allowed to enter Seminole country without a government permit. The agent and the president both realized that there were many Floridians who advocated the immediate seizure and enslavement of all blacks in the territory. They wisely refused to yield to their pressure, but in other respects their management of the Seminole removal was inept and provocative.[210]

After a series of meetings and private negotiations, Thompson finally, on April 23, 1835, gained the signature of 16 chiefs accepting the validity of the Treaty of Payne's Landing and agreeing to prepare for removal. But five of the most prominent leaders, including Micanopy, the head of the Alachuas, refused to sign. Angrily, Agent Thompson declared that henceforth, those five were no longer chiefs.[211] Thompson's purge was not only unwise but illegal, as agents lacked the authority to either appoint or remove Native American leaders. While Captain Sprague in his excellent history of the Seminole War blames Agent Phagan for its provocation, a strong case can be made that Thompson was equally if not more responsible for the outbreak of violence in 1835. He compounded the insult to the chiefs by prohibiting any further sales of arms or ammunition to Seminoles. He also withheld the annuity payments owed to the Seminoles under the previous treaty. Finally, he arrested and clamped in irons a 35-year-old Red Stick refugee known to whites as Billy Powell. Powell, the great nephew of the warrior prophet Peter McQueen, is better known to history as Osceola. It is not known exactly how he had offended the agent in an incident during a meeting in the agent's office that led to his shackling and incarceration, but contemporary sources relate that Osceola had not only denounced the ban on arms sales as degrading but threatened to "make the white man red with blood, and then blacken him in the sun and rain . . . the buzzard shall live on his flesh."[212] Thompson set Osceola free after his prisoner agreed to work with him to persuade other Seminoles that they must all now accept the new treaty of Payne's Landing and prepare to migrate westward.

Wiley Thompson did not understand the depth of Osceola's anger. As Osceola pretended to support his removal program, the agent even came to regard the Seminole militant as a friend and presented him with a very handsome rifle as a gift. Nor did Thompson understand fully the real threat posed by the Seminole resistance. Others were less optimistic. Rumors combined with some isolated clashes between whites and Seminoles had impelled the local commanding general Duncan Clinch to advise his superiors in early 1835 that he did not have adequate troops to defend the frontier against the uprising of Seminoles and their black allies he now saw as the likely outcome of current policy. The Indians, he warned, would not accept removal and would respond violently to any effort to carry out the president's threat to remove them from Florida by force. The general declared that if he did not receive reinforcements immediately, "the whole frontier may be laid waste by a combination of Indians, Indian negroes, and the negroes on the plantations." But Clinch was denied authority to call out the militia reserves and received only a few more regular troops.[213]

Jackson and his associates expected that with firmness and just a little muscle, the Seminole could easily be brought around. They were wrong. Old Hickory's former secretary of war John Henry Eaton, arriving in Florida to assume the governorship, joined others in the territory who warned that the Seminoles aided by blacks would put up a formidable resistance. He also raised questions about both the wisdom and the validity of the new removal treaty. To little avail. Jackson, grossly underestimating the threat, was unwilling to either reopen negotiations or to divert substantial military resources to the subduing of what he termed "a handful of savages." Old Hickory provoked a war he lacked the resources to fight. Historian John Mahon finds the failure to anticipate and prepare for a Second Seminole War "all but inexplicable."[214]

The war came late in 1835. The first clear warning of violent Seminole resistance to relocation in the west was the slaying, on November 26, of Charlie Emathla, a prominent chief who had just sold his cattle in preparation for migration. Despite his promise to Thompson not to make any more trouble, Osceola had continued to advocate that the Seminoles execute anyone and everyone who cooperated with the federal removal program. But the young militant did more than talk. Word that Charlie Emathla had been killed by a band of warriors riding with Osceola spread rapidly and led some pro-removal Seminole chiefs, accompanied by about 500 of their followers, to take refuge near a small American post named Fort Brooke. There they subsisted on rations supplied by the soldiers, and waited.

Osceola and other militants remained at large. After several minor but disturbing clashes between Seminoles and white settlers in various parts of the territory, full-scale hostilities broke out just before Christmas. On the Atlantic seaboard, Mikasuckis attacked and destroyed the sugar plantations south of St. Augustine, wiping out the entire industry and spreading panic through northeast Florida. Further west, on December 28, a band of Osceola's warriors annihilated a 100-man detachment under the command of Major Francis L. Dade bound for Fort King. On the same day, Osceola lay in wait outside the Agency Post for Wiley Thompson, shot him dead, and killed a number of his associates. Efforts in the following weeks to pursue and punish the insurgent Seminoles ended in failure.[215] General Clinch described Florida in early 1836: "It is truly distressing to witness the panic and sufferings of the white frontier inhabitants. Men, women and children are seen flying in every direction, and leaving everything behind them save a few articles of clothing" as their homes were "plundered and burned by small bands of Indians."[216]

When the Second Seminole War broke out, Andrew Jackson had only 15 months left in his final presidential term. He still regarded Seminole resistance as a minor problem and certainly did not expect a protracted conflict. Receiving a disturbing report from Florida early in the war, he demanded that the secretary of war explain what the local commander "Col. Clinch is about . . . why is he permitting outrageous depredations by the Indians without inflicting just punishment for outrages unpunished."[217] Although he finally ordered reinforcements for Florida, Jackson never quite grasped the nature of this conflict. Commenting in August 1836 on a dispute between two of his generals (Scott and Gaines) over the conduct of operations in Florida, Sharp Knife declared they should have "put this puny Indian war down in ten days."[218]

Jackson was wrong. This was not just a "puny Indian war" but the beginning of a long period of humiliation for this nation's military establishment. In the struggle against the Seminoles, one commander after another failed to comprehend fully the futility of trying to counter guerilla warfare with conventional battlefield strategies. (Among those commanders who failed in Florida were Duncan Clinch, Edmund P. Gaines, Winfield Scott, Richard Keith Call, Thomas Sidney Jesup, Zachary Taylor, Walter Keith Armistead, and William Jenkins Worth.) While over several years hundreds of Seminoles were captured (or induced to surrender) and then shipped westward, a substantial number retreated into southern Florida, into swamplands and hammocks not only uninhabited but uncharted.

Persuaded that Indians being rebels and savages did not deserve the protections accorded to military combatants and civilians, Jackson urged the army to use methods generally regarded as dishonorable. In a particularly notorious case, Osceola was taken prisoner in violation of a white flag of truce, then imprisoned under harsh circumstances first at St. Augustine, then in Charleston. After his death in captivity, his attending physician beheaded him and turned his skull into an ash tray. Osceola soon became an iconic figure not only for the Seminoles and other Indians but also for those whites over the years who celebrated Indian resistance, romanticized Indian warfare, and deplored Jacksonian Indian removal.

As leader, Osceola was quickly replaced by Wildcat and other insurgents. The resisters demonstrated a remarkable capacity to evade and then strike and get away. As Seminoles made their way into the largely uninhabited southern regions of the peninsula, federal army units and Florida militia units year after year floundered through unmapped swampy wilderness areas, forced to depend upon overextended supply lines that often failed them. They were unprepared for the scorching heat and stifling humidity that gripped Florida for more than half the year. The hot months they called the "sickly season," and, with the exception of a short campaign mounted late in the war by Colonel William Jenkins Worth, conducted no offensive actions during those months.

One commander after another, under three presidents, failed to put an end to Seminole resistance. The roster of failures included many of the nation's most outstanding military men, including among others Winfield Scott, Edmund Gaines, and Zachary Taylor. They were, without exception, appalled by a war they could not seem to win. Florida's governor Richard Keith Call demonized the Seminoles and cast the war as a conflict of good versus evil. The governor, who also commanded troops, declared "seldom in the history of savage warfare have such horrid scenes been exhibited." He described one such scene with "orphan children driving off the hogs from the mangled body of their lifeless mother while they witnessed the heart rending spectacle of seeing one of their brothers devoured by these animals."[219] But growing numbers of Americans doubted that the Jacksonians claim that the struggle against the Seminoles was a righteous one. Lt. Henry Prince, a West Point graduate and a career army man spent three years fighting to subdue and deport the Seminoles. At the end of his service in Florida, he recorded in his diary that it was "a Vile Country," whose white settlers were a "heartless population," unworthy of the sacrifices the army had made to protect their "plundering."[220] There were many who shared that view and came to the conviction that this was a dirty war waged for the benefit of profiteering white slave traders.[221]

Living in retirement at the Hermitage, Andrew Jackson continued to worry that the new administration was mishandling the Seminole matter. On August 27, 1837, he wrote to Van Buren's secretary of war Joel Poinsett to warn that his "long in dealing with Indians satisfies me that they are only to be well governed by their fears." He opined that Osceola had been treated much too leniently in the months before his capture by violation of the flag of truce. There should have been no negotiations with "that scoundrel," Jackson declaimed. Instead, he "ought to have been hung or kept in irons the moment he came in on account of his atrocious conduct." The rules of civilized warfare in Jackson's view ought not be observed in dealing with savages as such people are dishonorable by nature. To "put a speedy end to this expensive and shamefully prolonged war," Jackson advised that the generals should not restrict themselves to killing the warriors, but rather find out where their women and children were hiding, kill or capture those noncombatants and thereby break the resistance. In a detailed "memorandum on the Florida campaign," Sharp Knife complained that the commanders in Florida, by failing to go after the Seminole women, had mounted a campaign that "was like a combined operation to encompass a wolf in the hammock without knowing first where her den and whelps were."[222]

Ironically, despite Jackson's long-standing fame as an Indian fighter and as an expert negotiator, in his recommendations for dealing with the Seminoles, both before and after his presidency, he displayed not only an indifference to the grievances and continuing sufferings of the Seminole peoples but an apparent ignorance of the nature of their evolving socioeconomic system. This is remarkable given his trade and military relationships with a number of Cherokee, Creek, Seminole, Choctaw, and Chickasaw chiefs and warriors. His insistence on the merger of the Creek and Seminole may have reflected a lack of knowledge of their past and present interactions (although that is highly doubtful), but it was also an expression of his own stubborn determination to have his way in setting the terms of their continued existence as a people. In any case, the advice he gave to field commanders and to President Van Buren on the conduct of the Seminole War was less than helpful. It reflected his lifelong lack of respect for the nation's indigenous peoples. But Van Buren in all matters involving Indians deferred to the former president. During his term of office, no efforts were made to address any of the very real grievances of the Cherokee, Creek, Seminole, and others who had suffered both at the hands of deceitful and predatory whites, some of whom were agents of the federal government.

The Seminole War, arguably was the most controversial Indian war in our history. Troop morale was low and popular support divided, essentially along sectional lines. Jackson's northern opponents quickly labeled it a war fought for the benefit of the slave power. The cost in lives and wealth was staggering. When the war was finally terminated by the Tyler administration, most of the Seminole population of Florida had finally, at great cost, been deported from the territory. However, a remnant was never defeated but built a new homeland deep in the swamp country in the far southern reaches of the peninsula. Naval engagements against them in 1853–1858, sometimes termed "the Third Seminole War," captured and deported around 300 but failed to eliminate completely the Seminole community in the Everglades. Many of their descendants are still there.[223]

Overall, Jackson's removal policy achieved most of its immediate objectives in the south but failed to eliminate all of the Indian communities in other areas east of the Mississippi. Of the approximately 90,000 Indians affected by the 70 removal treaties negotiated during Jackson's two terms of office, around half were resettled in the west prior to his retirement. The remainders were left to Van Buren and in a few cases to his successors. The notorious Potawatomi Trail of Tears did not begin until 1838. The removal of the Miami from Indiana started in 1839 but was never actually completed. The expulsion of the Wyandot from Ohio got under way, after a decade of haggling and indecision, in 1843. The final removal treaties were negotiated in the 1850s. It is estimated that around 9,000 Indians, in the northern Great Lakes area, in New York in New England, and in isolated areas in the South, managed, by a variety of means, to avoid removal. A very few were rewarded for past loyalty and military service to the United States and exempted from removal. Others found sanctuary in mountains (Eastern Cherokee) or swamplands (Seminoles) remote from white settlement. Some tried to avail themselves of the government's offer to provide land grants to those Indians who chose to remain behind. As we have seen, that promise was seldom honored. But many thousands of Indians, now mostly landless and destitute, nonetheless remained in the South. Over the years, against all odds, they have not only survived but maintained their identity. The story of their cultural persistence and later resurgence is beyond the scope of this study, but it is a remarkable story, one that Andrew Jackson/Sharp Knife could never have anticipated.

Epilogue

Andrew Jackson, Ethnic Cleansing and Genocide

In his final message to Congress, on March 4, 1837, President Andrew Jackson proudly assured his fellow citizens that his administration had removed the final obstacle, which might "impede your march to the highest point of national prosperity." "The States, which had so long been retarded in their improvement by the Indian tribes living in the midst of them," Jackson explained, "are at last relieved of the evil of their presence. . . . The safety and comfort of our citizens have been greatly promoted by their removal." Moreover, Indians as well as whites had benefitted greatly from the process, as "the remnant of that ill-fated race has been at length beyond the reach or injury or oppression . . . the paternal care of the Government will thereafter watch over them and protect them."[1]

In earlier addresses to Congress, Jackson had argued that "Indians have neither the intelligence, the industry, the moral habits, nor the desire of improvement which are essential to any favorable change in their condition. Established in the midst of another and a superior race, and without appreciating the causes of their inferiority or seeking to control them, they must necessarily yield to the force of circumstance and ere long disappear." The central issue in Indian policy, as Jackson had defined it in his message to Congress in 1830, and repeated annually thereafter, was the conflict of civilization versus savagery, "What good man," Jackson had asked, "would prefer a country covered with forests and ranged by a few thousand savages to our extensive Republic, studded with cities, towns, and prosperous farms embellished with all the improvements which art can devise or industry execute, occupied by more than 12,000,000, and filled with all the blessings of liberty, civilization, and religion?" Indians must therefore give way so "good men" could do the work savages could not, or would not, do. Happily, there was, however, an alternative to waiting for their inevitable annihilation: the removal program. His administration, as we have noted, proposed to provide in exchange for their tribal lands a new Indian homeland in the west, beyond the boundaries of states. "Rightly considered," Jackson declared, "the policy of General government toward the Redman is not only liberal, but generous."[2]

Jackson's sweeping declaration of Indian racial incapacity is stunning, as is his insensitivity to the sufferings of the Trails of Tears. After reading documents that reflect and expose the greed, the bad faith, the lies, the corruption, the incompetence, and the hypocrisy that marked the work of many of those who executed Andrew Jackson's Indian removal program, Old Hickory's self-portrait as the great paternalistic benefactor of red men and whites alike is hard to stomach. Historian Gary Clayton Anderson, who has argued that Jacksonian Indian policy was not genocide, but rather "the crime of ethnic cleansing," notes cogently that an examination of Andrew Jackson's rhetoric makes it "difficult to suggest he held any serious sympathy for the plight of the Indian."[3] Historian Robert Remini believes Jackson's professed concern for Indian survival was sincere but concedes that because of his mismanagement of his removal program "thousands of men, women and children suffered not only the loss of their property but physical agony and even death."[4]

Jackson's scholarly defenders emphasize the limits on his power as president to intervene on behalf of the Indians. As he often stated, he had neither the military power nor the political support that would have been needed to coerce Georgia, Alabama, Mississippi, and other states determined to eliminate the Indian nations in their midst. That may well be true. But we need to ask another question. How did Jackson use such power and influence as he did have? The documentary evidence we have is damning. An affluent slave holding planter and aspiring southern gentleman, Jackson felt only contempt for the ignorant and slovenly frontier "roughs" who robbed and murdered the Indians whose lands and goods they coveted. But as a treaty negotiator he exploited the fears they inspired to persuade their victims to sell out and move on. As president, he made no use of the "bully pulpit" to urge justice for Indians. He consistently removed Indian agents deemed too sympathetic to Indians but generally refused to act to retrain others, less humane and honorable, who robbed and abused them. He insisted in one instance that an agent's resort to fraud and coercion did not invalidate an Indian land cession treaty. In another, he challenged an agent's right to hold his job, on the grounds that he was a Yankee and therefore not sufficiently sympathetic to the needs of white southerners. In a notorious miscarriage of justice, Jackson claimed he had no power as president to intervene to protect Creeks defrauded in land allotments, but soon thereafter acted to provide redress to white land claimants. The administration refused to honor pleas from white settlers that food be sent to starving, homeless Creeks, on the grounds that they must not be given any assistance that would encourage them to think they could remain east of the Mississippi. President Jackson's conduct as commander in chief during the Second Creek War as well as during the better known Second Seminole War cannot be considered honorable. Believing that the rules of civilized warfare did not apply to conflicts with "savages," Jackson, without congressional authorization, deported peaceful as well as belligerent Creeks westward sometimes in chains. Soon thereafter, frustrated by the persistence of Seminole resistance in what Sharp Knife termed "a puny little Indian war," he demanded that troops break Indian morale by targeting, kidnapping, or killing their women and children. Early in the conflict, he complained that rather than negotiating with Oseola, the army should have hung him immediately.

There is a clear pattern here, and it is one that suggests Jackson embraced genocide's foundation belief that, because of certain perceived racial, moral, intellectual, cultural, or religious deficiencies or tendencies, a targeted group within a given territory is not only unworthy of inclusion in the community or of its protection, but on occasion must be dealt with as an existential threat to its well-being. That sense of threat leads to actions, which to quote the UN definition, are "committed with intent to destroy, in whole or in part, a national, ethnical, racial, or religious group as such." There is no doubt that Andrew Jackson believed that the polities Marshall called "domestic dependent nations" such as the Cherokee nation, should not be permitted to remain within any of the states. His public and private statements, with their repeated insistence that Indians cannot be trusted because of certain inherent racial deficiencies, expose the basic premise that drove his Indian policy.

In implementing that policy, was Jackson guilty of genocide? Or should we call it ethnic cleansing? Ethnic cleansing, some assume, does not have physical extermination of its victims as the objective. But as we noted at the beginning, here we encounter a very difficult problem. The conditions under which victims are subjected to the process may not be explicitly designed to murder, but they invariably lead to increases in mortality, particularly among the young and the aged. In other words, ethnic cleansing kills. And in the case of the Jacksonian removals, the killing was not small scale. Men and women, all too often not provided with sufficient food, clothing, and shelter from snow and ice, collapsed and died by the hundreds, year after year. Demographers do not agree on the number, but it is thought that relatively few old people and very few infants survived the process. As you ponder the question, "what shall we call this?" bear this in mind. We've seen evidence in the preceding chapter that President Andrew Jackson and his circle knew this was happening. They could have intervened, enforced their own orders that Indians not be abused, provided shoes, a little more bread, answered letters from Indian chiefs, and heeded appeals from their own more honest underlings. But the priority was—do it fast and do it cheap.

Jackson's defenders argue that the absence of the conscious "intent" required in the UN resolution exempts him from the charge that he committed genocide. In a larger sense, this definition game does not matter. Sharp Knife was guilty of as serious an abuse of power as any president in our history sworn to uphold the Constitution and thereby enforce the laws and treaties protecting Native American nations, he betrayed his trust by serving the interests of those who saw great personal profit to be made in the stealing of yet more Indian land. Of course, he did not regard the taking of Indian land as theft, as Indians were, by his lights, inferior peoples in the way of progress whose disappearance, he declared, should occasion no regret. Perpetrators of genocide always characterized their victims as people of little use, unworthy of protection. Jackson, in his most candid moments, so characterized the American Indian.

Even so the key to Jackson's indifference to Indian lives, to the larger question of their survival as a people, is not to be found by examining his racist attitudes, even though he clearly regarded Indians as not only inferior but by nature also malicious. Disturbing as Jackson's racial attitudes were, they must be understood as a component in an evolutionary view of history, widely shared and seldom challenged by white Americans, during Jackson's day and long thereafter. In a brilliant new analysis of the portrayal of native peoples in the chronicles, narratives, and festivals of the frontier, historian James Buss argues that Indian removal was not merely a physical process of dislocation but also the expression of an ideology rooted in "linguistic forms of domination. . . . Since the early 19th century, the popularized image of the white yeoman pioneer, which first developed east of the Mississippi, has propped up a powerful American narrative about western expansion, an inclusive American democracy and unlimited national progress while disempowering and dispossessing America's indigenous peoples by historicizing them and writing them out of a narrative of modernization and progress."[5] Andrew Jackson, in arguing for his removal program, denied repeatedly and emphatically that Indians had anything to contribute to that "inclusive America democracy and unlimited national progress" that the faithful revered as "Jacksonian Democracy." To be sure, they held out the hope that one day, after long isolation from the superior race, Indians might show signs of progress. But, reading his words carefully, one senses that he was not particularly optimistic about that. As we have seen, Sharp Knife assured Congress and the electorate that they need not lament the Indians' passing. True "philanthropists," he advised, serenely accept the disappearance of inferior people. "Jacksonian philanthropy" offered cold comfort to the victims. But it no doubt offered comfort and even vindication to some of those who profited so greatly from removal. One recent writer, in a very thorough study of Old Hickory's relationship to the law assures us that that there is no reason "to doubt the sincerity of Jackson's belief in his own lawfulness, nor even the accuracy of that belief."[6] He was hardly alone in the conviction that the rules of international law, as they were understood in the early 19th century, offered little protection to "savage" peoples. The question "who's really the savage?" was seldom asked. It was not a question Jackson understood.

Notes

PREFACE

1. Gale Courtney Toensing, "Indian-Killer Andrew Jackson Deserves Top Spot on List of Worst US Presidents," *Indian County Today*, February 20, 2017. https://indiancountrymedianetwork.com/history/people/indian-killer-andrew-jackson-deserves-top-spot-on-list-of-worst-us-presidents/. ICMN Staff, "Andrew Jackson: Worst and Most Terrifying U.S. President," *Indian Country Today,* September 11, 2012. https://indiancountrymedianetwork.com/news/andrew-jackson-worst-and-most-terrifying-us-president/

2. Herman Melville, *Moby Dick* (Norwalk, CT: The Easton Press, 1977), 123–124. First published in 1851.

3. Frederick Jackson Turner, *The Frontier in American History* (New York: H. Holt, 1920), 268.

4. A Google search on June 7, 2016, found that Jackson was generally rated as number 5 or 6 in various historian polls conducted between 1948 and the early 1990s. But several surveys and ratings since then, more varied in their sampling, have placed him much lower, the worst being a ranking at number 33 by the *Huffington Post*, September 12, 2016. See also Arthur M. Schlesinger Jr., "Rating the Presidents: Washington to Clinton," *Political Science Quarterly* 11 (1997): 179–190; Robert K. Murray and Tim H. Blessing, "The Presidential Performance Study: A Progress Report," *Journal of American History* 70 (1983): 535–555; Lynn Hudson Parsons, *The Birth of Modern Politics: Andrew Jackson, John Quincy Adams and the Election of 1828* (New York: Oxford University Press, 2009), 203n.

5. Binyamin Appelbaum, "Here Are the New Faces of the $5, 10, 20 Bills," *New York Times*, April 21, 2016.

6. Kari Winter, "Tubman Will Replace Jackson on the $20 Bill," *The Washington Post*, April 21, 2016.

7. Eugene Robinson, "It Matters Who's on the Money and Harriet Tubman Fills the Bill," *The Washington Post*, April 22, 2016.

8. David Horsey, "As the $20 Bill Gets a New Face, Andrew Jackson's Sins Are Recalled," *The Los Angeles Times*, April 21, 2016.

9. Deepti Hajela and Errin Haines Whack, "Tubman Replacing Jackson on the $20 a Deeply Symbolic Move," Fort Worth *Star-Telegram*, April 21, 2016.

10. "Editorial: Putting Harriet Tubman on the $20 Bill Is Proof America Is Finally Recalibrating Its Image," *The Dallas Morning News*, April 21, 2016.

11. Horsey, "As the $20 bill Gets a New Face, Andrew Jackson's Sins Are Recalled."

12. Jillian Keenan Slate, "Keenan: The War Criminal on Our $20 Bill," *The Salt Lake Tribune*, April 27, 2016. This column was first published on March 4, 2014.

13. Alex Alvarez, *Native America and the Question of Genocide* (Lanham, MD: Rowman & Littlefield, 2014), 164–165.

14. Dan Barry, "A Heated Linguistic Debate: What Makes 'Redskins' a Slur?," *The New York Times,* May 22, 2016.

15. Jonah Engel Bromwich, "The Wild Inauguration of Andrew Jackson, Trump's Populist Predecessor," *New York Times*, January 20, 2017. On the day Trump moved into the White House, Andrew Jackson's portrait returned to the Oval Office.

16. Martin Shaw, *What Is Genocide?* 2nd ed. (London: Polity, 2015), 1.

17. Raphael Lemkin, *Axis Rule in Occupied Europe: Laws of Occupation, Analysis of Governments, Proposals for Redress* (Washington, DC: Carnegie Endowment for International Peace, 1944), 79. Lemkin's notebooks indicate he devised the term a year before the publication of his book.

18. For an intriguing, controversial, comparative study of this process, see Carroll P. Kakel, *The American West and the Nazi East* (New York: Palgrave Macmillan, 2013). Kakel finds some similarities between Andrew Jackson and Heinrich Himmler, in their attitudes toward ethnic purity and frontier expansion.

19. Shaw, *What Is Genocide?*, 16–17.

20. For an excellent and succinct biography of Lemkin, see Samantha Powers, *A Problem from Hell: America in the Age of Genocide* (New York: Basic Books, 2002), 1–60. Lemkin's *Totally Unofficial the Autobiography of Raphael Lemkin* (New Haven: Yale University Press, 2013) is sketchy and disappointing. But see also Philippe Sand, *East West Street: On the Origins of "Genocide" and "Crimes against Humanity"* (New York: Alfred A. Knopf, 2016),) and Douglas Irvin-Erikson, *Raphael Lemkin and the Concept of Genocide* (Philadelphia: University of Pennsylvania Press, 2017). Most of Lemkin's papers remain unpublished. But there is a very useable collection of some of his writings: Steven Leonard Jacobs, ed., *Lemkin on Genocide* (Lanham, MD: Lexington Books, 2008).

21. John Cooper, *Raphael Lemkin and the Struggle for the Genocide Convention* (New York: Palgrave Macmillan, 2008).

22. Adam Jones, *Genocide: A Comprehensive Introduction*, 2nd ed. (London: Routledge, 2011), 16–20.

23. Jeffrey Ostler "Genocide and American Indian History," *American History: Oxford Research Encyclopedias*, http//americanhistory.oxfordre.com/view/10.1093/ acrefore-9780199329175.001.0001/acrefore-9780199329175-e-3.

24. Documentation regarding the nature of Indian warfare, and of Jackson's own view of belligerent rights as applied to Indians, will be provided in the chapters to come. For the background history of that warfare and its impact on Euro-American society, see Peter Silver, *Our Savage Neighbors: How Indian War Transformed America* (New York: W.W. Norton, 2008); Robert G. Parkinson, *The Common Cause: Creating Race and Nation in the American Revolution* (Chapel Hill: University of North Carolina Press, 2016).

25. Ronald N. Satz, *American Indian Policy in the Jacksonian Era* (Lincoln: University of Nebraska Press, 2002), 9.

26. Fr. John Paul Prucha has been Jackson's strongest modern defender. See, in particular, his seminal article "Andrew Jackson's Indian Policy: A Reassessment," *Journal of American History* 56 (December 1969): 527–539. Robert Remini, the premier Jacksonian scholar of the past century, has been somewhat more critical of Old Hickory, but in the end endorses Jackson's own claim that he had rescued American Indians "from probable annihilation." *Andrew Jackson and His Indian Wars* (New York: Viking, 2001), 281. A far more critical assessment is found in Anthony F. C. Wallace, *The Long Bitter Trail: Andrew Jackson and the Indians* (New York: Hill and Wang, 1993). But this is a short, supplemental text for students, not a full-scope study. There is a detailed and critical analysis of Jackson's role in Wallace's *Jefferson and the Indians: The Tragic Fate of the First Americans* (Cambridge, MA: Belknap Press of Harvard University Press, 1999). On Jackson's early career as an Indian fighter, see David S. Heidler and Jeanne T. Heidler, *Old Hickory's War* (Mechanicsburg, PA: Stackpole Books, 1996); and John Buchanan, *Jackson's Way: Andrew Jackson and the People of the Western Waters* (New York: John Wiley and Sons, 2001). Buchanan's Jackson is a heroic figure. The Heidlers' is not.

27. Gary Clayton Anderson, *Ethnic Cleansing and the Indian: The Crime That Should Haunt America* (Norman: University of Oklahoma Press, 2015), 151–191. Anderson argues that the continuing belief in certain ethical principles prevented ethnic cleansing in America from generating into widespread exterminatory genocide. But he notes that several 19th-century governors in Texas and California advocated and sometimes implemented campaigns of extermination. See also Gary Clayton Anderson, *The Conquest of Texas: Ethnic Cleansing and the Promised Land 1820–1875* (Norman: University of Oklahoma Press, 2005).

28. Alfred A. Cave, *Lethal Encounters: Englishmen and Indians in Colonial Virginia* (Santa Barbara, CA: Praeger, 2011).

29. Christopher D. Haveman, *Rivers of Sand: Creek Indian Emigration, Relocation and Ethnic Cleansing* (Lincoln: University of Nebraska Press, 2016), 5.

30. Benjamin Lieberman, "'Ethnic Cleansing' versus Genocide," in Donald Bloxham and A. Dirk Moses, eds., *The Oxford Handbook of Genocide Studies* (New York: Oxford University Press, 2010), 42–60.

31. Walter L. Hixson, *American Settler Colonialism: A History* (New York: Palgrave Macmillan, 2013), 4.

32. Tony Barta, "*Relations of Genocide: Land and Lives in the Colonization of Australia*," in Isidor Wallman and Michael Dokosky, eds., *Genocide in the Modern Age: Etiology and Case Studies of Mass Death* (Syracuse: Syracuse University Press, 2000).

33. A. Dirk Moses, "Conceptual Blockages and Definitional Dilemmas in the Racial Century: Genocides of Indigenous Peoples and the Holocaust," in A. Dirk Moses and Dan Stone, eds., *Colonialism and Genocide* (London: Routledge, 2007), 164–165.

34. Lorenzo Veracini, "Settler Colonialism: Career of a Concept," *The Journal of Imperial and Commonwealth History* 41 (2013): 313–333.

CHAPTER 1

1. Of the many biographies of Jackson published over the years, two older works remain indispensable: James Parton's three-volume *Life of Andrew Jackson* (New York: Mason Brothers, 1861) for its treasure-trove of Jackson lore and Robert V. Remini's three volumes (*Andrew Jackson and the Course of American Empire 1767–1821* [Vol. 1, 1977], *Andrew Jackson and the Course of American Freedom 1822–1832* [Vol. 2, 1981], and *Andrew Jackson*

and the Course of American Democracy [Vol. 3, 1984]), all published by Harper & Row (New York), for their sure command of both the primary sources and the scholarly literature. The quotations are from Remini's one-volume abridged edition *Andrew Jackson* (New York: Harper & Row, 1988), 5, and Parton, *Andrew Jackson*, I: 64. Among the more recent biographies, W.H. Brands's *Andrew Jackson: His Life and Times* (New York: Doubleday, 2005) and Jon Meacham's *American Lion: Andrew Jackson in the White House* (New York: Random House, 2008) are notable for their scope. Andrew Burstein, *The Passions of Andrew Jackson* (New York: Alfred K. Knopf, 2003) offers both an excellent short account of his life and a very interesting assessment of his personal temperament and character.

2. Remini, *Andrew Jackson and the Course of American Empire 1767–1821*, 6–8.

3. Lorman A. Ratner, *Andrew Jackson and His Tennessee Lieutenants: A Study in Political Culture* (Westport, CT: Greenwood, 1997), 1, 22.

4. Andrew Jackson to Amos Kendall, January 9, 1844, quoted in Sam B. Smith and Harriet Chappell Owsley, eds., *Papers of Andrew Jackson* (Knoxville: University of Tennessee Press, 1980), I: 9, fn. 4. Hereafter cited as *Jackson Papers*.

5. Quoted in Buchanan, *Jackson's Way*, 5.

6. Andrew Jackson to Willie Blount, January 4, 1813, in John Spencer Bassett, ed., *The Correspondence of Andrew Jackson*, 6 vols. (Washington, DC: Carnegie Institution, 1926–1934), I: 254–255. Hereafter cited as *Jackson Correspondence*.

7. Susan Alexander, "The Fugitive from the Waxhaws," *National Intelligencer*, August 1, 29, 1845, quoted in Robert V. Remini, *Andrew Jackson and His Indian Wars* (New York: Viking, 2001), 13–14. Alexander's claim that one of Elizabeth Jackson's relatives, perhaps a son, had been killed in an Indian raid near their home cannot be verified, and probably isn't true. As biographer Hendrik Booraem notes "there had been no Native American attacks in the Waxhaws for some years before the Jacksons arrived and Andrew was born. The Catawbas were completely inoffensive." In fact, the tribe whose small reservation was adjacent to the Waxhaws, sent some warriors to the South Carolina militia to support the campaign to expel the British. Hendrik Booraem, *Young Hickory: The Making of Andrew Jackson* (Dallas: Taylor Publishing Company, 2001), 56, 194.

8. John Ridge to Elias Boudinot, May 21, 1831, in *Cherokee Phoenix*, 2–3.

9. Quoted in Mary Douglas, *Purity and Danger* (London: Routledge, 1966), 14.

10. Patrick Griffin, *American Leviathan: Empire, Nation and Revolutionary Frontier* (New York: Hill & Wang, 2007), 3–16.

11. See Peter Silver, *Our Savage Neighbors: How Indian War Transformed America* (New York: W.W. Norton, 2008); Robert G. Parkinson, *The Common Cause: Creating Race and Nation in the American Revolution* (Chapel Hill: University of North Carolina Press, 2016).

12. Andrew Jackson to John McKee, January 30, 1793, in Smith and Owsley, *Jackson Papers*, I: 40.

13. Michael Paul Rogin, *Fathers and Children: Andrew Jackson and the Subjugation of the American Indian* (New York: Vintage, 1976), 40. In this brilliant and controversial work, Rogin traces the origins of the psychodynamics that drove Jackson's Indian policies to the rage emanating from his troubled childhood and problematic relationship with his mother. Jackson, he argues, suffered from acute "separation anxiety." His use of Freudian psychoanalytic concepts is provocative but, in the judgment of this reader, not persuasive. The origins of Indian removal are better understood through examination of the interaction of racist ideology and economic self-interest than through speculation about Old Hickory's inner demons.

14. James Parton, *Life of Jackson* (New York: Mason Brothers, 1861), I: 104–109.

15. Ibid., I: 121–124.

16. For another critical assessment of this story, see John Buchanan, *Jackson's Way: Andrew Jackson and the People of the Western Waters* (New York: John Wiley and Sons, 2001), 48–50. Buchanan offers an excellent account of the racial violence that marked the expansion of white settlement in the Upper South.

17. Remini, *Andrew Jackson and the Course of American Empire 1767–1821*, 40.

18. Harriette S. Arnow, *Seedtime on the Cumberland* (New York: Palgrave Macmillan, 1960), 363.

19. Remini, *Andrew Jackson and the Course of American Empire 1767–1821*, 41.

20. Thomas P. Abernethy, *From Frontier to Plantation in Tennessee* [1932] (Westport, CT: Greenwood Press, 1979), 198–199.

21. Buchanan, *Jackson's Way*, 128.

22. A. W. Putnam, *History of Middle Tennessee* [1859] (New York: Arno Press, 1971), 318.

23. Remini, *Andrew Jackson and His Indian Wars*, 27.

24. Andrew Jackson to John McKee, May 16, 1794, in Smith and Owsley, *Jackson Papers*, I: 48.

25. Quoted in Christina Snyder, *Slavery in Indian Country* (Cambridge: Harvard University Press, 2010), 159.

26. Abernethy, *From Frontier to Plantation in Tennessee*, 53.

27. Abernethy, *From Frontier to Plantation in Tennessee*, 58–59.

28. Rogin, *Fathers and Children*, 82.

29. Remini, *Andrew Jackson and the Course of American Empire 1767–1821*, 45. For an analysis of Jackson's legal career, see James W. Ely Jr. and Theodore Brown Jr., eds., *Legal Papers of Andrew Jackson* (Knoxville: University of Tennessee Press, 1987), xxxvi-liv.

30. Amos Kendall, *Life of General Jackson* [1843] (Ann Arbor, MI: University Microfilms, 1974), 90.

31. Rogin, *Fathers and Children*, 82–83.

32. Ronald Takaki, *Iron Cages: Race and Culture in 19th Century America* (New York: Oxford University Press, 1979), 93–94.

33. John Overton to Andrew Jackson, March 8, 1795; Agreement with Joel Rice, April 5, 1795, in Smith and Owsley, *Jackson Papers*, I: 54–55.

34. Agreement with David Allison, May 14, 1795, in Smith and Owsley, *Jackson Papers*, I: 56–58.

35. Meeker, Cochran & Company to Andrew Jackson, August 11, 1795; John B. Evans & Company to Andrew Jackson, January 4, 1796, in Smith and Owsley, *Jackson Papers*, I: 64, 79.

36. Remini, *Andrew Jackson and the Course of American Empire 1767–1821*, 86–90. For some glimpses of Jackson's continuing difficulties over this matter see John Overton to Andrew Jackson, 18 December, 1796; Andrew Jackson to Thomas Overton, March 6, 1798; Statement Regarding the Allison Transaction, July 15, 1801, in Smith and Owsley, *Jackson Papers*, I: 64, 79, 104–105, 250–252.

37. Lynn Hudson Parsons, *The Birth of Modern Politics: Andrew Jackson, John Quincy Adams and the Election of 1828* (New York: Oxford University Press, 2009), 9.

38. Appointment as Mero District Attorney for the Southwest Territory, February 15, 1791, in Smith and Owsley, *Jackson Papers*, I: 26; Buchanan, *Jackson's Way*, 125.

39. "Andrew Jackson to John McKee," January 30, 1793; May 16, 1794, in Smith and Owsley, *Jackson Papers*, I: 40, 48–49.

40. Remini, *Andrew Jackson and the Course of American Empire 1767–1821*, 72; Buchanan, *Jackson's Way*, 115–117.

41. Andrew Jackson to Daniel Smith, February 13, 1789, in Smith and Owsley, *Jackson Papers*, I: 16–17.

42. Buckner F. Melton, *The First Impeachment: The Constitution's Framers and the Case of Senator William Blount* (Macon, GA: Mercer University Press, 1998).

43. Parton, *Jackson*, I: 196. Remini questions Gallatin's veracity, pointing out Jackson had hired a fine Philadelphia tailor and dressed like a gentleman. *Andrew Jackson and the Course of American Empire 1767–1821*, 92. But while Jackson may not have appeared on the senate floor clad in buckskin, he was hardly your typical Federalist era congressman.

44. "Speech before the House of Representatives, December 29, 1796," in Smith and Owsley, *Jackson Papers*, I: 106–107. For a detailed analysis of Jackson's role, see Remini, *Andrew Jackson and the Course of American Empire 1767–1821*, 94–99.

45. Remini, *Andrew Jackson and the Course of American Empire 1767–1821*, 109.

46. Parton, *Life of Jackson*, I: 219.

47. Jos Anderson, Andrew Jackson, William Charles Cole Claiborne to John Adams, March 5, 1798, in Smith and Owsley, *Jackson Papers*, I: 185–186.

48. Quoted in Remini, *Andrew Jackson and the Course of American Empire 1767–1821*, 111.

49. Ibid., 108–112.

50. Record of a Slave Sale, Washington County Court, November 17, 1798, in Smith and Owsley, *Andrew Jackson Papers*, I: 19; Remini, *Andrew Jackson and the Course of American Empire 1767–1821*, 57.

51. Quoted in Buchanan, *Jackson's Way*, 138.

52. Andrew Burstein, *The Passions of Andrew Jackson*, 15, notes that Indian men "turned to beating their wives and children, something unheard of in their matrilineal societies before the white intrusion."

53. Ratner, *Andrew Jackson and His Tennessee Lieutenants*, 35–48.

54. Remini, *Andrew Jackson and the Course of American Empire 1767–1821*, 135.

55. See the detailed analyses of the Jackson's finances in Mark R. Cheatham, *Andrew Jackson: Southerner* (Baton Rouge: Louisiana State University Press, 2013).

56. Abernethy, *From Frontier to Plantation in Tennessee*, 201–209.

57. Francis Baily, *Journal of a Tour of the Unsettled Parts of America in 1796 and 1797* (London: Baily Brothers, 1856), 416–426; Buchanan, *Jackson's Way*, 112–113.

58. Parton, *Jackson*, I: 227. On his career as a superior court judge, see Ely and Brown, *The Legal Papers of Andrew Jackson*, 101–318.

59. Parton, *Jackson*, I: 228–229.

60. For a very clear, concise account and analysis of the complicated events leading to the Jackson-Dickinson duel, see Remini, *Andrew Jackson and the Course of American Empire 1767–1821*, 136–143.

61. Parton, *Jackson*, I: 269.

62. Affidavit of Joseph Erwin re Forfeit in the Truxton-Ploughboy Race, in Moser et al., *Jackson Papers*, II: 79.

63. Thomas Swann to Andrew Jackson, January 3, 1806, in Moser et al., *Jackson Papers*, II: 78.

64. Andrew Jackson to Thomas Swann, January 7, 1806, in Moser et al., *Jackson Papers*, II: 79–81. Parton, *Andrew Jackson*, I: 269–283.

65. Thomas Swann to Andrew Jackson, January 12, 1806, in Moser et al., *Jackson Papers*, II: 82.

66. Parton, *Andrew Jackson*, I: 286–294. For Jackson's account of his dispute with Swann, see his letter to Thomas Eastin, February 10, 1806, in Moser et al., *The Jackson Papers*, II: 84–89.

67. Charles Henry Dickinson to Thomas Eastin, May 21, 1806, in Moser et al., *Jackson Papers*, II: 97–98.

68. Andrew Jackson to Charles Henry Dickinson, May 23, 1806, in Moser et al., *Jackson Papers*, II: 98.

69. Parton, *Jackson*, I: 295–306.

70. David S. Reynolds, *Waking Giant: America in the Age of Jackson* (New York: Harper, 2008), 7.

71. Jackson's self-defense is found in an undated letter, apparently unsent, to newspaper editor Thomas Eastin, in Moser et al., *Jackson Papers*, II: 106.

72. Parton, *Life of Jackson*, I: 305.

73. Remini, *Andrew Jackson and the Course of American Empire 1767–1821*, 132.

74. Excellent analyses of Andrew Jackson's financial affairs is to be found in Mark R. Cheathem, *Andrew Jackson Southerner* (Baton Rouge: Louisiana State University Press, 2013) and in Remini's three-volume biography of Jackson cited earlier.

75. Power of Attorney from James Buchanan, November 8, 1790, in Smith and Owsley, *Jackson Papers*, I: 24.

76. See, for example, Robert King to Andrew Jackson, October 23, 1793, in Smith and Owsley, *Jackson Papers*, I: 41; other cases involving Jackson either as an attorney or as a judge are found in Ely and Brown, *The Legal Papers of Andrew Jackson*, 28–31, 142–145; 207–211, 238–241.

77. Remini, *Andrew Jackson and the Course of American Empire 1767–1821*, 133. See, for examples, of Jackson's slave transactions his letter to John Overton, dated November 30, 1799, in which he arranges for the purchase of "a Negro fellow George and a wench," his letter to Stockley Donelson, March 26, 1802, complaining that a "Negro boy" he sold had not been paid for, a letter from Samuel Jackson, June 9, 1802, about Jackson's purchase of "five Negroes," and a subsequent letter from the same trader about another 10 he was transporting to Tennessee, in Smith and Owsley, *Jackson Papers*, I: 224–225, 290, 316.

78. Andrew Jackson to Andrew Hutchings, in Bassett, *Jackson Correspondence*, V: 105.

79. Andrew Jackson to Andrew Jackson Jr., July 4, 1829, and July 28, 1829, in Bassett, *Jackson Correspondence*, V: 49–50.

80. Quoted in Reynolds, *Waking Giant*, 6.

81. Andrew Jackson to Andrew Jackson Donelson, July 3, 1821, in Bassett, *Jackson Correspondence*, III: 87.

82. Andrew Jackson to James Crane Bronaugh, July 3, 1821, in Moser et al., *Jackson Papers*, V: 66–67.

83. Andrew Jackson to Andrew J. Donelson, July 3, 1821, in Bassett, *Jackson Correspondence*, III: 78.

84. Andrew Jackson to Andrew Hays, August 30, 1827; Andrew Hays to Andrew Jackson, August 31, 1827, in Moser et al., *Jackson Papers*, VI: 385–386. A political enemy accused Jackson of covering up the killing. In fact, he urged prosecution even after the coroner's jury dismissed the indictment on grounds that Walton acted in self-defense. Andrew Jackson to William Berkeley Lewis, August 5, 1828, in Moser et al., *Jackson Papers*, VI: 486–488; Matthew S. Warshauer, "Andrew Jackson: Chivalric Slave Master," *Tennessee Historical Quarterly* (65: Fall, 2006), 202–229.

85. Fredrick M. Binder, *The Color Problem in Early National History as Viewed by John Adams, Jefferson and Jackson* (The Hague: Mouton, 1968), 120–135.

86. Cheathem, *Andrew Jackson: Southerner*, 93.

87. Remini, *Andrew Jackson and the Course of American Empire 1767–1821*, 133.

88. Andrew Jackson to George Washington Campbell, October 15, 1812, in Moser et al., *Jackson Papers*, II: 334.

89. Andrew Jackson to Willie Blount, January 25, 1812, in Moser et al., *Jackson Papers*, II: 278.

90. Remini, *Andrew Jackson and the Course of American Empire 1767–1821*, 163–164.

91. John M. Belohlavek, *"Let the Eagle Soar!" The Foreign Policy of Andrew Jackson* (Lincoln: University of Nebraska Press, 1985), 72.

92. Andrew Jackson to John Sevier, May 8, 1797; John Sevier to Andrew Jackson, May 8, 1797; Andrew Jackson to John Sevier, May 10, 1797; John Sevier to Andrew Jackson, May 11, 1797, in Smith and Owsley, *Jackson Papers*, I: 136–142.

93. Andrew Jackson to John Sevier, March 27, 1802; Thomas Augustine Claiborne to Andrew Jackson, July 14, 1803; Andrew Jackson to Benjamin J. Bradford, July19, 1803, in Smith and Owsley, *Jackson Papers*, I: 290–291, 335–339; 342–347.

94. Andrew Jackson to John Sevier, October 2, 1803; John Sevier to Andrew Jackson, October 2, 1803; Andrew Jackson to John Sevier, October 3, 1803; John Sevier to Andrew Jackson, October 3, 1803, Andrew Jackson to John Sevier, October 11, 1803, in Smith and Owsley, *Jackson Papers*, I: 384–385, 367–369; 375–382; Remini, *Andrew Jackson and the Course of American Empire 1767–1821*, 121–123.

CHAPTER 2

1. General Order to the Militia, as to Spanish Threats, August 7, 1803, in Bassett, *Jackson Correspondence*, I: 68.

2. Order to Brigadier Generals of the 2nd Division, October 4, 1806, in Moser et al., *Jackson Papers*, II: 111–112.

3. David O. Stewart, *American Emperor: Aaron Burr's Challenge to Jefferson's America* (New York: Simon & Schuster, 2011), 14.

4. Andrew Jackson to [William Preston Anderson], October 4, 1806, in Moser et al., *Jackson Papers*, II: 110. The historical literature on the Burr conspiracy is voluminous. Many of the books on this matter are unreliable, but most recent accounts are both well documented and fairly judicious in their judgments. Even so, Burr's intentions remain somewhat unclear. It is safe to say that no one has unearthed any evidence whatsoever that he had any official authorization from the administration to mount a military campaign in the west. Nor is there conclusive evidence that he plotted secession of the west from the federal union, although that charge was leveled against him. There is, however, quite a bit of reasonably credible testimony suggesting his involvement or leadership of some very questionable schemes involving seizure of Spanish territories, including some testimony from Andrew Jackson. In sorting out the various claims, Milton Lomask's two volumes *Aaron Burr* (New York: Farrar, Straus & Giroux, 1979, 1982) remain very useful. The best recent account, in this writer's judgment, is in Nancy Isenberg, *Fallen Founder: The Life of Aaron Burr* (New York: Viking, 2007). Isenberg is more sympathetic to Burr than most past historians and biographers. But she is in full command of the available sources and avoids either demonizing or idealizing her "fallen founder."

5. Andrew Jackson to James Winchester, October 4, 1806, in Moser et al., *Jackson Papers*, II: 110–111.

6. See "Account with Aaron Burr," October 4, 1806, in Moser et al., *Jackson Papers*, II: 113–114.

7. Andrew Jackson to Daniel Smith, November 12, 1806, in Moser et al., *Jackson Papers*, II: 117–119.

8. Andrew Jackson to Thomas Jefferson, November 5, 1806, in Moser et al., *Jackson Papers*, II: 114–115.

9. Andrew Jackson to William Charles Cole Claiborne, November 12, 1806, in Moser et al., *Jackson Papers*, II: 116–117.

10. Henry Dearborn to Andrew Jackson, December 19, 1806, in Moser et al., *Jackson Papers*, II: 125.

11. Andrew Jackson to George Washington Campbell, January 15, 1807, in Moser et al., *Jackson Papers*, II: 149.

12. Andrew Jackson to Henry Dearborn, March 17, 1807, in Moser et al., *Jackson Papers*, II: 155–158.

13. The most persuasive summary and critique of the evidence, in this writer's judgment, is to be found in Isenberg, *Fallen Founder*.

14. Daniel Smith to Andrew Jackson, December 29, 1806, in Moser et al., *Jackson Papers*, II: 127.

15. Andrew Jackson to Daniel Smith, November 28, 1807, in Moser et al., *Jackson Papers*, II: 174–175. Although long the subject of rumor, definitive documentary proof from Spanish archives of Wilkinson's role as a paid Spanish agent came to light in 1854, some 29 years after his death.

16. Remini, *Andrew Jackson and the Course of American Empire*, 157–158.

17. Andrew Jackson to William Henry Harrison, November 18, 1811, in Moser et al., *Jackson Papers*, II: 270.

18. To the 2nd Division, March 7, 1812, in Moser et al., *Jackson Papers*, II: 290–293.

19. Remini, *Andrew Jackson and the Course of American Empire*, 169–171.

20. Willie Blount to Andrew Jackson, November 11, 1812, in Moser et al., *Jackson Papers*, II: 338–339.

21. Andrew Jackson to William Eustis, January 7, 1813, quoted in Buchanan, *Jackson's Way*, 200.

22. Andrew Jackson to John Armstrong, March 15, 1813, in Moser et al., *Jackson Papers*, II: 383–385. The government at first refused to pay Jackson's expenses, which would have ruined him financially, but Thomas Hart Benton persuaded Secretary Armstrong to reconsider. Buchanan, *Jackson's Way*, 203–204.

23. Remini, *Andrew Jackson and the Course of American Empire*, 171–179; Buchanan, *Jackson's Way*, 203.

24. Andrew Jackson to the Officers of the 2nd Division, April 20, 1808, in Moser et al., *Jackson Papers*, II: 190–191.

25. Andrew Jackson to Thomas Jefferson, April 20, 1808, in Moser et al., *Jackson Papers*, II: 191–194.

26. Andrew Jackson to Willie Blount, June 4, 1812, in Moser et al., *Jackson Papers*, II: 300–301.

27. Andrew Jackson to George Colbert, June 5, 1812, in Moser et al., *Jackson Papers*, II: 302–303.

28. "The Massacre at the Mouth of the Duck River," in Moser et al., *Jackson Papers*, II: 310–311.

29. Michael Paul Rogin, *Fathers and Children: Andrew Jackson and the Subjugation of the American Indian* (New York: Vintage, 1976), 147.

30. Dispatch from Benjamin Hawkins, May 25, 1812, in *American State Papers: Indian Affairs* 2 vols. (Washington, DC: Gales & Seton, 1832), I: 809. Hereafter cited as *ASPIA*.

31. Benjamin Hawkins to the Secretary of War, September 7, 1812, *ASPIA*, I: 811–812.

32. H.S. Halbert and T.H. Ball, *The Creek War of 1813 and 1814 [1895]* (Tuscaloosa: University of Alabama Press, 1995), 104.

33. Benjamin Hawkins to the Secretary of War, October 12, 1812, *ASPIA*, I: 813.

34. Benjamin Hawkins to James Monroe, January 11, 1813, and to John Armstrong, March 1, 1813, in C.L. Grant, ed., *Letters, Journals and Writings of Benjamin Hawkins*, 2 vols. (Savannah, GA: Beehive Press, 1980), II: 627.

35. There are a number of excellent studies of the Creek Indians, J. Leitch Wright Jr., *Creeks and Seminoles* (Lincoln: University of Nebraska Press, 1990), and Robbie Ethridge, *Creek Country: The Creek Indians and Their World* (Chapel Hill: University of North Carolina Press, 2003), provide useful overviews. As to the more specialized studies, three in particular are indispensable: Joel W. Martin, *Sacred Revolt: The Muskogees' Struggle for a New World* (Boston: Beacon Press, 1991); Kathryn H. Holland Braund, *Deerskins and Duffels: Creek Indian Trade with Anglo-America* (Lincoln: University of Nebraska Press, 1993) and Claudio Saunt, *A New Order of Things: Property, Power and the Transformation of the Creek Indians, 1733–1816* (Cambridge: Cambridge University Press, 1999). On Andrew Jackson's dealings with the Creeks over the years, see in particular O'Brien, *In Bitterness and in Tears*.

36. Verner W. Crane, *The Southern Frontier, 1670–1782* (Ann Arbor: University of Michigan Press, 1956), 260–263; Saunt, *A New Order of Things*, 26–27; Alfred A. Cave, *Prophets of the Great Spirit* (Lincoln: University of Nebraska Press, 2006), 157.

37. Braund, *Deerskins and Duffels*, 31–34; Alan Gallay, *The Indian Slave Trade: The Rise of the English Empire in the American South, 1670–1717* (New Haven, CT: Yale University Press, 2002); Christina Snyder, *Slavery in Indian Country: The Changing Face of Captivity in Early America* (Cambridge, MA: Harvard University Press, 2010), 1–78.

38. Reuben Gold Thwaites, ed., *The Jesuit Relations and Allied Documents* (Cleveland, OH: Burrow Brothers, 1896–1901), 61: 201–202.

39. Peter C. Mancall, *Deadly Medicine: Indians and Alcohol in Early America* (Ithaca, NY: Cornell University Press, 1995).

40. Saunt, *A New Order of Things*, 147–148.

41. Quoted in Braund, *Deerskins and Duffels*, 126.

42. Ibid., 131.

43. Ibid., 132.

44. Ibid., 72–75, 178; Cave, *Prophets of the Great Spirit*, 160.

45. Quoted in Florette Henri, *The Southern Indians and Benjamin Hawkins, 1796–1816* (Norman: University of Oklahoma Press, 1986), 85. That principle had been enunciated much earlier. It can be found in Thomas More's *Utopia* in the early 16th century and was fully developed in the writings of 18th-century commentators on "the Law on Nations."

46. Henri, *Benjamin Hawkins*, 84, 137.

47. Saunt, *A New Order of Things*, 79–80.

48. *ASPIA*, I: 604.

49. Minutes, treaty with the Creeks, June 9, 1802, ASPIA, I: 536.

50. William Blount to the Secretary of War, November 10, 1794, *ASPIA Papers, I*: 536.

51. Quoted in David Reynolds, *Waking Giant: America in the Age of Jackson* (New York: Harper, 2008), 91.

52. Henri, *Benjamin Hawkins*, 100, 106.

53. William Blount to James Carey, April 21, 1797, in *American State Papers: Foreign Affairs*, II: 77. Cited hereafter as ASPFA.

54. Henri, *The Southern Indians and Benjamin Hawkins*, 92–96, 227–228.

55. Ibid., 133.

56. Claudio Saunt, *A New Order of Things*, 272.

57. Cave, *Prophets of the Great Spirit*, 161.

58. On the controversy over the road, see Henry Deleon Southerland and Jerry Elisha Brown, *The Federal Road through Georgia, the Creek Nation and Alabama, 1806–1836* (Tuscaloosa: University of Alabama Press, 1989).

59. Benjamin Hawkins to William Eustis, June 23, 1812, and to David Mitchell, August 31, 1812, in Grant, *Letters, Journals and Writings of Benjamin Hawkins*, II: 610–611, 616.

60. Quoted in Buchanan, *Jackson's Way*, 210.

61. Frank L. Owsley Jr., *Struggle for the Gulf Borderlands: The Creek War and the Battles of New Orleans* (Tuscaloosa: University of Alabama Press, 2000), 15–17. For recent overviews of the Creek War and its aftermath, see David S. Heidler and Jeanne T. Heidler, *Old Hickory's War: Andrew Jackson and the Quest for Empire* (Mechanicsburg, PA: Stackpole, 1996) and Sean Michael O'Brien, *In Bitterness and in Tears: Andrew Jackson and the Destruction of the Creeks and Seminoles* (Westport, CT: Praeger, 2003).

62. Benjamin Hawkins to the chiefs of the Upper Creeks, March 25, 1813, in Grant, *Letters, Journals and Writings of Benjamin Hawkins*, II: 630–632.

63. Benjamin Hawkins to David B. Mitchell, April 26, 1813, in Grant, *Letters, Journals and Writings of Benjamin Hawkins*, II: 633–634; Nimrod Doyell to Benjamin Hawkins, May 13, 1813, *ASPIA*, I: 843.

64. Big Warrior to Benjamin Hawkins, April 26, 1813, *ASPIA*, I: 843. Alexander Cornells, a mixed blood Creek notable, served as interpreter and scribe for this letter.

65. Benjamin Hawkins to General Armstrong, May 10, 1813, *ASPIA*, I: 844.

66. Benjamin Hawkins to General Armstrong, June 7, 1813, *ASPIA*, I: 844–845.

67. Gregory A. Waselkov, *A Conquering Spirit: Fort Mims and the Redstick War of 1813–1814* (Tuscaloosa: University of Alabama Press, 2006), 89.

68. Report of Alexander Cornells, interpreter to Colonel Hawkins, June 22, 1813, *ASPIA*, I: 845–846.

69. Talosee Fixico, a Runner from Tuchabatchie to Colonel Hawkins, July 5, 1813, *ASPIA*, I: 847.

70. Benjamin Hawkins to the Secretary of War, July 28, 1813, *ASPIA*, I: 848–849.

71. Joel W. Martin, *Sacred Revolt*, 133–149; Cave, *Prophets of the Great Spirit*, 140–182: O'Brien, *In Bitterness and in Tears*, 37–62.

72. Buchanan, *Jackson's Way*, 213.

73. Henri, *Southern Indians and Benjamin Hawkins*, 281; Saunt, *A New Order of Things*, 256. Some claim the term "red stick" referred to bundles of painted sticks used to count days in order to coordinate offensive actions. A stick would be discarded each day. When all were gone, it was time to attack.

74. Henri, *Southern Indians and Benjamin Hawkins*, 281.

75. Halbert and Hall, *The Creek War*, 125–142; Waselkov, *A Conquering Spirit*, 100–191; Owsley, *Struggle for the Gulf Borderlands*, 30–32; O'Brien, *In Bitterness and in Tears*, 40–42.

76. Waselkov, *A Conquering Spirit*; Halbert and Hall, *The Creek War*, 143–176; O'Brien, *In Bitterness and in Tears*, xi–xv, 43–48, 51–52.

77. Benjamin Hawkins to John B. Floyd, September 30, 1813, in Grant, *Letters, Journals and Writings of Benjamin Hawkins*, II: 669.

78. Waselkov, *A Conquering Spirit*, 2.

79. Quoted in Waselkov, *A Conquering Spirit*, 97.

80. Owsley, *Struggle for the Gulf Borderlands*, 41, 44–45.

81. Weatherford, a mixed blood planter, later claimed that he had joined the Red Sticks out of expediency and had never really believed in their cause. That claim is suspect. For an incisive analysis of the evidence relating to Weatherford's relations with the Red Sticks, see Waselkov, *A Conquering Spirit*, 91–95.

82. Halbert and Hall, *The Creek War*, 177–211; Cave, *Prophets of the Great Spirit*, 174–175; Owsley, *Struggle for the Gulf Borderlands*, 47–48; O'Brien, *In Bitterness and in Tears*, 63–72.

83. Andrew Jackson to Willie Blount, July 31, 1813, in Moser et al., *Jackson Papers*, II: 416–418.

84. There are many accounts of this brawl. As always, Remini tells the story well. See Remini, *Andrew Jackson and the Course of American Empire*, 180–186.

85. To the Tennessee volunteers, September 24, 1813, in Moser et al., *Jackson Papers*, II: 427–428.

86. Andrew Jackson to John Coffee, September 29, 1813, in Moser et al., *Jackson Papers*, II: 431–432.

87. Andrew Jackson to John Coffee, October 7, 1813, in Moser et al., *Jackson Papers*, II: 435–436.

88. Quoted in Remini, *Andrew Jackson and the Course of American Empire*, 193.

89. Pathkiller to Andrew Jackson, October 22, 1813, in Moser et al., *Jackson Papers*, II: 440.

90. Andrew Jackson to Willie Blount, October 28, 1813, in Moser et al., *Jackson Papers*, II: 442.

91. Andrew Jackson to John Cocke, December 28, 1813, in Moser et al., *Jackson Papers*, II: 511.

92. Owsley, *Struggle for the Gulf Borderlands*, 50.

93. David Crockett, *A Narrative of the Life of David Crockett of the State of Tennessee* (Knoxville: University of Tennessee Press, 1973), 88–89; Herbert J. Doherty, *Richard Keith Call, Southern Unionist* (Gainesville: University of Florida Press, 1961), 6; O'Brien, *In Bitterness and in Tears*, 73–82.

94. Remini, *Andrew Jackson and the Course of American Empire*, 193.

95. Andrew Jackson to Rachel Jackson, November 4, 1813, in Moser et al., *Jackson Papers*, II: 444.

96. Andrew Jackson to Rachel Jackson, December 29, 1813, in Moser et al., *Jackson Papers*, II: 516. This passage is suggestive of Jackson's bitterness toward his own relatives in South Carolina. While he was not exactly alone in the world after his mother's death, he was not, it seems, given much real nurture and, as indicated earlier, later in life showed no interest in contact with his kinfolk.

97. Moser et al., *Jackson Papers*, II: 444, fn. 5.

98. Andrew Jackson to Rachel Jackson, February 21, 1814, in Moser et al., *Jackson Papers*, II: 516.

99. Parton, *Life of Andrew Jackson*, 439–440; Remini, *Andrew Jackson and the Course of American Empire*, 194; Mark R. Cheathem, *Andrew Jackson: Southerner* (Baton Rouge: Louisiana State University, 2013), 79–80.

Notes

100. Andrew Jackson to Rachel Jackson, November 12, 1813, in Moser et al., *Jackson Papers*, II: 449.

101. Thomas Flournoy to Andrew Jackson, November 9, 1813, in Moser et al., *Jackson Papers*, II: 447.

102. Waselkov, *A Conquering Spirit*, 148.

103. Andrew Jackson to Thomas Pinckney, March 7, 1814, in Moser et al., *Jackson Papers*, III: 41.

104. Andrew Jackson to Thomas Pinckney, March 2, 1814, in Moser et al., *Jackson Papers*, III: 35–36.

105. Thomas Pinckney to Andrew Jackson, March 11, 1814, in Moser et al., *Jackson Papers*, III: 46.

106. Andrew Jackson to Rachel Jackson, November 12, 1813; Remini, *Andrew Jackson and the Course of American Empire*, 194–198; Owsley, *Struggle for the Gulf Borderlands*, 64–67.

107. William Berkeley Lewis to Andrew Jackson, January 26, 1814, in Moser et al., *Jackson Papers*, III: 16. See also John Overton to Andrew Jackson, February 12, 1814, in Moser et al., *Jackson Papers*, III: 29.

108. Andrew Jackson to Rachel Jackson, February 1, 1814, in Moser et al., *Jackson Papers,* III: 23.

109. Willie Blount to Andrew Jackson, December 7, 1813, Jackson Papers, Library of Congress; Willie Blount to Andrew Jackson, December 22, 1813, in Moser et al., *Jackson Papers*, II: 498–499.

110. Andrew Jackson to Willie Blount, December 29, 1813, in Bassett, *Jackson Correspondence*, I: 416–420.

111. Andrew Jackson to Willie Blount, December 29, 1813, in Moser et al., *Jackson Papers*, January 2, 1813, III: 5.

112. Andrew Jackson to General Thomas Pinckney, January 29, 1814, in Bassett, *Jackson Correspondence*, I: 448. For the problems faced by the Georgia militia and by Claiborne, see Owsley, *Struggle for the Gulf Borderlands*, 42–60.

113. Andrew Jackson to Rachel Jackson, January 28, 1814, in Moser et al., *Jackson Papers*, III: 17–21; Remini, *Andrew Jackson and the Course of American Empire*, 209.

114. For Jackson's rejection of the condemned man's appeal, see Andrew Jackson to John Wood, March 14, 1814, in Moser et al., *Jackson Papers*, III: 48–49.

115. Andrew Jackson to Thomas Pinckney, March 23, 1814, in Moser et al., *Jackson Papers*, III: 50–51; Owsley, *Struggle for the Gulf Borderlands*, 77–78; Remini, *Andrew Jackson and the Course of American Empire*, 211–212.

116. Remini, *Andrew Jackson and the Course of America Empire*, 210–213; Owsley, *Struggle for the Gulf Borderlands*, 79; Buchanan, *Jackson's Way*, 283–284; O'Brien, *In Bitterness and in Tears*, 141–152.

117. Owsley, *Struggle for the Gulf Borderlands*, 79.

118. Andrew Jackson to Thomas Pinckney, March 28, 1814, in Moser et al., *Jackson Papers*, III: 52; Andrew Jackson to Rachel Jackson, April 1, 1814, in Moser et al., *Jackson Papers*, III: 54.

119. John Coffee to Andrew Jackson, April 1, 1814, in Moser et al., *Jackson Papers*, III: 55–57.

120. Andrew Jackson to Thomas Pinckney, March 28, 1814, in Moser et al., *Jackson Papers*, III: 52–53.

121. Robert Remini, *Andrew Jackson and His Indian Wars* (New York: Viking, 2001), 77.

122. For descriptions of the slaughter at Horseshoe bend, see O'Brien, *In Bitterness and in Tears*, 141–152; Owsley, *Struggle for the Gulf Borderlands*, 79–82; Buchanan, *Jackson's Way*, 279–290; James W. Holland, *Andrew Jackson and the Creek War: Victory at the Horseshoe* (Tuscaloosa: University of Alabama Press, 1968); Heidler and Heidler, *Old Hickory's War*, 19–20; Thomas Kanon, "'A Slow Laborious Slaughter': The Battle of Horseshoe Bend," *Tennessee Historical Quarterly* 58 (1999): 3–15.

123. Andrew Jackson to Rachel Jackson, April 1, 1814, in Moser et al., *Jackson Papers*, III: 54.

124. Andrew Jackson to Willie Blount, March 31, 1814, in Bassett, *Jackson Correspondence*, I: 489–92.

125. Quoted in Ronald Takaki, *Iron Cages: Race and Culture in 19th-Century America* (New York: Oxford University Press, 1990), 96.

126. Ibid., 96.

127. Andrew Jackson to David Holmes, April 18, 1814, in Bassett, *Jackson Correspondence*, I: 105.

128. Andrew Jackson to the Tennessee Troops in Mississippi Territory, April 2 and April 28, 1814, in Moser et al., *Jackson Papers*, III: 58, 65–66.

129. Heidler and Heidler, *Old Hickory's War*, 41.

130. Henry Adams, *History of the United States during the Administration of James Madison* [1891] (New York: The Library of America, 1986), 798; To counter the portrayal of Jackson as an Indian fighter of inhumane brutality, biographer James Parton insisted that Old Hickory was willing to spare those who heeded his call to surrender. It just happened, he explained, that no Red Stick warrior did so during the battle or during its immediate aftermath. Parton did hear a story of one wounded Red Stick captive who, while being treated sometime after the battle by Jackson's surgeons, complained that they "were curing him only to kill him later. The general, who was standing by, assured him that he had no such intention." Parton tells that the Red Stick recovered, and was afterwards "taken home by Jackson to Tennessee, where he learned a trade, married a colored woman, and established himself in business" (Parton, *Life of Andrew Jackson*, I: 504–506). That story cannot be confirmed and may have been nothing more than a fiction devised as part of the later propaganda campaign to create a mythic image of Old Hickory as the stern but humane father and friend of his Indian children. Or it may be that the first part of the story was true, but not the second. While there is no contemporary evidence of a Red Stick warrior taken back to the Hermitage by Jackson, he did on a few occasion spare captives, most famously in the case of the war chief William Weatherford (Red Eagle). Be that as it may, we do know this: Jackson's exhortations to his troops and his reports to his superiors during the Creek War consistently called for the "extermination" of the Red Sticks.

131. Andrew Jackson to Rachel Jackson, August 10, 1814, in Moser et al., *Jackson Papers*, III: 54.

132. Andrew Jackson to John Armstrong, May 8, 1814, in Moser et al., *Jackson Papers*, III: 54.

133. Colonel Hawkins, Agent for Indian Affairs, to Big Warrior, Little Prince and other chiefs of the Creek Nation, June 16, 1814, *ASPIA*, I: 845.

134. Andrew Jackson to Willie Blount, April 18, 1814, in Moser et al., *Jackson Papers*, III: 54. The stories of Weatherford's courage at his surrender and Jackson's gallantry to a hated foe have often been retold. To this writer, it seems more the stuff of legend than of fact. Both men had much to gain by the arrangement that made Weatherford a collaborator in securing an end to the Red Stick insurgency.

135. Jackson's correspondence contains repeated expressions of his preoccupation with present and future English and Spanish collusion with hostile Indians in the southeast. See, for examples, Moser et al., *Jackson Papers*, II: 194–125, 207, 270, 272, 300, 301, 304, 316, 431, 434, 435; III: 89, 90, 92, 95–102, 116, 119, 121, 122, 123, 128, 132, 179, 382.

136 Andrew Jackson to James Monroe, November 20, 1814, in Moser et al., *Jackson Papers*, III: 192.

137. "To the Tennessee Volunteers," September 24, 1813, in Moser et al., *Jackson Papers*, II: 228.

138. Andrew Jackson to Gideon Blackburn, December 3, 1813, in Moser et al., *Jackson Papers*, II: 464. As Bernard Sheehan has demonstrated, preoccupation with Indian cruelty, particularly in the torture of captives, was widespread in commentaries published from the late 18th century through most of the 19th. See *Seeds of Extinction: Jeffersonian Philanthropy and the American Indian* (Chapel Hill: University of North Carolina, 1973), 179–181.

139. Andrew Jackson to John Armstrong, December 16, 1813, in Moser et al., *Jackson Papers*, II: 493.

140. Andrew Jackson to Henry Atkinson, May 15, 1819, in Moser et al., *Jackson Papers*, IV: 298.

141. *Niles Register*, November 15, 1817, quoted in Rembert W. Patrick, *Florida Fiasco: Rampant Rebels on the Georgia-Florida Border*[1954] (Athens: University of Georgia Press, 2010), 48.

142. Quoted in Rogin, *Fathers and Children*, 6.

143. Quoted in William McLoughlin, *Cherokee Renascence in the New Republic* (Princeton: Princeton University Press, 1986), 35.

144. Cave, *Prophets of the Great Spirit*, 158–159; Henri, *The Southern Indians and Benjamin Hawkins*, 92–96, 227–228.

145. Quoted in Remini, *Andrew Jackson and His Indian Wars*, 115.

146. Thomas Jefferson to Henry Dearborn, August 28, 1897, in Lipscomb and Berg, *Writings of Thomas Jefferson*, II: 345–346.

147. Quoted in McLoughlin, *Cherokee Renascence in the New Republic*, 37.

148. Quoted in Nicholas Guyatt, *Bind Us Apart: How Enlightened Americans Invented Racial Segregation* (New York: Basic Books, 2016), 93.

149. Ibid., 146–147.

150. Christian B. Keller, "Philanthropy Betrayed: Thomas Jefferson, the Louisiana Purchase, and the Origins of Federal Indian Removal Policy," *Proceedings of the American Philosophical Society* 144 (2000): 39–66.

151. Quoted in Henri, *The Southern Indians and Benjamin Hawkins*, 258–259.

152. Andrew Jackson to George Washington Campbell, October 15, 1812, in Moser et al., *Jackson Papers*, II: 226–227.

153. Waselkov, *A Conquering Spirit*, 72–73.

154. Willie Blount to Andrew Jackson, December 28, 1809, in Moser et al., *Jackson Papers*, II: 226–227.

155. Quoted in A. J. Langguth, *Driven West: Andrew Jackson and the Trail of Tears to the Civil War* (New York: Simon & Schuster, 2011), 214.

156. For a defense of Jackson's removal program that argues that it was indeed benevolent in intent, see Francis Paul Prucha, "Andrew Jackson's Indian Policy: A Reassessment," *Journal of American History* 56 (1969): 527–539.

157. John Reid and John Henry Eaton, *The Life of Andrew Jackson* [1817] (Tuscaloosa: University of Alabama Press, 1974); Owsley, 13–14; 51, 64.

158. Burstein, *The Passions of Andrew Jackson*, 106.

CHAPTER 3

1. Quoted in Langguth, *Driven West*, 8.
2. Steve Inskeep, *Jacksonland: President Andrew Jackson, Cherokee Chief John Ross, and a Great American Land Grab* (New York: Penguin, 2015), 9. Two recent studies are of particular value in illuminating both the large-scale economic consequences of this transformation and its individual human aspects: Edward E. Baptist, *The Half Has Never Been Told: Slavery and the Making of American Capitalism* (New York: Basic Books, 2014); and Sven Beckert, *Empire of Cotton: A Global History* (New York: Alfred A. Knopf, 2014). Of enduring value is Eric Williams, *Capitalism and Slavery* (Chapel Hill: University of North Carolina Press, 1944).
3. Quoted in Merritt B. Pound, *Benjamin Hawkins: Indian Agent* (Athens: University of Georgia Press, 1951), 234–325.
4. John Coffee to W. B. Lewis, April 18, 1814, in Bassett, *Jackson Correspondence*, II: 4n.
5. Thomas Pinckney to Benjamin Hawkins, April 23, 1814, *ASPIA*, I: 857–858; Benjamin Hawkins to William Hawkins, April 26, 1814, in Grant, *Letters, Journals and Writings of Benjamin Hawkins*, II: 680. For Armstrong's instructions to Pinckney, see The Secretary of War to Major General Pinckney, March 17, 20, 1814, in *ASPIA*, I: 836–837.
6. Benjamin Hawkins to Thomas Pinckney, April 25, 1814, in *ASPIA Indian Affairs*, I: 858.
7. Andrew Jackson to Thomas Pinckney, May 18, 1814, in Bassett, *Jackson Correspondence*, II: 1–4. For another expression of Jackson's views on Indian settlement policy, see Andrew Jackson to John Williams, May 18, 1814, in Moser et al., *Jackson Papers*, III: 74–75.
8. Andrew Jackson to Robert Hays, January 25, 1798, in Smith and Owsley, *Jackson Papers*, I: 172–173.
9. Andrew Jackson to John Jackson, June 18, 1805, in Smith and Owsley, *Jackson Papers*, II: 61–62.
10. Andrew Jackson to John Williams, May 18, 1814, in Moser et al., *Jackson Papers*, III: 74–75.
11. Andrew Jackson to John Coffee, August 12, 1817, in Moser et al., *Jackson Papers*, IV: 32.
12. Cheathem, *Andrew Jackson: Southerner*, 94.
13. Henri, *The Southern Indians and Benjamin Hawkins*, 300–301.
14. Andrew Jackson to Benjamin Hawkins, July 11, 1814, in Bassett, *Jackson Correspondence*, II: 14–15.
15. Andrew Jackson to Big Warrior, August 7, 1814, in Moser et al., *Jackson Papers*, III: 109–111; Remini, *Andrew Jackson and the Course of American Empire*, 225–231; Heidler and Heidler, *Old Hickory's War*, 25–27; O' Brien, *In Bitterness and in Tears*, 161–164.
16. Reid and Eaton, *The Life of Andrew Jackson*, 172–173.
17. "Articles of Agreement and Capitulation . . ." August 9, 1814, in *ASPIA*, I: 826–827.
18. Andrew Jackson to Big Warrior, August 7, 1814, in Smith and Owsley, *Jackson Papers*, III: 109–111.
19. Rogin, *Fathers and Children*, 157–160, 191–193; Remini, *Andrew Jackson and His Indian Wars*, 88–99; Buchanan, *Jackson's Way*, 299–300; William J. McLoughlin, *Cherokee Renascence in the New Republic* (Princeton, NJ: Princeton University Press, 1986), 194–201.
20. Benjamin Hawkins to Andrew Jackson, August 6, 1814, in Grant, *Letters, Journals and Writings of Benjamin Hawkins*, II: 691–692.
21. Benjamin Hawkins to Secretary of War Armstrong, August 10, 1814, in Records of the Office of the Secretary of War, Letters Received, National Archives.

22. Heidler and Heidler, *Old Hickory's War*, 241, n. 73.
23. Owsley, *Struggle for the Gulf Borderlands*, 90–91.
24. Jesse Wharton to Andrew Jackson, February 16, 1815, in Moser et al., *Jackson Papers*, III: 280.
25. Andrew Jackson to Secretary Armstrong, June 13, 1814, in Bassett, *Jackson Correspondence*, II: 1–4.
26. Heidler and Heidler, *Old Hickory's War*, 239, n. 42; Martin, *Sacred Revolt*, 163.
27. Rembert Patrick, *Florida Fiasco: Rampant Rebels on the Georgia-Florida Border, 1810–1815* (Athens: University of Georgia Press, 1954); James Cusick, *The Other War of 1812: The Patriot War and the American Invasion of East Florida* (Gainesville: University Press of Florida, 2003).
28. Theda Purdue, *Slavery and the Evolution of Cherokee Society* (Knoxville: University of Tennessee Press, 1979); Kenneth W. Porter, *The Black Seminoles: History of a Freedom Seeking People* (Gainesville: University Press of Florida, 1996).
29. Cusick, *The Other War of 1812*, 214.
30. Quoted in Patrick, *Florida Fiasco*, 184.
31. Benjamin Hawkins to David B. Mitchell, September 7, 1812, in Grant, *Letters, Journals and Writings of Benjamin Hawkins*, II: 617.
32. Patrick, *Florida Fiasco*, 195–210.
33. Ibid., 229.
34. Ibid., 229–230.
35. Ibid., 226.
36. Ibid., 233–234.
37. Cusick, *The Other War of 1812,* 214–257; Patrick, *Florida Fiasco*, 202–210; Heidler and Heidler, *Old Hickory's War*, 37.
38. Annals of Congress, 12th Congress, 2nd Session, 504–535.
39. Patrick, *Florida Fiasco*, 282.
40. Benjamin Hawkins to Thomas Pinckney, May 17, 1814, in Grant, *Letters, Journals and Writings of Benjamin Hawkins*, II: 681.
41. Remini, *Andrew Jackson and His Indian Wars*, 94.
42. Heidler and Heidler, *Old Hickory's War*, 38–42; Remini, *Andrew Jackson and His Indian Wars*, 94–95; Buchanan, *Jackson's Way*, 306–312; Owsley, *Struggle for the Gulf Borderlands*, 98–119; O'Brien, *In Bitterness and in Tears*, 175–185.
43. Andrew Jackson to James Monroe, October 10, 1814, in Bassett, *Jackson Correspondence*, II: 70.
44. Andrew Jackson to John Armstrong, June 27, 1814, in Smith and Owsley, *Jackson Papers*, III: 83.
45. Andrew Jackson to John Armstrong, July 18, 1814, in Smith and Owsley, *Jackson Papers*, III: 83.
46. Remini, *Andrew Jackson and the Course of American Empire*, 225.
47. See, for example, "Report of the Supplies to the Indians by the British and Spaniards at Pensacola and Mouth of the Chattahoochee," enclosed in Benjamin Hawkins to Peter Early, June 15, 1814, in Grant, *Letters, Journals and Writings of Benjamin Hawkins*, II: 683–685.
48. Benjamin Hawkins to John Armstrong, August 16, 1814, in Grant, *Letters, Journals and Writings of Benjamin Hawkins*, II: 683–685.
49. Andrew Jackson to John Reid, August 27, 1814, in Smith and Owsley, *Jackson Papers*, III: 124–125.

50. Andrew Jackson to Gonzales Manrique, September 9, 1814, in Bassett, *Jackson Correspondence*, II: 44–46.

51. James Monroe to Andrew Jackson, October 21, 1814, in Smith and Owsley, *Jackson Papers*, III: 170–171.

52. Andrew Jackson to James Monroe, October 26, 1814, in Smith and Owsley, *Jackson Papers*, III: 170–171.

53. James Monroe to Andrew Jackson, December 7, 1814, in Smith and Owsley, *Jackson Papers*, III: 200–201.

54. Heidler and Heidler, *Old Hickory's War*, 42–49; Buchanan, *Jackson's Way*, 310–312; Owsley, *Struggle for the Gulf Borderlands*, 116–119; O'Brien, *In Bitterness and in Tears*, 178–180.

55. James Monroe to Andrew Jackson, December 7, 1814, in Smith and Owsley, *Jackson Papers*, III: 200–201.

56. John William Ward, *Andrew Jackson: Symbol for an Age* (New York: Oxford University Press, 1955), 8.

57. Ward, *Andrew Jackson: Symbol for an Age*, 13–29.

58. Daniel Walker Howe, *What Hath God Wrought: The Transformation of America, 1815–1848* (New York: Oxford, 2007), 15.

59. Quotations from Remini, *Andrew Jackson and the Course of American Empire*, 284 and Buchanan, *Jackson's Way*, 362. Of the voluminous literature on the Battle of New Orleans, the following are also particularly useful: Charles Brooks, *The Siege of New Orleans* (Seattle: University of Washington Press, 1961); Samuel Carter III, *Blaze of Glory: The Fight for New Orleans 1814–1815* (New York: St. Martin's, 1971); Robin Reilly, *The British at the Gates: The New Orleans Campaign in the War of 1812* (New York: G.P. Putnam, 1974); Robert V. Remini, *The Battle of New Orleans* (New York: Viking, 1999); Owsley, *Struggle for the Gulf Borderlands*, 123–196. One eyewitness account, from the British perspective, is highly recommended: George R. Gleig, *The Campaigns of the British Army at Washington and New Orleans* (London: John Murray, 1847). See also Hugh Rankin, ed., *The Battle of New Orleans: A British Perspective* (New Orleans, LA: Hauser Press, 1961).

60. Remini, *Andrew Jackson and the Course of American Empire*, 282.

61. Andrew Jackson, "To Troops on the Right Bank of the Mississippi River," January 8, 1815, in Bassett, *Jackson Correspondence*, II: 136.

62. William Charles Cole Claiborne to Andrew Jackson, August 14, 1814, in Moser et al., *Jackson Papers*, III: 115.

63. William Charles Cole Claiborne to Andrew Jackson, August 30, 1814, in Moser et al., *Jackson Papers*, III: 126.

64. Matthew Warshauer, *Andrew Jackson and the Politics of Marital Law* (Knoxville: University of Tennessee Press, 2007), 20–24.

65. Warshauer, *Andrew Jackson and the Politics of Marital Law*, 35–39, 181.

66. Alexander J. Dallas to Andrew Jackson, July 1, 1815, in Moser et al., *Jackson Papers*, III: 375; Warshauer, *Andrew Jackson and the Politics of Marital Law*, 41–43.

67. Warshauer, *Andrew Jackson and the Politics of Marital Law*, 40–177.

68. Bassett, *Jackson Correspondence*, II: 208–209.

69. Alexander J. Dallas to Andrew Jackson, June 12, 1815, in Clarence E. Carter, ed., *The Territorial Papers of the United States* (Washington, DC, 1934), XV: 62.

70. Edmund Pendleton Gaines to Andrew Jackson, June 8, 1815, in Moser et al., *Jackson Papers*, III: 361.

71. Benjamin Hawkins to Andrew Jackson, July 17, 1815, in Grant, *Letters, Journals and Writings of Benjamin Hawkins*, II: 742.

72. Benjamin Hawkins to Edmund P. Gaines, June 14, 1815, in Grant, *Letters, Journals and Writings of Benjamin Hawkins*, II: 736.

73. Benjamin Hawkins to Edward Nicolls, May 28, 1815, in Grant, *Letters, Journals and Writings of Benjamin Hawkins*, II: 734.

74. Benjamin Hawkins to George Graham, August 1, 1815, in Grant, *Letters, Journals and Writings of Benjamin Hawkins*, II: 744.

75. Benjamin Hawkins to Alexander Cornells, June 24, 1815, in Grant, *Letters, Journals and Writings of Benjamin Hawkins*, II: 736.

76. Heidler and Heidler, *Old Hickory's War*, 55; Remini, *Andrew Jackson and His Indian Wars*, 97–100.

77. Heidler and Heidler, *Old Hickory's War*, 57.

78. Remini, *Andrew Jackson and His Indian Wars*, 99.

79. Jackson's Talk to the Creeks, September 4, 1815, in Bassett, *Jackson Correspondence*, II: 328–329.

80. Chief Tustunnuggato to the Creek Council, September 18, 1815, Office of Indian Affairs, Record Group 75, Treaty File: Fort Jackson, microfilm, National Archives, Washington, DC.

81. Andrew Jackson to Secretary Dallas, June 20, 1815, in Bassett, *Jackson Correspondence*, II: 210–211.

82. William Crawford to Benjamin Hawkins, October 16, 1815, *Letters Sent by the Secretary of War Regarding Indian Affairs*, National Archives, Record Group 75, microfilm, National Archives, Washington, DC.

83. Heidler and Heidler, *Old Hickory's War*, 59.

84. Benjamin Hawkins to Andrew Jackson, July 17, 1815, in Grant, *Letters, Journals and Writings of Benjamin Hawkins*, II: 736; Andrew Jackson to Alexander Dallas, June 20, 1815, in Bassett, *Jackson Correspondence*, II: 210; Creek Annuity Statement, February 22, 1816, *ASPIA*, II: 29; Heidler and Heidler, *Old Hickory's War*, 59.

85. John Coffee to Andrew Jackson, February 8, 1816, in Bassett, *Jackson Correspondence*, II: 328–329.

86. I am not persuaded by Rogin's argument that Jackson and Coffee needed for psychological reasons to use those affidavits to convince themselves of their moral and legal right to that territory. Aggressors generally employ righteous rhetoric for public relations reasons, and there were those in Congress and elsewhere who needed to be persuaded. Recall the delay in the ratification of the Treaty of Fort Jackson. See Rogin, *Fathers and Children*, 171.

87. Rogin, *Fathers and Children*, 170–171; Remini, *Andrew Jackson and the Course of American Empire*, 322–323.

88. Andrew Jackson to George Colbert, February 16, 1816, in Moser et al., *Jackson Papers*, IV: 13.

89. William H. Crawford to Andrew Jackson, March 8, 1816, in Bassett, *Jackson Correspondence*, II: 235; Rogin, *Fathers and Children*, 171.

90. Andrew Jackson to James Monroe, May 12, 1816, in Moser et al., *Jackson Papers*, IV: 28–30; Protest of the Tennesseans, *ASPIA*, II: 89. William J. Crawford to Andrew Jackson, May 20, 1816, in Moser et al., *Jackson Papers*, IV: 32–33; Andrew Jackson to William H. Crawford, June 10, 13, 16, July 1, 24, 1816, in Bassett, *Jackson Correspondence*, II: 243–254, 255–256.

91. Andrew Jackson to William H. Crawford, July 24, 1816, in Bassett, *Jackson Correspondence*, II: 243–254, 255–256. As to the Cherokee damage claims, even a cursory analysis of Meigs's reply to Jackson, August 7, 1816, in Moser et al., *Jackson Papers*, IV: 55–58 indicates that, Jackson's bluster notwithstanding, they were clearly justified.

92. William G. McLoughlin, *Cherokee Renascence in the New Republic* (Princeton, NJ: Princeton University Press, 1986), 195.

93. Joseph McMinn to the Cherokees, December 18, 1818, in *ASPIA*, II: 485–486.

94. William Harris Crawford to Andrew Jackson, May 20, 1811, in Moser et al., *Jackson Papers*, IV: 32.

95. William J. Crawford to Andrew Jackson, July 1, 1816, in Moser et al., *Jackson Papers*, IV: 49.

96. William J. Crawford to Andrew Jackson, July 21, 1816, in Bassett, *Jackson Correspondence*, II: 254.

97. William H. Crawford to Andrew Jackson, July 5, 19, 1816, in *ASPIA*, II: 100–102, 112.

98. Return J. Meigs to William H. Crawford, August 19, 1816, in *ASPIA*, II: 113–114.

99. Andrew Jackson to John Coffee, July 19, 1816, in Bassett, *Jackson Correspondence*, II: 253.

100. Andrew Jackson to William H. Crawford, July 19, 1816, in *ASPIA*, II: 103; Andrew Jackson to John Coffee, September 19, 1816, in Bassett, *Jackson Correspondence*, II: 260.

101. McLoughlin, *Cherokee Renascence in the New Republic*, 154.

102. Arthur H. DeRosier, *The Removal of the Choctaw Indians* (Knoxville: University of Tennessee Press, 1970), 37.

103. Charles J. Kappler, ed., *Indian Affairs: Laws and Treaties* (Washington, DC: Government Printing Office, 1904), II: 137.

104. Journal of the Convention held in September 1816, Jackson Papers, Library of Congress; Remini, *Andrew Jackson and His Indian Wars*, 108–109.

105. Journal of the Convention held in September 1816, Jackson Papers, Library of Congress; Remini, *Andrew Jackson and His Indian Wars*, 110–111.

106. Andrew Jackson to William H. Crawford, July 20, 1816, *ASPIA*, II: 103; Andrew Jackson, D. Meriwether, and J. Franklin to William H. Crawford in Moser et al., *Jackson Papers*, IV: 65–67; September 20, 1816, in *ASPIA*, II: 104–105; Remini, *Andrew Jackson and His Indian Wars*, 111–112.

107. Journal of the Convention with the Cherokees, September, October 1816, *Jackson Papers*, Library of Congress; Instructions to a Deputation of Cherokee Warriors, September 17, 1817, *ASPIA*, II: 45; Remini, *Andrew Jackson and His Indian Wars*, 114.

108. Remini, *Andrew Jackson and His Indian Wars*, 124–125.

109. McLoughlin, *Cherokee Renascence*, 212–213, 230.

110. Andrew Jackson to John Coffee, July 13, 1817, in Bassett, ed., *Jackson Correspondence*, II: 307; McLoughlin, *Cherokee Renascence*, 230–231, 255–259.

111. Brian Hicks, *Toward the Setting Sun: John Ross, the Cherokees, and the Trail of Tears* (New York: Atlantic Monthly Press, 2011), 97.

112. John Ross et al. to James Monroe, March 5, 1819, in Moulton, ed., *The Papers of Chief John Ross* (Norman: University of Oklahoma Press, 1985), I: 34–35.

113. Gary E. Moulton, *John Ross, Cherokee Chief* (Athens: University of Georgia Press, 1978), 13–22, 97–103.

114. John C. Calhoun to the Cherokee Delegates, *ASPIA*, II: 190.

115. Andrew Jackson to John Coffee, August 12, 1817, in Moser et al., eds., *Jackson Papers*, IV: 132–133; Remini, *Andrew Jackson and His Indian Wars*, 130.

116. Howe, *What Hath God Wrought*, 126.
117. McLoughlin, *Cherokee Renascence*, 207.
118. Howe, *What Hath God Wrought*, 126; David S. Dupre, *Transforming the Cotton Frontier* (Baton Rouge: Louisiana State University Press, 1997), 86–87.
119. Eric Hobsbawm, *The British Industrial Revolution* (London: Routledge, 2000).
120. Baptist, *The Half Has Not Been Told*, xxi.
121. John Coffee to Andrew Jackson, December 27, 1815, Jackson Papers, Library of Congress; Andrew Jackson to John Coffee, February 2, 1816, Moser et al., eds., *Jackson Papers*, IV: 7.
122. Steve Inskeep, *Jacksonland* (New York: Penguin, 2015), 78–79.
123. Arthur Peronneau Hayne to Andrew Jackson, August 3, 1817, in Moser et al., eds., *Jackson Papers*, IV: 130–131.
124. Inskeep, *Jacksonland*, ß101.
125. Rogin, *Fathers and Children*, 13.
126. Andrew Jackson to James Monroe, March 4, 1817, in Moser et al., eds., *Jackson Papers*, IV: 93–97.
127. Theda Purdue and Michael D. Green, *The Cherokee Nation and the Trail of Tears* (New York: Penguin, 2007), 51–57.

CHAPTER 4

1. James Monroe to the House of Representatives of the United States, March 25, 1818, *ASPMA*, I: 680–681.
2. For a careful analysis of the legal ramifications and international consequences of Jackson's 1818 invasion of Florida, see Deborah A. Rosen, *Border Law: The First Seminole War and American Nationhood* (Cambridge, MA: Harvard University Press, 2015).
3. Edmund Gaines to Andrew Jackson, May 14, 1816, in Moser et al., *Jackson Papers*, IV: 31.
4. Benjamin Hawkins to William H. Crawford, February 10, 1816, quoted in Saunt, *A New Order of Things*, 285.
5. William H. Crawford to Andrew Jackson, March 16, 1816; Andrew Jackson to Mauricio de Zunega, April 26, 1813, in Moser et al., *Jackson Papers*, IV: 15–16, 22–23.
6. Mauricio de Zunega to Andrew Jackson, May 26, 1813, in Moser et al., *Jackson Papers*, IV: 22–23.
7. William H. Crawford to Andrew Jackson, March 16, 1816, in Moser et al., *Jackson Papers*, IV: 15.
8. Andrew Jackson to William H. Crawford, September 7, 1816, in Moser et al., *Jackson Papers*, III: 60–62; Heidler and Heidler, *Old Hickory's War*, 70–75; John Missall and Mary Lou Missall, *The Seminole Wars* (Gainesville: University Presses of Florida, 2004), 28–31; John Mahon, *The History of the Second Seminole War, 1835–1842* (Gainesville: University Presses of Florida, 1985), 19–24; Saunt, *A New Order of Things*, 285–289; T.D. Altman, *Finding Florida: The True History of the Sunshine State* (New York: Atlantic Monthly Press, 2013), 82–98.
9. "Negro Fort," *Niles Weekly Register*, November 20, 1819.
10. Altman, *Finding Florida*, 84.
11. Joshua R. Giddings, *The Exiles of Florida* (Columbus, OH: Follett, Foster and Company, 1858), 28–45; Altman, *Finding Florida*, 86–87.

12. Brigadier General Edmund P. Gaines to Andrew Jackson, August 31, 1817, in Bassett, *Jackson Correspondence*, II: 323–324; Gaines to Jackson, November 21, 1817, in Moser et al., *Jackson Papers*, IV: 150–151; Remini, *Andrew Jackson and His Indian Wars*, 133.

13. Edmund P. Gaines to Andrew Jackson, October 1, 1817, in Moser et al., *Jackson Papers*, IV: 141; Gaines to Jackson, November 21, 1817, in Moser et al., *Jackson Papers*, IV: 150–151.

14. Edmund Pendleton Gaines to the Secretary of War, December 9, 1817, *ASPMA*, I: 887–688; Gaines to Jackson, December 2, 1817, in Moser et al., *Jackson Papers*, IV: 153–154.

15. See Attorney General William Wirt's report "Slaves Imported by Indian Agent Contrary to the Law," January 21, 1821, in *American State Papers: Miscellaneous*.

16. Edmund P. Gaines to Andrew Jackson, April 2, 1817, in Moser et al., *Jackson Papers*, IV: 107. For a description of the attack on the Garret family, see Archibald Clark to General Gaines, February 26, 1817, *ASPIA*, II: 155.

17. Edmund P. Gaines to Andrew Jackson, October 1, 1817, in Moser et al., *Jackson Papers*, IV: 141.

18. David B. Mitchell to the Secretary of War, March 30, 1817, *ASPMA*, I: 683.

19. Quoted in Missall and Missall, *The Seminole Wars*, 38.

20. Archibald Clarke to General Gaines, February 26, 1817, *ASPMA*, I: 682.

21. Heidler and Heidler, *Old Hickory's War*, 59.

22. Seminole Chiefs to the commanding officer at Fort Hawkins, September 11, 1817, *ASPMA*, I: 686.

23. General Gaines to the secretary of war, November 9, 1817, *ASPMA*, I: 688.

24. Governor of Georgia to General Gaines, February 6, 1817, *ASPMA*, I: 681.

25. George Perryman to Lt. Sands, February 14, 1817, *ASPIA*, II: 155.

26. General Gaines to Secretary of War, April 3, 1817, *ASPIA*, II: 157.

27. Statement of King Hatchy, n.d., *ASPMA*, I: 723.

28. General Gaines to George Graham, November 9, 1817, *ASPMA*, I: 686; 688.

29. General Gaines to Andrew Jackson, November 21, 1817, in Moser et al., *Jackson Papers*, IV: 130–131.

30. George Graham to Edmund P. Gaines, December 2, 1817, *ASPMA*, I: 687.

31. John C. Calhoun to Edmund P. Gaines, December 16, 1817, *ASPMA*, I: 689.

32. John C. Calhoun to Andrew Jackson, December 26, 1817, *ASPMA*, I: 690.

33. Andrew Jackson to James Monroe, January 6, 1818, in Moser et al., *Jackson Papers*, IV: 166–167.

34. An extreme example of the claim that Jackson was lying is Richard R. Stenberg, "The Rhea Letter Hoax," *Journal of Southern History* 2 (November 1936), 480–482. See also Heidler and Heidler, *Old Hickory's War*, 120. The "silence as consent" explanation is favored by Remini. See *Andrew Jackson and His Indian Wars*, 138–140.

35. Daniel Feller, "The Seminole Controversy Revisited: A New Look at Andrew Jackson's 1818 Florida Campaign," *The Florida Historical Quarterly* 88 (Winter 2010), 309–325. A letter from Jackson to his wife, dated February 19, 1818, which came to light in 2008, contained the postscript "preserve with care the letter of Mr John Rhea which I enclose A.J."

36. Quoted in Remini, *Andrew Jackson and His Indian Wars*, 138.

37. For an overview of McIntosh's career, see Benjamin W. Griffith Jr., *McIntosh and Weatherford: Creek Indian Leaders* (Tuscaloosa: University of Alabama Press, 1988). For a broader perspective see Andrew K. Frank, *Creeks and Southerners: Biculturalism on the Early American Frontier* (Lincoln: University of Nebraska Press, 2005).

38. Andrew Jackson to Francisco Caso y Luengo, April 6, 1818, in Moser et al., *Jackson Papers*, IV: 186.

39. Heidler and Heidler, *Old Hickory's War*, 142–143.

40. Andrew Jackson to John C. Calhoun, April 8, 1818, in Moser et al., *Jackson Papers*, IV: 190.

41. Andrew Jackson to Francisco Caso y Luengo, (March) 6, April 1818, in Moser et al., *Jackson Papers*, IV: 186–187.

42. Francisco Caso y Luengo to Andrew Jackson, April 7, 1818, in Moser et al., *Jackson Papers*, IV: 188–189.

43. Andrew Jackson to John C. Calhoun, April 8, 1818, in Moser et al., *Papers of Andrew Jackson*, IV: 190; quotation from Heidler and Heidler, *Old Hickory's War*, 144.

44. Edmund Pendleton Gaines to Andrew Jackson, April 2, 1817, in Moser et al., *Jackson Papers*, IV: 107.

45. Andrew Jackson to John C. Calhoun, April 8, 1818, in Moser et al., *Jackson Papers*, IV: 190.

46. Alexander Arbuthnot to Edward Nicolls, "Minutes of the Proceedings of a Special Court, Fort St. Marks," *ASPMA*, I: 725.

47. Alexander Arbuthnot to Charles Bagot, January 1818, in "Minutes of the Proceedings of a Special Court, Fort St. Marks," *ASPMA*, I: 721.

48. Alexander Arbuthnot to General Mitchell, January 18, 1818, in *ASPFR*, IV: 591.

49. Andrew Jackson to John C. Calhoun, May 5, 1818, in Moser et al., *Jackson Papers*, IV: 197–199.

50. Remini, *Andrew Jackson and the Course of American Empire*, 352.

51. "Minutes of the Proceedings of a Special Court, Fort St. Marks," *ASPMA*, I: 721; Winslett, http://joancase.tripod.com/winslett.htm August 2, 2012.

52. The most useful account of the Arbuthnot and Ambrister cases is in Heidler and Heidler, *Old Hickory's War*, 146–156.

53. "Minutes of the Proceedings of a Special Court, Fort St. Marks," *ASPMA*, I: 722.

54. Ibid.: 722–723.

55. Alexander Arbuthnot to Charles Cameron, n.d., in "Minutes of the Proceedings of a Special Court," *ASPMA*, I: 722–723.

56. Heidler and Heidler, *Old Hickory's War*, 134–135.

57. "Minutes of the Proceedings of a Special Court," *ASPMA*, I: 727–730.

58. Ibid.: 730–731.

59. Andrew Jackson to John Caldwell Calhoun, May 24, 1818, in Moser et al., *Jackson Papers*, IV: 199.

60. Missall and Missall, *The Seminole Wars*, 34.

61. Remini, *Andrew Jackson and the Course of American Empire*, 352.

62. "Minutes of the Proceedings of a Special Court," *ASPMA*, I: 728–735.

63. Daniel Walker Howe, *What Hath God Wrought* (New York: Oxford, 2007), 102.

64. Andrew Jackson to Rachel Jackson, April 10, 1816, in Moser et al., *Jackson Papers*, IV: 191; Cave, *Prophets of the Great Spirit*, 178–179; Heidler and Heidler, *Old Hickory's War*, 145–146.

65. Andrew Jackson to John C. Calhoun, April 20, 1818, *ASPMA*, I: 700; Andrew Jackson to John C. Calhoun, April 26, 1818, in Bassett, *Jackson Correspondence*, II: 363–364; Heidler and Heidler, *Old Hickory's War*, 148; Wright, *Creeks and Seminoles*, 207–208; Remini, *Andrew Jackson and His Indian Wars*, 150–152.

66. Andrew Jackson to Rachel Jackson, in Bassett, *Jackson Correspondence*, II: 360.

67. Andrew Jackson to John C. Calhoun, April 20, 1818, in Bassett, *Jackson Correspondence*, II: 360–364.

68. Andrew Jackson to Rachel Jackson, March 26, 1818, in Moser et al., *Jackson Papers*, IV: 183–185.

69. William Bibb to John C. Calhoun, March 27, 1818, in *ASPMA*, I: 699; Heidler and Heidler, *Old Hickory's War*, 157.

70. For a thorough summary of this affair, see Heidler and Heidler, *Old Hickory's War*, 159–169.

71. Thomas Glascock to Andrew Jackson, April 30, 1818, in *ASPMA*, I: 702; Andrew Jackson to William Rabun, May 7, 1818, in Moser et al., *Jackson Papers*, IV: 202; Andrew Jackson to the Chehaws, May 7, 1818, *ASPMA*, I: 776–777; Remini, *Andrew Jackson and His Indian War*, 158–159; Heidler and Heidler, *Old Hickory's War*, 159–169; O'Brien, *In Bitterness and Tears*, 217–218.

72. Andrew Jackson to John C. Calhoun, May 9, 1818, in Moser et al., *Jackson Papers*, IV: 200.

73. Andrew Jackson to John C. Calhoun, May 9, 1818, in Moser et al., *Jackson Papers*, IV: 200. Jose Masot to Andrew Jackson, April 26, 1818, in Bassett, *Jackson Correspondence*, II: 354.

74. Andrew Jackson to John C. Calhoun, May 9, 1818, in Moser et al., *Jackson Papers* IV: 199–200. The correspondence with Masot to which Jackson alludes in his dispatch to Crawford may be found in Bassett, *Jackson Correspondence*, II: 355–356, 359–360.

75. Andrew Jackson to Jose Masot, April 27, 1818, *ASPMA*, I: 706–707.

76. Jose Masot to Andrew Jackson, May 18, 1818, in Moser et al., *Jackson Papers*, IV: 204.

77. Andrew Jackson to Jose Masot, May 23, 1818, in *ASPIA*, I: 712–713.

78. Andrew Jackson to Jose Masot, May 23, 1818, in Moser et al., *Jackson Papers*, IV: 206–209; Remini, *Andrew Jackson and His Indian Wars*, 161.

79. Andrew Jackson to James Monroe, June 2, 1818, Moser et al., *Jackson Papers*, IV: 215.

80. Andrew Jackson to Edmund P. Gaines, August 7, 1818, *ASPMA*, I: 744; John C. Calhoun to Edmund P. Gaines, September 1, 1818, *ASPMA*, I: 745; Heidler and Heidler, *Old Hickory's War*, 194–196.

81. Andrew Jackson to John C. Calhoun, November 28, 1818, in Moser et al., *Jackson Papers*, IV: 252.

82. Heidler and Heidler, *Old Hickory's War*, 196–197.

83. John C. Calhoun to James Monroe, September 21, 1818, in W. Edwin Hemphill, ed., *The Papers of John C. Calhoun* (Columbia: University of South Carolina Press, 1959), III: 148–149; Heidler and Heidler, *Old Hickory's War*, 197.

84. See the affidavits and depositions, September 13–17, 1818, in *ASPMA*, I: 716–717, 662–766; Andrew Jackson to George Campbell, October 5, 1818, in Bassett, *Jackson Correspondence*, I: 397; Heidler and Heidler, *Old Hickory's War*, 203.

85. Allan Nevins, ed., *The Diary of John Quincy Adams* (New York: Scribner's, 1951), 200–201 (entry of July 21, 1818); Heidler and Heidler, *Old Hickory's War*, 184–185.

86. Heidler and Heidler, *Old Hickory's War*, 194; James Gadsden, "'The Defense of the Florida,' A Report of Captain James Gadsden, Aide-de-Camp to General Jackson," *Florida Historical Quarterly* 15 (1937): 242–248.

87. Affidavit of John Donelson Jr., January 14, 1820, in Bassett, *Jackson Correspondence*, III: 6–7.

88. John Quincy Adams to Luis de Onís, July 18, 1818, *ASPFA*, IV: 497–499.

89. Fred N. Israel, *The State of the Union Messages of the Presidents, 1789–1966* (New York: Chelsea House, 1966), I: 157.

90. Report of the Committee on Military Affairs on the Seminole War, January 12, 1819, *ASPMA*, I: 735.

91. Minority Report of the Committee on Military Affairs on the Seminole War, January 12, 1819, *ASPMA*, 173–739. For the legal implications of Jackson's handling of those cases, see Deborah A. Rosen, "Wartime Prisoners and the Rule of Law: Andrew Jackson's Military Tribunals during the First Seminole War," *Journal of the Early Republic* 28 (Winter 2008): 559–595. Rosen argues Jackson anticipated the modern treatment of suspected terrorists.

92. *Annals of Congress* 15th Congress, 2nd Session, 584–588.

93. Ibid., 599–613.

94. Heidler and Heidler, *Old Hickory's War*, 218.

95. "Speech on the Seminole War," January 20, 1819, in James Hopkins, ed., *The Papers of Henry Clay* (Lexington: University of Kentucky Press, 1961), II: 636–662.

96. Robert Remini, *Henry Clay, Statesman for the Union* (New York: W. W. Norton, 1991), 165–166.

97. *Annals of Congress* 15th Congress, 2nd Session, 1136–1138.

98. Report of the Select Senate Committee, February 24, 1819, *ASPMA*, I: 739–760.

99. Rosen, *Border Law*, 209.

100. Andrew Jackson to William Berkley Lewis, January 30, 1819, in Moser et al., *Jackson Papers*, IV: 169.

101. Andrew Jackson to Isaac Shelby, August 11, 1818, in Moser et al., *Jackson Papers*, IV: 235.

102. Cave, *Prophets of the Great Spirit*, 141–142.

103. John C. Calhoun to Isaac Shelby and Andrew Jackson, May 2, 1818, *ASPIA*, II: 173–154.

104. Quoted in Remini, *Andrew Jackson's Indian Wars*, 169.

105. Andrew Jackson to James Colbert, July 24, 1818, in Moser et al., *Jackson Papers*, IV: 228–229.

106. Andrew Jackson, *Confidential Journal, Chickasaw Treaty*, September 29-October 20, *Jackson Papers*, Library of Congress; Remini, *Andrew Jackson and His Indian Wars*, 175.

107. Remini, *Andrew Jackson and His Indian Wars*, 176.

108. Andrew Jackson to Joseph McMinn, August 25, 1819, Bassett, *Jackson Correspondence*, II: 426. For a detailed explanation of Jackson's financial legerdemain with the Colbert reservation, see Remini, *Andrew Jackson and His Indian Wars*, 178.

109. Remini, *Andrew Jackson and His Indian Wars*, 185–186. Jackson's defense against John Williams's charges is to be found in Andrew Jackson to John Williams, September 25, 1819, Moser et al., *Jackson Papers*, IV: 325–328. The state legislature investigated and exonerated Jackson. Their report has been lost.

110. Remini, *Andrew Jackson and His Indian Wars*, 176–178.

111. Andrew Jackson, *Confidential Journal, Chickasaw Treaty*, Jackson Papers, Library of Congress.

112. Andrew Jackson to Isaac Shelby, November 24, 1818, in Moser et al., *Jackson Papers*, IV: 250.

113. On the origins and precontact history of the peoples who would later form the Choctaw Confederation, see Patricia Galloway, *Choctaw Genesis* (Lincoln: University of Nebraska Press, 1985).

114. Arthur DeRosier Jr., *The Removal of the Choctaw Indians* (Knoxville: University of Tennessee Press, 1970), viii, 14–37.

115. Mississippi *Star Gazette,* January 8, 1820, quoted in DeRosier Jr., *Removal of the Choctaw Indians,* 54.

116. DeRosier Jr., *Removal of the Choctaw Indians,* 22.

117. James Taylor Carson, *Searching for the Bright Path: The Mississippi Choctaws from Prehistory to Removal* (Lincoln: University of Nebraska Press, 1999), 95.

118. DeRosier Jr., *Removal of the Choctaw Indians,* 54.

119. John McKee to John C. Calhoun, October 27, 1818, letters received by the secretary of war, National Archives MSS; John C. Calhoun to John McKee, Indian Affairs, War Department: Letters Sent; DeRosier Jr., *Removal of the Choctaw Indians,* 47–48; Remini, *Andrew Jackson and His Indian Wars,* 181.

120. Andrew Jackson to John C. Calhoun, December 30, 1818; James Pitchlynn to Andrew Jackson, December 1818, in Bassett, *Jackson Correspondence,* II: 404–407; Remini, *Andrew Jackson and His Indian Wars,* 181–182.

121. John C. Calhoun to Andrew Jackson, March 29, 1819, Bassett, *Jackson Correspondence,* II: 414.

122. Andrew Jackson to John C. Calhoun, June 19, 1820, *ASPIA,* II: 230–231.

123. Andrew Jackson to John McKee, April 22, 1819, in Moser et al., *Jackson Papers,* IV: 288–289.

124. Margaret Zimmer Searcy, "Choctaw Subsistence, 1540–1830," in Carolyn Keller Reeves, ed., *The Choctaw before Removal* (Jackson: University Press of Mississippi, 1985), 32–52. On the economic and political history of the Choctaw in the 18th and early 19th centuries, the following are particularly valuable: Richard White, *The Roots of Dependency: Subsistence, Environment and Social Change among the Choctaw, Pawnees and Navahos* (Lincoln: University of Nebraska Press, 1983); Daniel H. Usner, *Indians, Settlers, & Slaves in an Exchange Economy: The Lower Mississippi Valley before 1783* (Chapel Hill: University of North Carolina Press, 1992); James Taylor Carson, *Searching for the Bright Path: The Mississippi Choctaws from Prehistory to Removal* (Lincoln: University of Nebraska Press, 1999); Greg O'Brien, *Choctaws in a Revolutionary Age* (Lincoln: University of Nebraska Press, 2002).

125. Carson, *Searching for the Bright Path,* 71. Carson uses the term "marketplace society" to contrast it from a fully developed market economy.

126. James Taylor Carson, "Native Americans the Market Revolution, and Culture Change: The Choctaw Cattle Economy, 1690–1830," in Greg O'Brien, *Pre-Removal Choctaw History: Exploring New Paths* (Norman: University of Oklahoma Press, 2008), 183. Women, who traditionally did not work with animals, apparently resolved a conflict with Choctaw conceptions of gender roles by defining domesticated livestock as plants. See Carson, *Searching for the Bright Path,* 76–78.

127. DeRosier, *Removal of the Choctaws,* 50.

128. Mushulatubbee and Pooshhamatawa to Monroe, August 12, 1819, *American State Papers, Indian Affairs,* II: 239. I have modernized the spelling of the chiefs' names in the text above.

129. Andrew Jackson to John C. Calhoun, August 24, 1819, Jackson MSS, Library of Congress.

130. DeRosier, *The Removal of the Choctaw Indians,* 51–52.

131. Andrew Jackson to John C. Calhoun, November 13, 1820, in Bassett, *Jackson Correspondence,* III: 33.

132. Andrew Jackson to John C. Calhoun, June 19, 1820, *ASPIA,* 230–231.

133. John C. Calhoun to Andrews Jackson, July 15, 1820, *ASPIA,* 2: 231.

134. Report from the Choctaw Treaty Grounds, October 8, 1820, *ASPIA*, II: 234.
135. Report from the Choctaw Treaty Grounds, October 10, 1820, *ASPIA*, II: 235–237.
136. Jackson and Hinds to the Choctaw, October 13, 1820, *ASPIA*, II: 238.
137. John McKee to Andrew Jackson, July 31, 1819, *ASPIA*, II: 230.
138. Andrew Jackson to Choctaw Indians, October 17, 1820, Moser et al., *Jackson Papers*, IV: 393–396.
139. John Rodgers Jr. to Andrew Jackson, June 7, 1820, Moser et al., *Jackson Papers*, IV: 371.
140. Carson, *Searching for the Right Path*, 86–98. Quotation on 88.
141. Ibid., 98.
142. Andrew Jackson to John C. Calhoun, June 15, July 26, November 30, 1820, in Bassett, *Jackson Correspondence*, III: 26, 30, 33–34.

CHAPTER 5

1. Allan Nevins, ed., *The Diary of John Quincy Adams, 1794–1845* (New York: Charles Scribner's Sons, 1951), 209.
2. Deborah A. Rosen, *Border Law: The First Seminole War and American Nationhood* (Cambridge, MA: Harvard University Press, 2005).
3. Andrew Jackson to James Monroe, January 15, 1820, in Bassett, *Jackson Correspondence*, III: 7.
4. Andrew Jackson to John C. Calhoun, January 10, 21, 1820, in Bassett, *Jackson Correspondence*, III: 2–6, 9–11.
5. John C. Calhoun to Andrew Jackson, February 5, 1820, in Bassett, *Jackson Correspondence*, III: 11n.
6. James Monroe to Andrew Jackson, January 24, 1821, in Moser et al., *Jackson Papers*, V: 9.
7. Andrew Jackson to Dr. James C. Bronaugh, February 11, 1821, in Bassett, *Jackson Correspondence*, III: 39.
8. Andrew Jackson to James Monroe, February 11, 1821, in Moser et al., *Jackson Papers*, V: 10.
9. Rachel Jackson to Elizabeth Kingsley, July 23, 1821, in Moser et al., *Jackson Papers*, V: 80.
10. Remini, *Andrew Jackson and the Course of American Empire*, 407.
11. Quoted in Remini, *Andrew Jackson and the Course of American Empire*, 414. Jackson's quarrels with former governor Callava and Judge Fromentin are discussed at great length in his correspondence with the principals and with his superiors in Washington, DC. He provides a particularly detailed account in two letters to Secretary of State Adams, dated August 26 and November 13, 1821, available in Bassett, *Jackson Correspondence*, III: 112–116, 126–132.
12. Herbert J. Doherty Jr., "The Governorship of Andrew Jackson," *Florida Historical Quarterly* 33(1954): 3–31.
13. Charles Vignoles, *Observations upon the Floridas* (New York: E. Bliss & E. White, 1823), 134–135.
14. William H. Simmons, *Notices of East Florida: With an Account of the Seminole Nation of Indians* [1822] (Gainesville: University of Florida Press, 1973), 89.
15. John K. Mahon, "The Treaty of Moultrie Creek, 1823," *Florida Historical Quarterly* 40 (1962): 355.
16. Andrew Jackson to John C. Calhoun, September 2, 17, 1821, in *ASPIA* II: 412, 414.

17. John C. Calhoun to Andrew Jackson, May 14, 1821, Jackson Papers, Library of Congress; Andrew Jackson to John C. Calhoun, September 20, 1821, Clarence E. Carter and John Porter Bloom, *Territorial Papers of the United States*, II: 210–213.

18. Jackson's Talk with Indian Chieftains, September 20, 1821, in Bassett, ed., *Jackson Correspondence*, III: 118–121.

19. Rembert W. Patrick, *Aristocrat in Uniform: General Duncan L. Clinch* (Gainesville: University of Florida Press, 1963), 68. For a very meticulous examination of the somewhat unclear evidence relating to this matter, see John K. Mahon, "The Treaty of Moultrie Creek, 1823," *The Florida Historical Quarterly* 40 (1962): 350–372.

20. James Gadsden to Andrew Jackson, July 30, 1823, in Moser et al., *Jackson Papers*, V: 285.

21. Report of the Committee on Indian Affairs, February 21, 1823, in *ASPIA*, II: 408–419.

22. Quoted in Thom Hatch, *Osceola and the Great Seminole War* (New York: St. Martins, 2012), 62.

23. Mahon, "Treaty of Moultrie Creek, 1823," 350–372; Hatch, *Osceola*, 60–61; Missal and Missal, *Seminole Wars*, 55.

24. Memorial to Congress from the Legislative Council, February 1832, *Territorial Papers*, Florida, XXIV: 667; "An Act to Prevent Indians from Wandering at Large." January 15, 1827, *Territorial Papers*, Florida, XXIII: 896.

25. Andrew Jackson to James Gadsden, December 6, 1821, in Bassett, ed., *Jackson Correspondence*, III: 141.

26. Remini, *Andrew Jackson and the Course of American Freedom*, 14–15.

27. Andrew Jackson to Richard Keith Call, June 29, 1822, in Moser et al., *Jackson Papers*, V: 199; Remini, *Andrew Jackson and the Course of American Freedom*, 36–38.

28. Charles G. Sellars, "Jackson Men with Feet of Clay," *American Historical Review* 42 (1955): 537–551.

29. Andrew Jackson to Rachel Jackson, December 7, 1823, in Bassett, *Jackson Correspondence*, III: 216.

30. Andrew Jackson to George Martin, in Bassett, *Jackson Correspondence*, III: 222.

31. Remini, *Andrew Jackson and the Course of American Freedom*, 60–62.

32. Jon Meacham, *American Lion: Andrew Jackson in the White House* (New York: Random House, 2008), 38.

33. Grace Webster quoted in Irvin H. Bartlett, *Daniel Webster* (New York: W.W. Norton, 1978), 89.

34. His votes are enumerated and described in Moser et al., *Jackson Papers*, V: 463–467. For an analysis of his overall Senate service, see Remini, *Andrew Jackson and the Course of American Freedom* (New York: Harper and Row, 1981), 55–73.

35. *A Dialogue between a Colonel of the Militia and a Militiaman in Relation to the Rights of Six Militiamen Shot by Order of General Jackson* (n.p., 1824).

36. *A Review of Gen. Jackson's Letters to Mr. Monroe* [n.p., n.d.].

37. John Henry Eaton, *The Letters of Wyoming, to the People of the United States, on the Presidential Election and in Support of Andrew Jackson* (Philadelphia: S. Simpson and J. Conrad, 1824).

38. On political corruption during the Monroe administration, see Remini, *Andrew Jackson and the Course of American Freedom*, Chapter 2. The Adams administration, however, was relatively free of scandal, despite Jacksonian assertion to the contrary.

39. Andrew Jackson to Rachel Jackson, February 6, 1824, in Moser et al., *Jackson Papers*, V: 352.

40. Andrew Jackson to Andrew Jackson Donaldson, January 21, 1824, in Moser et al., *Jackson Papers*, V: 225.
41. Andrew Jackson to John Coffee, January 6, 1825, in Moser et al., *Jackson Papers*, VI: 8.
42. Andrew Jackson to William B. Lewis, January 21, 1825, in Moser et al., *Jackson Papers*, VI: 17.
43. Robert Remini devotes a chapter in his monumental biography of Jackson to "the theft of the Presidency." See *Andrew Jackson and the Course of American Freedom, 1822–1823*, 74–99.
44. Donald Ratcliffe, *The One Party Presidential Contest: Adams, Jackson, and 1824's Five-Horse Race* (Lawrence: The University Press of Kansas, 2015), 201–277; Appendix 1.
45. Andrew Jackson to William B. Lewis, February 14, 1825, in Bassett, *Jackson Correspondence*, III: 276.
46. On the role of the "Corrupt Bargain" as "a launching point" for the new political party Jackson would organize and lead, see Kristopher Ray, "The Corrupt Bargain and the Rise of the Jacksonian Movement, 1825–1828," in Brian D. McKnight and James S. Humphrey, eds., *The Age of Andrew Jackson* (Kent, OH: Kent State University Press, 2011), 22–35.
47. Memorial of the State of Georgia to President Monroe, December 18, 1823, in *ASPIA*, II: 491.
48. Andrew Jackson to Edward G.W. Butler, July 25, 1825, in Bassett, *Jackson Correspondence*, III: 288–289. For a highly detailed and well-documented account of this affair, see William W. Winn, *The Triumph of the Ecunnau-Nuxulgee: Land Speculators, George M. Troup, States Rights, and the Removal of the Creek Indians from Georgia and Alabama, 1825–1838* (Macon, GA: Mercer University Press, 2015), 1–228.
49. "Journal of the Proceedings of the Commissioners Appointed to Deal with the Creek Indians, June 16-December 18, 1824," in *ASPIA*, II: 564–587.
50. *Niles Weekly Register*, December 4, 1824; Michael D. Green, *The Politics of Indian Removal: Creek Government and Society in Crisis* (Lincoln: University of Nebraska Press, 1982), 79–80; Winn, *Triumph of the Ecunnau-Nuxulgee*, 67–69.
51. Benjamin F. Griffith Jr., *McIntosh and Weatherford: Creek Indian Leaders* (Tuscaloosa: University of Alabama Press, 1988), 212–254; Green, *The Politics of Indian Removal*, 82–83; Winn, *Triumph of the Ecunnau-Nuxulgee*, 75–88.
52. Green, *The Politics of Indian Removal*, 81–84; Winn, *Triumph of the Ecunnau-Nuxulgee*, 95–99; Christopher D. Haveman, *Rivers of Sand: Creek Emigration, Relocation & Ethnic Cleansing in the American South* (Lincoln: University of Nebraska Press, 2016), 11–22.
53. "Memorial of the McIntosh Party to the President," January 25, 1825, in *ASPIA*, II: 579–580.
54. Green, *Politics of Indian Removal*, 75–77; Griffith, *McIntosh and Weatherford*, 213–223; William G. McLoughlin, *Cherokee Renascence in the New Republic* (Princeton: Princeton University Press, 1986), 305.
55. Duncan Campbell to John C. Calhoun, February 16, 1825, *ASPIA*, II: 584; Winn, *Triumph of the Ecunnau-Nuxulgee*, 94–132; Green, *The Politics of Indian Removal*, 84–88.
56. John Crowell to John C. Calhoun, February 18, 1825, in *House Executive Documents*, 19th Congress, 2nd Session, Doc. 59, 75–76.
57. Winn, *Triumph of the Ecunnau-Nuxulgee*; Griffith, *McIntosh and Weatherford*, 232–254; Green, *The Politics of Indian Removal*, 69–97.
58. Green, *The Politics of Indian Removal*, 108–112.
59. Green, *The Politics of Indian Removal*, 98–126; James W. Silver, "General Gaines Meets Governor Troup: A State-Federal Clash in 1825," *Georgia Historical Quarterly* 27

(1943), 248–270; Richard Hryniewicki, "The Creek Treaty of Washington, 1826," *The Georgia Historical Quarterly* 48 (1964): 425–441.

60. Adams, John Quincy, *Memoirs of John Quincy Adams*, Vol. VII, edited by Charles Francis Adams (Philadelphia: J.B. Lippincott and Co., 1875): 89–92.

61. Quoted in Langguth, *Driven West*, 53.

62. Andrew Jackson to Edward George Washington Butler, July 25, 1825, in Moser et al., *Jackson Papers*, VI: 94.

63. Andrew Jackson to John Dabney Terrell, July 29, 1826, in Moser et al., *Jackson Papers*, VI: 192. Jackson also advised that the Chickasaw be guaranteed permanent ownership of land in the west and promised that, should they become civilized, they might someday be granted statehood in the union.

64. Thomas Hart Benton, *Thirty Years' View* 2 vols. [1856] (New York: Greenwood Press, 1968), 58–59; Remini, *Andrew Jackson and His Indian Wars*, 223; Hryniewicki, "The Creek Treaty of Washington, 1826," 436.

65. Quoted in Howe, *What Hath God Wrought?*, 414.

66. The most useful analysis of Meigs's career as the Cherokee agent is in McLoughlin, *Cherokee Renascence in the New Republic*, 33–167. The following paragraphs draw heavily on his work.

67. Quoted in John A. Andrew III, *From Revivals to Removal: Jeremiah Edwards, the Cherokee Nation and the Search for the Soul of America* (Athens: The University of Georgia Press, 1992), 117.

68. Governor Troup to secretary of war, August 26, 1826, in *ASPIA*, II: 743. This source in the pages following contains a number of letters from Troup and others stating Georgia's claims to absolute control of the territory within her borders.

69. Quoted in Parsons, "A Perpetual Harrow upon My Feelings," 336–337.

70. Richardson, *Letters and Papers of the Presidents*, II: 373.

71. Andrew Jackson to John Henry Eaton, February 8, 1827, in Moser et al., *Jackson Papers*, VI: 287.

72. Samuel Carter III, *Cherokee Sunset: A Nation Betrayed* (Garden City, NJ: Doubleday, 1976), 83.

73. Quoted in McLoughlin, *Cherokee Renascence in the New Republic*, 425.

74. Quoted in Remini, *Andrew Jackson and the Course of American Freedom*, 172. For the most thorough and perceptive account of the 1828 election, see Lynn Hudson Parsons, *The Birth of Modern Politics: Andrew Jackson, John Quincy Adams and the Election of 1828* (New York: Oxford University Press, 2009).

75. Alan Nevins, ed., *The Diary of John Quincy Adams, 1794–1845* (New York: Charles Scribner's Sons, 1951), 216–217. Entry of June 4, 1819.

76. Quoted in Parsons, *Birth of Modern Politics*, 31.

77. Parsons, *Birth of Modern Politics*, xvii.

78. John William Ward, *Andrew Jackson: Symbol for an Age* (New York: Oxford University Press, 1963), 196.

79. The most extreme allegations of the campaign are best sampled in *Truth's Advocate and the Monthly Anti-Jackson Expositor* published from January 1828 to October in Cincinnati.

80. Henry, *An Examination of the Civil Administration of General Jackson in Florida* (Washington, DC: National Intelligencer, 1828).

81. Quoted in Cheathem, *Andrew Jackson: Southerner*, 109.

82. Quoted in Meacham, *American Lion: Andrew Jackson in the White House*, 5.

83. Quoted in Remini, *Andrew Jackson and the Course of American Freedom*, 154.

CHAPTER SIX

1. John C. Fitzpatrick, ed., *The Autobiography of Martin Van Buren* (Washington, DC: Government Printing Office, 1920), 295.

2. Regan Lutz, "West of Eden: The Historiography of the Trail of Tears," PhD Dissertation (The University of Toledo, 1995); John T. Ellisor, "Seeking the Mainstream: The Historiography of Indian Removal," in McKnight and Humphreys, *The Age of Andrew Jackson*, 64–78. For a pioneering and influential study of Jacksonian Indian policy, see Grant Foreman, *Indian Removal* (Norman: University of Oklahoma Press, 1932).

3. Arthur Schlesinger, Jr., *The Age of Jackson* (Boston: Little & Brown, 1945). The first detailed study of Old Hickory's administration to emphasize the importance of the Indian removal issue was Richard B. Latner, *The Presidency of Andrew Jackson* (Athens: University of Georgia Press, 1979).

4. Van Buren, *Autobiography*, 293.

5. Fred S. Rolater, "The American Indian and the Origin of the Second American Party System," *Wisconsin Magazine of History* 76 (1993): 160–203.

6. Report of General Gaines, 1827, in *ASPMA*, IV: 129–133.

7. James Silver, "A Counter-Proposal to the Indian Removal Policy of Andrew Jackson," *The Journal of Mississippi History* 4 (1942): 207–215. Gaines's correspondence quoted on 212 and 214.

8. Richardson, *Messages and Papers of the Presidents*, II: 72.

9. Ibid.: 280–283.

10. In 1817 in a letter to his close friend John Coffee, Jackson entertained the prospect of exempting from removal a very few Indians who had abandoned their "ancient customs and habits." Andrew Jackson to John Coffee, August 13, 1817, Moser et al., *Papers of Andrew Jackson*, IV: 126–127. Although he would hold out the possibility of state citizenship for Indians in his first message to Congress, it is apparent from his subsequent words and deeds that he no longer seriously considered that as a viable or desirable option, if indeed he ever really had.

11. William H. Crawford to the Senate of the United States, March 13, 1816, *ASPIA*, 2: 26–28. On Crawford's ideas concerning Indian policy, see Chase C. Mooney, *William H. Crawford 1772–1834* (Lexington: University Press of Kentucky: 1974), 85–90.

12. Andrew Jackson to William H. Crawford, [June 13, 1816], Bassett, *Jackson Correspondence*, II: 248.

13. Andrew Jackson to Marin Van Buren, August 12, 1829, in Feller et al., *Jackson Papers*, VII: 366.

14. Andrew Jackson to the Creek Indians, March 23, 1829, in Feller et al., *Jackson Papers*, VII: 112–113.

15. In response to the misconceived belief that his people would starve if they could not hunt, a Cherokee spokesman in a letter to Albert Gallatin in 1826 declared "I take pleasure to state, though cautiously, that there is not to my knowledge a single Cherokee to be found that depends upon the chase for subsistence." John Ridge quoted in Theda Purdue and Michael Green, *The Cherokee Removal: A Brief History with Documents*, 2nd ed. (Boston: Bedford/St. Martin's, 2005), 36.

16. That view was not original with Jackson. It was widely held by, among others, Henry Clay and John Quincy Adams. To place this in broader perspective, see Steven Conn, *History's Shadow Native Americans and Historical Consciousness in the Nineteenth Century* (Chicago: University of Chicago Press, 2004) and James Joseph Buss, *Winning the West*

with Words: Language and Conquest in the Lower Great Lakes (Norman: University of Oklahoma Press, 2001).

17. Andrew, *From Revivals to Removal*, 125.

18. On the history of that legislation, see Francis Paul Prucha, *American Indian Policy in the Formative Years: The Indian Trade and Intercourse Acts 1780–1834* (Cambridge: Harvard University Press, 1962).

19. Andrew Jackson to secretary of war, n.d., *Jackson Papers*, The Library of Congress.

20. The Georgia laws are reprinted in Perdue and Green, *The Cherokee Removal: A Brief History with Documents*, 76–79.

21. Jeremiah Evarts, *Cherokee Removal: The William Penn Essays and Other Writings*, ed., Francis Paul Prucha (Knoxville: University of Tennessee Press, 1981), 171.

22. Lutz, "West of Eden," 44–45.

23. Grant Foreman, *Indian Removal* (Norman: University of Oklahoma Press, 1972 [1932]), 45.

24. Foreman, *Indian Removal*, 246.

25. Secretary of War Eaton to the Cherokee Delegates, April 18, 1829, in Francis Paul Prucha, ed., *Documents of United States Indian Policy* (Lincoln: University of Nebraska Press, 2000), 44–46.

26. Quoted in Prucha, *American Indian Policy in the Formative Years*, 236–237.

27. This error is particularly extensive in textbooks. See Alfred A. Cave, "Abuse of Power: Andrew Jackson and the Indian Removal Act of 1830." *The Historian* 65 (2001): 1330–1331.

28. Andrew Jackson to John Overton, June 8, 1829, in Feller et al., *Jackson Papers*, VII: 270–271.

29. Andrew Jackson to the Creek Indians, March 23, 1829, in Feller et al., *Jackson Papers*, VII: 112–113.

30. Tuskeneath et al. to Andrew Jackson, March 20, 1829, in Feller et al., *Jackson Papers*, VII: 106–107.

31. Remini, *Andrew Jackson and His Indian Wars*, 227; Ronald N. Satz, *American Indian Policy in the Jacksonian Era* (Norman: University of Oklahoma Press, 1975), 12.

32. Richardson, *Messages and Papers of the Presidents*, 2: 248.

33. Andrew Jackson to James Gadsden, October 12, 1827, in Feller et al., *Jackson Papers*, VII: 491–492.

34. For the text of Jackson's first annual message see The American Presidency Project. www.presidency.edu.ucsb/ws/?pid=29471.

35. Mary Hershberger, "Mobilizing Women, Anticipating Abolition: The Struggle against Indian Removal in the 1830's," *Journal of American History* 86 (June 1999): 15–40.

36. On his life and work, see John A. Andrew 111, *From Revivals to Removal: Jeremiah Edwards, the Cherokee Nation and the Search for the Soul of America* (Athens: The University of Georgia Press, 1992).

37. Francis Paul Prucha, "Introduction" to Jeremiah Evarts, *Cherokee Removal: The William Penn Essays and Other Writings* (Knoxville: University of Tennessee Press, 1981), 6.

38. Evarts, *Cherokee Removal: The William Penn Essays and Other Writings*, 73.

39. Ibid., 54–55.

40. Ibid., 209–210.

41. Ibid., 51, 113.

42. Quoted in Evarts, *Cherokee Removal: The William Penn Essays and Other Writings*, 32.

43. *Christian Advocate and Journal*, December 25, 1829, quoted in Andrew, *From Revivals to Removal*, 205.

44. Lewis Cass, "Considerations of the Present State of the Indians and Their Removal to the West of the Mississippi," *North American Review* 30 (January 1830): 63–121. Cass had expressed reservations about Indian capacity in an earlier article. See "Remarks on the Policy and Practice of the United States and Great Britain in Their Treatment of the Indian," *North American Review* 27 (April, 1827): 3–78; on McKenney's views, see his 1829 Annual Report, in David S. and Jeanne Heidler, *Indian Removal: A Norton Case Book* (New York: W.W. Norton, 2007), 123–126. He would later disavow his support for Jackson's program, having been removed from office by Old Hickory.

45. Cass, "Considerations of the Present State of the Indians and Their Removal to the West of the Mississippi," 63–121. On Cass as an amateur ethnographer, see Doug Maitland, "Lewis Cass' Changing Views of Native Americans," MA Thesis (University of Toledo, 2004).

46. Isaac McCoy, *Remarks on the Practicability of Indian Reform, Embracing Their Colonization* (Boston: Lincoln & Edmunds, 1827); a second edition recommending Cherokee removal, appeared in the following year. See also Isaac McCoy, *History of the Baptist Indian Mission* (Washington, DC: William M. Morrison, 1840); George H. Schultz, *An Indian Canaan: Isaac McCoy and His Vision of an Indian State* (Norman: University of Oklahoma Press, 1972); Nicholas Guyatt, *Bind Us Apart: How Enlightenment America Invented Racial Segregation* (New York: Basic Books, 2016), 288–298.

47. See Francis Paul Prucha, "Thomas L. McKenney and the New York Indian Board," *Mississippi Valley Historical Review* 48 (March 1962): 625–655.

48. House Committee on Indian Affairs, HR227 (1830), 11.

49. The text of the act is widely available, for example, in Heidler and Heidler, *Indian Removal: A Norton Case Book*, 143–146.

50. *Speeches on the Passage of the Bill for the Removal of the Indians, Delivered in the Congress of the United States, April and May 1830* (Millwood, NY: Kraus Reprint Co., 1975), 4–6.

51. Cave, "Abuse of Power," 1332–1334.

52. Ibid., 1335.

53. Register of Debates, 21 Congress, 1st Session, May 18, 1830, 1132–1133.

54. Robert Remini, *The Legacy of Andrew Jackson: Essays on Democracy, Indian Removal, and Slavery* (Baton Rouge: Louisiana State University Press, 1988), 66.

55. Van Buren, *Autobiography*, 289.

56. On the sectional breakdown of the vote, see Rolater, "The American Indian and the Origins of the Second American Party System," 193. A statistical analysis of voting behavior concludes that "slaveholders, Democrats and advocates of cheap land were all more likely to support removal. Congressmen from the north and west who favored legalizing squatters' rights were more likely to support removing Indians from the old southwest." Leonard A. Carlson and Mark A. Roberts, "Indian Lands, 'Squatterism,' Economic Interests and the Passage of the Indian Removal Act of 1830," *Explorations in Economic History* 43 (2006): 502.

57. Andrew Jackson to John Pitchlynn, August 5, 1830, in Feller et al., *Jackson Papers*, VIII: 466.

58. "First Annual Message to Congress, Draft by Andrew Jackson," in Feller et al., *Jackson Papers*, VII: 609–610.

59. "Draft by John Henry Eaton on Indian Removal," in Feller et al., *Jackson Papers*, VII: 623–625.

60. Andrew Jackson, Second Annual Address to Congress. The American Presidency Project. www.presidency.ucsb.edu/ws/index.php?pid=29472.

61. Steven Salaita, *Inter/Nationalism: Decolonizing Native America and Palestine* (Minneapolis: University of Minnesota Press, 2016), 81.

62. Andrew Jackson to the Chickasaw Indians, August 23, 1830, in Feller et al., *Jackson Papers*, VIII: 507.

63. Andrew Jackson to William B. Lewis, August 25, 1830, in Feller et al., *Jackson Papers*, VIII: 501.

64. Remini, *Andrew Jackson and His Indian Wars*, 142–143.

65. Andrew Jackson to the Chickasaw Indians, August 23, 1830, in Feller et al., *Jackson Papers*, VIII: 497.

66. Journal of the Proceedings with the Chickasaws and Choctaw, August 23–25, 1830, in *Correspondence on the Subject of the Emigration of the Indians Senate Document 512* (Washington, DC, 1835), II: 246–247; Remini, *Andrew Jackson and His Indian Wars*, 244–245.

67. Journal of the Proceedings with the Chickasaws and Choctaw, August 23–25, 1830, in *Correspondence on the Subject of the Emigration of the Indians*, II: 247.

68. Andrew Jackson to the Chickasaw Indians, August 25, 1830, in Feller et al., *Jackson Papers*, VIII: 507.

69. Arrell Gibson, *The Chickasaws* (Norman: University of Oklahoma Press, 1971), 175.

70. Francis Paul Prucha, *American Indian Treaties: The History of a Political Anomaly* (Berkeley: University of California Press, 1994), 174–175.

71. Andrew Jackson to John Coffee, March 16, 1833, in Bassett, *Jackson Correspondence*, V: 39.

72. Many examples, including quotations from correspondence from Chickasaw leaders to Andrew Jackson, are provided in Amanda L. Paige, Fuller L. Bumpers, and Daniel Littlefield, Jr., *Chickasaw Removal* (Ada, OK: Chickasaw Press, 2010), 23–70.

73. The classic statement of this point of view is found in Francis Paul Prucha, "Andrew Jackson's Indian Policy: A Reassessment," *Journal of American History* 56 (1969): 527–539.

74. *Correspondence on the Subject of the Emigration of the Indians*, Document 512, of the U.S. Senate, 23rd Congress, 1st Session, I: 102.

75. George Gibson to J. H. Gardiner, June 28, 1832, in *Correspondence on the Subject of the Emigration of the Indians*, I: 102.

76. On the various sorts of disputes related to the rations provided during the removals, see, as examples, *Correspondence on the Subject of the Emigration of the Indians*, I: 102, 343–349, 481,816–817, 819–820, 837,842–843.

77. Joseph Kerr to Lewis Cass, June 14, 1832, *Correspondence on the Subject of the Emigration of the Indians*, I: 719–720. Kerr, a brigadier general in the Ohio militia during the War of 1812, had served several terms in the Ohio legislature, and one as United States senator, before emigrating first to Tennessee and then Louisiana in the 1820s. One of his sons died in the battle of the Alamo. Joseph Kerr, *Biographical Dictionary of the United States Congress* (Washington, DC: 2005).

78. Joseph Kerr to General George Gibson, August 17, 1832, *Correspondence on the Subject of the Emigration of the Indians*, I: 721–722. Mann charges that the Choctaw removal was an act of genocide, as those who traveled under federal supervision by steamship were knowingly transported right into the center of a raging cholera epidemic. Moreover, although medical authorities urged prompt vaccination of the travelers to prevent smallpox, removal officials did not take their recommendation, falsely claiming that the Choctaws

had asked for a delay; Mann, *Tainted Gift*, 19–42. Scrutiny of the evidence relating to the medical needs of the migrants indicates that some of the special agents, at minimum, were guilty of what we might well term "depraved indifference" for Choctaws lives. Others tried hard to protect their charges but were often not given the resources to do the job.

79. Ronald Satz, *American Indian Policy in the Jacksonian Era*, 80–81.

80. Ibid., 64–65.

81. For the correspondence between Colquhoun and his superiors, see *Correspondence on the Subject of the Emigration of the Indians*, Document 512, of the U.S. Senate, 23rd Congress, 1st Session, I: 547, 554–555, 558, 560, 562, 563, 568–569, 571-580, 581–583, 586–590, 592, 595–596, 598–602, 604–608, 610–611, 617–621, 662, 632, 641, 643, 650. These exchanges, beginning in April 1831 and terminating in November 1833, dealt mostly with routine matters, but they do provide a portrait of an honest, decent man trying to do a job under nearly impossible circumstances. They make it clear that the funding made available to removal agents was far from adequate, and that great suffering was inflicted on the Indians by the lack of even basic necessities. The efforts of the bureaucrats to suppress information of the real situation become apparent with a close reading of these letters.

82. Mann, *Tainted Gift*, 40.

83. Ibid., 33.

84. George Gibson to Lewis Cass, February 20, 1832, quoted in DeRosier, *The Removal of the Choctaw Indians*, 147.

85. Lewis Cass, "Removal Regulations," May 15, 1832, quoted in DeRosier, *The Removal of the Choctaw Indians*, 183–184.

86. DeRosier, *The Removal of the Choctaw Indians*, 158.

87. Virginia R. Anderson, "Medical Practice and Health in the Choctaw Nation, 1831–1883," *Chronicles of Oklahoma* 48 (1970): 124–143; Russell Thornton, *American Indian Holocaust and Survival: A Population History Since 1492* (Norman: University of Oklahoma Press, 1987), 114.

88. "Petition of Chippewa, Ottawa and Potawatomi Chiefs to AJ, March 10, 1835," quoted in Remini, *Andrew Jackson and His Indian Wars*, 280.

89. Satz, *American Indian Policy in the Jacksonian Era*, 147.

90. Tisinhaw-haw to Andrew Jackson, May 31, 1831, Office of Indian Affairs, Letters Received.

91. Spencer Darwin Pettis to Andrew Jackson, in Feller et al., *Jackson Papers*, VIII: 65–66; Cave, "Abuse of Power," 1344.

92. DeRosier, *The Removal of the Choctaw Indians*, 103.

93. William Ward to Andrew Jackson, October 11, 1830, in Feller et al., *Jackson Papers*, VIII: 553–554.

94. DeRosier, *The Removal of the Choctaw Indians*, 120.

95. Andrew Jackson to Francis P. Blair, July 3, 1838, in Bassett, *Jackson Correspondence*, V: 553.

96. John L. Allen to Andrew Jackson, January 23, 1830, in Feller et al., *Jackson Papers*, VII: 46–48; Rogin, *Fathers and Children*, 223.

97. John Mahon, *The Second Seminole War* (Gainesville: University of Florida Press, 1985), 84–85.

98. Andrew Jackson to the United States Senate, January 16, 1832, *Jackson Papers*, Library of Congress microfilm edition.

99. Silver, "A Counter-Proposal to the Indian Removal Policy of Andrew Jackson," 212.

100. Cave, "Abuse of Power," 1323–1343; Rogin, *Fathers and Children*, 228; Foreman, *Indian Removal*, 73–75; Satz, *American Indian Policy in the Jacksonian Era*, 84–96; Carson, *Searching for the Right Path*, 124. On the activities of speculators, and of Agent Ward, the depositions in *American State Papers: Public Lands,* VII: 641–643; 8: 337, 629–633, 691–693 [hereafter *ASPPL*] are particularly telling.

101. Lewis Cass to Franklin Plummer, May 23, 1832, *ASPPL*, VII: 611.

102. For an excellent summary of the details, see Mary Elizabeth Young, *Redskins, Ruffleshirts and Rednecks: Indian Allotments in Alabama and Mississippi, 1830–1860* (Norman, OK: University of Oklahoma Press, 1961), 47–73.

103. Young, *Redskins, Ruffle-shirts and Rednecks*, 47–72; Cave, "Abuse of Power," 1343–1344; Rogin, *Fathers and Children*, 230.

104. Green, *The Politics of Indian Removal*, 89.

105. Christopher D. Haveman, *Rivers of Sand: Creek Indian Emigration, Relocation, & Ethnic Cleansing in the American South* (Lincoln: University of Nebraska Press, 2016), 29, 40–41.

106. Captain J.S. McIntosh to James Barbour, January 18, 1827, Office of Indian Affairs, Letters Received.

107. Basil Hall, *Travels in North America, in the Years 1827 and 1828* 3 vols. (Edinburgh: Cadell and Company, 1829), III: 388–389.

108. Haveman, *Rivers of Sand*, 29.

109. Eneah Micco et al. to Andrew Jackson, January 21, 1830, in Feller et al., *Jackson Papers*, VIII: 43.

110. 7 Statutes at Large, 366–368. For a detailed account of the controversies and consequences of this treaty, see John T. Ellisor, *The Second Creek War: Multiethnic Conflict and Collusion on a Collapsing Frontier* (Lincoln: University of Nebraska Press, 2010), 47–97 as well as Young, *Redskins, Ruffleshirts, and Rednecks*, 73–98.

111. Neah Micco et al. to Lewis Cass, September 26, 1832, Senate Document 512, III: 464–470.

112. Robert Crawford to Lewis Cass, August 31, 1832, Senate Document 512, III: 420–431.

113. For a comprehensive study of the problems with the Cusseta Treaty, see Ellisor, *The Second Creek War*, 47–97.

114. Robert McHenry to Lewis Cass, May 25, 1835, in Senate Document 425, 24th Congress, 1st Session, 280–281; Cave, "Abuse of Power," 1345.

115. John B. Hogan to Lewis Cass, March 30, 1836, quoted in Rogan, *Fathers and Children*, 231.

116. Ellisor, *Second Creek War*, 64.

117. Enoch Parsons to Lewis Cass, January 25, 1833, Senate Document 412, IV: 43–44. Even if game had been plentiful, it would have done the Indians little good, as by state law they were forbidden to hunt.

118. Winn, *The Triumph of the Ecunnu-Nuxulugee*, 367–368; Ellisor, *Second Creek War*, 84–94. Frank L. Owsley, Jr., "Francis Scott Key's Mission to Alabama," *The Alabama Review* 23 (190): 181–192.

119. Ellisor, *Second Creek War*, 109.

120. Haverman, *Rivers of Sand*, 92.

121. Remini, *Andrew Jackson and His Indian Wars*, 272–273. For comprehensive accounts, see Ellisor, *The Second Creek War* and William W. Winn, *The Triumph of the Ecunnau-Nuxulgee* (Macon, GA: Mercer University Press, 2015). On removal, see Christopher

D. Haveman, *Rivers of Sand: Creek Indian Emigration Relocation & Ethnic Cleansing in the American South* (Lincoln: University of Nebraska Press, 2016). On the Creek War of 1836, in addition to the secondary sources cited above, the documents included in "Causes of the Hostilities of the Creek and Seminole Indians," *American State Papers: Military Affairs*, VI: 574–783 sheds much light on the origins of Creek and Seminole resistance.

122. Some of their descendants are known as the Poarch Creeks. See Anthony Paredes, "Back from Disappearance: The Alabama Indian Community," in Walter L. Williams, *Southeastern Indians since the Removal Era* (Athens: University of Georgia Press, 1979), 123–141.

123. Ellisor, *Second Creek War*, 297–334.

124. Quoted in Jil Nolgren, *The Cherokee Cases: The Confrontation of Law and Politics* (New York: McGraw Hill, 1998), 63.

125. Wilson Lumpkin to Andrew Jackson, February 9, 1835, in Bassett, *Jackson Correspondence*, V: 327. Lumpkin's two volume history of *The Removal of the Cherokee Indians from Georgia* (New York: Dodd Mead, 1902) blends professions of benevolent intent with expressions of vehement anti-Indian prejudices. Poorly written, rambling, and self-serving, it offers some interesting insights into the prejudices and convictions of his countrymen.

126. *Niles Weekly Register*, March 13, 1830, 53 reprints the text of their petition to Congress. For other Cherokee appeals to Congress during Jackson's presidency, see Moulton, *Papers of Chief John Ross*, I: 290, 298, 394, 419, 426.

127. Jill Nolgren, *The Cherokee Cases: The Confrontation of Law and Politics* (New York: McGraw Hill, 1996), 42. For another very perceptive study of the Marshall court's rulings on Indian rights, see Joseph C. Burke, "The Cherokee Cases: A Study in Law, Politics and Morality," *Stanford Law Review* 21 (February 1969): 500–531.

128. Nolgren, *The Cherokee Cases*, 87–92.

129. Ibid., 95–98, 155–164.

130. Ibid., 87–112.

131. Nolgren, *The Cherokee Cases*, 112–141; 170–186; Andrew Jackson to Wilson Lumpkin, June 22, 1832, in Bassett, *Correspondence of Andrew Jackson*, IV: 451; Lumpkin, *Removal of the Cherokee Indians*, I: 195–208; Burke, "The Cherokee Cases," 530.

132. The story seems to have originated with Horace Greeley who, after the Civil War, claimed that Massachusetts congressman George N. Briggs told him about Jackson's quip. See Greeley's *American Conflict: A History of the Great Rebellion in the United State of America* 2 vols. (Hartford, CT: D.C. Case, 1867), I: 106.

133. Andrew Jackson to John Coffee, June 22, 1832, in Bassett, *Jackson Correspondence*, IV: 430.

134. Tim Alan Garrison, *Legal Ideology of Removal: The Southern Judiciary and the Sovereignty of Native American Nations* (Athens: University of Georgia Press, 2009), 11.

135. John Ridge to Elias Boudinot, May 21, 1831, in *Cherokee Phoenix*, 2–3.

136. Quoted in Daniel Blake Smith, *An American Betrayal: Cherokee Patriots and the Trail of Tears* (New York: Henry Holt, 2011), 136.

137. John Ross to John Martin, John Ridge, and William S. Coody, December 1, 1831, in Moulton, *Papers of Chief John Ross*, I: 242–243.

138. Thurman Wilkins, *Cherokee Tragedy: The Ridge Family and the Decimation of a People* (Norman: University of Oklahoma Press, 1986), 233–241; Gary E. Moulton, *John Ross: Cherokee Chief* (Athens: University of Georgia Press, 1978), 50–51; Remini, *Andrew Jackson and His Indian Wars*, 261–262; Smith, *An American Betrayal*, 136–138.

139. John Ridge to John Ross, February 23, 1833, in Moulton, *Papers of Chief John Ross*, I: 260.

140. John Ross to John Quincy Adams, March 12, 1825, in Moulton, *Papers of John Ross*, I: 99–101.

141. "Annual Message," October 24, 1831, in Moulton, *Papers of John Ross*, I: 230.

142. "An Address to the Whites," in Theda Purdue, ed., *Cherokee Editor: The Writings of Elias Boudinot* (Athens: University of Georgia Press, 1996), 67–83.

143. Quoted in Wilkins, *Cherokee Tragedy*, 234.

144. Patrick Wolfe, "Settler Colonialism and the Elimination of the Native," *Journal of Genocide Research* 8 (2006): 396.

145. O'Brien, *In Bitterness and in Tears*, 229.

146. Leonard L. Richards, *The Life and Times of Congressman John Quincy Adams* (New York: Oxford University Press, 1986), 149.

147. Cave, "Abuse of Power," 1347.

148. Henry Clay to Daniel Webster, June 7, 1830, in Charles M. Wiltse, et al., *The Papers of Daniel Webster: Correspondence*, III: 80–82.

149. Stephen J. Valone, "William Seward, Whig Politician, and the Compromised Indian Removal Program in New York State, 1838–1843," *New York History* (Spring 2001): 107–139.

150. Burke, "The Cherokee Cases," 529–530.

151. Cave, "Abuse of Power," 1347–1350.

152. Quoted in John Ehle, *Trail of Tears: The Rise and Fall of the Cherokee Nation* (New York: Doubleday Anchor Books, 1988), 264.

153. Quoted in William L. Anderson, ed., *Cherokee Removal Before and After* (Athens: University of Georgia Press, 1991), 56.

154. Theda Purdue, "The Conflict Within: Cherokees and Removal," in Anderson, *Cherokee Removal Before and After*, 55–72.

155. A number of those incidents were reported in articles the *Cherokee Phoenix*, which are reprinted in Purdue, *Cherokee Editor*, 102–103, 105, 108–109, 111–114, 120–125, 128–132.

156. On his proposals to Andrew Jackson, March 12, 17, 28, 1834, in Moulton, *Papers of John Ross*, I: 277–284.

157. On Ross's negotiations with Jackson, see Remini, *Andrew Jackson and His Indian Wars*, 263–265; Hicks, *Toward the Setting Sun*, 111–208; Moulton, *John Ross*, 54–71; Wilkins, *Cherokee Tragedy*, 242–265.

158. John Ross, Annual Message to the Cherokees, October 24, 1831, in Moulton, *Papers of John Ross*, I: 230.

159. John Ross to David Crockett, January 13, 1831, in Moulton, *Papers of John Ross*, I: 211.

160. Andrew Jackson to B. F. Curry and David Montgomery, September 3, 1834; John Ross to Andrew Jackson, September 15, 1834, in Bassett, *Jackson Correspondence*, V: 288, 292–293.

161. For the strife within the Cherokee nation, Thurman Ridge, *Cherokee Tragedy: The Ridge Family and the Decimation of a People*, 2nd ed. (Norman: University of Oklahoma Press, 1986) remain indispensable.

162. Brian Hicks, *Toward the Setting Sun: John Ross, the Cherokees, and the Trail of Tears* (New York: Atlantic Monthly Press, 2011), 242.

163. John Ross et al., *Memorial to the Senate*, June 24, 1834, *Papers of Chief John Ross*, I: 299; *Cherokee Phoenix*, April 5, 1834, 3; Moulton, *John Ross*, 36; Langguth, *Driven West*, 214–215.

164. Jackson, "Talk to the Cherokee, March 1835, Jackson Papers, Library of Congress.

165. Marion L. Starkey, *The Cherokee Nation* (North Dighton, MA: JG Press, 1995), 236.

166. Quoted in Purdue and Green, *The Cherokee Removal*, 75.

167. Carl J. Vipperman, "The 'Particular Mission' of Wilson Lumpkin," *Georgia Historical Quarterly* 66 (Fall 1982), 295–316.

168. Wilson Lumpkin to Andrew Jackson, January 2, 1831; Feller et al., *Jackson Papers*, X: 10–13; Andrew Jackson to Wilson Lumpkin, June 22, 1832, in Feller et al., *Jackson Papers*, X: 316–317.

169. Purdue and Green, *Cherokee Removal*, 93.

170. "Memorial Protest of the Cherokee Nation," June 22, 1836, in House Document 286, 24th Congress, 1st Session; Purdue, *Cherokee Editor*, 27.

171. Mary Young, "The Exercise of Sovereignty in Cherokee Georgia," *Journal of the Early Republic* 10 (Spring 1990), 52.

172. Purdue and Green, *The Cherokee Removal*, 58–78.

173. On Schermerhorn's activities in the Cherokee nation, see James William Van Hooten, "Salvation and Indian Removal; The Career Biography of John William Schermerhorn: Indian Commissioner," PhD Dissertation (Vanderbilt University, 1972); Wilkins, *Cherokee Tragedy*, 267–287; Starkey, *Cherokee Nation*, 255–277; Moulton, *John Ross*, 63–68, 72–74. Among many Cherokee, he was reputed to be a womanizer, the butt of off-color jokes about horns. Historians have generally not dealt kindly with him, characterizing him as an opportunistic, dishonest, and stupid tool of the administration.

174. For the text of the Treaty of New Echota, see Royce, *Cherokee Nation of Indians*, 125–129.

175. Royce, *Cherokee Nation of Indians*, 162–163.

176. William Schley to Andrew Jackson, February 13, 1836, quoted in Perdue and Green, *The Cherokee Nation and the Trail of Tears*, 114.

177. Moulton, *Papers of Chief John Ross*, I: 381–382; 394–413.

178. *Niles Weekly Register*, January 24, 1835, 362.

179. Wilkins, *Cherokee Tragedy*, 266.

180. Ibid., 266–268.

181. Cave, "Abuse of Power," 1352.

182. Hicks, *Toward the Setting Sun*, 287.

183. Ibid., 269–276.

184. Ibid., 305.

185. James Mooney, *Historical Sketch of the Cherokee* (Chicago: Aldine, 1975), 100. First published in 1900.

186. Foreman, *Indian Removal*, 265.

187. Russell Thornton, *The Cherokee: A Population Estimate* (Lincoln: University of Nebraska Press, 1990); The "Demography of the Trail of Tears Period: A New Estimate of Cherokee Population Losses," in Anderson, *Cherokee Removal*, 75–94.

188. Vicki Rozema, ed., *Voices from the Trail of Tears* (Winston Salem, NC: John F. Blair Publisher, 2003), 140–141, 148.

189. John G. Burnett, "The Cherokee Removal through the Eyes of a Private Soldier," *Journal of Cherokee Studies* 3 (1978), 183.

190. James M. Mooney, *Historical Sketch of the Cherokee* (Chicago: Aldine Transaction, 1975), 124. First published in 1900.

191. Quoted in Thornton, "Demography of the Trail of Tears," 79.

192. Holman Hamilton, "Zachary Taylor and the Black Hawk War," *Wisconsin Magazine of History* 24 (1941): 305–315.

193. Roger J. Nichols, *Black Hawk and the Warriors Path* (Arlington Heights, IL: Harlan Davison, 1992), 21–61. This war is exceptionally well documented and has inspired a rich and provocative secondary literature. The primary sources are to be found in Ellen C. Whitney, ed., *The Black Hawk War, 1831–1832*, 2 vols. *Collections of the Illinois Historical Library*, Vols. 35–38 (Springfield: Illinois State Historical Library, 1970–1978). Black Hawk's own account of his life, as dictated to an interpreter, became an American literary classic, but its authenticity has been a matter of controversy. See Donald Jackson, ed., *Black Hawk: An Autobiography* (Urbana: University of Illinois Press, 1955). Scholarly studies of note include Cecil Eby, *That Disgraceful Affair: The Black Hawk War* (New York: W.W. Norton, 1973); Patrick J. Jung, *The Black Hawk War of 1832* (Norman: University of Oklahoma Press, 2007); Kerry A. Trask, *Black Hawk: The Battle for the Heart of America* (New York: Henry Holt, 2006).

194. For an excellent analysis of the history of intertribal alliances and animosities, see John A. Hall, *Uncommon Sense: Indian Allies and the Black Hawk Indian War* (Cambridge: Harvard University Press, 2009).

195. William T. Hagan, *The Sac and Fox Indians* (Norman: University of Oklahoma Press, 1958), 5–6.

196. Jung, *Black Hawk Indian War*, 118–119.

197. John Robb to Andrew Jackson, June 12, 1832, Feller et al., *Jackson Papers*, X: 303.

198. Quotation from Remini, *Andrew Jackson and His Indian Wars*, 258.

199. The foregoing and following paragraphs rely in particular on the following: Mahon, *Second Seminole War*; J. Leitch Wright, Jr., *Creeks and Seminoles* (Lincoln: University of Nebraska Press, 1986); Inwin C. McRenolds. *The Seminoles* (Norman: University of Oklahoma Press, 1957); James W. Covington, *The Seminoles of Florida* (Gainesville: University Presses of Florida, 1993); Kenneth W. Porter, *The Black Seminoles: History of a Freedom Seeking People* (Gainesville: University of Florida Press, 1996).

200. Mahon, *History of the Second Seminole War*, 58–71. For a detailed and meticulously documented study, see Kevin D. Kokomoor, "Indian Agent Gad Humphreys and the politics of slave claims on the Florida Frontier, 1822–1830," MA Thesis (University of South Florida, 2008).

201. Secretary of War to J. Gadsden, January 30, 1832, *American State Papers: Military Affairs*, VI: 473.

202. John K. Mahon, "Two Seminole Treaties: Payne's Landing, 1832 and Ft. Gibson, 1833," *The Florida Historical Quarterly* 41 (1962): 8.

203. Mahon, "Two Seminole Treaties," 8–14; Mahon, *History of the Second Seminole War*, 75–76; Edwin C. McReynolds, *The Seminoles* (Norman: University of Oklahoma Press, 1957), 123–126; John T. Sprague, *The Origin, Progress, and Conclusion of the Florida War* (New York: D. Appleton, 1847), 72–76.

204. Mahon, "Two Seminole Treaties," 16–18; Sprague, *The Origin, Progress, and Conclusion of the Florida War*, 72–76.

205. Report of the Secretary of War to the President, December 4, 1832, *ASPMA*, V: 23.

206. See, for example, Jackson's endorsement on the memorandum from Indian Agent Wiley Thompson to Superintendent of Indian Affairs Elbert Herring, October 28, 1834, in Clarence E. Carter, ed., *Territorial Papers of the United States: Florida* (New York: AMS Press, 1972), XXV: 63.

207. Covington, *The Seminoles*, 69–71; Edwin C. McReynolds, *The Seminoles*, 214–215.

208. Mahon, *Second Seminole War*, 87–100.

209. "Abstract of Council" *Senate Document 152*, October 25, 1834, 26–27.

210. "Jackson's Directive," July 7, 1835, *Office of Indian Affairs, Letters Sent;* Mahon, *Second Seminole War,* 93, 98.

211. Mahon, *Second Seminole War,* 91–97; Missell and Missell, *Seminole Wars,* 88–91; Covington, *The Seminoles of Florida,* 72–75.

212. Quotation in Sprague, *Origin, Progress, and Conclusion of the Florida War,* 86. Thom Hatch's *Osceola and the Great Seminole War: A Struggle for Justice and Freedom* (New York: St. Martin's, 2012) provides a lively and reliable account of the warrior's career that exemplifies the most recent stage in the transformation of Osceola from terrorist to freedom fighter in the American historical imagination, a transformation that began soon after his death.

213. Report of General Duncan Clinch, January 24, 1835, in Carter, *Territorial Papers of the United States: Florida,* 25: 182–189.

214. Mahon, *Second Seminole War,* 87–134, Quotation, 94.

215. Mahon, *Second Seminole War,* 87–134.

216. Report of General Duncan Clinch, Carter, Territorial Papers of the United States, Florida, 25: 209–210.

217. Quoted in Mahon, *Second Seminole War,* 103.

218. Andrew Jackson to Francis P. Blair, August 12, 1836, Bassett, *Correspondence of Andrew Jackson,* V: 419.

219. Joe Knetsch, "Strategy, Operations and Tactics in the Second Seminole War," in William S. Belko, ed., *America's Hundred Years War: U.S. Expansion to the Gulf Coast and the Fate of the Seminoles, 1763–1858* (Gainesville: University of Florida Press, 2000), 128–157.

220. Frank Laumer, ed., *Amidst a Storm of Bullets: The Diary of Lt. Henry Prince in Florida* (Tampa, FL: University of Tampa Press, 1998), 121.

221. See in particular Joshua Giddings, *The Exiles of Florida* (Gainesville: University of Florida Press, 1955). First published in 1858.

222. Andrew Jackson to Joel Poinsett, August 27, 1837, in Bassett, *Jackson Correspondence,* V: 222; "Memorandum on the Florida Campaign," April (?) 1837, in Bassett, *Jackson Correspondence,* V: 468–471.

223. James W. Covington, *The Seminoles of Florida* (Gainesville: University Press of Florida, 1993), 128–144; John and Mary Lou Missall, *The Seminole Wars* (Gainesville: University of Florida Press, 2004), 213–222.

EPILOGUE

1. Andrew Jackson, "Farewell Address," *The American Presidency Project,* http://www.presidency.ucsb.edu/?pid=67087.

2. Andrew Jackson, "Second Annual Message to Congress, 1830," "*The American Presidency Project,* http//www.presidency.ucsb.edu/?pid=67087.

3. Anderson, *Ethnic Cleansing and the Indian,* 151.

4. Remini, *Andrew Jackson and His Indian Wars,* 280.

5. James Joseph Buss, *Winning the west with Words: Language and Conquest in the Lower Great Lakes* (Norman: University of Oklahoma Press, 2011), 3–10.

6. J. M. Opal, *Avenging the People: Andrew Jackson, the Rule of Law, and the American Nation* (New York: Oxford University Press, 2017), 2.

Index

Abernathy, Thomas, 8
Adams–Onís Treaty, 113, 116
Adams, Henry, 45
Adams, John, 12–13
Adams, John Quincy
   abrogates Treaty of Indian Springs on grounds of fraud, 125
   conflict with Georgia, 125–26, 128–29
   "Corrupt Bargain" allegations, 121–22
   wins the presidency in 1824 election, 120–122
   loses 1828 presidential election, 131–132
   elected to Congress, presents 47-yard-long petition against Jackson's Indian removal program, 166
   Indian land rights, 47
   strengths and liabilities as president, 130
   denounces Treaty of New Echota, 173
Adams, Robert, 145
Albany Regency, 119
Alexander, Susan, 3
Allison, David, 9–10, 14
Alvarez, Alex, xii
American System, 119
Anderson, Gary Clayton, xvi–xvii, 190
Anderson, Joseph, 12
Anderson, William P., 22

Andrews, T. P., 125
Arbuckle, Matthew, 83
Arbuthnot, Alexander, 89–93
Armbrister, Robert, 91, 93
Armstrong, Francis W., 153
Armstrong, John, 28, 52
Atkinson, Henry, 178

Baily, Francis, 14
Baptist, Edward, xii
Barta, Tony, xviii
Battle at Calabree Creek, 38
Battle of Bad Axe, 178
Battle of Burnt Corn Creek, 37
Battle of Emuckfuw Creek, 43
Battle of Enitachopco, 43
Battle of Horseshoe Bend (Tohopeka), 39, 44
Battle of Stillman's Run, 178
Battle of Talladega, 42
Bean, Russell, 15
Benton, Thomas Hart, 118, 126
Berrien, John M., 138
Big Warrior, 55–56, 68
Black Hawk, 177–78
Black Hawk War, 175–78
Blount, William, 8, 10, 11, 48–49
Blount, Willie, 43, 45, 48

Blunt, 116
Boudinot, Elias, 164–65
Bowlegs, 57, 59, 89
Bowles, William Augustus, 33
Brandon, Gerard, 112
Braund, Kathryn H. Holland, 31
Brims, 29
Brown, Richard, 69
Buchanan, James, 145
Burnet, David, 106
Burnet, John C., 174–75
Burr, Aaron, 21–24
Buss, James, 192
Butler, Elizer, 162
Butrick, Daniel, 174

Caldwell v. Alabama, 163
Calhoun, John C.
   addressed by Jackson of need to keep American troops in Florida, 95–97
   addressed by Jackson that Choctaw leaders could be induced to give up land, 106–7
   candidate for president in 1824, withdraws, runs for vice presidency, elected, 119
   demands that Jackson be charged with gross insubordination, 99
   issues orders limiting military action in Spanish Florida, 86
   joins Jacksonian political faction, 129
   as secretary of war agrees with Cherokee complaints against Jackson but takes no action, 76–77
   spreads rumor that Jackson was speculating in Florida land, 98–99
Call, Richard Keith, 185
Callava, Jose, 115
Caller, James, 37
Campbell, David, 12
Campbell, Duncan, 123
Carey, James, 33
Carroll, William, 139
Carson, James, 111
Cass, Lewis
   advises Mississippi Congressman Plummer that Jackson will not enforce restriction on immediate occupation of Choctaw land, 156
   advises that tribal approval required to ratify the Treaty of Fort Gibson, disregarded, 181
   appointed secretary of war, reduces food rations for Indian removal, 153–54
   publishes *North America Review* article calling for Indian removal, declaring Indians incapable of civilization, 142–43
   sets requirements for Cherokee removal treaty, 171
Catawba, 3
Cheathem, Mark, 18
Cheever, George, 142
Cherokee, 68–71, 74–76, 112, 127–29, 136–37, 160
Cherokee Nation v. Georgia, 162
Cherokee Phoenix, 138
Chickamauga, 8, 11
Chickasaws, 72, 73, 74, 103–5, 126, 148, 150, 155
Chief Payne, 57–59
Choctaw removal, 153
Choctaws, 38–39, 73, 105–12, 156–57
Churchill, Ward, xii
Claiborne, William C., 12, 22–23
Clark, John, 125
Clay, Henry, 51, 101–2, 118, 121, 126, 166, 172
Clinch, Duncan, 83, 183–84
Cobb, Thomas, 100–101
Cocke, William, 11, 38, 42, 44
Coffee, John
   fights in Creek War, 40–41, 44
   forms partnership with Andrew Jackson, 17
   serves as Jackson's spokesman to Indians resisting removal, 138–39, 150
   surveys western and northern border of Fort Jackson treaty land cession, 68–69
Coffin Handbill, 131
Colbert, George, 69
Colbert, Levi, 150
Coles, Robert, 111
Colquhoun, William S., 152–53

Conway, George, 19
Cook, Peter, 92
Cooper, Thomas, 48
Cornells, Alexander, 35–37
Corrupt Bargain allegation, 121–22
Cotton Kingdom, 51–51, 78–79
Crawford, Thomas, 2
Crawford, William H.
   bypassed in appointment of boundary commission, 69–70
   calls for land grants for Indians within the states, 134–35
   calls for removal of squatters on Indian lands, 68
   presidential candidacy opposed by Jackson, 117–18
   proposes intermarriages with Indians, 48
Crawley, Mary, 27
Creeks, 30–57, 68, 125, 138, 157–60
Crockett, Davy, 40
Crowell, John, 125, 159
Cyprus Land Company, 99

Dade, Francis L., 184
Davis, W. W., 172
Dearborn, Henry, 22–23
DeRosier, Arthur, 154
Dickinson, Charles, 15–17
Dinsmore, Silas, 18, 154
Donaldson, Andrew Jackson, 18
Donelson, John, 8
Dragging Canoe, 8
Duval, William P., 116, 179–80

Eaton, John Henry
   appointed secretary of war, denies federal jurisdiction over Indians within the states, 137–38
   asks Georgia officials to avoid "harshness toward Indians" during Congressional debate on removal, 145
   author of *Letters of Wyoming,* 120
   biographer of Andrew Jackson, 50
   as governor of Florida warns against Seminole resistance to removal, 183–84

Election of 1824, 120–21
Election of 1828, 131–32
Emathla, Charlie, 184
Emathlochee, 116
Erwin, Joseph, 15
Ethnic Cleansing, xvi–xvii
Evarts, Jeremiah, 140–42

First Seminole War, 83–94
Fletcher v. Peck, 161
Flournoy, Thomas, 38, 41
Floyd, John, 38
Forbes Company, 60
Foreman, Grant, 137
Fort Mims Massacre, 37–38
Fort Scott, 83
Fowltown, 83
Franklin, Jesse, 71
Frelinghuysen, Theodore, 144–45
Fromentin, Eligius, 115, 117

Gadsden, James, 116, 139, 180
Gaines, Edmund P., 68, 81–82, 84–85, 86, 125, 128, 156
Gallitan, Albert, 11
Gardiner, James B., 153
Garrett, Obediah, 84
Genocide, controversies over definition, xiii–xv
Georgia Journal editorial opposing war against the Seminoles (1812), 58–59
Georgia v. Tassals, 163
Gibson, Arrell, 150
Gibson, George, 152
Goldsborough, Robert, 173
Griffin, Patrick, 3
Gwin, William, 156

Hagan, William T., 177
Hall, Augustus Dominick, 65
Hall, Basil, 157
Hambly, William, 92
Harrison, William Henry, 24–25, 176
Haveman, Christopher D., xvii
Hawkins, Benjamin, 28–29, 33–37, 49, 52–53, 58, 59, 60, 66, 155
Hayne, Arthur, 79

Hays, Robert, 53
Hemphill Amendment, 145–46
Hersey, John, 109
Hicks, Brian, 169
Hicks, Charles, 128
Hinds, Thomas, 109
Hitchcock, Ethan Allen, 181
Hixson, Walter L., xviii
Hobsbawm, Eric, 78
Holmes, John, 101
Homathlencio, 83
Humphreys, Gad, 179–81
Hunter, William, 59
Hunters of Kentucky, myth of, 63
Hutchings, John, 17

Indian Board for the Emigration, Preservation, and Improvement of the Aborigines of America, 144
Indian Civilization Fund, 136
Indian Country Media Network declares Andrew Jackson our "worst president," xi
Inskeep, Steve, 52, 79

Jackson, Andrew
  adolescence, 4–5
  appointed territorial governor of Florida, serves four months, 114–16
  asks Congress to support Indian removal, 139–40
  attempts after Creek War to negotiate total Choctaw, Chickasaw and Creek removal to lands west of the Mississippi, fails but obtains some concessions, 103–12
  attitude toward Indians, 3–7, 10–11, 46–47, 72, 103, 135–36, 139–40, 147
  attitude toward slavery, 17–19
  birth and family background, education, 2
  blames Adams and Clay for Rachel's death, 131–32
  cabinet divided over Jackson's Florida invasion, 99–100
  conflict over Cherokee land annexation, 69, 74
  conflicts with the Spanish authorities in Florida, 61–62, 89, 95–99
  controversy over the Rhea letter, 87
  defeats the Red Sticks in the First Creek War, 38–46
  distrust of James Wilkinson, 24–25
  duel with John Dickinson, 15–17
  elected major general of the Tennessee militia, 19
  elected president, 131–32
  elected to Tennessee Supreme Court, 13
  elected to the United States Senate, 12, 118
  evaluation of his Indian policies, x–xvii, 189–92
  executes Robert Armbrister, 93
  experiences during the American Revolution, 2–3
  feud with John Sevier, 19
  forces Creek to accept the Treaty of Fort Jackson, 51–56, 67
  governors of Georgia and Alabama oppose Jackson's Florida invasion, 94
  hangs Prophet Francis and Chief Homathlencio, 93
  House of Representatives debates censure of Jackson for actions in Florida,101–102
  passes part of the censure resolutions, 100–102
  imposes martial law in New Orleans, 65–66
  land speculations, 13–14, 53–54, 77–78, 98–99, 105
  law student in Salisbury, NC, 5
  moves to Tennessee, establishes connections with Blount faction, 8–9
  negotiates with the Cherokee, 160–73
  nominated for presidency by the Tennessee legislature, 118
  Old Hickory legend, 5–7, 16, 26, 50, 77
  opposes Cherokee damage claims, 70
  opposition to Jackson's Indian removal proposal, 140–46

organizes opposition to the Adams administration, 129–31
protests Georgia militia Captain Obed Wright's attack on the Creeks at Chehaw, 94–95
refuses, as president, to enforce federal legislation and treaties protecting Indian rights, 136–38, 146–50, 154, 158–60
relations with Aaron Burr, 21
relations with Black Hawk, 177–78
removes Indian agents and removal agents considered too sympathetic to the Indians, 154–57
in retirement at the Hermitage, prepares plan for invasion of Florida should Spain fail to implement Adams–Onís Treaty, 113
role in the Second Seminole War, 179, 181–86, 190–92
runs store and tavern, 17
Senate takes no action on Jackson censure, 102
serves in Congress, 11–13
supports Georgia's demand for total removal of all Indians, 160–68
trial and execution of Alexander Arbuthnot, 93
victory at New Orleans, 63–64
Warhawk, 25
wins plurality of electoral and popular votes in 1824 presidential election, but defeated in Congress by J. Q. Adams in 1825, 119–22
Jackson, Elizabeth, 2–3
Jackson, Hugh, 2
Jackson, Rachel, 8, 15, 41–42, 44–45, 114–15, 131–32
Jay's Treaty, 12
Jefferson, Thomas, 12, 26–27, 48
Jessup, Thomas, 160
Johnson, Richard M., 100
Johnson v. McIntosh, 161
Jung, Patrick J., 178

Keane, John, 63
Kerr, Joseph, 151–52

Key, Francis Scott, 159
Knox, Henry, 13–14, 47
Knoxville Gazette denies Indian land rights, 7

Laycock, Abner, 101
Lemkin, Raphael, xiii–xiv
Letters of Wyoming, 120
Lieberman, Benjamin, xii
Little Warrior, 34
Louaillier, Louis, 65
Luengo, Francisco Caso y, 89
Lumkin, Wilson, 161, 163, 170
Lyncoya, 41

Madison, James, 25, 81
Mahon, John, 184
Mann, Barbara, 153
Manrique, Don Matteo Gonzalez, 60–62
Marshall, John, 161–63
Masot, Jose, 95–98
Matthews, George, 57, 58
McCoy, Isaac, 141, 143–44
McGillivray, Alexander, 28–29, 32
McIntosh, William, 87–88, 123–25
McKee, John, 71, 106
McKenney, Thomas, 141–42, 144
McMinn, Joseph, 71, 74, 76, 104
McNairy, Nathaniel, 16
McQueen, Peter, 37, 94
Meacham, John, 118
Meigs, Return J., 72, 73, 76, 90, 127–28
Melville, Herman, xi
Meriwether, David, 71
Micanopy, 183
Mikasuckis, 83–84
Mitchell, David, 84–85
Monroe, James
abandons belief in the "civilization" program, favors voluntary Indian removal to West of the Mississippi, 134
appoints Jackson territorial governor of Florida, 114
orders Jackson to respect Spanish authority in Florida, 62

as president justifies Jackson's invasion of West Florida, 100
as secretary of war withdraws support from Florida "Patriots" after U.S. military intervention on the Alachua plain, 59–60
supported by Jackson for the Democratic–Republican presidential nomination in 1812, 25
Mooney, James, 174
Moses, A. Dirk, xviii
Mulatto King, 116
Mushulatubbee, 108

Nashville Clarion calls for "dismemberment" of the Creek Nation, 37–38
Nationalist Party (Cherokee), 168–69
Neamathla, 83–84, 86, 116
Negro Fort at Prospect Bluff, 81–82
Newman, Daniel, 58
New Orleans, Battle of, 63–64
Nicoles, Edward, 60–61, 66–67, 81, 90
Niles Register declares all Indians enemies to civilized society, 47
North Carolina land grab, 1783, 8

O'Brien, Sean Michael, 166
Oseola, 183–84, 186
Ostler, Jeffrey, xiv
Overton, John, 9, 138
Owsley, Frank, 35, 44

Packenham, Sir Edward, 63–64
Parton, James, 5–6, 17
Pathkiller, 40, 74
Patriots (Florida), 58–59
Perdue, Theda, 167
Phagan, John, 155, 180
Pickering, Timothy, 13
Pigot, Hugh, 60
Pinckney, Thomas, 38, 52–53, 59
Pitchlyn, James, 106–7, 148
Plains of Chalmette, 64
Plummer, Franklin, 156
Poindexter, George, 106–7
Primitive accumulation, 79–80
Prophet Francis, 93–94

Prospect Bluff, 60
Pushmataha, 108–9

Quick, Tom, 3–4

Randolph, John, 130
Ratcliffe, Donald, 121
Rayburn, William, 95
Red Sticks, 36–37, 44
Reid, John, 50
Remini, Robert, 42–44, 61, 105, 190
Rhea, John, 87
Rhea letter, 87
Richmond Junto, 119
Ridge, John, 163–66, 173
Ritchie, Thomas, 119
Robards, Lewis, 8
Roberts, John, 44
Robertson, James, 11, 35
Robinson, Eugene, xii
Rogin, Michael Paul, 79–80
Ross, Andrew, 169
Ross, John, 39, 76, 161, 164–65, 167, 173–73

Sac and Fox Indians, 175–78
Salaita, Steven, 147
Satz, Ronald, xv, 152
Saukenuk, 177–78
Saunt, Claudio, 34
Schernerhorn, John F., 171–72
Schley, William, 172
Searcy, Thomas, 5
Second Creek War, 160, 184–87
Seminoles, 56–59, 81, 83, 85, 88–89, 115–18, 178–87
and slavery, 58, 178
Sequoyah, 39
Settler Colonialism School, xvii
Sevier, John, 11–12, 19, 31, 68
Sharp Knife, xi, 45
Shelby, Issac, 103
Smith, Benjamin, 155
Smith, Daniel, 22–24
Sprague, John H., 181, 183
Stevenson, Andrew, 146

Stiggins, George, 30
Swann, Thomas, 15

Takaki, Ronald, 45
Tallushatchee Massacre, 40
Tarelton, Banastre, 1
Tariff of 1828, 130
Tassel, George, 162
Taylor, Zachary, 175
Tecumseh, 24, 34, 55, 103
Tennessee v. Foreman, 163
Third Seminole War, 187
Thompson, Wiley, 182–84
Thornton, Russell, 174
Tiger King, 95
Tochelar, 75
Tohopeka, 43
Treaty of Augusta, 32
Treaty of Cusseta, 158
Treaty of Dancing Rabbit Creek, 156
Treaty of Doak's Stand, 111–12
Treaty of Fort Gibson, 181–82
Treaty of Fort Jackson, 54–56
Treaty of Franklin, 149
Treaty of Galphinton, 32
Treaty of Ghent, 66–67
Treaty of Hopewell, 8
Treaty of Indian Springs, 88, 122–25
Treaty of Moultrie Creek, 118
Treaty of New Echota, 172
Treaty of Payne's Landing, 180
Treaty of Pontotoc, 150
Treaty of San Lorenzo, 13
Treaty of Shoulderbone Creek, 32
Treaty of Washington, 126
Treaty Party (Cherokee), 167
Troup, George M, 62–63, 125–26
Trump, Donald J., vii
Tubman, Harriet, xii
Turner, Frederick Jackson, xi
Tuskegee Warrior, 35
Tusli Hajo, 116

United Nations convention on genocide, xiv

Van Buren, Martin, 129, 133, 146
Vann, Joseph, 171
Veracini, Lorenzo, xviii

Wagaman, Thomas, 16
Walker, Tandy, 28
Walsh, Paddy, 46
Walton, Ira, 18
Ward, William, 106, 155–56
Warshauer, Matthew, 65
Waselkov, Gregory A., 37
Watson, Thomas, 17
Weatherford, William, 38, 46
Webster, Daniel, 12, 129–30
Webster, Daniel, Mrs., 118
Wescott, John D., Jr., 181
Wesley, John, 3
Wharton, Jesse, 56
White Path, 161
Wildcat, 185
Wilkinson, James, 23, 26
William Penn Essays, 140
Williams, John, 104
Winchester, James, 25
Winnebago Prophet, 177
Winter, Kari, xii
Wirt, William, 148, 161
Woodbine, George, 60
Worchester, Samuel, 162
Worchester v. Georgia, 162
Wright, Obed, 94–95

Young, William, 96

Zuniga, Mauricio de, 82

About the Author

Alfred A. Cave is professor emeritus of history at the University of Toledo, Toledo, Ohio. Some of his published works include *Lethal Encounters: Englishmen and Indians in Colonial Virginia* (Praeger), *The French and Indian War* (Greenwood), *Jacksonian Democracy and the Historians* (University Press of Florida), *Prophets of the Great Spirit: Native American Revitalization Movements in Eastern North America* (University of Nebraska Press), and *The Pequot War* (University of Massachusetts Press).